Foreign Exchange: Exchange Risk and Corporate International Finance

Foreign Exchange: Exchange Risk and Corporate International Finance

Dr. Anoop Pant

RANDOM

RANDOM PUBLICATIONS

NEW DELHI (INDIA)

Foreign Exchange:
Exchange Risk and Corporate International Finance

ISBN 978-93-5111-347-8

Published in 2014 in India by

RANDOM PUBLICATIONS

4376-A/4B, Gali Murari Lal, Ansari Road
New Delhi-110 002
Phone : +91-11-43580356, +91-11-23289044
e-mail: randomexports@gmail.com, sales@randompublications.com,
info@randompublications.com

Reprinted 2024

Type Setting by : Keystoneprintads, Delhi-110051
Digitally Printed at: Replika Press Pvt. Ltd.

Preface

The foreign exchange is a global decentralized market for the trading of currencies. The main participants in this market are the larger international banks. Financial centres around the world function as anchors of trading between a wide range of different types of buyers and sellers around the clock, with the exception of weekends. Electronic Broking Services (EBS) and Reuters 3000 Xtra are two main interbank FX trading platforms. The foreign exchange market determines the relative values of different currencies.

Globalization and increasing internationalization of financial transactions has profoundly transformed the Foreign Exchange Markets, not only in size, but also in complexity, variety of products, number of players, technology use and settlement processes. Given the volatility in these markets and the direct impact on profitability of the enterprise, managing the foreign exchange exposure remains a great challenge for any organization. With its focus on foreign exchange, the book acquaints the readers with new concepts of almost all aspects of Foreign management and issues associated with the same.

While the study is done with specific reference to Indian context, the findings and underlying principles and methods used are expected to be of general applicability. On the whole the book with its wide scope and concentrated presentation is expected to be of great use to students seeking a good guide to foreign exchange. It is also expected that every reader who reads the book attentively will find himself or herself, after a thorough perusal of the book, to have harvested several times the worth of his or her time and money invested in buying and reading this excellent book.

I would like to thank my team for standing beside me throughout my career and writing this book. My special thanks go to "Random Publications" who have published the book.

— Dr. Anoop Pant

Contents

1

Foreign Relations of India: An Introduction

AN OVERVIEW

India has formal diplomatic relations with most nations, as the world's second most populous country, the world's most-populous democracy and one of the fastest growing major economies in the world. With the world's tenth largest military expenditures, tenth largest economy by nominal rates and third largest by purchasing power parity; India is a regional power, and a potential Superpower. It is India's growing international influence that increasingly gives it a more prominent voice in global affairs.

India is a newly industrialized country; it has a long history of collaboration with several countries and is considered a leader of the developing world. India was one of the founding members of several international organizations, most notably the United Nations, the Asian Development Bank, G20 industrial nations and the founder of the Non-aligned movement.

India has also played an important and influential role in other international organizations like:

- East Asia Summit,
- World Trade Organization,
- International Monetary Fund (IMF),
- G8+5 and
- IBSA Dialogue Forum.

Regional organizations India is a part of include SAARC and BIMSTEC. India has taken part in several UN peacekeeping missions and in 2007; it was the second-largest troop contributor to the United Nations. India is currently seeking a permanent seat in the UN Security Council, along with the G4 nations.

HISTORY

Even before independence, the Government of British India maintained semi-autonomous diplomatic relations. It had colonies (such as the Aden Settlement), sent and received full diplomatic missions, and was a founder member of both the League of Nations and the United Nations. After India gained independence from the United Kingdom in 1947, it soon joined the Commonwealth of Nations and strongly supported independence movements in other colonies, like the Indonesian National Revolution. The partition and various territorial disputes, particularly which over Kashmir, would strain its relations with Pakistan for years to come. During the Cold War, India adopted a foreign policy of not aligning itself with any major power bloc. However, India developed close ties with the Soviet Union and received extensive military support from it.

The end of the Cold War significantly affected India's foreign policy, as it did for much of the world. The country now seeks to strengthen its diplomatic and economic ties with the United States, the People's Republic of China, the European Union, Japan, Israel, Mexico, and Brazil. India has also forged close ties with the member states of the Association of Southeast Asian Nations, the African Union, the Arab League and Iran.

Though India continues to have a military relationship with Russia, Israel has emerged as India's second largest military partner while India has built a strong strategic partnership with the United States. The Indo-US civilian nuclear agreement, signed and implemented in 2008, highlighted the growing sophistication of the Indo-American relations.

POLICY

India's foreign policy has always regarded the concept of neighbourhood as one of widening concentric circles, around a central axis of historical and cultural commonalities.

The guiding principles of India's Foreign Policy have been founded on Panchsheel, pragmatism and pursuit of national interest. In a period of rapid and continuing change, foreign policy must be capable of responding optimally to new challenges and opportunities. It has to be an integral part of the larger effort of building the nation's capabilities through economic development, strengthening social fabric and well-being of the people and protecting India's sovereignty and territorial integrity. India's foreign policy is a forward-looking engagement with the rest of the world, sandeep based on a rigorous, realistic and contemporary assessment of the bilateral, regional and global geopolitical and economic milieu.

As many as 20 million people of Indian origin live and work abroad and constitute an important link with the mother country. An important role of India's foreign policy has been to ensure their welfare and well being within the framework of the laws of the country where they live.

ROLE OF THE PRIME MINISTER

Jawaharlal Nehru, India's first Prime Minister, promoted a strong personal role for the Prime Minister but a weak institutional structure. Nehru served concurrently as Prime Minister and Minister of External Affairs; he made all major foreign policy decisions himself after consulting with his advisers and then entrusted the conduct of international affairs to senior members of the Indian Foreign Service. His successors continued to exercise considerable control over India's international dealings, although they generally appointed separate ministers of external affairs.

India's second prime minister, Lal Bahadur Shastri (1964–66), expanded the Prime Minister Office (sometimes called the Prime Minister's Secretariat) and enlarged its powers. By the 1970s, the Office of the Prime Minister had become the de facto coordinator and supraministry of the Indian government. The enhanced role of the office strengthened the prime minister's control over foreign policy making at the expense of the Ministry of External Affairs. Advisers in the office provided channels of information and policy recommendations in addition to those offered by the Ministry of External Affairs.

A subordinate part of the office—the Research and Analysis Wing (RAW)—functioned in ways that significantly expanded the information available to the prime minister and his advisers. The RAW gathered intelligence, provided intelligence analysis to the Office of the Prime Minister, and conducted covert operations abroad.

The prime minister's control and reliance on personal advisers in the Office of the Prime Minister was particularly strong under the tenures of Indira Gandhi (1966–77 and 1980–84) and her son, Rajiv (1984–89), who succeeded her, and weaker during the periods of coalition governments. Observers find it difficult to determine whether the locus of decision-making authority on any particular issue lies with the Ministry of External Affairs, the Council of Ministers, the Office of the Prime Minister, or the prime minister himself.

The Prime Minister is however free to appoint advisers and special committees to examine various foreign policy options and areas of interest. In a recent instance, Manmohan Singh appointed K. Subrahmanyam in 2005 to head a special government task force to study 'Global Strategic Developments' over the next decade. The Task Force submitted its conclusions to the Prime Minister in 2006. The report has not yet been released in the public domain.

MINISTRY OF EXTERNAL AFFAIRS

The Ministry of External Affairs is the Indian government's agency responsible for the foreign relations of India. The Minister of External Affairs holds cabinet rank as a member of the Council of Ministers.

S. M. Krishna is current Minister of External Affairs. The Ministry has two Ministers of State Preneet Kaur and E. Ahamed. The Indian Foreign Secretary is the head of Indian Foreign Service (IFS) and therefore, serves as the head of all Indian ambassadors and high commissioners. Ranjan Mathai is the current Foreign Secretary of India.

GENERAL IDEA

India's relations with the world have evolved since the British Raj (1857–1947), when the British Empire monopolized external and defence relations. When India gained independence in 1947, few Indians had experience in making or conducting foreign policy. However, the country's oldest political party, the Indian National Congress, had established a small foreign department in 1925 to make overseas contacts and to publicize its freedom struggle. From the late 1920s on, Jawaharlal Nehru, who had a long-standing interest in world affairs among independence leaders, formulated the Congress stance on international issues. As a member of the interim government in 1946, Nehru articulated India's approach to the world.

India's international influence varied over the years after independence. Indian prestige and moral authority were high in the 1950s and facilitated the acquisition of developmental assistance from both East and West. Although the prestige stemmed from India's nonaligned stance, the nation was unable to prevent Cold War politics from becoming intertwined with interstate relations in South Asia.

Sardar Swaran Singh was India's foreign minister from 1964 to 1966. In the 1960s and 1970s, India's international position among developed and developing countries faded in the course of wars with China and Pakistan, disputes with other countries in South Asia, and India's attempt to balance Pakistan's support from the United States and China by signing the Indo-Soviet Treaty of Friendship and Cooperation in August 1971.

Although India obtained substantial Soviet military and economic aid, which helped to strengthen the nation, India's influence was undercut regionally and internationally by the perception that its friendship with the Soviet Union prevented a more forthright condemnation of the Soviet presence in Afghanistan. In the late 1980s, India improved relations with the United States, other developed countries, and China while continuing close ties with the Soviet Union. Relations with its South Asian neighbours, especially Pakistan, Sri Lanka, and Nepal, occupied much of the energies of the Ministry of External Affairs.

In the 1990s, India's economic problems and the demise of the bipolar world political system forced India to reassess its foreign policy and adjust its foreign relations. Previous policies proved inadequate to cope with the serious domestic and international problems facing India. The end of the Cold War gutted the core meaning of nonalignment and left Indian foreign policy without significant direction.

The hard, pragmatic considerations of the early 1990s were still viewed within the nonaligned framework of the past, but the disintegration of the Soviet Union removed much of India's international leverage, for which relations with Russia and the other post-Soviet states could not compensate. After the dissolution of the Soviet Union, India improved its relations with the United States, Canada, France, Japan and Germany. In 1992, India established formal diplomatic relations with Israel and this relationship grew during the tenures of the Bharatiya Janata Party (BJP) government and the subsequent UPA (United Progressive Alliance) governments.

In the mid-1990s, India attracted the world attention towards the alleged Pakistan-backed terrorism in Kashmir. The Kargil War resulted in a major diplomatic victory for India. The United States and European Union recognized the fact that Pakistani military had illegally infiltrated into Indian territory and pressurized Pakistan to withdraw from Kargil. Several anti-India militant groups based in Pakistan were labelled as terrorist groups by the United States and European Union.

In 1998, India tested nuclear weapons for the second time which resulted in several U.S., Japanese and European sanctions on India. India's then defence minister, George Fernandes, said that India's nuclear programme was necessary as it provided a deterrence to potential Chinese nuclear threat. Most of the sanctions imposed on India were removed by 2001.

After the 11 September attacks in 2001, Indian intelligence agencies provided the U.S. with significant information on Al-Qaeda and related groups' activities in Pakistan and Afghanistan. India's extensive contribution to the War on Terrorism, coupled with a surge in its economy, has helped India's diplomatic relations with several countries. Over the past three years, India has held numerous joint military exercises with U.S. and European nations that have resulted in a strengthened U.S.-India and E.U.-India bilateral relationship. India's bilateral trade with Europe and U.S. has more than doubled in the last five years.

India has been pushing for reforms in the UN and WTO with mixed results. India's candidature for a permanent seat at the UN Security Council is currently backed by several countries including France, Russia, the United Kingdom, Germany, Japan, Brazil, Australia and UAE. In 2004, the United States signed a nuclear co-operation agreement with India even though the latter is not a part of the Nuclear Non-Proliferation Treaty.

The US argued that India's strong nuclear non-proliferation record made it an exception, however this has not persuaded other Nuclear Suppliers Group members to sign similar deals with India. During a state visit to India in November 2010, US president Barack Obama announced US support for India's bid for permanent membership to UN Security Council as well as India's entry to Nuclear Suppliers Group, Wassenaar Arrangement, Australia Group and Missile Technology Control Regime.

STRATEGIC PARTNERS

India's growing economy, strategic location, friendly foreign policy and large and vibrant diaspora has won it more allies than enemies. India has friendly relations with several countries in the developing world. Though India is not a part of any major military alliance, it has close strategic and military relationship with most of the major powers.

Countries considered India's closest include the Russian Federation, Israel, Afghanistan, France, Bhutan and Bangladesh. Russia is the largest supplier of military equipment to India, followed by Israel and France. Israel is set to overtake Russia as India's largest military and strategic partner.

The two countries also collaborate extensively in the sphere of counter-terrorism and space technology. India also enjoys strong military relations with several other countries, including the United Kingdom, the United States, Japan, Singapore, Brazil, South Africa and Italy. In addition, India operates an airbase in Tajikistan and signed a landmark defence accord with Qatar in 2008.

India has also forged relationships with developing countries, especially South Africa, Brazil, and Mexico. These countries often represent the interests of the developing countries through economic forums such as the G8+5, IBSA and WTO. India was seen as one of the standard bearers of the developing world and claimed to speak for a collection of more than 30 other developing nations at the Doha Development Round. India's "Look East" Policy has helped it develop greater economic and strategic partnership with Southeast Asian countries, South Korea, Japan, and Taiwan. India also enjoys friendly relations with the Persian Gulf countries and most members of the African Union.

INTERNATIONAL ORGANIZATIONS

India participates in the following international organisations:

- *ADB*: Asian Development Bank
- *AfDB*: African Development Bank (non-regional members)
- ASEAN Regional Forum
- ASEAN (dialogue partner)
- *BIMSTEC*: Bay of Bengal Initiative for Multisectoral Technical and Economic Cooperation
- *BIS*: Bank for International Settlements
- Commonwealth of Nations
- *CERN*: European Organization for Nuclear Research (observer)
- *CP*: Colombo Plan
- *EAS*: East Asia Summit
- *FAO*: Food and Agriculture Organization
- G-15
- G-24
- G-77
- *IAEA*: International Atomic Energy Agency
- *IBRD*: International Bank for Reconstruction and Development (World Bank)

- *ICAO*: International Civil Aviation Organization
- *ICC*: International Chamber of Commerce
- *ICRM*: International Red Cross and Red Crescent Movement
- *IDA*: International Development Association
- *IFAD*: International Fund for Agricultural Development
- *IFC*: International Finance Corporation
- *IFRCS*: International Federation of Red Cross and Red Crescent Societies
- *IHO*: International Hydrographic Organization
- *ILO*: International Labour Organization
- *IMF*: International Monetary Fund
- *IMO*: International Maritime Organization
- *IMSO*: International Mobile Satellite Organization
- *Interpol*: International Criminal Police Organization
- *IOC*: International Olympic Committee
- *IOM*: International Organization for Migration (observer)
- *IPU*: Inter-parliamentary Union
- *ISO*: International Organization for Standardization
- *ITSO*: International Telecommunications Satellite Organization
- *ITU*: International Telecommunication Union
- *ITUC*: International Trade Union Confederation (the successor to ICFTU (International Confederation of Free Trade Unions) and the WCL (World Confederation of Labour))
- *LAS*: League of Arab States (observer)
- *MIGA*: Multilateral Investment Guarantee Agency
- *MONUC*: United Nations Organization Mission in the Democratic Republic of the Congo
- *NAM*: Nonaligned Movement
- *OAS*: Organization of American States (observer)
- *OPCW*: Organization for the Prohibition of Chemical Weapons
- *PCA*: Permanent Court of Arbitration
- *PIF*: Pacific Islands Forum (partner)
- *SAARC*: South Asian Association for Regional Cooperation
- *SACEP*: South Asia Co-operative Environment Programme
- *SCO*: Shanghai Cooperation Organization (observer)
- *UN*: United Nations
- *UNCTAD*: United Nations Conference on Trade and Development
- *UNDOF*: United Nations Disengagement Observer Force
- *UNESCO*: United Nations Educational, Scientific, and Cultural Organization
- *UNHCR*: United Nations High Commissioner for Refugees
- *UNIDO*: United Nations Industrial Development Organization
- *UNIFIL*: United Nations Interim Force in Lebanon
- UNMEE: United Nations Mission in Ethiopia and Eritrea

- *UNMIS*: United Nations Mission in Sudan
- *UNOCI*: United Nations Operation in Côte d'Ivoire
- *UNWTO*: World Tourism Organization
- *UPU*: Universal Postal Union
- *WCL*: World Confederation of Labour
- *WCO*: World Customs Organization
- *WFTU*: World Federation of Trade Unions
- *WHO*: World Health Organization
- *WIPO*: World Intellectual Property Organization
- *WMO*: World Meteorological Organization
- *WTO*: World Trade Organization

NON-ALIGNED MOVEMENT

Nonalignment had its origins in India's colonial experience and the nonviolent Indian independence struggle led by the Congress, which left India determined to be the master of its fate in an international system dominated politically by Cold War alliances and economically by Western capitalism. The principles of nonalignment, as articulated by Nehru and his successors, were preservation of India's freedom of action internationally through refusal to align India with any bloc or alliance, particularly those led by the United States or the Soviet Union; nonviolence and international cooperation as a means of settling international disputes. Nonalignment was a consistent feature of Indian foreign policy by the late 1940s and enjoyed strong, almost unquestioning support among the Indian elite.

The term "Non-Alignment" itself was coined by Indian Prime Minister Jawaharlal Nehru during his speech in 1954 in Colombo, Sri Lanka.

UNITED NATIONS

As a founder member of the United Nations, India has been a firm supporter of the Purposes and Principles of the United Nations, and has made significant contributions to the furtherance and implementation of these noble aims, and to the evolution and functioning of its various specialized programmes.

It stood at the forefront during the UN's tumultuous years of struggle against colonialism and apartheid, its struggle towards global disarmament and the ending of the arms race, and towards the creation of a more equitable international economic order. At the very first session of the UN, India had raised its voice against colonialism and apartheid, two issues which have been among the most significant of the UN's successes in the last half century. India exulted in the UN's triumph, and saw in the UN's victory, a vindication of the policy relentlessly pursued by it from its initial days at the world forum.

India has been a participant in all its peace-keeping operations including those in Korea, Egypt and Congo in earlier years and in Somalia, Angola and Rwanda in recent years. India has also played an active role in the deliberations of the United Nations on the creation of a more equitable international economic order. It has been an active member of the Group of 77, and later the core group of the G-15 nations. Other issues, such as environmentally sustainable development and the promotion and protection of human rights, have also been an important focus of India's foreign policy in international forums.

WORLD TRADE ORGANIZATION

Described by WTO chief Pascal Lamy as one of the organization's "big brothers", India was instrumental in bringing down the Doha round of talks in 2008. It has played an important role of representing as many as 100 developing nations during WTO summits.

SAARC

Certain aspects of India's relations within the subcontinent are conducted through the South Asian Association for Regional Cooperation (SAARC). Its members are Afghanistan, Bangladesh, Bhutan, India, Maldives, Nepal, Pakistan, and Sri Lanka. Established in 1985, SAARC encourages cooperation in agriculture, rural development, science and technology, culture, health, population control, narcotics control and anti-terrorism.

SAARC has intentionally stressed these "core issues" and avoided more divisive political issues, although political dialogue is often conducted on the margins of SAARC meetings. In 1993, India and its SAARC partners signed an agreement to gradually lower tariffs within the region. Forward movement in SAARC has come to a standstill because of the tension between India and Pakistan, and the SAARC Summit originally scheduled for, but not held in, November 1999 has not been rescheduled. The Fourteenth SAARC Summit was held during 3–4 April 2007 in New Delhi.

INTERNATIONAL DISPUTES

India's territorial disputes with neighbouring Pakistan and People's Republic of China have played a crucial role in its foreign policy. India is also involved in minor territorial disputes with neighbouring Bangladesh, Nepal and Maldives. India currently maintains two manned stations in Antarctica but has made some unofficial territorial claims, which are yet to be clarified.

BANGLADESH

6.5 km of the border between India and Bangladesh remains to be demarcated.

Ongoing discussions with Bangladesh to exchange 162 minuscule enclaves between the two.

NEPAL

Kalapani village of India is claimed by Nepal and Nawalparasi district of Nepal is claimed by India.

The dispute between India and Nepal involves about 75 km (29 sq mi) of area in Kalapani, where China, India, and Nepal meet. Indian forces occupied the area in 1962 after China and India fought their border war. Three villages are located in the disputed zone: Kuti, Gunji, and Knabe. India and Nepal disagree about how to interpret the 1816 Sugauli treaty between the British East India Company and Nepal, which delimited the boundary along the Maha Kali River (Sarda River in India).

The dispute intensified in 1997 as the Nepali parliament considered a treaty on hydro-electric development of the river. India and Nepal differ as to which stream constitutes the source of the river. Nepal regards the Limpiyadhura as the source; India claims the Lipu Lekh. Nepal has reportedly tabled an 1856 map from the British India Office to support its position. The countries have held several meetings about the dispute and discussed jointly surveying to resolve the issue. Although the Indo-Nepali dispute appears to be minor, it was aggravated in 1962 by tensions between China and India. Because the disputed area lies near the Sino-Indian frontier, it gains strategic value.

BRITISH INDIAN OCEAN TERRITORIES

Dispute over the British Indian Ocean Territories and the Cocos (Keeling) Islands with the former colonial powers. India regards these islands as part of its Lakshadweep Indosphere strategy as part of its oceanic vicinity of its sovereignty and a threat to its integrity of its emerging geo-political might, and does not recognise the crown's rule over these "Indian" islands.

MALDIVES

Dispute over Minicoy Island with Maldives. However, Maldives and India have made arrangements to allow Maldivians to travel directly to Minicoy without a visa. The Framework Agreement on Cooperation for Development, which was signed by Maldivian President Mohamed Nasheed and Indian Prime Minister Manmohan Singh during his recent visit to the Maldives, includes an article on establishing a transport network between the Maldives and Minicoy.

The earlier policy required Maldivians to get a visa from New Delhi before boarding a ferry en route to Minicoy from India's Kochi. The Government of the Maldives has stressed that the ferry service to be established between Kulhudhuffushi in Haa Dhaal atoll and Minicoy will also allow cargo to be transported between the Maldives and Minicoy. President Nasheed also expressed hope to start a regular passenger cargo ferry service between the Maldives and Minicoy in the near future. This has regularised the issue of Minicoy and although Maldives continues to claim Minicoy, friction about this atoll has lessened considerably

PAKISTAN

The unresolved Kashmir dispute and the status of Kashmir with Pakistan, involving the illegally occupied region in Kashmir, India claims the disputed territory from Pakistan occupied Kashmir.

- Dispute over Sir Creek and the maritime boundary regarding the Rann of Kachchh area of India.
- Water-sharing problems with Pakistan over the Indus River (Wular Barrage). *(Indus Water Treaty)*
- Pakistani sponsorship of terrorism in India

PEOPLE'S REPUBLIC OF CHINA

India claims Aksai Chin and Trans-Karakoram Tract, as part of Jammu and Kashmir.

China claims most of Arunachal Pradesh, a contested disputed territory of north-east India by not recognising the McMahon Line.

Two regions are claimed by both India and China. Aksai Chin is in the disputed territory of Kashmir, at the junction of India, Tibet and Pakistan-Occupied Kashmir. India claims the 38,000-square-kilometre territory, currently administered by China.

India also considers the cessation of Shaksam Valley to China by Pakistan as illegal and a part of its territory. Arunachal Pradesh is a state of India in the country's northeast, bordering on Bhutan, Myanmar and China. Though it is under Indian administration, China calls the 90,000-square-kilometre area as South Tibet. Also the boundary between the North Indian states of Himachal Pradesh and Uttaranchal with China's Tibet is not properly demarcated with some portions under de-facto administration of India.

LOOK EAST POLICY

In the post cold war era, a significant aspect of India's foreign policy is the Look East Policy. During the cold war, India's relations with its South East Asian neighbours was not very strong. After the end of the cold war, the government of India particularly realised the importance of redressing this imbalance in India's foreign policy. Consequently, the Narsimha Rao government in the early nineties of the last century unveiled the look east policy. Initially it focused on renewing political and economic contacts with the countries of East and South-East Asia.

At present, under the Look East Policy, the Government of India is giving special emphasis on the economic development of backward north eastern region of India taking advantage of huge market of ASEAN as well as of the energy resources available in some of the member countries of ASEAN like Myanmar. Look-east policy was launched in 1992 just after the end of the cold war, following the dissolution of the Soviet Union. After the start of liberalization, it was a very strategic policy decision taken by the government in the foreign policy. To quote Prime Minister Manmohan Singh "it was also a strategic shift in India's vision of the world and India's place in the evolving global economy".

The policy was given an initial thrust with the then Prime Minister Narasimha Rao visiting China, Japan, South Korea, Vietnam and Singapore and India becoming an important dialogue partner with ASEAN in 1992. Since the beginning of this century, India has given a big push to this policy by becoming a summit level partner of ASEAN (2002) and getting involved in some regional initiatives such as the BIMSTEC and the Ganga–Mekong Cooperation and now becoming a member of the East Asia Summit (EAS) in December, 2005.

INDIA–ASEAN

India's interaction with ASEAN in the cold war era was very limited. India declined to get associated with ASEAN in the 1960s when full membership was offered even before the grouping was formed.

It is only with the formulation of the Look-East policy in the last decade (1992), India had started giving this region due importance in the foreign policy. India became a sectoral dialogue partner with ASEAN in 1992, a full dialogue partner in 1995, a member of the ASEAN Regional Forum (ARF) in 1996, and a summit level partner (on par with China, Japan and Korea) in 2002.

The first India-ASEAN Business Summit was held at New Delhi in October 2002. The then Prime Minister A.B. Vajpayee addressed this meet and since then this business summit has become an annual feature before the India-ASEAN Summits, as a forum for networking and exchange of business experiences between policy makers and business leaders from ASEAN and India.

Four India-ASEAN Summits, first in 2002 at Phnom Penh (Cambodia), second in 2003 at Bali (Indonesia), third in 2004 at Vientiane (Laos) and the fourth in 2005 at Kuala Lumpur (Malaysia), have taken place till date.

The following agreements have been entered into with ASEAN:

- Framework Agreement on Comprehensive Economic Cooperation (for establishing a FTA in a time frame of 10 years) was concluded in Bali in 2003.
- An ASEAN-India Joint Declaration for Cooperation to Combat International Terrorism has been adopted.
- India has acceded to the Treaty of Amity and Cooperation (TAC) in 2003, on which ASEAN was formed initially (in 1967).
- Agreement on "India-ASEAN Partnership for Peace, Progress and Shared Prosperity" was signed at the 3rd ASEAN-India Summit in Nov 2004.
- Setting up of Entrepreneurship Development Centres in ASEAN member states – Cambodia, Myanmar, Laos and Vietnam. (The one in Laos is already functional)

The following proposals were announced by the Prime Minister at the 4th ASEAN-India Summit:

- Setting up centres for English Language Training (ELT) in Cambodia, Laos, Myanmar and Vietnam.

- Setting up a tele-medicine and tele-education network for Cambodia, Myanmar, Laos and Vietnam.
- Organising special training courses for diplomats from ASEAN countries.
- Organising an India-ASEAN Technology Summit in 2006.
- Organising education fairs and road shows in ASEAN countries.
- Conducting an India-ASEAN IT Ministerial and Industry Forum in 2006.

The ASEAN region has an abundance of natural resources and significant technological skills. These provide a natural base for the integration between ASEAN and India in both trade and investment. The present level of bilateral trade with ASEAN of nearly US $ 18 billion is reportedly increasing by about 25% per year. India hopes to reach the level of US $ 30 billion by 2007. India is also improving its relations with the help of other policy decisions like offers of lines of credit, better connectivity through air (open skies policy), rail and road links.

2

Challenge to Indian Foreign Policy

A subversive pragmatic vision is increasingly challenging some of the key foundations of India's traditional nationalist and left-of-center foreign policy, diluting the consensus that shaped the policy, and raising new possibilities especially for India's relations with the United States and global nuclear arms control. This debate between two centrist foreign policy perspectives is not yet settled.

The two are described here as "traditional nationalist" and "pragmatist," with the former representing the established and dominant perspective, and the latter as the emerging challenger. Actual Indian policy mostly splits the difference, mouthing traditional nationalist slogans while following pragmatist prescriptions. One major result has been the widening of political space for closer relations with the United States, even without a stable consensus.

These taxonomies are ideal types: it is very unlikely that those characterized as either nationalist or pragmatist would agree with or accept every tenet of these categories. The categorizations are designed to provide an outline of the competing lines of argumentation about Indian foreign policy, rather than identify nationalists or pragmatists *per se*. It also is important to note that it is difficult right now in India to associate these perspectives with particular political parties, think tanks, or ministries. Thus, these perspectives are individualistic and do not correspond to particular organizations.

They do, however, represent the views of important public intellectuals, policy analysts, academics, journalists, diplomats, and government officials.

THE NATIONALIST PERSPECTIVE

The nationalist perspective traces its roots to India's traditional Cold War foreign policy. Shaped by India's anti-colonial independence movement, it emphasizes national sovereignty as well as autonomy, and sought common cause with other third-world countries and non-alignment with either side in the Cold War, instincts that still guide the nationalists.

INDEPENDENCE OF FOREIGN POLICY

India's capacity for autonomous action in foreign policy is of fundamental importance to nationalists. This has taken on different policy manifestations at different times, including as "non-alignment" during the Cold War and more recently as "strategic autonomy." As Foreign Minister S.M. Krishna noted in a September 2009 speech, "Our main objective is ensuring a conducive international environment for consolidating our strategic autonomy." Nationalists tend to see New Delhi as being under constant pressure to submit India's interests to those of other major powers.

This usually means from the United States, though at different times it has also meant from the West in general or China. Nationalists see foreign policy as an arena of conflict, with major powers constantly seeking to subvert India's pursuit of its national interest to force New Delhi to follow policies that are in the interests of other powers.

For example, some commentators charged that India's passivity towards Pakistan over the last decade, despite evidence of Pakistani complicity in terrorism directed at India, was made at the behest of the United States because of Pakistan's importance to U.S. interests—in other words, that Indian policy was being dictated by Washington. This criticism is often invoked by nationalists on issues as varied as India's position at the Cancun climate change summit in December 2010, where India was seen as bending to U.S. pressure to accept legally-binding emission cuts, or its February 2006 vote to refer Iran to the UN Security Council. This was also one of the key objections that nationalists had to the U.S.—India civil nuclear deal. As one analyst noted, "We are forgetting that we are being sucked into a situation that will hobble the independence of our foreign policy." Nevertheless, it is important to note that there were some differences within the nationalist camp on the nuclear deal, and some who could be characterized as nationalist did support the deal.

The fear of losing independence in foreign policy is the primary reason why nationalists oppose any alliance-alliances are seen as a way of subverting Indian interests to those of others. It was this deeply-held value that Prime Minister Manmohan Singh was referring to in September 2010 when he said that "India is too large a country to be boxed into any alliance." The idea that alliances are constraining rather than a way of security burden-sharing explains the Delhi elite's enduring suspicion of great powers, especially the United States. This does not mean that India has no interests in common with other powers, but such common interests are likely to be on particular issues rather than in general. Thus, nationalists prefer foreign policy cooperation on a case-by-case basis to long-term alliance relationships which could tie India down.

OPPOSITION TO POWER POLITICS

Nationalist opposition to balance of power politics has its roots in the tradition of Jawaharlal Nehru, the country's first prime minister. Even though Nehru's ideological reasoning may have withered away, an analyst recently noted that "the Nehruvian instinct of staying away from balance of power considerations has not.... it is fair to say that balance of power is not the default common sense of Indian strategic thinking." Jasjit Singh, a leading Indian strategist, echoed that thought, saying, "Indian strategic culture does not accept conflict as inevitable." Writing about India's policy towards China, Singh continued that India's central goal in relation to other powers is "to address potential adversarial relations through political and diplomatic efforts to improve relations and rely on cooperative engagement as the primary instrument of strategy... [N]onalignment itself was pursued as a strategy to diffuse the strategic challenge posed by China." This opposition to power politics grows out of the strongly held belief that "India can and must play its role as conscience-keeper of the world." Thus, there is frequent invocation of alternative paradigms such as "comprehensive security" that are designed to be "cooperative, multilayered and multilateralized."

The nationalist opposition to power politics also makes for continuing controversy and considerable discomfort about episodes in which India has reached out to other countries to counter a threat. Nehru's desperate plea to President John F. Kennedy for U.S. military assistance to deal with the Chinese invasion in the fall of 1962 is particularly noteworthy because the opposition to power politics owes so much to Nehru himself.

The streak of moralism which runs through this opposition to power politics has another manifestation: a strong and abiding commitment to global nuclear disarmament. India's commitment to nuclear disarmament is usually treated with some skepticism outside the country, and indeed even by some within the country. But even if there is posturing in India's diplomatic positions, there can be little doubt about the sincerity of the sentiment regarding nuclear disarmament among sections of the Indian strategic elite.

INDIA'S INNATE IMPORTANCE

India's economic growth, information technology prowess, and rising power have reshaped global perceptions of India and India's perception of itself. A decade after India's nuclear tests, India's global relations have dramatically improved and New Delhi is increasingly wooed by major powers. Indian commentators have not been slow to notice that leaders from all of the permanent members of the UN Security Council visited India in 2010. For nationalists, this was a recognition of India's importance which called for a "noiseless celebration."

The possibility exists, however, that at least some of India's strategic elite are inflating India's capabilities and attractiveness. Yashwant Sinha, a senior Bharatiya Janata Party (BJP) leader and former Minister for External

Affairs, expressed this overconfidence well when he argued, in the context of the recent visit by President Obama to India, that "the U.S. needs India more" than India needs the United States.

For instance, the United States was forced to lift the sanctions it imposed on India after the 1998 Indian nuclear tests because "these sanctions were causing more damage to the U.S. than India." This belief that India was so important that other powers would not stand by idly if India was invaded-possibly even leading to a world war is presumably one of the reasons why Nehru thought that China would not attack India militarily in 1962. The sense of India's intrinsic importance is also reflected in India's push for a permanent seat on the UN Security Council. Though all shades of foreign policy opinion in India broadly support a permanent seat for India, nationalists tend to emphasize such demands more.

EQUITY AND DEMOCRATIC GLOBAL GOVERNANCE

A key determinant of nationalist positions on specific foreign policy issues is their claim that India must stand for democratic global governance. Nationalists support the UN as the key global multilateral forum "which embodies the collective will of its member states and the rule of law." What this means in the abstract is not often clear, but it is usually invoked in reference to the actions of other global powers rather than to India's own behaviour.

For example, though nationalists strongly support multilateralism, this rarely extends to issues that might impact Indian interests and sovereignty such as Kashmir or arms control. Nationalists generally tend to equate democratization of world politics with multi-polarity. Thus, nationalists propose working together with other powers in groups such as the IBSA Dialogue Forum towards a multi-polar world order. Equity in international interactions is another fundamental concern of nationalists, leading many times to legalist rather than political arguments on international issues. This should not be surprising since the Indian government has often been criticized for just such a predilection, and many of those who would hold nationalist views are former Indian diplomats.

This was the basis of much of the opposition to the U.S.—India nuclear deal among some nationalists, who joined with other critics from both the left and the right of the political spectrum in parsing every statement and document for signs of U.S. perfidy. For example, they pointed out that the United States had unilaterally altered or reinterpreted a previous nuclear cooperation agreement for the supply of nuclear reactors to the Tarapur nuclear plant in the 1970s.This emphasis on equity can also be seen in the focus on the rights of states, especially developing ones, rather than obligations. Such legalism tends to make nationalists inflexible and dismissive of arguments based on political changes.

RISING PRAGMATISM

The end of the Cold War led to new challenges and new debates about India's foreign policy. Some Indian strategists, referred to here as the pragmatists, argued that India's traditional foreign policy was no longer relevant to the post-Cold War world, and pushed for the unabashed consideration of the Indian national interest rather than global justice or ethics.

THE PRIMACY OF NATIONAL INTEREST

One of the key arguments made by the new pragmatists is that Indian foreign policy has for far too long been driven by ideological positions which have not promoted India's national interest. Therefore, they argue that national interest rather than global concerns or ideology should guide Indian policy. Pragmatists have, for example, wondered why India is so committed to the UN. T.P. Srinivasan, a former Indian diplomat, noted that "India's commitment to multilateralism and the U.N. is firm and absolute... And yet, India has very little to show in reciprocal advantages, which India has gained over the years from the U.N." Pragmatists tend to be skeptical of the UN in general, though they are not averse to the idea of India in the UN Security Council. They tend to be much more realistic about the prospects of any such entry in the future, however, and dismissive of the urgency with which such demands are made in the Indian debate, characterizing these as "immature yearnings."

MORALITY AND COMPROMISE

Pragmatists tend to be impatient with moral claims in foreign policy. As Shashi Tharoor, who would become India's junior foreign minister, put it once, traditionally India "seemed to take greater satisfaction in being right than being diplomatic." More recently—and controversially—he criticized Nehruvian foreign policy for being a "moralistic running commentary." But direct criticism is not the only tack that pragmatists have used to argue against the moralism in Indian foreign policy.

Others have argued that Indian foreign policy was actually not particularly moralistic, which also is an argument to suggest that there is little reason for Indian foreign policy today to try to live up to such traditions. Pragmatists tend to blame misplaced moralism for India's previous strategic missteps, such as not conducting a nuclear test in the 1960s so that India could join the nuclear Non-Proliferation Treaty (NPT) as a nuclear weapon state. In contrast, nationalists dismiss these new claims, suggesting that those who proclaim themselves as realists have "little awareness of what real politic means."

Pragmatists argue that India should be flexible in the pursuit of its national interests, especially on ideological issues. They believe that Indian policy is often geared towards consistency with past positions without recognizing India's changed circumstances, especially in the aftermath of the 1998 nuclear tests. This is particularly visible in India's nuclear policies. Pragmatists find the deeply held Indian opposition to the Comprehensive Test Ban Treaty (CTBT) and many other nuclear arms control policies outdated and suggest that India take a fresh look at such issues.

But as strategist C. Raja Mohan suggested, Indian foreign policy debates are so focused on semantics that "they have little time for the 'grammar' of global power politics." He argues that this focus on semantics was understandable when India was weak, when "rhetoric compensated for power," but unnecessary for an India that has become far more consequential in global affairs. Pragmatists think that New Delhi should carefully weigh foreign policy choices, assessing the overall benefit rather than costs alone.

ALLIANCES

Pragmatists are much less doctrinaire about alliances than nationalists are. While nationalists make non-alignment the basis for Indian foreign policy, pragmatists are not as concerned about that foreign policy heritage. Although they are critics of the excessive focus on non-alignment, pragmatists do not necessarily suggest that India needs to align with other powers.

For example, while pragmatists tend to be strong supporters of closer U.S.—India relations, they do not see the relationship as an alliance. A hostile China may bring the United States and India together in the near term, but "it is far from certain on which side of the U.S.—China divide India's long-term interests lie." Nevertheless, pragmatists suggest much closer U.S.— India cooperation not only on political and military issues, but also on issues of the global commons. But pragmatists also suggest closer military ties with powers other than the United States, such as Russia, as a way of hedging against any potential threat from China. In essence, though they have not suggested that India should ally with other powers, this appears to be more because they do not yet see the necessity for such alliances rather than because of any ideological opposition.

INTERNATIONAL TREATIES

Pragmatists do not share the suspicion which nationalists have of many international treaties or agreements. For pragmatists, while there might have been good reasons for India not to accede to particular international agreements in the past, India's changed global circumstances should also lead to changes in its approaches to international treaties. This is particularly true for various arms control agreements and initiatives. Pragmatists have not only supported signing the CTBT, but also initiatives such as the Proliferation Security Initiative (PSI). Similarly, pragmatists suggest that India should prepare the groundwork for the Fissile Material Control Treaty (FMCT) rather than simply opposing the treaty. Since the key objection to the treaty is not having sufficient fissile materials, India should decide how much fissile material it needs and how to acquire it prior to an FMCT coming into force.

OPPOSING PERSPECTIVES, DISPUTED POLICIES AND IMPLICATIONS

These opposing perspectives have led to far greater disagreements over India's foreign policy than at any time in the past. Below are four specific policy disputes, all of which have particular policy relevance for the United States.

U.S. RELATIONS

India's policy towards the United States has become increasingly contested. Pragmatists want closer ties—they see the United States as being useful to India right now—while nationalists remain suspicious that the United States seeks to contain India.

For the nationalists, "there is a fundamental contradiction between U.S. and Indian long-term foreign policy objectives" because while "the U.S. wants the current so-called unipolar world order to continue, India believes that the world should be multipolar, with India itself as one of the poles." Others suggest that the key problem is the U.S. dependence on Pakistan. As a former Indian Foreign Secretary asked, "If the U.S. has a long-term strategic partnership with a Pakistan that remains unremittingly hostile to India, how does it reconcile that reality with its strategic partnership with India?" Pragmatists, on the other hand, are willing to push for closer relations with the United States, even if that increases the possibility that it could lead to greater difficulties with other powers such as China.

They suggest that it is in India's interest to build up ties with the United States, given the close relations that China has had with Pakistan for decades and the fact that India is an attractive partner for the United States, both because of U.S. worries about a rising China and the clout of India's burgeoning market.

The debate over the U.S.—India civil nuclear deal is an illustration of the growing clout of the pragmatists. The Indian decision to go ahead with the deal finally owed more to Prime Minister Singh's determination to push it through than to pragmatist success in the public debate over the issue. Nevertheless, the debate over the nuclear deal demonstrated for the first time that the pragmatists could mount a credible challenge to the traditionalist dominance over a key area of foreign policy. There is little indication that the dispute over the appropriate type of relations which India needs to have with the United States will be resolved in the near future.

ARMS CONTROL

India's arms control policy is a second area of conflict between these two perspectives. Nationalists continue to be suspicious of many arms control agreements, holding out for nuclear disarmament as the right way forward. To the extent that they are willing to consider arms control measures, they require that such treaties directly contribute to nuclear disarmament rather than simply be stand-alone measures. Nationalists tend to be particularly opposed to treaties such as the CTBT and the FMCT, which are seen as non-proliferation measures rather than steps towards nuclear disarmament.

On CTBT, for example, nationalists would suggest that India should not sign the treaty unless all others do and add conditions such as the treaty being nondiscriminatory with a clearly-established link to nuclear disarmament. In essence, these conditions would suggest that India will not sign the CTBT in the foreseeable future. But pragmatists want India to be more open to considering a different approach. For example, arguing that India took the lead on CTBT in the 1950s, pragmatists have argued that India should rejoin discussions about nuclear non-proliferation rather than dismiss them. Similarly, pragmatists suggest that India should be more open to working with the nuclear non-proliferation regime, even if the NPT itself is considered unacceptable.

IRAN

India's position on Iran, specifically on Iran's dispute with the United States and the international community on the nuclear issue, has become another hotly contested foreign policy issue. The most serious conflict over Iran is between the pragmatists and leftist opinion-makers, who see the Iran nuclear issue through their traditional anti-American prism. The left has traditionally had little influence on Indian foreign policy, but was influential in the first Singh government because Communist parties were part of the ruling coalition and the government depended on their support to stay in power.

The nationalists have made common cause with leftists on this issue, dismissing U.S. claims that Iran is seeking nuclear weapons and supporting Iran's right to develop civilian nuclear technology. The nationalists are not necessarily united in their views on Iran, however. Some see Iran as "a neighbour with which India is linked by many centuries of economic, cultural and even civilizational ties." Other nationalists tend to worry about Iran's links to Pakistan, especially on the nuclear black market, and are suspicious of Iran's efforts to compare their illegal nuclear programme with India's.

It is not that nationalists are particularly supportive of closer ties with Iran, but their objection is to what they perceive as U.S. pressure on Indian foreign policy, of which Iran is only one manifestation. Writing about the purported U.S. pressure on the stillborn Iran—Pakistan—India gas pipeline project, one former senior official wrote that "the pipeline never was really a brilliant idea... But that apart, it was India's decision—good or bad, right or wrong."

Thus, India's Iran policy has become an important test of whether Indian foreign policy is sufficiently independent from the United States, with critics of the government claiming that New Delhi kowtows to Washington. Pragmatists tend to defend India's taking a position against the Iranian nuclear programme, such as voting against Iran at the International Atomic Energy Agency (IAEA), by pointing out that Iran had not lived up to its obligations and India had little reason to support Iran. Rejecting charges that such a position represented giving in to U.S. pressure, one analyst characterized the Indian position as "Enlightened Independence." This is another dispute that shows little sign of ebbing.

THE THIRD WORLD AND THE NON-ALIGNED MOVEMENT (NAM)

The Third-World and the NAM have become less important in India's foreign policy framework. Nevertheless, nationalists continue to argue that the NAM and third-world solidarity are useful for India. They tend to see various new coalitions, such as the IBSA, BRIC (Brazil—Russia—India—China), and BASIC (Brazil—South Africa—India—China), as carrying forward the task of developing the third-world unity which the NAM performed in the Cold War, characterizing this collectivity as the "new NAM." But pragmatists tend to dismiss such prospects, pointing to internal weaknesses within these coalitions and their inability—at least for India—to deal with the rise of China.

However, the disagreement over this issue is somewhat less serious, and likely to become increasingly marginal, because there is greater recognition that third-world solidarity or even these new coalitions are unlikely to be serious foreign policy options for India.

CONTINUING COMMONALITIES AND IMPLICATIONS

Though the nationalist and pragmatist perspectives are locked in serious disagreements, they are essentially both centrist perspectives. Thus, significant common areas exist where Indian foreign policy is relatively uncontroversial. Five of these areas follow:

CHINA

For different reasons, both nationalists and pragmatists want closer ties with Beijing, even as both are wary of China. Pragmatists see China as a power with which India can and must deal. Strategist C. Raja Mohan argues that "the nuclear tests of May 1998, the improved economic performance of the 1990s, and the positive evolution of India's relations with the United States in the changed international and regional context after the Cold War have given India an opportunity for a realistic and productive engagement with China in the coming decades." Meanwhile, though nationalists draw their perspectives from Nehru, they share none of the Nehruvian romanticism about Sino—Indian "brotherhood." As one put it, "We have to remember that all talk of harmonious development and peaceful neighbourhood notwithstanding, China will not give us space voluntarily. We have to make that space ourselves."

Nationalists would prefer that New Delhi use its own resources to deal with China rather than depend on others, while the pragmatists see the United States as a possible partner. Despite their suspicions, nationalists also tend to see strong similarities between India and China, suggesting that these similarities also suggest mutual interests. While they remain uncertain about how Sino—Indian relations will evolve, they are willing to seek out areas of common interest, such as trade, and hope that such interests will help ameliorate future conflict.

Pragmatists would also agree that India has to seek cooperation while also being prepared. As one pragmatist put it, India should be "seeking positive interaction while making itself powerful enough to shape or cope with China's behaviour." Another analyst went even further, expressing the sentiment well when he observed that "China's recent assertiveness is symbolic of not just its rise, but it also signals that Beijing will be in the future, at best, our greatest challenge and, at worst, a security nightmare." As suggested earlier, pragmatists are willing to consider closer ties with the United States as a way to counter the possible threat from China. Thus, although they may seek different ways to deal with the challenge, for both nationalists and pragmatists, China remains a threat and a concern.

PAKISTAN

Both nationalists and pragmatists see Pakistan as a key problem, but both see very little chance of a solution other than patience. After the November 2008 Mumbai terrorist attack, there was greater willingness among many analysts to consider military measures against Pakistan, even if that could involve possible nuclear escalation. Still, among both nationalists and pragmatists there is consensus that India has few options but to keep engaging with Pakistan, despite repeated acts of violence against India by Pakistani-supported terrorists.

Pragmatists recognize, as a well-respected former Indian diplomat put it, that "limited retaliation would likely fuel more terrorism" and "full retaliation is not our way." India simply lacks the conventional superiority that it needs to take military action against Pakistan, in addition to the risk of nuclear escalation.

Nationalists similarly argue that India cannot undertake counterterrorist military actions, as the United States has in Afghanistan, for a variety of reasons including the fact that India has neighbours who provide active support and sanctuary to terrorist groups. As one commentator noted, "India carries its burden of combating terrorism on its own. It would need to act alone to force a change of attitude and conviction in Pakistan..." There is an occasional suggestion that India should retaliate against Pakistan for acts of terrorism perpetrated by Pakistani-based groups, but these are notable for their rarity. Thus, on the critical issue of India's policy towards Pakistan, there is both increasing frustration but also broad consensus between the two perspectives.

DIPLOMACY AND FORCE

It follows from the above that both nationalists and pragmatists tilt heavily towards diplomacy in the grand strategic force—diplomacy equation. Indian analysts are exploring the consequences of nuclearization on the military balance in South Asia with increasing sophistication. Nevertheless, the predominant opinion across the political spectrum is that India does not really have much of a military option in dealing with either Pakistan or China. On the other hand, there are ruminations, at least among some pragmatists, about the necessity for India to develop an expeditionary military capability. Understandably, there has been some support for such proposals from the military. But given the predominant consensus on diplomacy rather than force, there is unlikely to be an Indian version of the "parabellum paradigm," a hard realist approach to strategy.

NUCLEAR NONPROLIFERATION TREATY

Pragmatists suggest that India needs to be less rigid in its approach to arms control issues such as the PSI and even on the CTBT. But this second look does not extend to the NPT itself. Pragmatists do see the possibility, and even the need, for India to work within the non-proliferation regime because nuclear proliferation is as much a threat to India as it is to the global community.

Nevertheless, they would not go so far as to suggest that India consider joining the NPT as it is currently structured, meaning as a non-nuclear weapon state. In practical terms, this approach matches that of the nationalists, who would not countenance any compromise with the NPT. Nationalist opposition to the NPT, however, is much broader, more rigid, and inflexible, seeing little point in even working within the existing non-proliferation order. They dismiss the argument that India can cooperate with the non-proliferation regime without actually joining the treaty itself. Since the NPT does not recognize India as a nuclear-weapon state, India's cooperation with the broader non-proliferation regime will neither reduce India's costs nor increase its benefits.

MYANMAR

Another issue on which nationalists and pragmatists agree is Indian policy towards Myanmar, a country that is likely to grow in importance for India. Nationalists do not accept notions of democracy promotion. Indeed, democracy promotion has never been a part of Indian strategy. In his

November 2010 speech to the Indian parliament, President Obama noted that "in international fora, India has often shied away" from issues such as democracy and human rights. As Raja Mohan has pointed out, "Much of the world sees a profound commitment to democracy amidst bewildering diversity as the defining feature of modern India. Yet, democracy as a political priority has largely been absent from India's foreign policy."

This is particularly true of India's policy towards Myanmar. Both nationalists and pragmatists see it as more important to compete with China, as well as deal with Indian insurgents in Myanmar. Pragmatists argue that there is little reason for India to justify its policies to powers such as the United States and United Kingdom "that have long coddled military dictators in India's South Asian neighbourhood, notably in Pakistan." This suggests that, however squeamish India gets about the military dictators in Yangon, there is unlikely to be any change in Indian policy.

A FRACTURING INDIAN FOREIGN POLICY CONSENSUS

While consensus on these five critical issues exists, the increasingly active contestations over Indian foreign policy debates means many other foreign policy choices are now open to challenge, and it is likely that the number of such contested foreign policy issues will increase in the coming years. While there have been some struggles in the past over India's policy towards the United States, there are also likely to be disputes over Indian policies towards China, Japan, and even Russia in the coming years.

One implication is that New Delhi might have more foreign policy options to consider. Domestic contestation provides policymakers with some cover to consider options which might not have been previously deliberated. It is too early to suggest that this process might lead to a new consensus, but what appears clear is that the traditional nationalist consensus over Indian foreign policy no longer holds.

For Washington, this implies that Indian foreign policy might become even more flexible. U.S. diplomacy has so far been both relatively adept and patient in dealing with the raucous Indian debate, advancing U.S. perspectives on various policy issues, usually without offending Indian sensibilities. But in Washington itself, Indian public debate has played little part in policy formulations, especially on larger Asian and global policy issues. New Delhi, of course, is not alone in being ignored in the U.S. foreign policy debate—other capitals are equally disregarded. As Washington's margin for error decreases with its relative decline, it becomes even more important for the United States to pay greater attention to the emerging debates in New Delhi.

The shift in Indian foreign policy discourse also suggests that India's global role might be more flexible than previously considered. India is not self-consciously debating its future global role in the centralized manner that China might be, but in a democratic and chaotic manner typical to India. But the debate itself is unmistakable.

An alternate possibility is that these increasingly acrimonious debates might slow down critical foreign policy decisions, or indeed even lead to policy paralysis. For instance, despite widespread global concern that India was being rewarded by the United States with the nuclear deal, Indian domestic opposition almost scuttled the deal more than once. At the same time, it is important to recognize that the debate itself represents a move away from the old consensus, which had tethered India for decades. It cannot be said right now that a new consensus is emerging. It is possible that Indian foreign policy might remain contested for a considerable period. This might be a good thing: the old consensus was the consequence of India's fairly stable international positioning for decades. The debate today is made possible precisely because India's global position is so dynamic. Until it stabilizes, it is unlikely that a new consensus will emerge.

3

Risk Management

In a world of stable currency exchange rates, there is no need for risk management. In a world of limited volatility and infrequent changes in a system of fixed exchange rates, there may be some interest in risk management. In a world of wide swings in currency exchange rates, risk management becomes a necessity.

This is a world of increasing volatility in currency exchange rates. Volatility, in general, is associated with instability. This, in itself, is a testament to our seemingly growing incapacity to control our created economic and financial systems. We first declared gold and silver to be deemed money. Currencies, which were convertible into gold and silver, eventually gave way to another man-made system of infrequently adjusted fixed rates of exchange among the leading currencies where one currency, the U.S. dollar, was convertible into gold. Then this system gave way to another predominantly "dirty" managed system of floating exchange rates, where a currency is convertible only into another currency.

Many of the world currencies have limited convertibility to other currencies. Companies doing business in these nations have to adapt their financial affairs to fit the situation. That is to say, the conduct of business is guided, among other things, with an eye on how much currency is being accumulated. Even for convertible currencies associated with industrialized nations, the conduct of business is influenced by which currencies are being accumulated and which are being liquidated. Changes in currency exchange rates since the early 1970s have been significant. Therefore, these changes have significantly impacted the reported profitability of subsidiaries and affiliates when their financial reports were translated to the standard currency of the parent company.

CONTROLLABLE AND UNCONTROLLABLE LOSSES

Running a business has its inherent risks. Many of these risks cannot be managed—that is, they are beyond the control of management. These include the risk of a general downturn in business activity that reduces the volume of sales and the risk of competitors slashing prices to aggressively expand their market share. A company must face the risk of competitors transforming the nature of the market by introducing an improved, or a new, version of a product that makes a company's product dated or obsolete. There is the risk of adverse government legislation, regulatory requirements, barriers to trade, and product liability suits. The list goes on, but added to this list is volatility in currency exchange rates. A receivable due in ninety days may not have the anticipated value in the domestic currency of a company that was envisioned when the transaction was consummated.

The risk of a currency exchange loss is a risk that has been dealt with by financial managers since the early 1970s. One might consider this potential loss of value in a financial transaction as uncontrollable in the sense that management cannot influence future currency exchange rates. Indeed, this is not so. Unlike a downward step in general business activity, an industry-wide price war, or a new product introduced by a competitor, there are ways for a company to protect itself against potential adverse changes in currency exchange rates. The availability of financial instruments to deal with this risk makes it controllable and gives meaning to the phrase "risk management."

PRICE VOLATILITY AS A MARK OF THE TIMES

Increased volatility transcends currency exchange rates. Prices of certain commodities that once were stable are now volatile. For example, the price of gold was constant from 1934, when President Franklin Roosevelt set the price of gold at $35 per ounce, until President Nixon shut the gold window in 1971. Although gold is not a commodity that affects the operations of most companies, its shift from a stable-priced commodity to one subject to wide swings in prices is instructive as to the nature of the problem of price volatility facing modern managers.

The purchasing managers of gold-consuming companies experienced a nearly forty-year history of paying $35 per ounce. During this time, the demands on the financial acumen of the purchasers to minimize the acquisition cost of gold were not overwhelming.

Little thought had to be given to inventory valuations and the potential of an inventory loss. Since 1971, the purchasing managers have had to endure the transition from purchasing gold at a fixed price to a price that is influenced by the supply and demand balance of gold and market perceptions of changes in that relationship. The percentage change, a measure of volatility, is the annual price swing divided by the mid-price for gold for the indicated year.

Daily quotes can be higher or lower than indicated. In 1980, spot gold spiked at over $800 per ounce for a short period of time. This is hidden in calculating monthly averages. Monthly or annual averages tend to mask the true nature of the volatility that is present in the daily, or spot, market. Purchasing managers focus on the current, or daily, market and must react to volatility on a daily, not on a monthly or annual, basis.

Volatility is better expressed as a percentage change from a base value than as an absolute difference between high and low quotes. The 1983 swing in prices of $102 per ounce appears to have greater volatility, or change, than the 1975 swing in prices of $37. Yet the volatility, as measured by the degree of change from the mid-value, is the same for both years. The $102 swing in prices in 1983, when compared to the mid-price of $439, is a measure of volatility of 23 percent. This is the same measure of volatility in 1975 when the $37 swing is compared to the mid-price of $162.

VOLATILITY IMPACTS PROFITABILITY

Nevertheless, the volatility of gold prices is going to affect the profitability of a company that consumes gold in its operations in two ways. Gold purchased in 1980 at an average price of $600 per ounce generated either operating losses or inventory write-downs when gold subsequently fell to $400 per ounce. Therefore, the task of management takes on a new dimension of meaning compared to what it was when the price of gold was fixed by government fiat. Poorly timed purchases of gold as a raw material with respect to the selling of the gold product can lead to substantial operating or inventory valuation losses, a risk not present when the price of gold was stable.

Loss from operations caused by a severe downturn in general business activity might be considered by managers to be beyond their control. An inventory loss may or may not fall into this category. Inventory is necessary for the smooth operations of a company and inventory requires management attention in terms of its quantity and safekeeping. So while a manager is focusing his or her attention on what he or she considers to be more important matters concerning marketing, production and financing, a loss may suddenly emanate from the warehouse. In his or her mind, this should not occur because one would not expect that something safely stored in a well-operated warehouse could generate a loss. Yet it can, if the price of whatever is stored in the warehouse declines substantially. Obviously, this uncontrollable loss becomes a controllable loss when managers accept the responsibility to minimize potential inventory losses and have some means of preventing the loss from occurring. For most inventories, management's tools may be limited to managing the quantity of inventory and, perhaps, terms of sales. But for other types of inventories, including inventories of currencies, there are means of insuring against such a loss. For generic forms of inventories such as metals, foodstuffs, energy, and currencies, there are a variety of risk management products available to reduce or contain the magnitude of a potential loss in the carrying value of an inventory.

VOLATILITY IMPACTS INVESTMENT DECISIONS

The discussion so far has been primarily from the buyer's perspective, where volatility introduces the potential for operating and inventory valuation losses. The other perspective is that of the seller, in this case, a gold mining company. Another complication arising from volatile gold prices is loss of confidence in the financial analysis associated with the decision-making process leading to a capital investment. When prices are constant, the projected revenue of a financial analysis of making a major capital investment in mining capacity can be viewed with a fair degree of confidence. As long as costs are reasonably accurate, and most companies have a fairly good handle on costs, a financial analysis with constancy of prices is reasonably reliable as long as the volume of output is realizable.

Instability in prices affects the confidence that management has in the validity of investment decision models. In 1940, one would confidently project a continued price of $35 per ounce in the decision-making process on making an investment in a gold mine. What price would one assume in 1980 to hold for the next ten to twenty years in order to justify the capital investment in expanding mining capacity? Five hundred dollars per ounce might have been considered reasonable at that time, but one would lack confidence in that price holding for the next decade or so because of past price volatility. In subsequent years, an average projected value of $500 per ounce turned out to be wrong. A capital project whose financing costs depended on an average price of $500 per ounce would certainly have impacted negatively on a company's earnings, and conceivably could have led to its bankruptcy. Therefore, volatility detracts from the confidence management can place in the underlying financial analysis of the investment decision process.

VOLATILITY COMMON IN TODAY'S WORLD

Increasing volatility is not restricted to currency exchange rates or gold. The cost of energy, as reflected in the cost for oil, was essentially constant at close to $2 per barrel from the 1930s until 1972. Interest rates were also stable up to this time. Yet by reviewing this table, one can see that there are times of general calm, and other times of tumult, in price volatility. The degree of volatility from year to year is itself volatile and unpredictable. This is an important point that adds to the challenge of risk management—hedging generally should be put in place before tumult in prices strikes the market. However, hedging during times of relative calm is sure to raise some questions as to its cost and need.

In viewing the table, islands of stability in a sea of volatility can be seen for interest rates from 1975 to 1978 and from 1985 to 1988. The price of oil was relatively stable from 1974 to 1978 and from 1982 to 1985. Other periods exhibited enormous volatility. It was no fun being a corporate borrower from 1977 to 1981 or purchasing oil from 1973 to 1974, or from 1978 to 1979. But there is always the other side of the coin. Those with savings seeking interest income would not consider 1982 to 1985 memorable times nor do oil producers have fond memories of 1985 to 1986, or 1987 to 1988. Viewing price changes from the two perspectives of buyers and sellers creates a potential market for risk management products. The seller is interested in fixing the sales price so that he or she does not have to worry about falling prices eroding profit. A buyer is interested in fixing cost so that he or she does not have to worry about rising costs eroding profit. What appears to be an adverse change in price for one party is considered by the other to be an opportunity. This makes it possible for those involved as middlemen or market makers in risk management products to put a deal together, because each party has a different view of the consequences of the same price change.

The airlines have historically flown on thin profit margins because of competitive pressures within this industry. Airline executives learned about the impact of price volatility on profits the hard way. Both the cost of money and jet fuel are important in an airline's operations. With thin profit margins, 25 percent jumps in interest rates (10 percent to 12.5 percent) or jet fuel costs (60 to 75 cents per gallon) are sufficient to obliterate profit margins. During the 1970s, both jet fuel prices and short-term interest rates spiked at three times, or 300 percent, their levels at the start of the 1970s.

The normal "knee-jerk" response to higher prices is to jack up the airfares. Airline executives learned that such enormous increases in the costs of money and fuel could not be entirely passed on to the consumer in the form of hikes in airline fares. Although the business traveller may be relatively indifferent to the cost of airfare, the vacationing public is not. The vacationing public makes up a sizable portion of airline traffic and is, in general, sensitive to the price of a ticket. As airlines raised ticket prices to compensate for these unheard of swings in the cost of money and fuel, the vacationing public stopped buying airline tickets. The vacation in Europe gave way to a vacation on the Jersey shore. The reduced number of passengers made it impossible for the airlines to recoup the incremental costs. The volatility in the cost of money and fuel on air fares and the ensuing loss of passenger volume was more than sufficient to destroy the profitability of the industry and to drive certain airlines into bankruptcy. Airlines that did protect themselves partially from these changes in costs through shrewd management of the risks that they faced found themselves at a competitive advantage. They number among the survivors.

Yet during those times of relative stability in prices for gold, interest, and currency exchange rates prior to the 1970s, managers of certain industries had to deal in a world of price instability. Lumber, copper, and foodstuffs were, and still are, exposed to the vagaries of sharp price swings. Managers of firms that bought or sold these commodities were keen to protect themselves from adverse price changes through risk management. Financial instruments have been around for over a century to address this need. These financial instruments were expanded in scope, and modified as necessary, as price volatility spread to precious metals, energy, and interest and currency exchange rates.

A discussion on risk management can be easily adapted from one commodity to another. Risk management techniques can be applied to tangibles (grain, lumber, oil, and metals) and to intangibles (interest rates, stock prices, and currency exchange rates). A proposed risk management product can be tailored to anything that exhibits sufficient price volatility to create a need for individuals as normal buyers or sellers of the tangible or intangible item to seek protection from such price swings. In addition, a proposed risk management product should be attractive enough for speculators to assume risk in their quest for personal gain. A proposed risk management product requires an acceptable means of settlement and a large number of actively trading participants. Their trading activity in hedging or speculating provides the revenue to cover the cost of operations and the requisite liquidity for the buying and selling of the risk management product.

Both hedgers and speculators are required for the successful laying off of risk among the participants. The presence of speculators adds depth to the market, by their volume of buying and selling. They are said to bring information to the market by taking positions based on their analysis of available data, which, in turn, influences prices. They often are the mainstay of balancing orders when the "legitimate" hedgers are primarily on one side of the market. For instance, when gold was $800 per ounce, mining companies may have been eager to fix their future production at a price around $800. Consumers of gold may not have been so eager to fix their costs at $800. There is now a mismatch between the number of buyers and sellers. The transference of risk, which is the purpose of risk management products, cannot be accomplished because the market has become one-sided. However, the presence of speculators provides the mining companies with the opportunity to enter into financial transactions that would stabilize their future revenue by transferring the opportunity of further gain in prices to the speculators.

In this example, gold mining companies who entered into futures contracts to fix the price of future production at $800 per ounce turned out to have made the right decision. Consumers of gold and speculators who represented the other side of the transaction lived to regret their decision. Risk management products are a means by which the risk of a rise or fall in a price, or the opportunity associated therewith, is passed from one party to another. Risk management products do not obviate the risk; no more than fire insurance stops fires.

CURRENCY RISK MANAGEMENT

Currency risk management has to do with taking action to avert the risk of loss because of the nature of the currency held by a company and because of the nature of future commercial transactions that lead to an exposure to a currency. Currency risk management is more complex than risk management of a commodity such as copper. A global company must think about its exposure in a hundred currencies, whereas a company dealing in copper has one commodity to worry about. Management views of a currency as favorable or unfavorable depend on whether it is strengthening or weakening in relation to other currencies and on whether a company is long (held in reserves) or short (owed to others). A copper mining company with inventory to be sold and a copper using company with copper in a warehouse to be consumed do not as readily shift between a long or short position as does a global company with a hundred affiliates dealing in a hundred currencies.

A copper-consuming company can easily quantify its exposure. Copper on hand, plus anticipated receipts and commitments less planned shipments, pretty much measures the exposure. Besides dealing in many currencies, a global company has two types of currency exposures: transactions and translations. Although transaction exposure is more easily understood, as payables and receivables in various currencies, translation exposure involves other aspects of the balance sheet. Moreover, the nature of the consolidation process affects the magnitude of translation risk.

Management usually tries to simplify the confusion over currencies by referencing all currencies to one currency—the currency of the nation of domicile. An American-based company's management thinks of all currencies in terms of a dollar equivalent. British, German, and Japanese managers view currencies in their pound, deutschemark, or yen equivalents. There is also a tendency to reduce excess holdings in various currencies to the currency of the company's nation of domicile. Although understandable, it is possible that holding cash reserves in the nation of domicile may not be the optimal course of action. If the pound or dollar is weakening with respect to the deutschemark and yen, is it wise to convert all deutschemark and yen holdings to pounds or dollars as quickly as possible just because management happens to be British or American? One aspect of the transition from a multinational company to a truly global company may be in the way the company thinks of currencies. A global company may not think in terms of a single dominating currency, but in terms of several major currencies with changing attitudes on which to hold. Perhaps its financial records and earnings reports may not be in a single currency.

But for now, it is easier to discuss currency risk management in terms of a single currency in relation to others. The discussion that follows is based on a U.S. domiciled company, but the principles are similar to those of companies domiciled in other nations.

TRANSACTION EXPOSURE

A common practice for affiliates operating in various countries is to receive payment for goods sold in the currency of its nation of domicile. Suppose that a company consists of three affiliates operating in the United States, Germany, and France. These affiliates buy and sell among themselves and normally, but not always, expect payment in their currency of domicile. Normally, when the American affiliat (A) purchases goods from the German affiliate (G), it generates a deutsche-mark (DM) payable. When it purchases goods from the French affiliate (F), the American affiliate generates a French franc (FF) payable. Similarly when the German or the French affiliates purchase goods from the American affiliate, the American affiliate has dollar receivables.

Although this is common practice, it is possible for an affiliate to buy goods from another affiliate and pay for it in its own currency, and to sell goods to another affiliate and receive payment in the affiliate's currency of domicile. It is also possible that a third currency not related to either of the affiliates may be used as a means of settlement. Suppose, at a point in time, the inter company receivables and payables.

Managers of a U.S. domiciled company would view these currency transactions in terms of dollar equivalents. Translating these payables and receivables in terms of a deutschemark being worth about $0.60 and a French franc about These receivables and payables can be combined as in A to obtain the net exposure to each currency.

Receivables and payables in the same currency are natural hedges. Thousands of individual receivables and payables can be combined to obtain the actual exposure of a company to a particular currency. In this example, the actual exposure of the company consisting of three affiliates in terms of inter company buying and selling is a long position of $54 worth of deutschemarks (90 DM), a short position of $300 of French francs (1,500 FF), and a long position of $40 (U.S.). Once the natural hedges within, and without, a company have been combined, management is in a position to evaluate its actual exposure to various currencies and to decide on a course of action to reduce potential currency exchange losses.

Some commercial banks offer a "netting" or payment-clearing service to companies with global operations. All the affiliates of a company enter their inter company receivables and payables, in terms of the actual currencies to be received or paid, through a telecommunications system into a common computer data bank. On a periodic basis, and under management control, all inter company receivables and payables are netted and an affiliate receives, or owes, one payment. As an example, a Belgian affiliate may have dealings with a hundred different affiliates in as many nations. Generally speaking, most payables are in the currency of the nation of domicile of the affiliate and most receivables are in Belgian francs, but this may not be true for all transactions. At specified periods such as a month, and assuming that there are more in receivables than in payables in these inter company transactions, the Belgian affiliate receives one payment in Belgian francs. All associated inter company receivables and payables contained within the computer data base, which could number in the tens, the hundreds, or even the thousands, are thereby liquidated with the issuance of a single payment. If the Belgian affiliate has more payables than receivables, then it makes one payment in Belgian francs, and again all associated receivables and payables are liquidated. The bank makes all spot conversions of currencies necessary for the affiliates to receive or pay in their respective currencies of domicile.

Management can incorporate projected payables and receivables into the system in addition to actual payables and receivables in order to improve its measurement of exposure to various currencies from inter company transfers. The netting service provides management with a full range of reports such as currency exposure, cash balance, transaction, consolidation, and working capital reports. These reports are used for control purposes, for cash management, and for measuring a company's current and projected exposure to various currencies from inter company transfers. A full measurement of exposure also requires projected payables and receivables to other companies outside the netting system.

It is also conceivable that several global companies could join together in such a system, further reducing the administrative processing costs of making individual payments to affiliates in the same global company and to affiliates in other global companies. Conceptually, this is not unlike credit cards where individuals make one monthly payment, which covers a multitude of individual purchases from many merchants, and where merchants receive one monthly payment from the credit card company, which represents the purchases of many individuals.

TRANSLATION EXPOSURE

Currency translation exposure applies to balance sheets and income statements denominated in a different currency than the company's nation of domicile. Translation exposure is determined by applying the appropriate exchange rate to the various items of the balance sheet and income statements. The rules regarding which exchange rate is to be applied to individual line items of a balance sheet and income statement differ with the consolidation method. Therefore, the amount and treatment of translation gains or losses vary with the method of consolidation.

As an example of the possibility of obtaining different measures of exposure to translation gains or losses, suppose that a company has an affiliate in country X and management is fearful of a 20 percent devaluation of the local currency (LC). For a U.S. company, however, there are two possible methods of consolidation. One is the current rate method (Financial Accounting Standards Board [FASB] 52) and the other is the temporal method (FASB 8).

If, on the other hand, management had determined that the functional currency was the U.S. dollar, the temporal method of translation would be applicable as prescribed by FASB 8. The temporal method must also be selected as the method of consolidation if the affiliate is operating in a hyperinflationary economy, which is defined as one where the currency has a three-year cumulative inflation exceeding 100 percent. Cash and accounts receivable total 1.9 billion LC and liabilities total 3.2 billion LC, resulting in a negative exposure, or short position, of 1.3 billion LC. Under FASB 8, inventories and fixed assets are recorded at historical values and are not exposed to changes in currency exchange rates. This short position, or negative exposure, of 1.3 billion LC will result in a translation gain of $26 million (1.3 billion LC x $0.02 LC/dollar change in the currency exchange rate). This gain is reflected in the income statement, not directly in the equity portion of the balance sheet.

Under FASB 8, the inventory is still recorded at the historic rate of $0.10. This means that in subsequent periods of operation, sales will be translated at 1 LC equal to $0.08, but cost of sales, as goods are withdrawn from the "old" inventory, will be translated at a rate of 1 LC being equal to $0. 10 until the "old" inventory is depleted. New additions to the inventory will be translated at 1 LC equal to $0.08. The existence of the "old" inventory has a negative

impact on future translated profit until it is depleted. In addition, depreciation expense on existing fixed assets at the time of the devaluation is translated at the rate of $0.10 to the LC after the devaluation, further depressing translated profitability.

Both the exposure to translation gain or loss and the accounting treatment of gain or loss differ widely between FASB 8 and FASB 52. The course of action pursued by management in its anticipation of a devaluation of the LC is, in this example, dramatically different as a consequence of the method of consolidation. In one case, there is a risk to translation loss that impacts the equity portion of the balance sheet. In the other, there is a translation gain with negative ramifications on future income.

FURTHER COMPLICATIONS

All assets and liabilities in the previous discussion are denominated in LC. The reason for this is that management is referring to the income statement and balance sheet as presented by the affiliate to the parent. The affiliate has translated all currencies contained in its financial statements to LC before presenting them to the parent organization. However, in today's global business environment, an affiliate usually deals in many currencies. Suppose that the affiliate in country X sells to local, Japanese, Thai, and U.S. markets and that the temporal method of consolidation (FASB 8) applies. Accordingly, cash, receivables, and liabilities are exposed to the risk of a revaluation or devaluation.

There is no net exposure to the U.S. dollar because assets and liabilities already denominated in U.S. dollars do not require further attention. Certain non-balancesheet adjustments have to be made for management to realise the actual exposure to various currencies. One adjustment is the omission of cash on hand, because cash on hand is usually the minimum necessary to operate the business on a day-to-day basis. That being the case, management does not have to take action to protect these minimal, and necessary, holdings. Other adjustments involve the effect of known future transactions, which are not yet reflected on the balance sheet, such as future sales contracts, firm commitments, and operating lease payments.

If it happens that the long exposure in one currency equals the short exposure in another, the two cannot be offset against each other. They both must be dealt with separately because it is unlikely that any two currencies will move in tandem. Exposures are expressed in dollars because it is assumed that the company is U.S. domiciled. Managers of a corporation can more readily grasp the magnitude of the exposures if they are expressed in the common currency of the company.

The analysis of exposure performed by British management would be in pounds and the risk of translation exposure would take into consideration the U.K. method of consolidation. This would hold for all nations of domicile.Including non-balance-sheet items such as future sales, purchase commitments, and leases changes the exposure to various currencies. In this example, the long position in Japanese yen has increased, the long position in Thai baht has decreased, and the short position in LC has increased.

The data base is now complete for management to take an overview of the situation and consider what actions, if any, are necessary to protect the company with regard to its exposure to various currencies.Measuring the exposure to transaction and translation risk requires a centralized information system in order for management to determine its exposure to various currencies. Without this information, managers involved in risk management are not able to act effectively. This information must be presented on a timely basis because it is possible for a company's exposure to a particular currency to swing from a long to short, or from a short to long, position in a brief period of time. Usually, monthly reports from all affiliates are consolidated and analyzed on a global basis for management to have a continual measure of the actual exposure of a company to all currencies.Affiliates may report their exposure to various currencies by telecommunications means using a specified electronic spreadsheet format. Once the parent has the spreadsheet reports from the affiliates, they can then be combined into one master spreadsheet that calculates the company's global exposure to all currencies. Besides timeliness of data and ease of display for measurement of exposure, such an information system places the management of the parent in a position to exercise control over the financial decisions being made by the affiliates to prevent them from taking actions that would make managing exposure to transaction and translation risk more difficult.

MANAGEMENT MEANS TO DEAL WITH CURRENCY EXPOSURE

Management may feel comfortable being exposed to certain currencies that it feels will maintain or increase in value with respect to the currency of domicile of the company. For those currencies where management fears a loss of purchasing power, various methods can be employed to reduce the exposure to these currencies, which are briefly described below.

- Local cash balances should be kept to a minimum level consistent with cash needs necessary for the operation of the business. Excess cash and profits should be remitted as quickly as possible from the subsidiary or affiliate to the parent by increasing the frequency or size of dividends, royalties, and licencing and management fees, remaining cognizant, of course, of tax considerations and local currency exchange controls.

- If management believes that a devaluation is imminent, one possible course of action may be to raise selling prices. In a competitive pricing environment, this will depress the sales volume, reduce receivables, and increase inventory. This, of course, is against the natural inclination of local management because raising prices to this extent also depresses profits. But this course of action is not intended to depress profits, but to reduce the potential of loss from an imminent devaluation.

  Investment in inventory, as a non-monetary asset, is a means of protection against the financial loss of a devaluation associated with cash balances and receivables. Transforming cash and receivables into tangible assets reduces the extent of write-downs of liquid assets. If FASB 8 applies, inventories are not written down because they are carried at historic cost. In addition, tangible assets tend to preserve their value as a currency loses purchasing power because they can be sold for a higher price after the devaluation. Once the impact of the devaluation on the local economy is over, selling prices can be reduced to competitive levels to enhance sales and reduce inventory. Of course, these price hikes have to take into account any local price control regulations that may be in effect.
- Speeding up collection of receivables, and for that matter, slowing down payment of payables, would result in higher cash balances, which might then be invested, along with any other excess cash, in increased inventory or other tangible assets. However, as everyone's receivable is someone else's payable, the net result of this course of action might be a nationwide stalemate on paying bills until after the devaluation. Excess cash holdings can also be invested in a strong currency foreign asset, such as an investment in a related affiliate or in a new subsidiary. Local government regulations on currency exchange may constrain or eliminate this latter option.
- Sometimes companies engage in "back-to-back" loans as a means of trying to reduce the impact of a devaluation, or a series of anticipated devaluations. Suppose that parent A has affiliate A operating in a nation where the local currency cannot be exchanged for a more desirable currency. One way to reduce the exposure to the local currency is to engage in back-to-back loans by lending surplus local currency to an affiliate (affiliate B) of a non-related company (parent B) that needs the local currency for its own

purposes. Simultaneously, parent B makes a hard currency loan to parent A. In a typical arrangement, both of these loans are paid off at a stipulated future date in their respective currencies. This exchange of cash for a receivable in a local currency at least has the benefit of making hard currency available to parent A at a negotiated interest rate that is usually advantageous to parent A. This gives parent A some slight benefit in its holdings of a local currency. The problem of what to do with excess holdings of the local currency has been deferred, but not solved.

- Leads or lags are timing differences in the payment or settlement of payables and receivables. This technique has two purposes. One is the funding of affiliates. Suppose that a Korean company sells $100,000 worth of goods to a Spanish company monthly. If these goods are sold on 60-day terms, the Spanish company owes the Korean company $200,000 on a permanent basis. If the Spanish company requires more funds, this can be accomplished by changing the terms to 120 days, that is, increasing the lag. This will increase the amount payable to the Korean company to $400,000 on a permanent basis. If the Korean company requires funds, then the Spanish company can pay currently, or, perhaps, in advance, which is known as a lead.

The other purpose of leads and lags is to shift the currency exposure between two nations. Suppose that management believes that the Spanish peseta will devalue in the near future. The Spanish affiliate could be instructed to speed up inter company payments; that is increase the lead, and obtain whatever financing is required from local lenders to make this possible. This reduces the exposure of the company in pesetas, before the devaluation occurs, by reducing its cash reserves of pesetas and increasing its payables in pesetas in the form of bank loans. The caveat here is that if all companies are making bank loans for the purpose of converting the proceeds to a different currency, then interest rates for these loans can become quite high, negating some of the benefit of reducing the exposure to currency exchange losses. Moreover, if everyone is joining in the rush to get out of pesetas, the devaluation becomes a self-fulfilling prophecy.

FINANCIAL ENGINEERING AND RISK MANAGEMENT PRODUCTS

The techniques just described can seldom accomplish all of management's objectives. To add to management's arsenal of tools to manage the risk associated with adverse changes in currency exchange rates, interest rates, and commodity prices, a host of risk management products have been devised by financial engineers. J. D. Finnerty, a professorat Fordham University, in an article titled "Financial Engineering in Corporate Finance: An Overview," appearing in the Winter 1988 issue of *Financial Management*, defined "financial engineering" as follows:

Financial engineering involves the design, the develop-ment, and the implementation of innovative financial instruments and processes, and the formulation of creative solutions to problems in finance.

Financial engineers work closely with a client firm to first identify and measure the potential exposure to risk and then create a solution to obtain a desired outcome. Some financial engineers specialize in the quantitative analysis of determining the exposure to risk. Others are responsible for coming up with what may be an innovative and creative solution. Still others are involved with the practical aspects of implementing the solution. Financial engineering usually requires the services of accountants, lawyers, tax specialists, analysts, modeling professionals, programmers, and information specialists.

Financial engineering is a sign of the times—as volatility of prices and interest and currency exchange rates increases, so does the risk of potential loss faced by corporations, and, therefore, the need for outside expertise to manage the risk of potential loss. The efficacy of financial engineering depends on modern methods of communication and the interfacing of communications and computers for the dissemination of information on various financial and commodity markets. Modern technology in the networking of computers allows multiple users to tap the same data base and use the same spreadsheet financial models for rapid analysis in preparing timely and effective recommendations to clients, both internal and external.

One interesting example of the technological impact of computers and telecommunications on financial markets is "programme trading." Stock market index futures are used by portfolio managers as insurance, or protection, against a falling market. Suppose that a mutual fund manager is worried about a falloff in the stock market. By shorting the index futures, any falloff in the stock market, which creates portfolio losses, is compensated by profits made in the index futures. Programme trading is the exploitation of discrepancies between the price of stock market index futures and the underlying market value of the stocks represented by these futures. Speed of execution of orders, computerized matching of buy and sell orders, buying and selling of "baskets" of securities, and rapid analysis of the complex mathematics associated with identifying pricing discrepancies are necessary technological preconditions for the existence of programme trading.

Stock market index futures can be viewed as a financial tool, devised by financial engineers for stock portfolio managers to protect themselves against volatility in stock prices. But financial engineers are also hard at work devising innovative and creative ways for individuals and firms to increase their yield on investments. By examining the spread between index futures and the underlying value of the basket of securities, financial engineers can provide the necessary information and the means to buy one and short the other, locking in a superior return over investing in other securities such as Treasury bills. This particular financial tool, created by financial engineers to protect portfolio managers against adverse changes in stock prices, is also exploited by financial engineers to enhance the return on investment for investors. The irony of the situation is that the exploitation of a financial instrument to enhance yield may also be responsible for increasing the volatility of stock prices. If this is the case, then the medicine is both treating and contributing to the disease.

The ability to gather information promptly and accurately, and disseminate the information immediately throughout the world can be considered a risk management tool. This, too, may be responsible for increased volatility. A manager of a chocolate factory who first learned about a cocoa crop failure in West Africa in the nineteenth century from a captain of a sailing vessel probably had sufficient time to act on this information to protect his company's interest in cocoa beans before his competitors learned about it. His individual buying of cocoa beans would probably not affect the market to any great degree. The slow dissemination of the information about the crop failure allows for an orderly adjustment of prices.

Nathan Rothschild supposedly learned of the defeat of Napoleon at Waterloo by homing pigeon. This allowed him to buy depressed stocks in London before anyone else knew of the allied victory and sell them when everyone else knew. Leaving aside the moral implications of having sole access to vital information, the buying and selling by Rothschild probably reduced the volatility in the London stock market because his buying occurred when everyone was selling and his selling occurred when everyone was buying. In today's world, all those who deal in cocoa beans and stocks and everything else are tapped into the same source of news. No one has a timing advantage, which means that all act in unison, and by so doing, increase the volatility of prices.

CONNECTION BETWEEN CURRENCY EXCHANGE AND INTEREST RATES

There is a connection between futures in currency exchange rates and interest rates. This connection ties these two markets, which allows financial engineers to devise ways of hedging in interest rates by means of hedges in currencies and vice versa. Suppose that an American has $1,000,000 to invest and six-month (180-day) U.S. Treasury bills offer an annual yield of 4.0 percent. If the investor completes this transaction, he would have approximately $1,020,000 at the end of the 180-day period. Suppose, however, that the investor notes that a French government security is yielding 4.5 percent in 180 days. If he converts his dollars to francs, he will earn more interest, but will be faced with a currency exchange risk at the maturity of the French security.

Suppose that the current spot rate for francs is 5.527 francs to the dollar and the 180-day forward contract is 5.538 francs to the dollar. The investor could convert his dollars to francs, receiving 5,527,000 francs, which when invested in the French 180-day note, yields 5,651,358 francs (5,527,000 x 4.5 percent x 180/360). Simultaneously with the conversion of dollars into francs, the investor also sells a 5,651,358 forward contract at the 180-day forward rate of 5.538 francs to the dollar. Upon receipt of the 5,651,358 francs in 180 days with the maturing of the French debt security, the investor fulfills his obligation under the forward contract by converting 5,651,358 francs to $1,020,469. This is in excess of the $1,020,000 he would have received had he invested in the U.S. Treasury 180-day bill.

The forward or futures rate for a currency is set not by the market impact of investors attempting to maximize their return as much as by arbitragers seeking a riskless return. An arbitrager enters into a riskless covered interest arbitrage by borrowing funds in one country, converting to another currency, investing the funds in another country, and selling a forward contract to cover the conversion back into the original currency to repay the loan. An arbitrager would continue entering into such transactions until the difference between the currency exchange spot and forward rates narrows sufficiently to remove the riskless profit

of entering into such transactions. This is accomplished by the continual buying of spot contracts and selling of forward contracts, which causes the price of the former to rise and the price of the latter to fall until the riskless profit differential disappears. The role of investors in maximizing returns on their assets and arbitragers in seeking riskless profit opportunities establishes a link between interest rates and the spread between spot and forward currency exchange rates. This makes it possible for financial engineers to devise ingenuous solutions to interest rate exposure by entering into a currency exchange contract or to manage a currency exchange risk through an interest rate contract.

It also makes it possible for financial engineers to reduce interest costs by having a company borrow from financial institutions in other countries without exposing the company to a currency exchange loss. For instance, a Canadian company was able to borrow in yen from a Japanese financial institution at a favorable interest rate, which exposed the company to the possibility of an adverse change in the Japanese yen/Canadian dollar exchange rate. Financial engineers addressed that risk by having the company enter into a long-term currency exchange contract. The net effect of these two transactions was a lower effective interest rate to the company by borrowing in Japan and hedging the currency exchange risk rather than by borrowing directly in the Canadian capital market.

FUTURES AND FORWARDS

The terms "futures" and "forwards" are oftentimes used interchangeably for contracts between two parties that require a specific action to be taken at some later date. As these contracts generally take the form of a delivery of an underlying asset such as a certain amount of currency or a quantity of a physical asset, they are sometimes referred to as contracts for deferred delivery. There are, however, important differences between futures and forwards.

A futures contract is traded on public exchanges with highly standardized terms other than the price of the contract, which is set by the market. A forward contract is traded in "over-thecounter" dealer markets where all terms, including price, must be negotiated between the buyer and seller. Over the counter means that a formal exchange or clearing house is not involved in a forward contract—deals are done on an individual basis with a dealer playing the role of a middleman or broker.

A clearing house or association stands between the parties of a futures contract, which removes the necessity of identifying the parties involved in the futures contract. This is similar to the trading of stock on a stock exchange—it is done between brokerage houses with the brokerage houses responsible for making the final settlement between the ultimate buyer and seller of the shares of stock. In a forward contract, each party is directly responsible for the fulfillment of the agreed terms and, therefore, their identity is a critical factor in the negotiation process leading up to the mutual agreement of contractual terms and conditions.

Futures markets, like the stock markets, are government regulated, whereas forward markets are not. The financial integrity of the futures market is ensured by each party to a futures contract maintaining the required margin, which can be likened to a performance bond. No such mechanism exists in the forward market. This is another reason why the identity of the parties, and their reputation, is a critical part of a forward contract.

In addition, the active market in futures contracts makes it easy to terminate a transaction by buying back the futures or entering into another that offsets the original transaction. In a forward contract where terms and conditions are uniquely defined for each contract, such ease of termination is not only difficult but may be impossible. There is liquidity in the continual buying and selling of futures in the futures market, whereas there is virtually no liquidity in the forwards market.

On the surface, one would wonder why anyone would enter into a forward contract rather than a futures contract. The primary reason is that the futures contract, being a highly standardized contract, may not fit the particular needs of an individual or company. Suppose that an importer must pay 20 million Japanese yen in forty-nine days. A futures contract is in units of 12.5 million yen to be settled thirty, sixty, and ninety days in the future. The futures contract does not meet the importer's specific needs. Rather than over or under hedge either in the amount of yen and the duration of time, by taking a position in futures on the futures exchange, the importer might negotiate a deal that meets his or her precise requirements with a forward contract arranged in the over-thecounter market.

SWAPS

Swaps are financial products originated by financial engineers in response to the growing instability in prices and in interest and currency exchange rates during the 1980s. Started in 1979, swaps became a popular financial instrument in 1981 because of the publicity associated with a currency swap arranged by Salomon Brothers between the World Bank and IBM. Currency swaps rapidly spread to swaps in interest rates and commodities. Swaps are built around the same basic structure as forwards and have been described as a series of forward contracts. Two parties, called counterparties, agree to one or more exchange(s) of specified quantities of underly-ing tangibles or intangibles, sometimes called notionals if there is a cash rather than a physical exchange of the underlying asset. Cash payments are the usual means of settlements between the counterparties of a swap.

A swap is usually arranged by a financial intermediary that negotiates a final deal between two counterparties entering into a swap. The intermediary, known as a swap dealer or market maker, receives his or her remuneration in the bidasked spread between the two counterparties. Three illustrations are provided to explain the principal "plain vanilla" swaps.

Interest Rate Swap

Counterparty A is a company that requires $10 million to construct a factory. The creditworthiness of the company is not sufficient for an issue of fixed rate interest debt, but a bank is willing to lend the company $10 million on a floating rate basis. Counterparty A worries about the floating rate interest rate increasing over the next ten years and wants to hedge, or protect itself, against this risk. Counterparty A is willing to sacrifice the opportunity of having to pay less in interest expense if floating rates fall in order to safeguard itself from the risk of having to pay higher than the fixed rate that can be arranged through a swap.

Counterparty B is a company, or a financial institution, whose creditworthiness is sufficient for it to issue fixed interest rate debt. Suppose that counterparty B borrows on the basis of its own creditworthiness $10 million at a fixed interest rate of 10 percent. It could lend the money to counterparty A, but then counterparty B assumes the credit risk of counterparty A repaying the loan. Instead of lending the money to counterparty A, counterparty B deposits the funds in a floating rate account. Suppose that the floating rate is currently 8 percent. Counterparty B transfers the interest income of 8 percent on its $10 million deposit to the swap dealer in return for a fixed rate of 10.3 percent.

Counterparty B neither makes nor loses money on the floating rate deposit and makes a 0.3 percent spread on its capacity to issue fixed rate debt. Counterparty B has no credit risk in borrowing the $10 million in that the proceeds of the loan have been placed in a floating rate deposit that is sufficient to pay off the principal of the fixed rate debt.

The swap dealer passes the floating rate interest payment received from counterparty B to counterparty A. In return, counterparty A pays the swap dealer 10.4 percent fixed rate of interest. The difference between receiving 10.4 percent interest from counterparty A and paying 10.3 percent interest to counterparty B is the swap dealer's remuneration. Counterparty A takes the floating rate interest of 8 percent and pays the floating rate interest plus any applicable spread to its lending institution. If the interest rate on counterparty A's loan is the floating rate plus a spread of 0.75 percent, then counterparty A is actually paying 8.75 percent on its loan. Therefore, the net cost of interest to counterparty A is the 0.75 percent differential to be paid on the floating rate loan plus the fixed 10.4 percent to the swap dealer.

There is no point in counterparty A paying 10.4 percent to the swap dealer and receiving the floating rate of 8 percent from the swap dealer. It is easier to net the difference and pay that to the swap dealer. Under the circumstances, counterparty A pays the difference between 10.4 percent and 8 percent to the swap dealer, or 2.4 percent applied against the notional amount of the interest rate swap, in this case, $10 million. Counterparty A pays less if the floating interest rate rises. If the floating rate goes above the fixed rate, counterparty A will receive money from the swap dealer. This extra money will be used to pay the higher interest charge associated with counterparty A's floating rate loan.

Therefore, counterparty A has accomplished his purpose of swapping a floating rate for a fixed rate loan. His cost of interest is the fixed rate of 10.4% plus the spread of 0.75% on the floating rate loan. He is no longer at risk in having floating rates rise to a level that may imperil his financial survivability. For this, he has foregone any opportunity to benefit from floating interest rates being less than the arranged fixed rate.

A single payment is also made between counterparty B, representing the difference between the 10.3 percent to be received from the swap dealer and the floating rate to be paid to the swap dealer. The swap dealer simply passes the payment between the two counterparties extracting his piece of the action. The swap dealer is making 0.1 percent interest spread between counterparty B receiving 10.3 percent and counterparty A paying 10.4 percent on the notional amount of the principal. He has accomplished his objective in arranging the swap.

Counterparty B has borrowed funds at 10 percent and has lent them out at 10.3 percent with the difference being remuneration for entering into the transaction. This fulfills counterparty B's objective in entering into the swap. However, in entering this swap, counterparty B has given up any benefit from rising interest rates. He has deposited the funds from a fixed rate loan in a floating rate account and turns the interest earnings over to the swap dealer. If the floating rate were to go to 20 percent on funds borrowed at 10 percent, counterparty B would have been better off not entering into the swap.

Counterparty B can undo the transaction by purchasing an interest rate futures, but from the point of view of the swap, he has given up the benefit of rising floating interest rates. Therefore, he might have been reluctant to enter into the swap if he had strong feelings that floating interest rates would rise. However, by counterparty B depositing the funds from the fixed rate loan in a floating rate account, whether floating rates rise or fall, counterparty B has locked in his return. This is the spread between the fixed rate paid by the swap dealer and the fixed rate being paid on the incurred debt.

It is possible that counterparty B does not borrow the funds at a fixed rate of interest. Counterparty B may be a financial institution that feels that interest rates are going to fall and may delay arranging its fixed debt financing. It is possible that it does not intend to arrange any borrowings, but to cover itself through the purchase of interest rate futures should interest rates begin to rise. If counterparty B perceives this to be a desired course of action, then the swap dealer would definitely find it easier to put the swap together if both counterparties have opposite viewpoints on the future direction of floating interest rates.

The swap can be considered as a series of forward contracts in which the termination of each individual contract occurs at the time of payment of the interest rate differential, say, every six months. Collectively, in this example, the swap represents a series of twenty forward contracts that cover ten years of interest payments. Credit risk is not transferred in a swap. Both counterparties A and B have arranged their floating and fixed rate loans based on their individual

creditworthiness. Each is responsible for the repayment of the underlying principal of the loan. If, by change, counterparty B did not arrange a fixed rate loan, then its creditworthiness must be sufficient to cover the differential in interest rates should its assessment on the future direction of rates be proven wrong. Even here, there are means for counterparty B to minimize, or avoid, losses.

The only connection between the two counterparties is the net payment representing the difference between the floating and fixed rates of interest. The bankruptcy of one of the counterparties affects only the interest rate differential payment between the two counterparties. In addition to the potential bankruptcy of a counterparty, swap dealers such as Drexel, Burnham, Lambert of junk bond fame, have gone bankrupt. The U.S. Bankruptcy Code has been amended to ensure that netting provisions of swaps be honored by the bankruptcy courts in the event of the bankruptcy of counterparties and swap dealers. Interest rate swaps have become so common that the plain vanilla variety are frequently arranged directly between banks without the services of a swap dealer.

Currency Swap

A currency swap can be arranged when one of the counterparties has more advantageous access to a financial market. Suppose that an American company desires to finance a factory to be built in Germany in deutschemarks at a fixed rate of interest. Further suppose that a German company has access to lower. fixed rate interest financing in Germany than the American company. To complete the picture, suppose that the German company desires to borrow in U.S. dollars for its business purposes, at a floating rate of interest and the American company is in a position to borrow in the United States for less than a German-based company can do on its own. This situation of each party having access to lower cost loans than the other party permits the origination of a swap, where the German company borrows deutschemarks from a German financial institution at a lesser interest rate than what would be charged to the American company. The American company borrows a like amount of dollars for a lesser interest charge than what the German company could have negotiated.

A swap dealer then arranges a currency swap whereby the two companies can take advantage of borrowing at lesser cost in different markets. Each swaps the principal amounts of the loans, which are the same, and each makes interest payments to the swap dealer as agreed, with the American company making deutschemark payments that are sufficient for the German company to pay off its loan and the German company making dollar payments sufficient for the American company to pay off its loan. The swap dealer takes a little out of the middle.

A plain vanilla currency swap does not involve an exchange of a credit risk. Both companies borrow on the basis of their own creditworthiness. Each merely exchanges, or swaps, the payment of debt and interest such that the American company ends up paying a fixed rate German denominated debt, which it desired,

and the German company ends up paying the type of dollar denominated debt, which it desired. Three exchanges are necessary. The first is the exchange of the principal of the loan, then the interest payments, and, at the end of the swap period, the final repayment of principal of the respective loans. Although currency swaps are usually floating/fixed rates of interest—that is, one counterparty paying a floating rate of interest and the other a fixed rate of interest—currency swaps can also be floating/floating and fixed/fixed.

This plain vanilla currency swap is also called an exchange of borrowings because that is exactly what it is. Its origin lies in each company's advantage in borrowing in its respective domestic market. However, the plain vanilla can easily become a more sophisticated variant because the exchange of borrowings may not exactly fit the desires of the two counterparties. An interest rate swap may have to be arranged along with the currency swap to change a floating rate loan to a desired fixed rate loan. The tenor, or the length of the repayment period, or the amount of the loan, may not entirely match the desires of each counterparty.

The swap dealer may turn to a financial engineer to introduce a new level of complexity to transform an undesirable cash flow stream into one that is desired by the two counterparties to the currency swap. It is possible for the repayment of principal to be amortized with the regular payments of interest similar to a level payment type of financing common for home mortgages. By combining swaps with other swaps or with other financial instruments, all sorts of variants can be created, limited only to the imagination of the financial engineers and the needs of client firms.

Commodity Swap

Counterparty A is an oil producer who has financed his wells with loans. If oil falls below a certain price, he will not be able to generate the earnings necessary to pay the financing charges associated with drilling and developing the oil wells. This may force the oil producer into bankruptcy. Counterparty B is a refinery operator who sold a portion of his output at a fixed price and wants to stabilize the price of oil required to be purchased in the future in order to preserve the profit margin of these fixed priced contracts. Counterparty B worries about an increase in the price of oil that would destroy the economic worth of his fixed price contracts.

A swap dealer, being in touch with both individuals, can arrange a plain vanilla swap. The oil producer sells his actual output, called "actuals," into the spot oil market and receives the spot price, which may be higher or lower than the agreed fixed price of the swap. If higher, he must pay the difference between what he receives and the agreed fixed price to the swap dealer. If lower, the producer will receive the difference from the swap dealer. On the other side of the swap dealer's ledger is counterparty B, the refiner. Counterparty B buys his oil needs, or actuals, from the spot market and pays the spot price. If the spot price is higher than the agreed swap price, counterparty B receives what the

producer has paid to the swap dealer. If the spot price for oil is lower than the swap price, then the refiner pays the difference to the swap dealer, which is passed on to the refiner. In order to avoid disagreements between the two counterparties as to what is the spot market price, the counterparties agree to base the spot price, not on actual purchases and sales, but on a spot price from a published source, such as the monthly average spot price for oil quoted in the financial press.

No matter in what direction the net payment is flowing, the swap dealer takes out a margin for his or her trouble, before passing the money to the other party. The swap dealer assumes no risk, which is why both the oil producer and the refinery operator must refer to the same published source for spot market quotes, such as a monthly average, to remove day-to-day price fluctuations, and other causes of price differences from becoming part of the calculation of what is to be paid between the two counterparties.

Otherwise, the swap dealer would become embroiled in disputes over price differentials between what an oil producer receives when he sells and what a refinery operator pays when he buys. Although the producer is selling his output to the spot market and the refiner is buying his input from the spot market, the net effect is that they are essentially buying and selling from each other at the swap price. The swap can go on for as long as the two counterparties desire, again illustrating the point that a swap can be considered a series of forward contracts.

The question may arise as to why the producer and the refiner did not enter into a contract with one another directly, as is practiced by banks for plain vanilla interest rate swaps. First of all, the buyer and seller may not have known of each other's presence or need—this is the classic role of the middleman. It is easier for a bank to canvass the market for interest rate swaps if there are relatively few banks providing the fixed rate portion of an interest rate swap. In the oil business, where there are hundreds of producers and refiners, a middleman or swap dealer, may be needed for the sorting out process of identifying and bringing together the two counterparties.

Another reason for having a swap dealer involved in a transaction is that frequently the needs of the producer and refiner do not exactly match. The producer may want to fix the price of oil for a quantity and for a duration of time that does not exactly fit the refiner's needs.

A deal cannot be directly negotiated between the two counterparties. However, a swap dealer can set up a swap that does match each of the two counterparties' needs. To do so, he or she may have to arrange another swap to take care of the differences in quantity and timing, or hedge the position for his or her own account.

Swap Variants

Swaps have grown from nothing in 1979 to a level of about several trillion in notional outstandings in the early 1990s. Notional outstandings do not necessarily mean actual deposits of funds in banks or assets in warehouses. Notionals are reference points from which the amount of payment between counterparties is calculated. In the previous case of a plain vanilla interest rate swap, the notional amount of the swap of $10 million was the reference point from which the interest rate differential payments between the counterparties were calculated. Plain vanilla swaps have given way to all sorts of variants that have been created to meet the specific needs of the counterparties to a swap. Variants to the plain vanilla swaps are as plentiful as mutations in a jar of fruit flies; a sampling follows.

An accreting swap is one where the notional principal increases, and an amortization swap is one where the notional principal decreases, over the life of the swap. An annuity swap transforms an irregular cash flow payment stream to a regular one. An asset swap is based on assets rather than liabilities. A basis swap deals with a mismatch between assets and liabilities. A blended interest rate swap combines two swaps to produce a more attractive overall rate. A callable and puttable swap gives one or the other counterparty the right to terminate the swap after a specified time. A capped swap is a swap with a cap, or a maximum limit, on the floating payment side of a swap. A cross currency swap is an exchange of cash flows of one currency for another that reverses at some point during the swap period. A debt-equity swap isn't even a swap, but a substitution of equity in local companies in lieu of interest or principal payments of a heavily indebted nation.

A deferred swap is one where the payments are deferred for a specified period, whereas a delayed LIBOR reset swap is one where the floating payment is based on a future rather than the present London Interbank rate. A differential swap is the swapping of floating interest rate payments referenced to different currencies. A discount swap has a large balloon payment at the end of the swap period to take into account the discount on the regular payments as opposed to a highcoupon swap where the fixed payments are above the market rate with some sort of compensating adjustment at the end of the swap period. A dual currency swap contains rights to repay principal and interest in a choice of currencies at preset exchange rates. An escalating rate swap permits the fixed rate side of a swap to escalate with time. An extendable swap contains the right for the payer to extend the swap. A forward swap is one that is arranged at some point before the start date. A naked swap is one without a corresponding asset or liability, an interesting concept. A reversible swap gives one side the option to alter the payment basis after a certain period as compared to a reverse floating swap where the floating rate payments are inversely proportional to interest rates.

The roller coaster swap alternates the counterparties between paying fixed and floating rates. The seasonal swap is one where the notional amount varies with the time of the year to fit the needs of companies that borrow on a seasonal basis. A spreadlock swap has one payment stream referenced to a fixed spread over a benchmark rate. The tax-exempt swap has its fixed rate interest tied to tax-exempt bonds. The warrant-driven swap is a swap with a warrant allowing an issuer of a bond to extend a swap if it exercises a similar warrant on a bond. The yield curve swap is one where the two interest rates reflect different points on a mutually agreed yield curve. The zero-coupon swap is one where one or both counterparties make one payment at maturity.

Finally, there is the swaption. A swaption is an option on a swap. The swap is set up in all respects except for the starting date. One of the counterparties to the swap pays a swaption premium for the right to start the swap at any point during the swaption period, say, in six months. If he or she does not exercise the swaption, the swap terminates without execution at the end of the swaption period. Swaptions have their family of variants.

Swap dealers are not in business to accept risk, but to transfer the nature of risk between the two counterparties. Swap dealers work off their "swap book" to tailor a swap to meet the needs of the two counterparties. In so doing, they may introduce an element of risk into their swap books. Swap dealers then enter into other swaps or hedges to remove the element of risk that may be present in their swap books. Swap dealers usually wish to neutralize any risk in their swap books to protect their remuneration, which is in the bid-ask spread between the two counterparties of a swap. However, if the swap dealers are confident about the emergence or continuation of a price trend, they may accept a degree of risk in their swap books to profit thereby.

PUTS AND CALLS

Futures and forwards are contractually binding agreements. Swaps, as a continuing series of forwards, are also contractually binding. These contractually binding agreements mean that each party must transfer a specified underlying asset, or a cash equivalent thereof, at known points in time. Puts and calls are options where the purchaser of a put or call has the right, but not the obligation, to buy or sell an underlying asset. A buyer of a call has the right, but not the obligation, to purchase something at a stipulated price, whereas the buyer of a put has the right, but not the obligation, to sell something at a stipulated price. However, the seller of a call or a put does have an obligation to sell the underlying asset at the stipulated price when the call is exercised or to buy the underlying asset at the stipulated price when the put is exercised. An American option can be exercised from the time it is written until the time it expires. A European option differs in that its exercise period is limited to a short period of time before its expiration date.

Staying with American options, pricing of options depends on several factors. One is the exercise price in relation to the underlying value of the asset. If the exercise price is $20 and the underlying value of the asset is $22, then the option has an intrinsic value of $2 and is described as being "in the money." If the underlying value is $20, the same as the exercise price, the option is described as being "at the money." If the underlying value is $18, the call option has no intrinsic value, but still has extrinsic value. Extrinsic value depends on the difference between the market and exercise prices, the remaining time to expiration, and the volatility of the price of the underlying asset. The smaller the

difference between market and exercise prices, the longer the time to expiration, and the greater the volatility of the price of the underlying asset, the greater the extrinsic value of the option even though it may have no intrinsic, or inherent, value. Another factor in the pricing of options is interest rates, because a grantor, or a writer, of an option is seeking income by writing calls. Generally speaking, an option writer grants options on an owned asset. As an alternative, he or she can sell the owned asset and invest the proceeds in a secure interest bearing financial instrument. Because the grantor has the choice to sell the asset and invest in interest-bearing financial instruments or underwrite options, option writing premium income must be attractively priced in relation to interest-bearing securities.

All of these factors are built into the first complete option pricing model developed by two professors, Fisher Black and Myron Scholes, in 1973. Options are generally priced based on models derived or adapted from the original BlackScholes model. The model is a mathematical expression containing the difference between the current price of the underlying asset and the strike price, a measure of past volatility in the price of the underlying asset, time to expiration and the interest rate on a secure deposit. The purpose of the model is to determine a theoretical price for an option. Dealers sometimes use the Black-Scholes model to examine prices being quoted by grantors or writers of options, by reversing the model to obtain the implied volatility in the quote. Some dealers use the implied volatility to differentiate quotes on different options for the same asset. By being able to identify options with differently implied volatilities for the same underlying asset, dealers can use this information for putting deals together or in hedging their own portfolios. Moreover, implied volatility can be charted and analyzed as to what feelings participants in the option markets have toward volatility. A period of falling implied volatility can be interpreted to mean that participants in the market feel that prices are approaching an island of stability in a sea of volatility. Rising implied volatility means that participants see storm clouds on the horizon. This information is of value for market makers in options.

OPTIONS IN RISK MANAGEMENT

From the perspective of a company attempting to manage the risk of price volatility, options can be used to change the cost profile of an asset in a way that serves the interest of the company. Suppose that a company buys an asset that management feels can vary in price from $15 to $25 per unit and the current price is $20. The company does not want to find itself in a position of paying much over $20 per unit for the asset. It buys a call option for $1 per unit with an exercise price of $20. For that portion of its needs covered by the call option, the company has changed the cost profile.

A company wanting to contain its costs to $21 per unit for the asset has done so by purchasing the option. The profit from the call option compensates for the extra cost of purchasing the asset. This protects the company whenever the price of the asset moves above $20. If the asset does not move above $20 per unit, the company has added $1 to unit to its acquisition cost. This can be likened to the premium cost of an insurance policy to protect against paying a higher than desired price for the asset. A company must weigh the cost of protection against the benefit of having the protection.

Suppose that a company has acquired a large supply of inventory at $20 and wishes to insure itself against a loss in value. The company buys a put option with an exercise price of $20 for $1. If the market value of the asset declines, the intrinsic value of the put will increase.

The company, in wanting to protect itself against loss, has maintained the value of the inventory at $19 per unit regardless how low the market value of the asset may sink. The profit from the put option compensates for the loss in inventory value. The cost of this protection is $1 per unit, which one can view as an insurance premium if the value of the asset remains above $20 per unit.

The portion of the inventory that is protected by the put is said to be hedged against a price decline.

Suppose that the price of the commodity is $20 and the company buys a put and a call, called a straddle, for $1 per option.

If the price of the asset falls below $18, the profit from the put can be used to hedge against a write-down of the inventory. If the price rises, the profit from the call can be used to hedge against paying above $22 per unit. If the price of the asset hovers between $18 and $22, the company would have been better off not purchasing the straddle. Straddles are useful when management expects increased volatility in the price of the asset but is unsure of the direction of change in price. The straddle offers double protection in limiting the maximum amount to be paid for the asset and in limiting the maximum amount of loss of holding the asset in inventory. In offering more protection, the insurance premium also costs more.

Suppose that the company decides to buy a call option with an exercise price of $20 for $1 and sells a call option with an exercise price of $22 for $0.50. The net cost of buying and selling the options is $0.50. What would be profit profile of this course of action?

The idea of selling the second call is to reduce the cost of the hedge by the amount of premium earned on the selling of the call. A company would employ such a strategy of buying and selling a call option at different strike, or exercise, prices if it was worried about a rise in price in the commodity, but was convinced that such a rise would not go over $23. If management were proven wrong and the price did exceed $23, it could buy its way out by purchasing another call option to compensate for the "loss" associated with the call that was sold. Once a company begins to protect itself against price rises or declines through some sort of hedging technique, there is a tendency to keep purchasing and selling options to "undo" those past hedging positions that are costing the company money. In time, a relatively simple hedging position can become quite complex.

If the two call options in the previous example expire at the same time, it is called a vertical bull spread. If the call with the lower strike price is sold and the one with the higher strike price is bought, there would be premium income and the strategy would be called a vertical bear spread. If the expiration dates are not the same, but the exercise price is the same for the two options, these strategies are called a horizontal bull or bear spread depending on the expiration dates of the purchased and sold options. If there is a mix of expiration dates and strike prices, the strategy is known as a diagonal spread. To show that there is virtually no limit to the imagination, a butterfly spread would involve four options. All have the same expiration date. Two options with the same strike price are sold, whereas one with a higher strike price is purchased along with one with a lower strike price. If the buying and selling of the options are reversed, this is called a reverse butterfly or a sandwich spread.

What risk does management fear the most? The financial engineers can dream up a solution. There are barrier options (four major types including knock-in and knock-out options), basket options, binary and digital options, call and put spreads, chooser options, compound options, condors, cylinders, difference options, embedded options, forward start options, hi-low options, lookback or path-dependent options, straddles and strangles, table tops, and tunnels, which are similar to cylinders. Someone in the company better have a firm understanding of where the company stands when the price of the underlying asset changes. Although there is no commitment undertaken by the company when options are purchased, there is certainly a commitment associated with sold options as there are with swaps, futures, and forwards. Therefore, there should also be someone in a company with a firm handle on what commitments have been undertaken by a company in its hedging programme. This someone should not be the person directing the company's risk management programme.

RISK MANAGEMENT FOR OPTION MARKET MAKERS

The role of market makers in options is to have a balanced position in options with little exposed risk. They are not in the options market to assume a risk. Their role is to be intermediaries in the exchange of risk between two parties. In this role, they may have to assume some risk in order to complete a deal. Then they take action to neutralize, or hedge, the risk assumed in putting the deal together. A hedged portfolio of options may no longer be fully hedged because the price of the underlying asset changes. Price changes in the underlying asset can transform out-of-the-money options to in-the-money ones and vice versa.

As a matter of interest, option market makers themselves have a risk management challenge in maintaining a neutral position and living off commissions and bid-ask spreads between buyers and sellers of options. To do this, they depend on a world of Greek letters. Delta is the price sensitivity of an option to price changes of the underlying asset. When an option is deeply out of the money, a move in the price of the underlying asset has little or no effect on its price (delta = 0). For an option deep in the money, there is an exact one-for-one relationship between its price and the price of the underlying asset. On a per unit basis, as the price goes up by one, the value of a call would also increase by one (delta = 1).

For puts that are in the money, an increase in the underlying value of the asset reduces their value by one (delta = -1). The delta associated with a short call in the money would be -1 and the delta associated with a short put in the money would be +1. For options where the market price is approaching the exercise price, there is an intermediate, not a one-for-one, relationship between changes in underlying value and in the value of the option.

Therefore, delta values vary between 0 and 1 for long calls and short puts, and between 0 and -1 for short calls and long puts.

The net risk of a dealer's exposure to options on the same underlying tangible or intangible asset can be quantified by totaling the deltas of all the options. A "delta neutral" portfolio of options would be one where the sum of all deltas is near zero. However, there are complications associated with maintaining a delta neutral portfolio of options because, as just discussed, the delta of an option varies with the underlying price of the asset. The rate of change of delta with respect to changes in the price of the underlying value is measured by gamma. Theta measures the erosion of an options premium as the expiration date nears. Theta can be positive or negative depending on whether there is a long and short position. Rho measures the sensitivity of the option's price to changes in interest rates, whereas kappa, or vega (not a Greek letter, but an old Chevy car model) measures the change in an option's price with respect to changes to the volatility of the price of the underlying asset.

Needless to say, delta, gamma, theta, kappa or vega, and rho measures of a portfolio of options are not calculated by hand. In addition, there are other Greek letters in a dealer's lexicon—beta trading is used by option traders to take advantage of similar financial instruments having diverging volatility, whereas omega is the risk associated with a buyer or seller of an option where the accounting of the option will be in a different currency than the option.

OPTIONS IN FUTURES

In addition, financial engineers have originated futures options. Calls and puts can be exercised calling for the delivery or sale of the underlying asset. Futures options are puts and calls on futures. A review of the U.S. financial press shows that one can buy and sell puts and calls on futures of U.S. Treasury notes and bonds, various currencies with both American and European variants including a cross trade between German marks and Japanese yen, various agricultural products, metals, various stock indices, and crude oil and oil products. Settlement of futures options is in cash, not a delivery or acceptance of an underlying asset. A futures option out of the money at the time of expiration is worthless.

EXCHANGE FOR PHYSICALS

There should be a strong linkage between an expiring futures contract and the cash price of the physical asset for futures to be effective as a hedging tool. Very few expiring futures end up with an exchange of physical assets. Usually, a long position is liquidated by selling the futures and a short position is liquidated by buying futures. But the possibility of a long position ending up with the physical possession of the underlying asset ensures that expiring prices and cash prices are very close to one another. For instance, an expiring copper future could end up with a change in ownership as 25,000 pounds of copper. The copper futures market has an associated warehouse holding a sufficient quantity of copper of the specified purity to provide for a change of ownership between the owner of an expiring futures contract and its seller.

Oil is a much less "homogenous" market than copper. The cash market in crude oil is based on commonly traded types of oil such as Saudi Arabian Light, North Sea, and West Texas Intermediate. The futures in crude oil traded on the New York Mercantile Exchange calls for delivery "at any pipeline or storage facility with pipeline access to Arco, Cushing Storage, or Texaco Trading & Transportation Inc...." In the world of oil, this is a rather limited transformation of "paper" barrels to "wet" barrels. To take into account the wide variety of grades of oil and time and place of delivery, the financial engineers devised exchange for physicals (EFPs). EFPs extend the circumstances surrounding delivery of futures by permitting buyers and sellers of futures to agree to the exact buyer and seller, the nature of the crude oil, and place, volume, time, and other details of delivery. Payment is made by exchanging long and short positions in expiring futures.

BACKWARDATION AND CONTANGO

The relationship between the futures and the cash markets determines whether a market is in backwardation or contango. When a futures contract is selling for less than the current cash price, the market is said to be in backwardation. Using oil as an example, a backwardation market permits an oil company to sell a part of its inventory that is to be refined in the future in the cash market and buy a, say, two-month future. In two month's time, the "paper" barrel is transformed to a "wet" barrel through an EFP, if necessary, to process the oil. This would only occur if the discount for the futures compared to the cash price is sufficient to make this a profitable transaction. In calculating this profitability, one must bear in mind that an oil company can invest the cash proceeds of selling oil in inventory in an interest-bearing security. There are also transfer, shipping, and other costs involved with the delivery of the futures, or the EFP, that have to be taken into account.

A contango market is one where there is a premium on the futures in relation to the cash price. If the premium on the futures contract is large enough, and if there is sufficient storage capacity at the oil company refinery, it may be to the oil company's advantage to buy extra oil in the cash market and short a futures contract. On the maturing of the futures contract, the oil company delivers the oil rather than making a cash settlement. The spread between the cash and futures market has to be sufficient to cover the storage costs and the interest costs of investing in what amounts to extra inventory.

CAPS, FLOORS, AND COLLARS

Calls and puts have a finite life usually measured in months. Rarely do their expiration times exceed one year. Another example of financial engineering creativity are multi period options. These were created to address the need for providing a maximum rate of interest on a loan, called an interest rate cap. Loans usually run for more than a year and, therefore, calls and puts with an expiration time of one year or less do not provide a solution for a company that desires to hedge against rising interest rates on a multiyear floating rate loan. The writer of an interest rate cap agrees to pay the holder of the cap the difference between a reference rate above the ceiling rate, applied against a notional principal, every six months during the two to five year tenor, or length of time, of the cap, or any other agreeable tenor. The reference rate is a published rate such as the London Interbank or U.S. Treasury bill rates.

The ceiling rate is the maximum rate the holder of the cap will pay on a loan covered by the notional principal of the cap. For this protection, the cap holder pays an upfront fee. The effective interest rate has the appearance of a multi period call. The amortization of the upfront premium over the life of the cap is analogous to the premium paid for a series of single period calls. If interest rates do not rise to the ceiling rate, the holder of the cap is simply paying a higher effective

interest rate. This is analogous to the previous example of illustrating how a call limits the maximum amount to be paid for some underlying asset. If the price does not rise to this limit, the premium for the call increases the effective acquisition cost for the underlying asset.

If interest rates rise above the ceiling rate, the profit from the cap offsets the higher cost of interest effectively capping interest at the ceiling rate. Obviously, the closer the ceiling rate is to current interest rates, the higher its cost. This holds true for call—the closer the exercise price is to the current price of the asset, the higher the premium. A buyer of a call, or a cap, must decide on the amount of premium and the protection afforded by that premium in covering his or her perceived risks. Interest rate caps are sometimes combined with interest rate swaps or with currency swaps to produce an interest or a currency rate capped swap. Caps can be assignable with the owner's permission, much as a call can be sold when its protection is no longer needed.

An interest rate floor is similar to a cap except that the purchaser of a floor receives payment when the reference rate drops below the contract rate. The classic use of a floor is an insurance company borrowing fixed rate money to be loaned out at a floating rate. In so doing, the insurance company is betting on an upswing in interest rates. If interest rates fall, the insurance company may not earn enough to service its policy holders. An insurance company can protect against this risk by purchasing an interest rate floor, which guarantees a minimum interest rate should the floating rate fall below the contract, or floor, rate.

Caps and floors do not involve the exchange of a credit risk. They are cash settlements at prescribed times whereby a purchaser of a cap does not pay more than the ceiling rate and the purchaser of a floor does not earn less than the floor rate. Because the principal covered by a cap or floor is not exchanged, the cash payments are based on a notional amount of a loan. If a cap is 10 percent and the referenced floating rate is 12 percent, and the notional amount is $10 million (MM) and settlements are made every six months, then the purchaser of the cap will receive the difference (2 percent × $10 MM × six months/twelve months) or $100,000 from the market maker. He then applies this against his floating rate loan, reducing its net interest cost from 12 percent to 10 percent. If the floor is 8 percent and the referenced floating rate falls to 6 percent, then the seller of the floor has to pay the market maker $100,000. This raises his effective interest cost from 6 percent to 8 percent, thus fixing his minimum interest rate at 8 percent.

A financial engineer can create collars from caps and floors. A collar is the purchase of a cap coupled with the sale of a floor. The proceeds from the sale of the floor reduce the cost of the cap. What this effectively does is lock the interest rate between the floor and ceiling rates. If a company has a floating rate loan on a certain amount of principal, a collar on the same notional amount of the loan fixes both the maximum and minimum interest rates. If floating interest rates exceed the ceiling rate, the company will receive a cash payment that compensates it for the incremental interest expense that is above the ceiling rate,

thus capping the interest rate on the loan at the ceiling rate. If floating rates fall below the floor rate, the company will not benefit from the lower interest costs because it is obligated to pay the difference between the floating rate and the floor rate, applied against the notional amount of the collar, to the market maker. If interest rates stay between the floor and ceiling rates, the lender has increased his effective interest rate in the amortization of the cost of acquisition of the collar.

The concept of the interest rate collar as a multi period option to set a ceiling and a floor rate for interest rates can be applied to currencies and commodities. A currency collar is a series of multi period cash settlements, where the holder of the collar limits his exchange rate within a prescribed band. This is accomplished by a cash settlement representing the differences in actual currency exchange transactions and the contractual upper and lower exchange rate limits-the ceiling and floor rates of conversion. For a premium, a company can collar, so to speak, the currency exchange rates on, say, Swiss franc to dollar conversion within a prescribed upper and lower rate of exchange based on a stipulated notional amount of currency. This is a powerful financial tool in managing the long-term exposure to a currency risk.

The collar is applied to commodities. For the payment of a premium, the holder of a collar, sometimes referred to as a range forward, can limit his purchases of a commodity, such as oil, to a prescribed band. Using a publicly available source of pricing for oil as a means of measuring spot purchases, a holder of a range forward receives money from the market maker when spot purchase prices exceed the upper limit or ceiling price. When spot purchase prices fall below the lower limit or floor price, the holder of the range forward must pay the difference to the market maker. When prices are between the floor and ceiling prices, the effective cost of oil is the spot price plus the premium paid for the collar, or range forward. The buyer of a collar or a range forward is obtaining protection against paying more than the ceiling price, but, in so doing, gives up the opportunity of buying for less than the floor price. He has, in effect, avoided a risk that he cannot endure by giving up an opportunity that he could enjoy.

RISK MANAGEMENT ACCOUNTING ISSUES

FASB 52 sets forth a series of conditions for accounting for currency exchange futures as hedges, avoiding having to "mark to market" the value of a futures on the last day of each accounting period. Mark-to-market gains and losses flow through the income statement, which adds to the volatility of earnings. Managers take a dim view of the mark-to-market accounting treatment of futures because of its unpredictable impact on earnings. Earnings, in the mind of many managers, should reflect the result of operations and not be distorted by the "snapshot" valuation of futures contracts. FASB 52 also accords the same accounting treatment to currency exchange forward contracts as to currency exchange futures contracts.

In 1984, FASB 80, "Accounting for Futures Contracts," was issued to deal with futures contracts for other than currency such as stock index, commodities, and interest rates. FASB 80 defers the loss or gain of a futures contract if the company owns, or is liable for, the delivery of the underlying asset. The gain or loss of a futures contract can also be deferred if there is a legally enforceable obligation to make or accept delivery of the underlying asset. And the third criterion for deferring a gain or loss is entering into a futures or forward contract on the basis of an anticipated transaction. This transaction need not be legally enforceable. In other words, if in management's judgment, there is sufficient probability of some transaction occurring to warrant entering into a futures or forward contract, and even if there is nothing legally binding to enforce the consummation of the contract, the gains and losses of the associated futures or forward contract can be deferred.

Under FASB 52, deferral of gains and losses can occur only if the currency exchange forward or futures contract reduces the risk of loss of a specified transaction. FASB 80 has a much broader interpretation of the conditions permitting deferral of gains and losses associated with other forms of futures and forward contracts. In particular, hedging based on anticipated transactions, in addition to exposure to risk of existing conditions and firm commitments, is permitted deferral of gains and losses. Mark to market, or the immediate recognition of gains and losses associated with non-currency-exchange futures and forward contracts, is required only when the futures and forward contract cannot be related to any underlying or anticipated exposure to risk. In essence, FASB 52, which applies only to currency exchange futures and forward contracts, and FASB 80, which applies to all other futures and forward contracts, are inconsistent in the accounting treatment of futures and forward contracts. This, not surprisingly, has sparked a continuing controversy among accounting professionals.

Neither FASB 52 nor FASB 80 addresses options. In 1984, the American Institute of Certified Public Accountants (AICPA) began to study this issue, which led to the publication of the "Options Issues Paper" in 1986. The paper tends to apply the principles underlying FASB 80, rather than FASB 52, to options. That is, using options to hedge against anticipated happenings should be treated similar to the treatment of futures and forward contracts in FASB 80. The "Options Issues Paper" has neither been endorsed by the Securities and Exchange Commission nor has there been follow-up in the form of a published FASB statement. Therefore, the issue of accounting for options is essentially yet to be fully resolved. Hedge accounting frequently has the effect of shifting reported gains or losses from one period to another. Given that the rules of accounting for hedges involving options are still evolving, management must be accordingly cautious on their approach to accounting for hedges.

In 1990, FASB 105, "Disclosure of Information about Financial Instruments with Off-Balance-Sheet Risk and Financial Instruments with Concentrations of Credit Risk," came into effect. Futures, options, and financial swaps fall within the definition of a financial instrument as set forth by FASB 105. The purpose of FASB 105 is not to specify accounting principles applicable to these financial instruments. Its purpose is footnote disclosure of the off-balance sheet risk associated with certain financial instruments and also concentrations of credit risk. Off-balance-sheet risk is the risk of an accounting loss that exceeds the amount recognized as an asset or liability on the balance sheet.

Prior to FASB 105, a company could have entered into a speculative futures contract that might have resulted in a potential loss far exceeding the amount of investment that would be recorded on the balance sheet. No further special accounting or disclosure was required. Normal accounting treatment would handle any gain or loss attributed to the futures contract. With the adoption of FASB 105, footnote disclosure is now required if a company takes a speculative position in a financial instrument that can result in a loss exceeding the acquisition or carrying cost of the financial instrument. FASB 105 describes the nature of the footnote disclosure and also requires disclosure of credit risk where financial instruments are concentrated by geographic regions, industries, or customer groups that have common exposure to adverse economic developments.

The 1990 annual report of the Coca-Cola Company contains these required footnote disclosures. The company's exposure to credit risk of its associated bottlers and customers. Note the reference to outstanding interest rate swaps.

Note 4 to Coca-Cola 1990 Annual Report

- Finance Subsidiary. Coca-Cola Financial Corporation (CCFC) provides loans and other forms of financing to Coca-Cola bottlers and customers for the acqui-sition of sales-related equipment and for other business purposes. The approximate contractual maturities of finance receivables for the five years succeeding December 31, 1990, are as follows (in thousands):

1991	$38,199
1992	30,609
1993	20,156
1994	11,290
1995	7,111

These amounts do not reflect possible prepayments or renewals. Finance receivables include amounts due from Johnston of $56 million and $59 million at December 31, 1990 and 1989, respectively.

At December 31, 1990, CCFC had outstanding interest rate swap agreements which effectively change CCFCs' float- ing interest exposure on $60 million of commercial paper to a fixed rate of approximately 8.2 percent.

Note 7 of the same annual report, discloses non-U. S. dollar denominated debts, which are acting as hedges against the company's investments in these countries. Note 8 discloses that the company has entered into a substantial amount of foreign currency exchange and interest rate contracts, which are subject to the risk of loss if there is a change in rates. Because "such changes would generally be offset by opposite effects on the items being hedged," there is no speculative aspect associated with these financial instruments.

Notes 7 and 8 to Coca-Cola 1990 Annual Report

Notes outstanding at December 31, 1990, were issued outside the United States and are redeemable at the Company's option under certain condition related to U.S. and foreign tax laws. The 5 ¾ percent notes due to April 24, 1996, are donominated in Japanese yen and the 5 ¾ percent notes due March 25, 1998, are denominated in German marks.

Portions of such notes have been swapped for U.S. dollar, Swiss franc and Belgian franc denominated liabilities. The Company has designated such foreign currency borrowing as hedges against its net investments in those respective countries.

Other long-term debt consists of various mortgages and notes with maturity dates ranging from 1991 to 2013. Interest on a portion of this debt varies with the changes in the prime rate, and the weighted average interest rate applicable to the remainder is approximately 12.7 percent.

Maturities of long-term debt for the five years succeeding December 31, 1990, are as follows (in thousand):

1991	$97,272
1992	78,353
1993	24,750
1994	14,103
1995	8,009

The above notes include various restrictions, none of which are presently significant to the Company. At December 31, 1990, the Company is contingently liable for guarantees of indebtedness owed by third parties of $139 million, of which $82 million, is related to independent bottling licensees. Interest paid was approximately $233 million, $319 mil- lion and $250 million in 1990, 1989 and 1988, respectively.

Financial Instruments. The Company has various financial instruments with off-balance-sheet risk for the primary purpose of reducing its exposure to fluctuations in foreign currency exchange rates and interest rates. White these financial instruments are subject to the risk that market rates may change subsequent to the acquisition of the financial instrument, such changes would generally be offset by opposite effects on the items being hedged. The Company's financial instruments typically mature within one year of origination and are transacted at rates which reflect the market rate at the date of contract. At December 31, 1990, the Company had $1.3 billion of foreign currency financial instruments, substantially all of which were forward exchange contracts to purchase or sell foreign currency (primarily French francs, German marks and Japanese yen). These instruments were employed to hedge balance sheet and transactional exposure.

TAX ACCOUNTING

There is a question whether gains and losses associated with futures and options purchased for a business purpose ought to be treated, for tax purposes, as ordinary income or as capital gains. If treated as ordinary income, losses associated with futures and options reduce the company's overall tax liability. If treated as capital gains or losses, capital losses can only be netted against capital gains. Because most companies have little in capital gains, the effect is little, or no, tax loss benefit for net losses associated with futures and options. In other words, a gain associated with a futures or option would be taxed as a capital gain. A loss associated with futures or options can only be netted against a capital gain. If there are no offsetting capital gains, the loss remains on the books as a capital loss and cannot be used to reduce taxes currently. Basically, a company finds itself paying taxes on net gains of holding positions in futures and options, but not being able to shield income if there are net losses associated with futures and options. This is sometimes termed as "asymmetric" treatment of gains and losses.

The tax treatment of futures and options acquired for business purposes has traditionally been to match gains or losses against ordinary income. However, in 1988, the Supreme Court made a decision with regard to the *Arkansas Best* case, which has been interpreted by the Internal Revenue Service to mean that such gains or losses should be treated as capital gains or losses. This has opened up Pandora's box, as the IRS audits past corporate income tax returns and recasts the tax treatment of futures and options, as well as forwards and swaps. These tax adjustments have been estimated by one expert to be $2 billion. Congressional legislation is required to clear up the situation.

RISK MANAGEMENT STRATEGIC CONSIDERATIONS

A U.S. based company sells a product for a million British pounds, to be paid in six months, with a current exchange rate of $1.80 per pound. The financial advisors to the company feel that the pound is likely to fluctuate in a range of $1.70 to $1.90 per pound. A futures contract can be purchased to guarantee conversion at $1.78 per pound, indicating some negative feelings about the prospects for the pound by those selling futures. What should be done? There are two pure strategies: do nothing or hedge everything. The do nothing approach is simple—do nothing. In six months, the pound might be worth $1.70, meaning that the company will receive $100,000 less than what it anticipated when the goods were sold for 1 million pounds. The hedge everything approach is just as simple. This would commit the company to honoring a futures contract that would, in effect, lock the proceeds from the sale of goods at $1,780,000. Many financial managers subscribe to the latter course of action because a fully hedged portfolio "let's them sleep peacefully at night." The cost of a futures contract is small, being the brokerage fee associated with buying the contract. So the peaceful sleep costs the company little, unless, of course, one wants to overlook the loss of opportunity gain associated with the pound moving up to $1.90. In this case, the true cost of the peaceful night's sleep could escalate from the small brokerage fee up to about $100,000. This is a very expensive tranquilizer.

A less expensive tranquilizer might be a futures option to establish a minimum exchange rate for a million pounds, while letting the company benefit if the British pound gains in value. This costs more in the form of an upfront premium than a futures contract, but there may be offsetting opportunity gains associated with a strengthening British pound that could justify the extra cost. Between these two extremes are all sorts of mixed strategies where the individual hedge does not cover the entire million pounds, or where the strike, or option price, does not match the current exchange rate.

The key question is which of these myriad of possibilities does one follow? Utility theory allows the mathematical modeling of risk aversion, or fear, on the part of managers. What kind of a disaster awaits the company if the pound should fall to $1.70? Suppose this sale has a profit element of $300,000 with the pound at $1.80. The worst that can happen is that the profit element is reduced to $200,000. That may be acceptable given that, by doing nothing, the profit element may grow as large as $400,000 if the pound rises in value to $1.90.

On the other hand, perhaps the profit element in the transaction is not the main concern to the manager. Perhaps, the receipt of the $1.8 million is crucial for the firm continuing as a going concern. Suppose that approximately $1.78 million must be dedicated to repaying a loan and bankruptcy looms if the company does not repay the loan in full. Now there is no question that the company had better lock in the $1.78 million through a futures contract; the financial officer has good reason to buy a futures contract to guarantee a peaceful night's slumber.

No manager actually knows the future price of a commodity or the exchange rate of a currency. If so, he or she would be better off giving up his or her position and taking a speculative position in the asset. But managers do know the consequences if the price of a commodity, the interest rate on a loan, or the exchange rate of a currency reaches certain levels. These thresholds of financial pain vary with the circumstances of every company, and with the perceptions of every executive.

As an example, a public bus company consumes an enormous quantity of diesel fuel oil. The last thing the bus depot manager wants is to have to go before the town budget committee and beg for more money because diesel fuel costs have gone beyond his budgetary allotment. Risk management provides the financial means, such as a range forward, to avoid this pain. The fact that he might end up paying more for fuel if it falls below the floor rate is not of any great concern; the manager is still within his budgetary limit. Pain is on the side of high prices, not low prices. He may forego the opportunity to enjoy lower prices in order to avoid the pain of paying higher prices.

A manager of the fuel purchases for an airline cannot afford to pay more for jet fuel than some stipulated amount. On the other hand, he has no authority for paying upfront premiums for protection. A market maker in the jet fuel offers the airline a participating forward where the airline will not pay more than a ceiling price on the purchase of jet fuel. However, when the price of jet fuel is less than the ceiling price, the airline pays some premium over the market price. For instance, the price of jet fuel may be adjusted upward by half the difference between the spot and ceiling prices. This, of course, is the hidden premium for this risk management product because, in the world of finance, there is no free lunch. In this case, there are two pains. One is the pain associated with jet fuel prices escalating above a certain level. Pain is also in requesting upfront premium fees to pay for this risk management product. The financial engineers created a remedy for both pains by devising the participating forward contract.

Financial engineers or market makers stand between the oil producers and the oil consumers. An oil producer has a large amount of debt. He cannot afford to have oil fall below a certain price because he will not generate the earnings necessary to repay his loans. He is an obvious candidate for entering into some sort of arrangement that fixes the price at which he can sell his oil. The bus company and the airline and a host of other companies want to fix their cost of oil products. A financial engineer has to devise hedging tools not just in crude oil but also in gasoline, heating oil, and other petroleum products. Once these financial tools are developed, a market maker can stand between the various parties making up the oil industry fixing revenue, fixing cost, to everyone's heart's content, even devising clever schemes to hide the premiums. With financial engineers creating futures in crude oil, gasoline, heating oil, and jet fuel, a market maker can now approach an oil refiner and induce him to sell futures in gasoline and heating oil and buy futures in crude oil and fix his margin. That is, the refinery operator can lock in his operational profit margin through risk management products. When risk management is used in ways that lock in profit margins, it is sometimes referred to as economic management.

An example of economic management is a copper mining company wanting to borrow funds to expand its capacity. Lenders are wary of the project because of the inherent volatility in copper prices. A falling copper price will jeopardize the repayment of the loans. To combat this risk, the copper mine operator can use a risk management product to enter into a swap that stabilizes the price he is going to receive for his copper production. Since the economic risk of a falling copper price is no longer of concern to the bankers, they offer a floating rate interest loan to finance the mine project.

Now it is the copper mine operator's turn to worry about the financial risk of a rising floating rate interest destroying his profitability, now that his revenue is fixed by virtue of the copper swap. To accommodate the mine operator's perception of risk, another risk management product, an interest rate swap, can be set up to fix the rate of interest. If by chance, different currencies were involved between the selling of the copper and the financing of the loan, a currency swap can also be part of the picture. With both the copper price and the interest rate, along with any possible currency exchanges involved with the project, fixed, the projected cash flow can be sufficiently stabilized to proceed with the development of the mine. The economic risks associated with the project were addressed by an assortment of risk management products. Once in place, they made the project financially viable.

Another example of economic management is a U.S. exporter competing in the global market. His non-U.S. based competitors quote in different currencies. The U.S. exporter quotes only in dollars. He perceives this to be a competitive disadvantage. One way to address the marketing risk of not satisfying the needs of customers is to enter into currency exchange rate swaptions, or other financial instruments, based on estimates of sales in these currencies. If these currency exchange risk management products can be properly designed, a company can quote in different currencies and not be exposed to a currency exchange loss.

SYNTHETICS

Finally, the financial engineers can set up synthetic instruments. Synthetics use risk management products not directly related to the underlying asset. The use of currency exchange futures to hedge interest rate positions and vice versa are examples of synthetic instruments. Suppose that there is no way to hedge against currency X. However, in tracking past movements of currency X, and comparing these movements with those of currency Y, it is noted that there is good correlation between the two.

That is to say, the two currencies move more or less in tandem. If there is a market for risk management products in currency Y, then it is possible for financial engineers to devise a hedging vehicle for currency X using risk management products based on currency Y. The problem here is that future movements of currency X may not correlate, or be in tandem, with currency Y. In which case, the hedge may not only be ineffective, but may be a financial disaster.

One example of a synthetic instrument that failed to perform as intended was the use of heating oil futures as a synthetic hedge for jet fuel futures by airlines before the development of jet fuel futures. The synthetic instrument had previously shown a good degree of correlation between the prices of heating oil and jet fuel.

Their respective prices more or less moved in tandem. Unfortunately, one day the two diverged. Jet fuel prices went up and heating oil futures went down. Not only did the heating oil futures fail to provide any protection against rising jet fuel prices, but the heating oil futures themselves were liquidated at a loss.

MODELING AND MANAGEMENT JUDGMENT

To manage risk, management must first have an assessment of its exposure to a particular risk. A financial reporting and control system could have a projection of the financial statement and balance sheet projection of a company set up using nominal values for those currency exchange rates, interest rates and commodity prices that are of importance in the operation of a company. This does not have to be an integral part of an financial reporting and control system per se. It could be done on a spreadsheet where a single change in the value of one of these key variables can be transmitted throughout the income statement and balance sheet in such a way that management can see the associated impact of a change on reported profitability and cash flow.

The company is now in a position to play what if scenarios for different values of the key variables whose volatility can be addressed by risk management products. By keeping all variables at their nominal value and adjusting one at a time for likely changes in value, exposure to risk can be quantified for each variable and ranked in importance. Such an analysis can also lead to determining those values of key variables that approach a threshold of financial pain. That is, if the floating interest rate rose to a certain level, if a particular currency exchange rate fell to some other level, if the price of an important commodity rose or fell to another level, then the earnings would not be sufficient to satisfy the cash needs of the company. This defines the threshold of financial pain. Presumably, management is willing to pay for some degree of coverage to avoid the threshold of financial pain.

If the spreadsheet is designed to handle futures and options, and this is no small task, then it would be possible for management to compare a futures with a call from the point of view of avoiding financial pain for a given cost. A sophisticated spreadsheet may be able to provide information for management on how much coverage, and what form of coverage, should be taken to financially safeguard the company. A simulation is a very large number of what if scenarios. This, too, can be used as a risk management tool in deciding on the requisite degree of coverage. Simulations have been used to sort out the efficacy of various hedging programs relying on historic price fluctuations. The problem with this approach is the underlying assumption that the past is a prelude to the future. The fact that a specific hedging programme worked best in the last five years is no guarantee that it is the best choice for the coming year.

Several companies have developed an in-house capability to analyse their exposure to risk and measure the effectiveness of various hedging techniques. Other companies rely on outside vendors who sell systems that are adaptable to the particulars of a company. Some of these systems are dedicated to handling currency exchange risk, because this is a risk faced by all global companies.

Others cover a broader range of currency, interest, and commodity risks. Some confine their output to exposure to risk and tracking of hedges in place. Others provide analysis of alternatives, and some are better described as decision support systems because their output offers suggested optimal risk management strategies. There are about thirty software companies offering risk management systems. In addition, certain banks offer tracking and analysis systems to their clients.

Regardless of the nature of the software systems, the simplicity or complexity of what if spreadsheet models, or the nature of other computer aids, their purpose is to provide quantitative data to decision makers. There is little question that a well-designed quantitative model improves the quality of decisions. The designing of such models enhances the understanding of the participants in the inner financial workings of a corporation. On the other hand, models cannot run companies unless human judgment can be reduced to a series of 0's and 1's, the language of computers.

Judgment is more than 0's and 1's. Judgment is required in "what if" analysis because there must be management inputs on the perceived direction rates or prices may take in orchestrating the what if scenarios. Judgment is necessary in assessing volatility.

Volatility itself must be judged by people because volatility is not predictable. Periods of calm with relative stability in prices or rates follow and precede periods of tumult. Management judgment is required in deciding on what must be avoided; that is, what is the threshold of financial pain for a company. Judgment also comes into play in deciding the degree and cost of the risk management product coverage necessary to avoid this pain.

The final decision on which risk management programme to implement must be made by management. No computer programme can perceive the world better than a human mind, which, after all, is also the programmer of the computer. Therefore, risk management, like all management functions, is ultimately as effective as the people making the decisions.

RISKS IN FINANCIAL INTERMEDIATION

The Case of Asia: The Asia crisis has revealed a number of weaknesses in the supervision of financial institutions in Asia. Coincidentally, this has taken place at a time when supervisors in mature economies are confronted with new risks and are revising their approach.

By and large, Asia's financial intermediaries still operate as fairly unsophisticated moneylenders and rely on antiquated risk management tools. While the new financial tools that are presently the focus of supervisors and raters in mature economies have yet to pose a serious threat to the balance sheets of Asian financial institutions, enough of those tools have become accessible to them for Asian supervisors to take notice. But this matter in fact represents considerably more of a danger in Asia than in regions with advanced banking systems, simply because there is, among Asian financiers, a general lack of skill in risk management and control.

An impending financial crisis in the early 1990s and how new financial tools and broader access to international financing have compounded the problem. The sorry state of risk management in Asia, on the failure of many local authorities to rehabilitate the banking system and on why simple but drastic solutions are disregarded.

Moneylenders are highly geared companies that enjoy the recognition of and a degree of protection from supervisors in exchange for the provision of financial services to the community under strict rules. The rules take the shape of capital and liquidity ratios, while a number of regulations affect the risk profile of the financial institutions' assets, especially their loan assets. On that front alone, supervisors made considerable mistakes in Asia prior to the 1997 crisis. Perhaps would it be useful at this point to clarify that the 1997 crisis was in reality a market panic that, through the transmission belt of exchange rates and stock market valuations, served to reveal the weaknesses of many Asian countries. But the banking crisis started well before the 1997 panic. Japan's banking crisis started in 1991. The Korean banking system was on its knees as early as 1993 or 1994. The liquidity profile of Thailand's banks was so fragile that by 1995 a major rating company-Thomson Financial

Bank Watch-took the unprecedented step of gathering the 15 Thai banks for tea and cookies to tell them that a major crisis would hit them sooner or later. That the banks survived until the July 1997 crisis is simply a miracle. Malaysia was less of a problem, and the misallocation of capital would only have hit the country in about 1999, if not for the 1997 contagion. The same goes, paradoxically, for Indonesia where the local banks, for all their mistakes and the flouting of some prudential rules, were not in immediate danger. The Philippines banking system was not scheduled to crash until the year 2000. Taiwan had-and still has-a remarkably fragile banking system in an otherwise healthy economy. Most banks in China, Vietnam and the Indian subcontinent have been happily operating with negative equity for years.

How did the regulators fare? The regulators' job is to keep the banks on the straight and narrow. They must catch delinquent institutions before their mistakes start to costinflict depositors, creditors or taxpayers. When a private-sector bank is about to lose its last chunk of free equity, it should be forced to mend its ways and inject fresh capital funds. Should it fail to do so, the authorities should step in, force a reduction of capital and, if no fresh investment funds can be located, nationalise the institution partly or entirely. It comes as a surprise that, after the mid 1980s when Malaysia acted that way in respect of three small banks, no Asian country used such powers to clean the banking system until Thailand made a belated attempt in 1998. The regulators failed in their duties, but in all fairness it should be stressed that politics went into play and they were largely prevented from doing their job.

Beyond control by the ratios, the regulators failed in another way: they disregarded the all-important risk management and control. This is where the new tools-the new toys is perhaps a more appropriate description-came into play: derivatives and large international risk-taking activities. It would be possible today for relatively small financial institutions to go bankrupt within two weeks, and there would be little the regulators could do. But it would also be possible for them to collapse suddenly under the weight of accumulated mistakes that no external observer could have foreseen. Managers themselves often fail to acknowledge the existence of such mistakes. Beyond the ratios, regulators should be able to gauge the skills and the tools of the risk managers in the financial institutions they control. If the managers of a bank adequately control the bank's risks, there should be no need for external supervision, beyond basic ratios. If the bank managers know what they are doing, there should be no risk-except at the tail end of the risk spectrum-that they could not manage and contain. A major weakness of the Asia banking systems in recent years is that financial institutions have been allowed to take risks that they do not understand and have been unable to control. From Thai banks borrowing short-term dollars to finance long-term baht investments in unneeded real estate, to tiny Korean merchant banks lending dollars to unsafe Brazilian or Indonesian corporate borrowers, to Hong Kong-based banks lending to Malaysian companies for risky investments in the steel industry of the Philippines, the list is long of obvious mistakes in risk management.

The huge losses posted by many banks in the aftermath of the 1997 crisis should have at least prompted the authorities to take a fresh look at those matters, and to start a new era of better controls, beyond traditional ratio monitoring. But here also the countries have failed: the rehabilitation of the banking systems has been far from harmonious.

Governments and bank regulators across much of Asia have been desperately trying to fix banking systems that in many cases are arguably beyond repair. Efforts to date amount to little more than creative accounting techniques designed to mask insolvency. Regrettably, received wisdom has centred on the principle of merging unsound banks with those perceived to be sound, with the expectation that reducing their number will somehow give rise to miracles. I would suggest that, to the contrary, now is the time to allow the creation of brand new commercial banks across the region. A case could be made that it would be best to create new banks rather than rehabilitate moribund financial institutions. Asian governments, swayed by international trends in the consolidation of banking systems, do not seem interested in the idea, but that is another story.

The capital funds that are presently missing from commercial banks represent between 15 per cent and 45 per cent of GDP, depending on the country. It is simply not realistic to expect that the missing capital funds can be easily found. So banks must cook the books. In truth, using stringent international accounting practices, most banks in Thailand, Indonesia and Korea would exhibit negative capital ratios. In many cases they are beyond repair. This has a number of implications.

From an investor's point of view, it would theoretically be more appropriate to start a new bank rather than to invest in a bankrupt financial institution and see the best part of the fresh injection of capital devoted to writing off bad loans.

From the bank owner's point of view, there is nothing more to lose. With no more downside risk, moral hazard is at its highest. The temptation exists to increase both reward and risk. Little fresh lending is likely to be directed at safe borrowers.

From the regulator's point of view, it is preferable to let the owners of the ailing banks make an attempt at rehabilitation. This is because liquidating the bank at this stage would carry social and perhaps political implications. Once the capital funds are exhausted, depositors, creditors and taxpayers will share the cost of the failure. It is often the case that a bank operating as a going concern, in the hands of those who wrote the credits in the first place, is likely to be more successful than liquidators in pursuing recalcitrant borrowers. It is also likely to be more successful than government bodies taking over such assets.

The Basle Committee's approach to capital ratios, in its original 1988 form and with subsequent revisions, may exhibit some weaknesses, but it is an important step forward. Its adoption in Asia, however, has become a source of creative accounting for banks in that, since it is the focus of all rehabilitation gauging, no effort is spared to fake solvency. The valuation of assets is inaccurate and the regulators often conspire with banks to conceal the extent of the damage. Banks post inflated capital ratios. Loan losses are concealed that, if recognised, would eat away at Tier I, the most precious part of capital funds, as opposed to the more fuzzy capital attracted under Tier II.

Now that capital funds have become acutely restricted, the banks will, for the first time in Asia, face trade-off decisions between various risks that may lead them to lending decisions that could become socially undesirable or economically suboptimal, simply because they have lost the power to choose.

Meanwhile problem loans in aggregate have reached catastrophic levels and created a huge gap in equity. Compounding this difficulty is the very manner in which problem loans are identified. The classification of problem loans is not only changing, being lenient and inconsistent across the region, but is also often subject to unwholesome influence by authorities. The same problem applies to the provisions that these banks need to put aside against such loans. Provisioning decisions seem to be dictated not so much by prudence or the recognition of loan defaults, but by what banks can afford without recording embarrassing losses.

Banks have traditionally hidden huge amounts of non-performing loans simply by rescheduling the terms of their interest and/or principal payments, despite the bleak future prospects of such repayment. There can, of course, be, valid situations in which borrowers have legitimate cause to seek a restructuring of their obligations. In Asia, however, such reasons are generally rare. Rescheduling allows banks to skimp on prudent provisions while simultaneously recording interest income that never was, and is never likely to be, earned. This explains why a bankrupt bank can often look profitable. While acknowledging that improving economic conditions could restore the cash flows of some distressed borrowers and their ability to service their debt obligations, the banks' practices remain an unacceptable gamble.

Another expedient-and more acceptable-practice involves the transfer of non-performing loans to asset management companies. The main characteristic of such financial vehicles in Asia is that, beyond the liquidation of loans in a more efficient manner, they ensure the transfer of wealth from taxpayers to banks in a discreet and seemingly painless way.

Most banks in South Korea, Thailand, Indonesia and Malaysia are now at the mercy of their governments for their very survival. Either the governments own the banks outright, or they have a moral obligation to support them, sometimes as a price paid to the banks for their help in rescuing the weaker constituents of the financial system. Such Faustian arrangements are not new to Asia. The governments of Indonesia, South Korea, the Peoples' Republic of China, Vietnam and the countries of the Indian subcontinent have long controlled most of the larger commercial banks. Under government control, banks can more easily fake solvency. They conceal bad loans. In lieu of capital, government bonds are lodged on the books.

The aforementioned practices are merely accounting illusions. At best they allow banks to post the minimum regulatory ratios to keep them alive, so that they can fulfil their role as moneylenders. At worst they perpetuate mediocrity and moral hazard.

However viewed the present efforts to rehabilitate banks in Asia are but a transfer of enormous wealth from the many to the few. The major shareholders and managers of failed banks have not only escaped just punishment generally but often profit from the artificial rescue of their banks.

Clearly the regulators have been forced to go along with expedient decisions dictated by political and often practical considerations. Beyond capital ratios, there are many pressing problems to fix in the financial systems throughout Asia; namely credit culture, transparency, disclosure and corporate governance. More important still, Asia should pay more attention to the development of its capital markets. Meanwhile substantial efforts are needed for a quick resolution of the present credit crunch. Asia needs ruthless regulators and supervisors who will not allow private sector banks to resume their wild chase for market share or elusive profits. One possible development would be the creation of brand new banks, an option to which nobody gives serious consideration. The sad truth, perhaps, is that the lessons of the painful Asian crisis will not translate into any substantial improvement in the way banks are supervised.

THE ROLE OF THE FINANCIAL STABILITY

INSTITUTE OF THE BANK FOR INTERNATIONAL SETTLEMENTS

The height of that concern the G-7 has supported a number of actions to put in place disciplines to promote greater stability, and the worlds economic growth prospects are now substantially better. To some degree a sense of complacency has grown that should cause concern. We must not forget that the instability of 1998 saw the fastest growing economies in East Asia suffering contractions in output that were even greater than that experienced during the Great Depression of the 1930s; Russia going into default beneath its cloud of corruption; in the US, the mounting of one of the biggest ever emergency refinancings, not for a bank but for a hedge fund; free enterprise Hong Kong taking publicly owned stakes in all of its private companies; and Japan nationalising its banks. The causes of the problem, about which there is general agreement, include excessive indebtedness, both public and private; the inappropriate nature of that indebtedness, with its tilt towards short-term maturities in non-domestic currencies; high levels of leverage, not just in the financial system, but also in the debt to equity ratio in the industrial sector; and the nearly universal weakness of developing nations' domestic financial systems. It is almost impossible to pick up a newspaper or magazine these days without confronting another set of proposals to reform the 'international financial architecture', proposals that sweep the horizon of reform and include:

- The creation of an international deposit insurance corporation.
- The formation of an international bankruptcy courts.
- A rethink of the generalised antipathy towards controls on capital outflow.
- Chilean-style controls on inflows.

The creation of a single global super-regulator of financial markets and institutions. The creation of a world central bank with responsibility for overseeing a new global. The selection of the IMF to perform the functions of a lender of last resort, a suggestion packaged along with a wide range of improvements to the existing structure of the international financial institutions (IFIs).

The Council on Foreign Relations created a task force (of which the author was a member) and recently published its findings in a report entitled 'Safeguarding Prosperity in a Global Financial System: The Future International Financial Architecture', which put forward seven key recommendations:

- The IMF should lend on more favourable terms to countries that take effective steps to reduce their crisis vulnerability, and should publish an assessment of these steps so that the market can take note.
- Emerging economies with fragile financial systems should take transparent and non-discriminatory tax measures to discourage short-term capital inflows.
- The private sector should promote fair burden sharing and market discipline.
- Emerging economies should reject pegged exchange rates.
- The IMF should adhere consistently to normal lending limits and abandon huge rescue packages.
- The IMF and the World Bank should revert to their basic historical roles.
- Political support for financial reform should be generated.

Most of these schemes have fatal flaws. Some suggestions, ranging from the unrealistic to the surreal, are politically infeasible given the absence of a supranational legal authority; some could substantially increase costs to lenders or add protection for borrowers, and thus would lead to a sharp contraction of capital flows to developing nations; and those that shift risk away from creditors, thus leading to an increase in capital flows, are likely to be followed by a wave of greater risk taking, followed by another wave of defaults.

It seems to me that all these suggestions possess bits that could be recalibrated and, if taken together, would be helpful in designing solutions. However any attempt to find a sweeping one-size-fits-all answer is bound to fail. After all, each situation is different and needs to be evaluated in light of its particular circumstances. In my view solutions must be designed on a case-by-case basis, combined with smaller packages from the IFIs and accompanied by a reduction of bailout expectations (the moral hazard issue); more private sector involvement early on with terms that incentivise the private sector to participate; the recognition that solutions cannot be forced, since countries make their own decisions, the acceptability of which are priced into the market; and limit restructuring to the most difficult cases when insolvency threatens. There is of course considerable disagreement about any and all of the solutions save one the need to strengthen the financial sector of developing nations. All commentators, all committee reports, public and private, agree that this is key to financial stability. Since the mid 1970s we have seen time and time again that:

- Poor macroeconomic policies coupled with a weak financial sector is a recipe for disaster.
- Even when a country has a reasonably decent macro policy mix, if it has a weak financial sector any external shock is quickly transformed into disaster.
- A country may have a poor macro policy mix, but if it has a strong and vibrant financial sector there may be big problems, but disaster is averted.

The financial sector should be a stabilising influence, but as we have seen in Asia, Russia and elsewhere it has acted as a multiplier, making bad problems worse.

Since there is general agreement that strengthening the financial sector is critical, there is an unfortunate tendency within the official community to assume that sufficient attention and resources are being paid to fixing this problem. Some efforts along these lines have been made in the past and are being made by a variety of central banks and international financial agencies-but not nearly enough.

Improving the financial sector fundamentally requires substantial upgrading of financial supervisory systems. Theoretically, change could and should be implemented by the private sector in recognition of best practice and in response to competitive pressures. But this has not happened. Many reasons have been cited-including structural and cultural issues, which are usually used as an excuse for not meeting best practice-for their inability to change. The fact remains that those institutions wished to enjoy the benefits of global markets without accepting global standards.

In recognition of the need to improve the functioning of financial intermediation, the Basel Committee on Banking Supervision (BCBS) adopted the Core Principles of Banking Supervision, which were designed to guide supervisors on the standards they should require when examining a bank in order to judge the safety, soundness and prudent management of that institution. Since the private sector had abdicated the role of self-improvement, the financial supervisors recognised that it fell on their shoulders to become the agents of change.

Upgrading financial supervision in any country is a long-term project, one that will take years of diligent implementation to succeed. In the US it takes about five years to train a good bank examiner. And good bank examiners are exactly what are needed. On-site supervision is key to determining the strength or weakness of any individual financial institution, and on-site means on-site bank examiners. Off-site examination, favoured by some, is only valid if off-site is the sum of skilled on-site examination. If it is not, then off-site calculations are often corrupted by incomplete and often misleading information.

In many of these countries there is an overwhelming shortage of trained and experienced bank examiners. Furthermore many of these supervisory agencies are starved of the financial resources needed to provide a competitive wage for professional staff and purchase support mechanisms such as information technology. These agencies do not receive the necessary political support, which precedes financial support, to upgrade their capacity to do the job.

Many of the G10 central banks and banking supervisory agencies have been active in training bank examiners from developing nations. This has been helpful, but not all the G10 banking supervisory agencies have a similar view on the techniques needed to implement the core principles. Furthermore the training provided has been coloured by the practices and procedures used in the country in question. As a result, hundreds of men and women have been sent back to their home countries with some element of training but, as a group, without a common understanding of techniques and goals. It is imperative that we create a broad set of international standards that are accepted, implemented and enforced across the global financial system. We need a common understanding of the root meanings of the Core Principles and a common measure for their implementation and enforcement. It is to be hoped that this will be furthered by the final adoption of the Core Principles Methodology by the BCBS.

The Financial Stability Forum (FSF), under the chairman-ship of Andrew Crockett, the general manager of the BIS, and in cooperation with the IMF and the World Bank, has begun to collect data on the various training courses being offered to banking supervisors. Prior to this effort, no compendium of courses was available. This is an important first step in the process of providing assistance for financial supervisory improvement.

The IMF has agreed to undertake, in the course of its Article IV consultations, a review of the state of financial supervision. That should prove to be enormously helpful, but much more is needed. Identification of problems is an important first step towards their correction, but it must be accompanied by sources of education, training and assistance to which countries can turn in order to improve financial supervision. It is towards this end that the Bank for International Settlements (BIS) and the BCBS created the Financial Stability Institute (FSI) of the BIS. The FSI's mandate is to help improve and strengthen financial intermediation in the developing nations and those in transition. For the most part this means working with banking supervisors, since financial intermediation in these countries is heavily concentrated in the commercial banking system. For the most part capital markets are virtually non-existent or are only in the earliest phases of development.

The FSI is pursuing this task through a variety of symposia, meetings and workshops for the leaders of financial supervisory agencies. Leadership is key. We know that we must convince the agency heads of the validity and timeliness of our programmes so that they will encourage, even order, their associates to attend the courses that have been designed for them.

An integral part of the FSI's programme is the holding of workshops and meetings, many of them regional, for middle-level members of the supervisory agencies-the men and women who are responsible for the examination process. The programme began with the leadership, but it must reach out to professional staff so that they too can receive the benefit of FSI programming.

At the very heart of the FSI's work will be the Core Principles and the Core Principles Methodology, when finally adopted by the BCBS. This is particularly important since the IMF's Article IV consultation will include an assessment of adherence, implementation and enforcement of the methodology.

During 2000 the FSI held a series of workshops on methodology in Basel and the regions. It has also offered workshops on fraud detection, consolidated supervision, governance, asset and liability management, information technology, financial innovation, deposit insurance, capital flows and, last but not least, risk management, credit risk, and market risk.

It is the FSI's practice to use supervisors from around the world to lecture on subjects that are primarily supervisory in nature, and for the private sector to provide the lecturers for subjects that are directly market related.

The FSI recognises that at this stage much of what it is doing is somewhat experimental. Early in its existence it sent a survey to the heads of supervision and the central bank governors of all the non-G-10 countries to find out what they needed. Most encouragingly, it received a response rate of slightly over 75 per cent. This impressive result overwhel-mingly indicated the need for assistance. The programme for 2000, which focused on risk management, consolidated supervision and core principles methodology, reflected their priorities.

Prior to 2000 the FSI had held four workshops, attended by 129 persons from 74 countries. Their level of sophistication and experience was broadly spread from a very few with near state of the art capacity to those who had just begun seriously to improve their supervisory skills. Nearly all of those with whom the ESI has been in contact have been seeking a substantive upgrade for their agencies. They wished to have the same basic competence as that which presently exists within the G10. And they realistically recognised that it would take some time to get there.

Therefore the task of the FSI is twofold: to give supervisors a grasp of the end result they wish to achieve; and to provide them with the tools that will help them to achieve that goal, not only in the long term but in the short term as well. It is not good enough just to outline the landscape of the promised land of banking supervision. They have continuing responsibilities and must examine and pass judgement on banks tomorrow. The FSI must provide them with the necessary tools to help them manage their ongoing responsibilities as they travel the long road to the promised land. This is easier said than done. Whatever is suggested for immediate implementation must be in concert with long-term, presently unachievable goals. The FSI is attempting to resolve this dilemma by stressing basics, coupled with techniques for an immediate assessment of an institution's ability to meet minimum standards. The FSI's course on market risk explains the benefits of and the techniques for stress testing and measurement tools such as VaR-all of this done by private sector experts, complemented by supervisors with this particular expertise-and simultaneously provides them with questions that will help them to determine the scope and reach of an institution's market risk management. In many countries, supervisors simply do not have enough trained professionals to evaluate the more sophisticated techniques designed by the G10 supervisors. Therefore the questions the FSI gives them are designed quickly to reveal the state of management's capacity to manage risk without requiring the supervisor to field an army of experienced examiners backed up by state of the art technology. For example, at the beginning of an examination the examiner could ask the CEO the following questions (there are follow-up questions depending upon the answers):

- What is the tolerable level of loss your board of directors has agreed is an acceptable level of risk?
- Please show me how you decompose your profit and loss statement between risk- and non-risk-related activities. Also, may I see your log of extraordinary gains and losses for the past six or 12 months with the accompanying explanations?

These questions are simple but not simplistic. If the board of directors has not set a tolerable loss limit, the supervisor knows there is a basic governance issue. If the profit and loss statement is not decomposed and if there is no log of extraordinary gains and losses, then the supervisor knows there is no effective risk management in that institution even if a risk management box appears on the organisation's chart. Since most supervisors have the power to inspect the institution's records, including board minutes, the answers given are easily verified by inspection. The FSI recognises that the path to global improvement of financial supervision is long and arduous. Most nations with which it has been in contact seem serious about improving their financial supervisory capacity. But no doubt some of those who say they are will not commit the necessary resources to accomplish the task. Adherence to principles is not necessarily compliance with principles. The FSI does not prejudge the motives of any nation in this respect. Over time it will become apparent to the FSI and the international financial community which nations are seriously trying to improve and those which are just paying lip service. As that becomes apparent, and it surely will, then international financial institutions and the capital markets will take progress, or the lack of it, into account and act accordingly.

TURBULENCE, CRISES AND RISK MANAGEMENT

Balance sheets are opaque concepts. In more than one way, the individual instruments in a balance sheet have no meaning by themselves. What is more, most large financial institutions carry a very large number of diverse instruments on their balance sheets, in many different branches and subsidiaries around the world. Even a careful analysis of financial tables and balance sheets will not show the exact positions and exposures the financial institution has taken. This is even before one can ask how one would value these positions.

Quantitative methods of risk management are perhaps the only reasonable way of assessing the potential losses institutions may face in the event of financial turbulence. In this introduction we illustrate why this is so by discussing the difficulties of managing risks using non-quantitative approaches. We do this using two examples, both of which relate to options. Options exist in explicit and implicit form. They are often implicit in very common contracts that never draw attention. For example, annuity contracts often contain significant optionality. Another case in point is bonds, most of which usually come with call or put options. Call loans on the other hand, are loans that contain complex implicit options. Looked at from this angle, explicit options that are either written over the counter or traded in organised exchanges are an exception.

All these aside, some of the more popular derivatives that have attained a huge volume contain options. Caps, floors and swaptions form the largest part of derivatives books in financial institutions.

They are basically options on interest rates. Selling or buying an option appears to an outsider as a very risky activity. After all, the seller of a call on interest rates or currencies faces the (gross) payoff at expiration.

Clearly it looks as though the trader who is short faces very high risks and may lose unlimited sums if the interest rates move against him or her! Yet this way of looking at option risks is misleading. As soon as a trader sells an option he or she buys an appropriate amount of the underlying asset. For example in this case he or she buys Eurodollar futures, whose value is:

$$Ft = 100(1-0.\ 25r_t)$$

where r t is the three-month Libor for example. If the contract is entered into when, say $r_{t'} = r$, then this position looks like the one. Here the slope of the payoff is 0. 25 times the number of futures contracts sold, which in general is equal to $C_3^0/0.25$ the slope of the option position at point C^0.

The two quantities are approximately equal, especially if r is small. This means that the option buyer (seller) has hedged his or her risk.

Hence if we look at the balance sheet of this institution we will see a long position in options, which we may think is risky. We will also see a short position in the underlying asset, which we may also find risky. But put together these risks cancel out.

Does this mean that the positions are not risky? Nothing could be further from the truth. The option holder faces volatility, or vega risk. If the actual volatility in the market turns out to be less than expected, the trader may lose money.

The trader is long the underlying asset, he is long an at-the-money put and short an at-the-money call. Considered separately, the instruments appear to be very risky and the trader has a high probability of losing money. But put together the position is not risky at all. In fact traders use these types of riskless positions to arbitrage between markets. They will 'buy' an instrument and, using appropriate call and put options, 'sell' it at a higher price. The spread is their profit. Their position is not any riskier than the activity of a new car dealer.

Yet suppose the prices move and the trader mistakenly sells the put, which has become profitable. Then the whole position reduces to a short put, which carries unlimited risks. This shows that the closing of a position may affect the risks of other assets in the portfolio

How can the institution tell whether such indirect exposures are created by the thousands of transactions carried out on a given trading day? Clearly this is not an easy operation.

The current methods of risk management and provides one answer to the above questions. The main concepts and tools. The next section discusses some standard ways of measuring risk.

This is followed by a discussion of the types of assets financial institutions deal with and their relevance from the point of view of risk management. The next two sections deal with the complications that one may encounter when applying these tools, and with the new avenues.

MANAGING RISKS

Risk management can be seen as having two broad branches. The first, and the one with which we are mainly concerned, is market risk management. The second, and equally important, is credit risk management-we shall comment on this rapidly developing domain as well.

We begin by considering a simple example in order to define the basic concepts, which are essentially the same across markets and credit risk management. Consider a default-free zero coupon bond with price B 0 with maturity T and yield R T. This could be a treasury bond, or more exactly a STRIP. Because the bond is default-free the holder of this instrument is guaranteed to receive 100 units of a certain currency at T, which for simplicity we assume is the US dollar. Assuming that the future default-free short rates are given by (*r t*, *t* = 0, 1. . , *T* 1), the arbitrage-free price of this bond will equal

$$B_0 = E^P \left(\frac{100}{(1 + r_0)(1 + r_1)..(1 + r_{T-1})} \right)$$

where P is the risk-neutral probability measure. This price can also be written in terms of the corresponding yield.

Here the R T, r t and the exchange rate, e T, between the US dollar and some relevant variables will alter the value of the asset in question. Market risk has to do with losses that may be caused by changes in these market risk factors. There are in fact three major ways in which changes in risk factors can affect the value of a portfolio.

We shall discuss these within the context of the same example. The first effect is the portfolio or asset's delta. The yield, R T, is a random variable and it will change by R T as time t passes. This change can be large and may cause significant drops in the value of the bond. In a portfolio that has long bonds, the losses will be proportional to increases in R T. This proportion (called the delta of the instrument) will be greater the longer the maturity of the bond.

Here we see the first type of market risk, namely the first order price risk of the bond portfolio, and this is clearly caused by random movements in the risk-free yield.

The secondary effects of movements in risk factors is the gamma effect. An institution that is long (short) the bond, or some other instrument, may have hedged the delta risk, however. This can be done by selling (buying) T-bonds, T-bills or other appropriate interest rate futures. But in some cases, such as Eurodollar futures, the futures price is a linear function of the interest rates, whereas the bond price is a non-linear function of R T, as can be seen from the formula above. Thus the institution may have exposure to the second derivative with respect to yield: This risk is called the gamma risk and is another type of market risk created by the inability of a linear instrument to hedge fully for the nonlinear effects of random changes in the risk factor R T. Note that in this particular case the gamma risk is of the opposite sign to the delta risk. Hence if one has exposure to a particular delta, ignoring the gamma risk will be equivalent to adopting a conservative approach.

CREDIT RISK

THE NEW FRONTIER OF RISK MANAGEMENT

The art of market risk measurement and control has reached a state today that is impressive by any standard. Recent academic developments (notably based on option pricing), new tools (VaR and its variations), new instruments (with the continuously renewed derivative contracts), new institutions (for example the importance assumed by risk management departments in banks) have all converged to provide a remarkable understanding and mastery of market risk, whether interest rate, foreign exchange or stock markets. Of course our deepened understanding has also confirmed what we cannot understand-forecasting and asset pricing have particularly been under stress. But overall the advancement of finance in market risk is both obvious and a guarantee of further advancements in the field, and other the clear promise of rocket science discoveries continuously to upgrade our knowledge and techniques. It is thus unfortunate that what is arguably the largest single risk class in volume today ($4. 6 trillion of public debt in the US in 1996 alone and easily $2. 9 trillion in corporate loans in the same country) and arguably the major risk for all economic agents in the business world-the risk of default-is far from being as well understood. Credit risk is also very pervasive. Most of the huge derivatives markets, for example, are OTC (over-the-counter) contracts and as such present a credit risk-the possibility of default by one counterparty. Banks have had to manage credit risk (risk of default on the loans they provide) for centuries. The fact that they are much less sophisticated at doing this than they are at managing their (comparatively more recent) FX or interest rate exposures, and also lack advanced techniques and instruments to do so, may therefore come as a surprise-but actually it should not do so. Credit risk is a complex topic that requires all our intellectual, technical and institutional abilities, and even then it does not lend itself to easy solutions. What should also be clear is that hoping to manage risk without managing credit risk is hopeless.

This is the risk to manage. It pervades all financial contracts and it perverts market risk, for example a portfolio believed to be fully hedged with swap or forward contracts against an FX or an interest risk may suddenly find itself at risk again because of credit risk.

What we propose to do here is to give a sense of why credit risk is so difficult to apprehend, what traditional methods are telling us, how modern techniques, inspired by the most advanced market risk techniques, are being used to look at the problem from a new angle, and how new instruments and new institutions are emerging that may help us to manage credit risk better in the near future.

THE COMPLEXITY OF CREDIT RISK

Credit risk is extremely complex and presents a greater challenge than both market risk (one needs to understand market risk in order to predict when and under what conditions a counterparty might default) and purely exogenous risks such as operational risk.

Indeed credit risk depends on market risk, but while market risk can be made homogeneous by category (interest rate, FX and so on), credit risk is deeply fragmented. First, credit risk is fragmented by product. For example banks hold loans while mutual funds hold bonds on what might appear to be the same credit risk (a company) but it actually leads to a very different outcome in the event of default (technically, while the probability of default may be similar across products for a one company exposure, the loss given default, and thus the credit risk that is a combination of these two dimensions, will differ widely and is usually not well determined ex ante but a consequence of complex negotiations). Second, credit risk is fragmented geographically. Most institutions lend and invest primarily in their own back yards. Global players, and those trying to design management techniques that will be applicable worldwide, have long discovered that default in the US, default in Switzerland and default in Japan are three very different things, with different economic outcomes and different uncertainties about the outcome, not to mention the complex interaction between the credit risk of the country and the credit risk of the company.

Third, credit risk is fragmented in time. On the investor's side it is fragmented by maturity horizon. Bank loans often mature within five years, while life insurance companies invest in 10- to 30-year bonds. These exposures are usually analysed by means of the same long-term rating system. The relationship between credit risk and time is not well understood, but as we shall see later, credit risk can increase or decrease with maturity, in a highly non-linear fashion.

This fragmentation can lead to excessive risk taking and inefficient pricing. If one adds to this fragmentation the proliferation of credit enhancement methods (from collateralisation to AAA subsidiaries via credit risk insurance), which make the issue even more confusing, the problematic heterogeneity of this risk starts to become evident.

On a more technical note, most market risk models (such as asset selection and the efficient frontier, the CAPM and other asset pricing models, and more recently most of the models in the option pricing literature) are based on an assumption of normal distribution. Unfortunately this assumption (and the rather simplified mathematical conclusions it produces) does not carry well for credit risk.

A holder of a credit instrument such as a bond can expect to receive the principal plus interest if the instrument is held until maturity, or even to have a limited upside if the credit instrument is upgraded in rating. The downside occurs, usually with a low probability, when either the obligor defaults or the instrument is downgraded in rating. Therefore the return from a credit instrument is highly skewed. In contrast the return from an equity instrument is fairly smooth and symmetrical and can be assumed to be normally distributed. Because of the highly skewed nature of returns from credit instruments, the calculation of value-at-risk (VAR) requires a different approach from the traditional market risk methods (from derivative pricing to VaR), where a normal distribution of returns is assumed. Note that this difference in statistical behaviour is linked to the relationship between credit risk and market risk and to the nature of credit risk itself.

One way of looking at credit risk, which those used to option theory will recognise, is to plot the profile of a bond that is subject to credit risk versus the value of the assets of the firm. The profile differs between a bond that is subject to interest rate risk and the reimbursement value of the same bond, depending on the capacity of the firm to honour its commitments. To these conceptual issues we have to add a practical consideration: lack of data. While there are some data on ratings, these are not frequently updated, nor are they necessarily a good representation of default probability.

They have no explanatory power for loss, given default. Yields on publicly traded instruments can be observed but they are instrument-dependent. Also, unlike with market risk, the correlation between the returns on credit instruments is not directly observable, which makes it difficult to calculate the credit risk of a portfolio. The current lack of data (something that could be partly remedied by effort on the part of banks and regulatory bodies) thus makes a conceptually difficult task even more problematic.

It is therefore to the credit of those working in the field that our knowledge and techniques have advanced dramatically since the late 1990s. Before examining these techniques we shall look at the difficulties that arise with the most frequently used traditional instrument: ratings.

DIFFICULTIES THAT ARISE WITH RATINGS

Traditionally ratings have been used as the starting point in credit risk analysis. Ratings are a simple way to transform a discrete event (default) into a more continuous variable (rating changes). It is well known that continuous variables are easier to handle and to obtain the dynamics of than discrete events. This transformation is thus welcome if it is valid. The following brief example illustrates the functioning of ratings. Suppose you have a long position in a bond that is rated AA. The risk you face is that of being downgraded. Hence to calculate the credit risk of your position you need to calculate:

- The probability of a downgrade.
- The bond's value in the event of a downgrade.
- The recovery rate in the event of the ultimate downgrade: default.

Hence the use of transition matrices, which plot the probability of moving to another rating. They are useful for measuring and managing credit risk in that they can be used to ascertain the dynamics of ratings over time.

The transition matrices can be calculated from past data by calculating (over a period of 15-20 years) the number of AAAs that have remained AAA, the number of AAAs that have become AA, and so on. More recent work tries to integrate the credit cycle instead of using only historical data, but obvious challenge of the methodology is its dependence on the latter (and its failure to consider outside factors such as macroeconomic variables).

How good are ratings at capturing credit risk information? Several researchers have addressed the problem, with mixed results. For example Lucas and Lonski analysed the ratings of 6000 issuers over the period 1970-90 and found that ratings are not stable, and that even their instability is not stable. Ratings volatility doubled from 6 per cent of changes per calendar year in the 1970s to 12 per cent in the 1980s. There was a clear downward trend in quality that makes credit risk analysis all the more important today. The ratio of downgrades to upgrades went from 1. 17 (almost balanced) to 2. 17 for long-term debt over the period in question, that is there were twice as many downgrades than upgrades at the end of the period.

Some authors defend the idea that there is no useful information to be obtained from ratings as they are too slow to adjust and reflect rating agencies' management as much as true credit changes. Others have strongly defended ratings as the only true source of information available. Using a sample of 1500 industrial firms during the period 1985-95, that there is little information content in rating upgrades (all the information has already been incorporated into market prices) but there is some in rating downgrades. This study shows that neither the antirating nor the prorating lobbies are right-the reality is more complex.

Several studies have shown that neither of the two agencies truly dominates the other as far as the information content of their ratings goes. Indeed, if one considers split ratings, it can be shown that taking into consideration the two ratings has more information content than taking either one. Stability (or instability) of rating migrations and established a methodology to adapt rating migrations to changes in the business cycle, the country or the industrial sector.

In short, the information content of credit ratings is minimal at best, even in the US, where ratings are extensive.

Note that credit risk depends not only on the probability of default (captured to a certain extent by ratings) but also on the recovery rate (or conversely the loss, given default), and information on this variable is even hardly to crime. There are huge differences across industries-for some industries the recovery rate can be as high as 80 per cent while for others it barely goes over the 10 per cent mark. Different recovery rates should lead to different credit risks, a fact not well represented in ratings and for which we lack even the most basic information, especially in Europe. From a practical viewpoint, the usual instruments of credit risk measurement seem limited and their relationship to actual pricing is difficult to assess as complex, non-linear relationships are sure to be present.

RECENT THEORETICAL LITERATURE ON CREDIT RISK PRICING

During the last few years, academic research has shed new light on the complexity of the credit risk problem and on ways to approach and treat it.

Two major lines of research have evolved (with some overlap): the contingent claim approach and the reduced form approach.

The first approach was pioneered in 1974 by Robert C. Merton (who won a Nobel Prize in 1997). Merton proposed that in a simple setting (a firm with only one issue of zero-coupon debt) the stock of the firm can be seen as a call option on the assets of the firm and hence the credit risk on the debt issue can be compared to a short position on a put option. Thus contingent claims analysis (option pricing) can be used to value the component parts of a firm's liability mix. In general, the value of each component will depend upon the stochastic variables that determine the evolution of the firm's asset value, the evolution of the interest rate, the payouts (dividends, coupons and so on) to the various claimants, and the division of the firm at any point of reorganisation (for example bankruptcy). The method makes it possible to analyse and measure the impact on credit risk spreads of a change in asset volatility, a change in interest rate volatility, different maturities of debt and so on.

The payoff structure for levered corporate equity is isomorphic to the one for a call option on a share of stock where the maturity date of the firm's debt, T, corresponds to the expiry date of the option, the promised payment on the debt, B, corresponds to the exercise price of the option and the firm's value, V, corresponds to the underlying security. As a consequence the terminal payoff to debt is functionally equivalent to owning the assets of the firm and being short a call option on those assets with an exercise price of B. (Alternatively the debtholders can be considered to have lent money risklessly at face value B and gone short a put option on the assets of the firm with an exercise price of B.)

We can thus use option pricing to value credit risky bonds. The theory provides for interesting and unexpected consequences, such as the fact that volatility and credit spreads may be two contradictory measures of credit risk (they may rank instruments differently as to their risk) and the fact that in high-yield debt, longer maturity may be associated with a lower credit risk, all else being equal.

The methodology has been extended in various ways to take into account non-constant interest rates, several debt issues, more complex instruments (including credit derivatives), the presence of collateral, the presence of gaming when there are bankruptcy costs and so on, but it becomes very difficult to handle mathematically when these different complexities are cumulated. It is nonetheless a full theory of credit risk with, notably, an endogenous recovery rate.

The reduced-form approach is quite different. Although it focuses on arbitrage-free models (and thus differentiates itself from the plain actuarial ratings-based approach), it treats bankruptcy as an exogenous rather than an endogenous process. From a theoretical point of view this is not a welcome departure, but it does allow for easier treatment of practical cases (with the weakness of ignoring the financial economics behind the determination of the bankruptcy process). Many recent papers have followed this assumption. The papers allow for somewhat easier pricing of complex instruments. They also allow models to be fitted in a clean way to past data. On the other hand the models are limited to exogenous times to default and exogenous recovery rates. Although very sophisticated mathematically and of great use in practice, the models do not provide a full theory and thus may be taken to be at fault in a highly unstable environment. Put together the two theories give us a much better picture of what credit risk is about and how this risk moves with different variables. They allow for a more precise pricing of credit risk and should prove highly useful as the market for credit risk evolves (notably with credit derivatives such as credit default swaps).

CREDIT RISK MEASUREMENT FOR PORTFOLIOS

Financial institutions are required by the regulatory authorities (The Bank for International Settlements and the national governing bodies) to hold a certain amount of funds in reserve to cover the risk of their assets. Determining the amount to be held is an important regulatory challenge, but knowledge of the amount of risk an institution is ex manage their portfolio and risks.

Since the financial performance of a company is influenced to a large extent by market conditions, the credit risk of the company (the possibility of downgrade or default) depends on market conditions.

Simply adding together market risk and credit risk may lead to double counting. At the same time a sudden increase in the riskiness of large 'market makers' can influence the overall market conditions. Ideally, therefore, in order to quantify the amount of risk there should be a holistic approach to risk measurement, capturing both aspects. Since the theoretical models for this are too complex for easy implementation, financial institutions are using separate models to evaluate the two aspects of risk.

Of the many models available to evaluate credit risk, the following four are dominant.

CREDITMETRICS

Creditmetrics, which was initially promoted by J. P. Morgan and is now marketed by an independent company (Riskmetrics), measures changes in the value of an asset due to the migration of its credit rating.

It starts by assigning a credit rating to an asset/obligor. The range of changes in the value of the asset is calculated on the basis of the probability of the asset changing its credit rating or defaulting over a certain period. Than the value at risk at a given confidence level is derived as the value of the return on the asset at that confidence level. Credit rating agencies such as S&P and Moody's publish data on the credit ratings of assets, their transition probabilities and the recovery rates in case of default.

CREDITRISK

Credit Suisse's CreditRisk+ is derived from the model used by insurance companies to evaluate their risks and relies on a two-state model of an asset-the asset is either in default or not in default. In this sense it is close to reduced-form models. The model does not consider risks due to the downgrading of the credit rating of the obligor. No assumption is made about the causes of default: obligor A is either in default, with probability P A or is not in default, with probability.

Losses (exposures, net of recovery) are divided into bands, with the level of exposure in each band being approximated by a single number. Default rates, their volatility and the recovery rates of obligors are obtained from the credit rating charts published by rating agencies or the financial institution itself. To calculate a loss due to the default of a portfolio of assets, the model divides the assets into bands, based on exposures. The total portfolio is then regarded as a portfolio of these bands. Value at risk at a certain confidence level is then calculated as the expected loss due to default at that confidence level.

CREDIT MONITOR MODEL

The Credit Monitor model is based on Merton's option model of a firm, where both the stockholders' and bondholders' claims on the firm's assets are considered as options. If the volatility of a firm's equity is known, its value and the firm's capital structure, value of the firm's assets and its volatility can be calculated. The value of the risky debt can then be calculated using the option pricing model.

Using historical data on the behaviour of defaulting firms, the credit-measuring company KMV has concluded that the critical threshold for default (The 'default point') is not the point where the value of a firm's assets falls below the value of its liabilities, but where the firm's value reaches the par value of current liabilities to be serviced over a time horizon plus half its long-term debt.

The model then computes the index, distance to default (DD) as the number of standard deviations between the mean of distribution of the asset value, and the default point. Unlike the Creditmetrics model, where firms with the same credit rating are expected to have the same default and transition probabilities, which are equal to the average historical rate, the Credit Monitor model allows us to look at the default probability of a specific firm.

Also, since rating agencies take time to upgrade and downgrade the credit ratings of firms, the default rates they report may not accurately reflect the actual default rates. In fact there are examples of the EDF (expected default frequency) becoming the leading indicator of default or a tall in the creditworthiness of obligors.

CREDITPORTFOLIO

The CreditPortfolio model incorporates macroeconomic factors into the calculation of default rates and the probability of credit rating transitions. The probability of default is calculated as a function of various macroeconomic factors and the speculative grade of the obligor. Provided there is enough historical data to calibrate the model-that is to establish coefficients for the influence of a particular factor on probability-this model can be used to calculate the riskiness of assets in any country or industry. The econometric consistency of the model thus becomes essential, but its theoretical base is weaker than those of the other models.

It should be noted that none of these models can deal with market risk at the same time as credit risk (for example none can deal with non-constant interest rates) and none can deal with non-linear instruments such as options, hence they are very limited. However, they do represent an important advance on the usual practices. For example they allow for portfolio optimisation of high-yield portfolios, something that has not been done before. When new instruments to manage credit risk emerge, such as credit derivatives, knowl

edge of how to manage portfolios and transform their exposure to credit risk will offer a major competitive advantage as the flexibility of exposure management becomes increasingly important. The most widely used credit derivatives (credit default swaps-basically default insurance-and total return swaps, whereby a safe return is swapped for a credit risky return) as well as new instruments (default spread options and futures) will render the credit risk exposure of financial intermediaries more flexible than they have ever been. Understanding what they want in terms of credit exposure and the value of that exposure are thus becoming essential concerns for financial intermediaries in respect of competitiveness.

PRESSURE TO INNOVATE AND RESTRUCTURE

The financial sector will face tremendous challenges in the coming years. Globalisation and information technology are the twin forces transforming the industry-indeed the world economy-at a pace never experienced before.

GLOBALISATION

It might sound like a cliché, but we are in the midst of the greatest economic transformation in the history of mankind. Since the early 1980s, thanks to new technology and globalisation, around one billion people have been lifted from abject poverty to some kind of global middle-class status. Globalisation has proceeded in steps: via freer trade, deregulation of the capital markets to today's rapid transformation and diffusion of technology to all corners of the world.

As a result the old trade-off between quality and quantity is changing. Some decades ago, when deciding on their production base global companies could choose between high-cost, high-quality production in industrialised countries and cheap, low-quality production in Third World countries. Today, however, courtesy of globalisation, new information technology and the collapse of communism, it is quite possible to produce high-quality goods and services in emerging economies-and much more cheaply than in industrialised countries. This of course means more rapid global growth, but also new challenges to the industrialised world and its old companies.

For the small and open economies of this new world there is no control room in the Ministries of Finance, where ministers can push buttons or pull levers and feel certain of controlling their national economies. As a matter of fact most national economies are merging into a single, comprehensive global economy.

In this new global economy the Anglo-Saxon free market model has triumphed over the planned economy, and also over the welfare state and the Asian model. Hence there is increasing pressure for deregulation and free markets in just about all countries. Tax structures are converging as tax bases become more mobile. The number of independent currencies is diminishing, due to currency unions, currency boards and dollarisation. New fashions and cultural trends are spreading rapidly via new media, global television, fax machines and the Internet-even to the remotest villages. Young people are increasingly influenced by global trends and by other young people all over the world, rather than by their local elders. We are truly becoming one world.

THE IT REVOLUTION

In this global environment a new revolution is taking place in information technology, a revolution that is in turn helping to propel both growth and globalisation. In my opinion the IT upheaval is a third industrial revolution-following the first industrialisation process, based on the steam engine, and the second wave, based upon the electrical motor and the internal combustion engine. There is of course no scientific or exact definition of what constitutes an industrial revolution. However economists and historians seem to agree that one important characteristic is the development of a generic technology, which is then exploited and employed in numerous sectors, creating spin-offs and 'developmental blocks' in important ways that were totally unforeseen by the original innovators.

We all know the story of the dynamo and the electrical motor; how it started as a big, clumsy machine at the centre of the factory floor but gradually evolved over decades to become more efficient, smaller and universal. Today there are literally hundreds of electrical motors in each home, in our kitchen appliances, vacuum cleaners and other gadgets that have transformed everyday life. The same is true of the internal combustion engine, which radically transformed transporta-tion, distribution, housing and living. And in time the manu-facture of cars, the construction of houses and the production of television sets, refrigerators and so on created economic growth and mass prosperity on an unprecedented scale.

I believe the same thing will happen again as a result of the IT revolution. Its symbol is the silicon chip and the glass-fibre cable. Some 20 years ago, when computers started to be used in industry, they were rather bulky and slow and were usually handled-in closed-off rooms-by men in white coats, speaking unintelligible techno-lingo. The productivity effect was low or hardly discernible. I guess we all remember Solow's quip: 'Computers are everywhere but in the productivity statistics'. Now, however, computers are literally everywhere and the man-machine interface is much easier to handle, and when millions of computers are interconnected through high-speed cable the productivity effects are much greater.

They are bound to be even greater in the future. While the engines of the earlier industrial revolutions simplified physical human work or replaced it with machines, the chip and the cable will replace or simplify mental and intellectual work. In doing so they will transform our lives in ways we cannot imagine today.

HEADING TECHNOLOGY

The technical change brought about by the IT revolution has just begun. Over the next few years we will see rapid development in several areas.

- Moore's law (exponential growth of computing capacity) will apply at least for the next couple of years. Processors will be faster, and memory capacity will rapidly increase. Computers and chips will become even smaller and smarter.
- Bandwidth will expand. The sending and receiving of immense amounts of information via the Internet is increasing much more rapidly than was thought possible only a couple of years ago. The bottleneck is the last thread out to the individual household, but here also experimentation and innovation are moving fast.
- The man-machine interface will become even simpler and easier to handle. We have become used to a screen, a mouse and a keyboard, but in the near future we will be able to interact with the computer through speech (or even via sensors applied to our bodies). The screens will be thinner, bendable or foldable and transportable. This means that e-mail and Internet connections will be easier to handle and will function faster from any place in the world with the help of a number of gadgets.
- All this opens up true interactivity. Not only will we be able to interact sequentially, but together we will be able to work on the same project or design, in real time, irrespective of where in the world we are.
- The communication explosion will propel the rapid development of filters, screening and push technologies.
- IT will, in simpler and less conspicuous ways, become embedded in all kinds of products and processes, which will become 'intelligent' or at least self-regulated, like thermostats. We can already see this in durable consumer goods, for example antilocking brakes and

automatic traction systems in cars. In the financial markets we can see it in automatic trading programs and their various selling and buying orders. In manufacturing, electronics are being gradually linked to electromechanical micromotors with sensors and switches, which work in a mechanical environment in machines and products of all kinds.

- Huge resources are being spent on combining such techniques with medical technology. Self-regulating medication and medical treatment, even operations, via remote control is already here. Simulations and similar technology can also be utilised to revolu-tionise education.
- In manufacturing and the service sector it is increasingly possible to mass produce tailor-made products, paradoxical as that may sound. Compute-rised control of production, inventories and supplies is being used already and is spreading to more and more industries.

Generally, means of group communication and communication over large distances will be more widely available and easy to use, as well as more sophisticated.

GROWTH-BUT STILL LOW INFLATION

All of this has already affected the macro economy, and it will have an even greater impact in the future. In the words of Joseph Schumpeter, earlier revolutions started long waves of growth and credit expansion.

The pattern is not completely clear, and it has repeatedly been disturbed by external shocks (wars and political disruption) and internal boom-bust cycles. Nonetheless, beneath the surface of day-to-day events it is quite possible to see a secular trend. Consequently, part of the rapid growth of the postwar period can be explained by the transformation of society through commercialisation of the electrical motor and the internal combustion engine.

The gradual economic retardation during the 1970s and early 1980s was partly due to external shocks (oil crises) and politics (deficit financing and inflation), but it can also, or at least partially, be explained by the fact that these technologies had matured to such an extent that they had lost much of their creative and transforming effects.

If the hypothesis about a third industrial revolution proves correct, we are now on the threshold of a new period of growth, but nobody knows how lasting or how strong it will be. Even though there will certainly be setbacks every now and then, I believe that it will take decades for the new technologies to make enough breakthroughs to lose their power. If such optimism is justified, we will see a better-functioning economy for several years in the western economies:

- Technical development will cut costs.
- Consumers will be stronger, better informed and more likely to shop around for the best buy.
- Quality of information and the more rapid processing of information will help cut transaction costs.

There is a clear possibility that the next decade will be characterised by strong growth and low inflation in many countries outside the US. It is impossible to quantify the growth effect, not least because statistical aggregates have a hard time capturing the development of the service sector. In particular, national accounts tend to underestimate improvements in the quality of goods and services. This is crucial to the knowledge-based economy that is now emerging. Nonetheless it is a good bet that growth in Europe and elsewhere will be stronger in the first decade of the twenty-first century than it was during the last 25 years of the previous century.

Furthermore there is a fair chance that inflation will stay low. Central banks have become more independent and they are likely to continue their inflation-bashing. They will be supported in this by the breakthrough of new cost-cutting and competition-enhancing technologies. More rapid productivity growth, improved market transparency and globalisation all speak in favour of low inflation. It is true that serious and stringent academic economists are uncertain of the quantitative effects, telling us sternly that this is not really a retardation of inflation rate per se, but rather a one-off effect on the price level. They may be right-in theory. But in real life it will take years for these one-off effects to make their full impact, and to any non-economist, therefore, they are naturally interpreted as a lower rate of inflation. All practical businessmen see the effects in real life in the increasing difficulty of raising prices. We can no longer push cost increases onto the consumer; instead we have to increase productivity. It is difficult to see this trend being reversed in the foreseeable future.

The combination of tight monetary policies, rapid industrial transformation (the scrapping of obsolete capital) and stiffer competition will also transform wage formation and labour markets, not least in Europe. The labour market will become more fragmented as union power decreases. Salaries are being set according to productivity rather than determined by distribution or egalitarian quarrels. Clearly, cost pressures from the labour market will tend to decrease as a result.

All in all it is fair to assume that growth can be strong without inflation picking up as a result. This does not necessarily mean that a 'new economy' is replacing an 'old' economy or that old economic laws have suddenly stopped working. Rather, old patterns are being stretched somewhat because of the great number of technological and structural changes. There is nothing strange about that.

It should be stressed that the effects of these new technologies, although beneficial at the global level, will not be perceived as beneficial by some people. Schumpeter aptly coined the term 'creative destruction' to depict the turbulent forces that tear down and build up in one single process. Rigid companies will be severely hit by industrial transformation. Regions that are highly dependent on such old companies will experience increased unemployment. On average, people with poor or old-fashioned educational backgrounds will fare worse than highly educated people. Wage differentials will change as new professions are created and old ones become obsolete. The leaders and stars of the new markets and technologies will be able to heap huge rewards, while others fall behind. Equity valuations will soar-and crash, as they always do during period of intense innovation and creative destruction. Of course, this will cause strains-for individuals as well as for elected politicians. There is a risk of political turbulence and short-sighted political reactions.

Market change at the micro level In many respects the micro effects on individual markets will be more far-reaching than the macro effects. Many markets will function more efficiently. As already stated, improved information and lower transaction costs will make it possible for consumers to shop around, choosing suppliers in a more efficient way. But beyond that it is interesting to note that markets in the communication and information sectors often tend to show more fundamental changes. In this new 'network economy', markets often show four characteristics:

- Products are more valuable if many people have access to them. A single phone or fax is not worth anything. But the more common they are, the more valuable they become since they can be linked to each other and communicate. This is a fascinating example of how the traditional textbook rule of declining marginal utility is turned on its head-utility actually increases sharply as more machines are linked to the network.
- Economies of scale cause unit costs to drop in several of these markets. The first product (software programme, musical recording, computer game and so on.) is expensive to manufacture, whereas mass production-that is, digitally copying the first product-is extremely cheap. Here also the traditional hypothesis about decreasing returns seems to be wrong.
- In order to enable users of fax machines, computers, cellular phones, pagers and so on to meet and communicate, the various products and systems must be able to communicate with each other. Thus industry standards must be established, spontaneously or through regulation.
- All this creates strong incentives for the emergence of (perhaps temporary) monopolies. Individual companies that conquer a dominant market position can set market standards and hence make it virtually impossible for any competitor to challenge them. This makes it profitable to act extremely aggressively in order to gain market share as fast as possible.

It can be said that the supply and demand relations of network markets are different from those prevailing in ordinary markets. If the value of a product increases with the number of people who have access to it, the demand curve is upward sloping. Consequently large economies of scale mean that the slope of supply curves may be negative. Some analysts see these peculiarities as so important that we should accept a 'new economy' paradigm-alas with a new economic theory as well. Most economists, however, see such network markets as special cases of the all-encompassing traditional micro theory of economics.

MANAGEMENT FACES NEW CHALLENGES

Obviously, these huge changes will have a profound impact on management. Developments in information technology will affect the very core of management as well as the company itself. Information is a decisive factor for client relations, brand name and the value chain of production. Until now information on the corporation and its products has primarily been embedded in the products themselves. But as the electronic networks evolve, information can be decoupled from the physical content and location of the products. This entails new business opportunities as information and products can be separated and reconnected in new combinations. In management literature this is called 'unbundling'. The traditional value chain is broken up and put together again in new ways.

In this respect the IT revolution constitutes a disruptive change to existing business on a scale never seen before. One effect is that the success and market capitalisation of firms can undergo sharp swings. In times of rapid change, new technologies and new products can suddenly ruin even very well-managed and successful companies, which just happen to be on the losing side of the new technologies. The other side of the coin is that upstarts that happen to be at the right place at the right time can suddenly be extremely successful and rewarded with a market capitalisation that-at least for a while -looks downright ridiculous. Such evaluations need not be long-lived; in this uncertain world new information rapidly has an effect on market capitalisation. But even though stock market valuations are volatile, the long-term economic and social effects of the new technology remains-as do the effects on business models and management.

There are many consequences for management emanating from these facts. One glaringly obvious conclusion is that hierarchical companies will tend to become less efficient. On the other hand flat organisations with a rich flow of information in easy-to-access networks will foster creativity; independent and small business units are the natural building blocks of the modern corporation. But the link between the corporation and its clients will also be affected. It is possible to provide more customers with information all over the world, irrespective of where production takes place or the products are sold. Consequently the role of the middleman or intermediary has abruptly changed. The customer and the supplier can find each other faster and easier, provided the information system can screen, filter and select. Traditional wholesale middlemen will soon be a defunct species unless they transform themselves into electronic information specialists and navigators. However, if they are successful in this, there is a new, booming market to catch.

One extremely important aspect of the new information technologies is the possibility of 'data mining', that is, exploiting all the new possibilities to learn about the customer. Intelligent data information systems make it much easier to collect information about clients' needs and purchasing patterns, making it possible to customise advertising, target special offers and adjust the product mix in an ever-more fragmented world. It also opens the possibility of price differentiation, which is all the more important in a world of cut-throat competition.

Given the high costs of information systems and the emergence of (albeit short-lived) technological monopolies, there are high risks involved in being locked into dependence on systems that become both costly and obsolete far more rapidly than expected. The obvious conclusion is to avoid such a locking-in. As product cycles get shorter it is also important to be more flexible in as many areas as possible. It is quite dangerous to put all one's eggs in one basket; firms that are dependent on a single technology are extremely vulnerable. The conclusion is that experimentation is vital. The firm must test many solutions and be prepared to incur losses in the process. It must allocate resources to make such experiments possible. To encourage creativity and overcome resistance from established departments, it is often advisable to set up special units to develop and test new technologies. This should be done even if they compete head-on with the (former) core activities of the firm.

STRONG TRANSFORMATION PRESSURE IN THE FINANCIAL SECTOR

The financial industry is one of those sectors that will see the greatest and most rapid upheavals. The reason is obvious. The sector's bread and butter is to process information and the IT revolution makes it easy to unbundle its products. The new technology makes it possible not only to change old patterns, but also to create totally new products and channels of distribution.

Retail banking is facing huge changes. Yesterday's banking was a vertically integrated value chain, where a number of different products were packaged, distributed and sold via a system of branch offices. This has been changed by electronic banking. It is seen by many as mainly a new and cheaper channel of distribution. But if my description of the trends facing us is correct, the changes will be much greater.

As the networks grow and become more sophisticated, more customers will be able to access information through new channels and to choose more freely among various services. The supply of personal financial management software is rapidly improving, while at the same time advanced analysis and updated information in real time is available more or less free from several sources, often via the most popular portals. It is probably only a question of time before alliances are formed between software producers, portals and other Web-sites on the one hand, and a number of banks and financial institutions on the other.

Free software and direct access to banks, as well as streaming video and audio will make it possible to see and listen to different financial advisers on the Internet-and to compare their advice. This makes the customer's freedom of choice much more real. The customer will soon be able to choose all sorts of services on the Internet. Until recently the general perception was that the market would be segmented into two main groups: cheap and quick transactions via the Internet; and more sophisticated, personalised and expensive financial advice, sold for a (hefty) fee in special, plush branch offices. However, the borderline between these markets is becoming increasingly blurred as clients are demanding to pick and choose between services and combinations of services.

It seems as though all big players must be able to provide their customers with all kinds of Internet-based services. Consequently the most sophisticated financial advisory services are being subjected to intense pressure to transform themselves. Commercial banking and corporate banking have already experienced great changes. Previously stable relations between banks and corporate clients have been severed as disintermediation and niche strategies have fragmented the markets. E-commerce is creating new channels for corporate clients of all sizes, which can now find each other easier and faster without traditional intermediaries. The new technologies that are transforming the financial sector

- Three enabling techniques. Advances in the performance and cost-efficiency of three interrelated technologies (computing power, data storage and data transmission bandwidth) are dramatically reducing the cost of collecting and processing information.
- Exploding connectivity and plummeting transaction costs. The fall in the cost of information is reducing transaction costs and increasing the demand for improved connectivity, creating a self-reinforcing cycle of reducted transaction costs.
- Substitution of information for hierarchy. The falling cost of delivering information instantaneously through-out the organisation is resulting in formal organisa-tional hierarchies giving way to more nimble, decentralised, network-based structures.
- Interactive customer relationships. The plummeting cost of interaction and connectivity is enabling companies to capture unprecedented amounts of data on their customers and to deliver increasingly individualised value propositions.
- Transformation of value chains to value webs. Lower transaction costs, increased connectivity and open standards are reducing coordination costs among multiple, disparate entities; as a result the traditional value chain is being replaced by web-like structures of coordinated, value added activity.

- Scale economies are increasing-and decreasing. Increasing connectivity, increasing information intensity of production factors and declining transaction costs are undermining traditional scale economies in marketing and distribution, while increasing economies of scale in digital production.
- Network effects and serial monopoly. There is an increase in the prevalence of network effects, which exist when the utility that a user derives from the consumption of a good increases with the number of fellow users, leading to monopolistic business systems-until replaced by rival product systems with displacing network effects.
- Digitial substitution and unbundling. The Information component of physical (or analog) products and services is being replaced by digital substitutes, often with radically different development trajectories, cost structures and distribution capabilities.
- Disintermediation and reintermediation. Some middlemen (retailers, agents and distributors) are being disintermediated or displaced by direct (typically electronic) buyer-seller trade; others are reintermediating markets by expanding their role as third-party information brokers or market makers.
- Channel disruption. Traditional physical or personal sales channels are being disrupted by lower-cost e-commerce alternatives and by consumers' increasing preference for scattering purchase activities across multiple channels.
- Infomediation. Traditional sales and distribution intermediaries that exploit information asymmetries are being replaced by electronic intermediaries that provide information and match buyers and sellers.
- Demand aggregation. The Internet and other information networks are enabling buyers to aggregate individual purchasing and 'put out to bid' transactions, transferring pricing power to the demand side and transforming suppliers into explicit price takers.
- Trading is obviously undergoing similar changes due to the introduction of electronic trading. Markets have become more transparent and information is flowing more freely, so traditional full-service brokers have become increasingly squeezed.

As a result of these changes-and of low interest rates and low inflation-it has become more difficult to make a profit on payments systems, using the float. Instead credit analysis is becoming more important as low inflation puts pressure on interest rates and corporate restructuring takes giant leaps.

THE SEB'S EXPERIENCE

The Skandinaviska Enskilda Banken (SEB) has undergone a rapid transition during the past few years. It has traditionally been the dominant commercial bank for large Swedish exporting companies, as well as the bank of choice for many wealthy Swedes. It is the biggest trader of currencies, bonds and securities in the Nordic region, and consequently is at the centre of the current reshaping of the financial markets due to globalisation and the IT revolution. In terms of size, it is large by Nordic standards but small in global or even pan-European terms. The pressure to transform is extremely strong and the SEB is facing this pressure head-on. It has embarked on a path of rapid technological renewal and transformation, concentra-ting on the booming savings markets and the possibilities offered Internet banking, in which area it intends to exploit its expertise in a European perspective.

The bank's Nordic focus is visible in the sense that it has acquired the Swedish insurance company Trygg-Hansa (and then divested the non-life operations) and Gyllenberg, a Finnish private bank. It entered Denmark through an alliance with Codan, an insurance company, and expanded into the Baltic region through ownership of three banks in the three Baltic countries, and recently also by acquiring a Polish bank. As a result its assets under management have more than trebled in three years, from SEK 190 billion in 1996 to SEK 950 billion in the third quarter of 2000. At the same time the number of Internet clients has increased 70-fold, from 10 000 to almost 700 000.

This last development illustrates the SEB's relentless pursuit of technological advancement, new distribution systems and new products. To a large extent its acquisitions have been prompted by its wish to channel its new products into new markets, for instance it is busy setting up an Internet bank in Denmark. It has also bought BfG Bank, the fifth largest privately owned bank in Germany, which the SEB hopes will create a platform for rapid expansion into Internet banking in Europe.

This is well in line with its (albeit short) Internet tradition. The SEB was among the very first to set up an independent Internet bank (in December 1996), although to a certain extent it cannibalised existing business and the retail branch offices. It was deliberately created as a separate entity to ensure its independent growth and aggressive expansion, even at the expense of other business of the bank. This reflects the experience in other areas, where new, disruptive technologies can threaten the entire business unless new units are allowed to be creative and to experiment, even though their activities seem to be at odds with the rest of the organisation. Now that e-banking is well established and more mature, it is being integrated into the different business areas more fully.

The SEB e-banking activity offers a complete range of banking and insurance services to private clients and small businesses alike-from account information to bill payment mutual funds and stock brokerage. The results have exceeded the bank's expectations. The bank now has more customer visits on the web than in its branch network in Sweden.

Even in the Baltic region, which is very small and has a far lower average income than Scandinavia, there has been a surprisingly rapid increase in e-banking. This demonstrates the possibility of starting from a 'low' technological base and moving directly to the most modern forms of production and distribution, that is, skipping a few of the normal steps of technical development and going straight for the frontier.

Encouraged by these events, and in order to sharpen its focus even further, the bank has set a high goal for its Internet service: it intends to have 5 000 000 Internet clients by 2005. This may sound overly optimistic; but the point is that setting such a seemingly impossible target will force the entire organisation to rethink its full range of processes and products. It will foster creativity, since it will demonstrate that the old ways of doing business will not suffice if the bank is to survive, let alone thrive, in the new global economy.

One example of the bank's high-tech approach is the development of an Internet Trading Station. This is an on-line service directed at all corporate clients, but perhaps is most beneficial to medium-sized trading clients that lack large financial departments. Physically, this is simply a computer terminal, but the client has access to all of the SEB's research, trading services and facilities. When using the Trading Station the customer can be certain that deals will be automatically passed to clients' financial systems via a common system interface. Decision support and the execution of deals are available globally through one channel, the Internet. Controlled deal entry enables clients to let administrative staff execute trades. As a result, human errors are reduced and costs are cut as real-time financial information is provided to all users within the company at low cost. In effect the Trading Station moves the bank's trading floor-the largest in Northern Europe-right into the office of the client.

Here, growth has been even more spectacular than in private banking. After only two years, the Internet accounts for some 50 per cent of total FX transactions in Sweden. Great interest has been expressed by other banks in franchising this service. During my 25 years in finance I have never seen technological breakthrough as rapid as this one. According to analysts the SEB is one of the world leaders in the use of modern IT in banking and financial services, and it intends to maintain its technological lead. One obvious task is to launch its IT distribution model in Europe. This can be done through mergers and acquisitions, using acquired firms as vehicles to spread the bank's knowledge. It can also be achieved through organic growth. Both these strategies are currently being used.

FROM BANK TO PORTAL

All these activities are tied together in a long-term e-centric strategy. The breakthroughs in IT are applicable on a global scale, whereas the existing banking systems and client bases are still largely local. The SEB's aim is to link global technological change to local clients by introducing new technologies through several channels. It intends to create a standardised Internet platform with three main characteristics:

- An Internet bank that offers private clients a wide range of services-payments and transactions, savings and borrowing, advice and investment.
- An interface that is easy to use, takes advantage of the bank's global technological expertise and is adapted to local needs.
- Technical solutions to payment and transaction systems tied to local/national payments systems.

This means that the bank's global system must be standardised and able to cope with local solutions, which may initially look different. Local solutions and interface, linked to data mining, will reduce customer acquisition costs and lead to long-term growth of the client base. Technically the process is intended to move from the local to the global as banking and financial markets become more integrated.

In a somewhat longer-term perspective, one task is to evolve from a service channel to a valuable portal, supplying clients with investment services, on-line banking and advisory services, but also leveraging the bank's valuable client base to other services and providers, financial as well as non-financial. This process has already started. The bank has launched a 'travel square' on its Web site as a first step. It is based upon a partnership with the Amadeus booking system and supplies its Internet banking customers with the opportunity to search, book and pay for travel on-line. It offers the bank the possibility of broadening its client base, it provides clients with additional services, and it provides airlines with the possibility of selling more tickets, not least excess capacity tickets, to an attractive customer segment. The bank's clients enjoy lower-priced tickets, and both the bank's and the booking system's client bases become more valuable.

This is seen as only the starting point. More services will be added, and the bank plans to cooperate more closely with a number of other service providers, leveraging each other's services. New technology and the links to existing client groups will be used to create new affinity groups, where the bank's will act as an entry point for special client groups to gain access to numerous other service providers. One example of this is the recent creation of a 'Senior Net' for older clients with special needs and demands in respect of housing, travel, medicine and so on. Another aspect of the recent developments is the increasing speed and accessibility of services. Currently, most electronic transactions go via PCs, but an increasing amount of business will soon be carried out via cell phones. The new WAP technology will make it possible to use mobile phones not only for conversation, but also for e-mail, automatic market updates and the transmission of buy and sell orders to stockbrokers. It will soon be easy to programme WAP phones to carry out just about everything that a top-of-the-range PC with modem can do today, no matter where you are in the world. At this point the trading floor will have moved not only to the office of the corporate client but also to the coat pocket of private customers-the branch office and the portal to many other services will literally be in the client's pocket.

4

Legal Environment

In India there are several Acts and legislations enacted by the Government of India for regulation of industries in the country. These enactments play a very important role in the country's overall progress and economic development. These legislations are amended from time to time in accordance with the changing circumstances and environment. The most important Act is the Companies Act, 1956 which relates to setting up and operation of companies in India. It empowers the Central Government to regulate the formation, financing, functioning and winding up of companies. It contains the mechanism regarding organisational, financial, managerial and all the relevant aspects of a company.

In order to provide the Central Government with the means to implement its industrial policies, several legislations have been enacted. The most important being the Industries (Development and Regulation) Act, 1951 (IDRA). The main objectives of the Act is to empower the Government to take necessary steps for the development of industries; to regulate the pattern and direction of industrial development; and to control the activities, performance and results of industrial undertakings in the public interest.

The bulk of the transactions in trade, commerce and industry are based on contracts. In India, the Indian Contract Act,1872 is the governing legislation for contracts, which lays down the general principles relating to formation, performance and enforceability of contracts and the rules relating to certain special types of contracts like Indemnity and Guarantee; Bailment and Pledge; as well as Agency. Another important aspect of legislations is the industrial relations, which involves various aspects of interactions between the employer and the employees; among the employees as well as between the employers. In such relations whenever there is a clash of interest, it may result in dissatisfaction for either of the parties involved and hence lead to industrial disputes or conflicts.

The Industrial Disputes Act, 1947 is the main legislation for investigation and settlement of all industrial disputes. The Act enumerates the contingencies when a strike or lock-out can be lawfully resorted to, when they can be declared illegal or unlawful, conditions for laying off, retrenching, discharging or dismissing a workman, circumstances under which an industrial unit can be closed down and several other matters related to industrial employees and employers.

Trade unions are also an important part of an industrial set up. The legislation regulating these trade unions is the Indian Trade Unions Act, 1926. The Act deals with the registration of trade unions, their rights, their liabilities and responsibilities as well as ensures that their funds are utilised properly.

It gives legal and corporate status to the registered trade unions. It also seeks to protect them from civil or criminal prosecution so that they could carry on their legitimate activities for the benefit of the working class.

MRTP, FEMA, EXIM IN LIGHT OF LIBERALIZATION POLICIES

Economic development can only result from state-led policies designed to address the numerous production failures and bottlenecks that characterize the economies of underdeveloped countries. SEZ is one such state led policy.

SEZs are benefited, apart from general fiscal and non fiscal concessions to firms, from the following:

- Location-specific advantage.
- Modern and efficient infrastructure.
- Better governance due to single window facilities to ensure corruption and red tape free business environment.

SEZs thus make up for infrastructural deficiencies and procedural complexities that characterize developing countries and offer a more conducive investment climate. Trade related infrastructure and institutional framework are generally deficient in developing countries. Besides, too many windows in the administrative set up, bureaucratic hassles and barriers raised by monetary, trade, fiscal, taxation, tariff and labour policies further increase production and transaction costs of exports. Since country-wide development of infrastructure is expensive and implementation of structural reforms require time due to socio-economic and political realities, Special Economic Zones SEZs or Export Processing Zones (EPZs) are considered an strategic tool for the promotion of exports in developing economies such as those of India, China, Bangladesh etc. The SEZ offers quality infrastructure and hassle free business environment permitting an economy to promote and diversify exports and develop a competitive industrial base.

However, given the limited technological and marketing capabilities of developing countries, the zones may not affect exports substantially unless they attract FDI also. Due to easy access to proprietary technology of their parents and international marketing network, MNCs affiliates are likely to be more competitive in international markets. Furthermore, in this era of globalization, MNCs restructuring their operations to avail economies of scale and scope by internalizing the economies of specialization through the integration of assets, production and marketing activities across countries to advance the core competencies in the global markets. The vision of SEZs/ EPZs in an export oriented regime is to establish a viable internationally competitive platform that is capable of attracting export oriented FDI to promote exports.

SEZs are industrial clusters of companies that are concentrated in a geographic region. These companies share economic infrastructure, a pool of skilled human capital, and governmental and other institutions that provide education, specialized training, information and technical support. Also, these companies may co-operate to create joint companies, distribution agreement, technology transfer agreements and common manufacturing agreements. External economies of scale and other advantages of the cluster help the operating firms in reducing costs, acquiring competitive advantages and attracting foreign direct investment.

To sum up, SEZs play a crucial initiating role in the development of national industrial capacity by: 1) offering a platform for internationally mobile productive units, 2) creating an environment conducive to promote investment and exports, 3) initiating a shift in the orientation of the domestic private sector towards export activities, 4) leading government to adapt a more proactive and responsive attitude towards private sector's requirements of regulatory and administrative efficiency.

Evolution

India initiated the process of industrial growth in 1948 (immediately after the political independence), when it announced its first Industrial Policy Resolution, IPR 1948. The strategy adopted was one of import-substitution industrialization across all sectors. Export promotion had also been a concern of the government. Thus, attempts to promote the EPZ as an export platform on the basis of economic incentives, such as the provision of better infrastructure and tax holidays became a feature of Indian development. The first zone was set up in 1965 at Kandla, Gujarat. The country has had four phases in the evolution of the EPZ policy since then. Following is a brief overview of the evolution of the EPZ policy in India through these four phases.

Initial Phase: 1965-1985

The first zone was set up in Kandla in a highly backward region of Kutch in Gujarat as early as in 1965. It was followed by the Santacruz export processing zone in Mumbai which came into operation in 1973. There was however no clarity of objectives that the government wanted to achieve. Kandla and Santacruz EPZs were set up with different sets of objectives. Operationally, an overall inward looking trade policy with umpteen controls and regulations influenced the EPZ policy also. The policies were rigid and the package of incentives and facilities was not attractive. Zone authorities had limited powers. There was no single window facility within the zone. Entrepreneurs had to acquire individual clearances from various state government and central government departments. Day-to-day operations were subjected to rigorous controls. Custom procedures for bonding, bank guarantees and movement of goods were rigid. FDI policy was also highly restrictive.

The business environment rating index which rated investment climate in 43 countries on the basis of 18 independent factors, Indian, zones were placed at the bottom for FDI (TCS 1976). In 1980 the government introduced the Export Oriented Units Plan (EOU). This plan facilitates the setting up of EOUs beyond the boundaries of EPZs. The responsibility of administering these units was also entrusted with the zone administration.

Expansionary Phase: 1985-1991

Towards the end of the 1970s, India's failure to step up significantly the volume of her manufactured exports in the background of the Second Oil Price Shock began to worry the policy makers. To provide fillip to exports, the government decided to establish four more zones in 1984. These were at Noida (Uttar Pradesh), Falta (West Bengal) Cochin (Kerala) and Chennai (Tamil Nadu).

Thereafter, Visakhapatnam EPZ in Andhra Pradesh was established in 1989, though it could not become operational before 1994. All these zones with the exception of Chennai were set up in industrially backward regions. The primary objectives of the zones were still not specified and there were no significant changes in other laws and procedures pertaining to the EPZs.

Consolidating Phase: 1991-2000

In 1991, a massive dose of liberalization was administered in the Indian economy. In this context, wide-ranging measures were initiated by the government for revamping and restructuring EPZs also. This phase was thus marked by progressive liberalization of policy provisions and relaxation in the severity of controls and simplification of procedures. The focus had been on delegating powers to zone authorities, providing additional fiscal incentives, simplifying policy provisions and providing greater facilities. The scope and coverage of the EPZ/EOU plan was enlarged in 1992 by permitting the agriculture, horticulture and aqua culture sector unit also. In 1994, trading, re-engineering and re-conditioning units were also permitted to be set up.

Emergence Phase: 2000 Onwards

This period has witnessed a major shift in direction, thrust and approach. The EXIM Policy (1997-2002) has introduced a new plan from April 1, 2000 for establishment of the Special Economic Zones (SEZs) in different parts of the country. SEZ is an almost self contained area with high class infrastructure for commercial as well as residential inhabitation. SEZs are permitted to be set up in the public, private, joint sector or by the State Governments with a minimum size of not less than 1000 hectares.

The number of incentives both fiscal and non fiscal has also been extended to the units operating in SEZs. Several measures have been adopted to improve the quality of governance of the zones. These include relaxation in the conditions for approval process and simplifying custom rules. More recently, Development Commissioners are given the labour commissioner's powers. SEZ policy is thus the most significant thrust towards ensuring the success of export processing zones.

From November 1, 2000 the Export Processing Zones at Kandla, Santa Cruz (Mumbai), Cochin and Surat have been converted into SEZs. In 2003, other existing EPZs namely, Noida, Falta, Chennai, Vizag were also converted into SEZs. In addition, approval has been given for the setting up of SEZs in various parts of the country in the private/ joint sectors or by the state.

SEZ POLICY

Section 5 of SEZ Act, 2005 specifies objectives of setting up of SEZs. The Central Government, while notifying any area as a Special Economic Zone or an additional area to be included in the Special Economic Zone in the Special Economic Zone and discharging its functions under this Act, shall be guided by the following, namely:

- Generation of additional economic activity;
- Promotion of exports of goods and services;
- Promotion of investment from domestic and foreign sources;
- Creation of employment opportunities;
- Development of infrastructure facilities;
- Maintenance of sovereignty and integrity of India, the security of the State and friendly relations with foreign States.

The salient features of SEZ Act, 2005 are as follows:

- An SEZ can be established either jointly or severally by the Central Government or any person for manufacture of goods or rendering services or for both or as an FTWZ.
- Any person who intends to set up can make a proposal to the State Government concerned which in turn sends the proposal to Board of Approvals
- First time the option has been given to the developers to make a proposal directly to BOA also.
- Central Government can set up the SEZ suo moto after consulting the State Government concerned.
- Central Government may prescribe the minimum area of land.
- Central Government has also been empowered to prescribe different minimum area of land for a class or classes of SEZs.
- Central Government is empowered to approve more than one

developer in an SEZ in cases where one developer does not have in his possession the minimum area of contiguous land.

- SEZ developers have been given full freedom to levy user charges on agreed terms and can allocate space or built up area.

Exemptions from Taxes, Duties or Cess

Any goods or services exported out of or imported into or procured from the DTA by:

- A unit in SEZ; or
- A developer

Shall be exempt from payment of taxes, duties or cess under all enactments specified in the First Schedule.

- First Schedule includes 21 Enactments
- This list includes the Agriculture Produce Cess Act, the Coffee Act, the Rubber Act, the Tea Act, the Mica Act, the Textile Committee Act, the MPEDA Act, the Agriculture & Processed Food Export Cess Act, the Spices Act, etc.

Special Provisions for SEZs

- Duty free goods for development of SEZ as well as for SEZ units
- Supply from DTA to SEZ treated as physical export.
- Exemption from Service Tax.
- Exemption from CST.
- Exemption from securities transaction tax.
- Exemption from Income Tax to SEZ units for 15 years (100% exemption for first 5 years, 50% of income exempted for the next 5 years and then in the next 5 years the 50% of the profits which are ploughed back in the capital investment would be exempted).
- Existing SEZ unit to get income tax exemption for the balance period. No income tax exemption if 10 years IT benefit already availed.
- IT exemption extended to export of services which would include trading as well.
- SEZ developers given IT exemption for 10 consecutive assessment years out of first 15 years of its operations.
- OBU entitled for IT exemption for 10 years (100% exemption for first 5 years and next 5 years 50% exemption).
- Unit of an International Financial Service Centre entitled for IT exemption fro a period of 10 years (100% exemption for first 5 years
- For the purpose of IT exemption manufacture shall have the same meaning as assigned in the SEZ Act.
- Exemption from capital gains in case of transfer of undertaking from an urban/ rural area of SEZ.
- Sale in the DTA on payment of full applicable duty.
- Exemption from MAT to SEZ developers and SEZ units.
- SEZ units and developers exempted from Dividend Distribution Tax.

- Exemption of interest income of NRI in respect of deposits in OBUs.

Miscellaneous:

- The Central Government may by notification direct any of the provisions of any other central act or any rules or regulations made there under or nay notification or orders issued or directions give there under shall not apply to an SEZ or a class of SEZ or all SEZs.
- State Governments may notify policies for developers and units and take suitable steps for enactment of any law.
  - Granting exemption from the state taxes, levies and duties to the developers or the entrepreneurs
  - Delegating the power conferred upon any person or authority under any state act, to the Development Commissioner.
- The provisions of this Act shall have affect not withstanding anything inconsistent therewith contained in any other law for the time being enforced.
- An SEZ shall be deemed to be a Port, Airport, ICD, Land Station and Land Customs Station, as the case may be, under Section 7 of the Customs Act.
- Central Government empowered to carry out amendment in Insurance Act, 1938, Banking Regulation Act, 1949 and Indian Stamp Act, 1989.

Other Non-fiscal Incentives in SEZs:

- Exemption from industrial licensing for manufacture of items reserved for SSIs.
- 100 per cent FDI investment through automatic route to manufacturing SEZ units (barring a handful of sensitive industries).
- Facility to retain 100% foreign exchange receipts in EEFC Account.
- Facility to realise and repatriate export proceeds within 12 months.
- No cap on foreign investment for SSI reserved items.
- Re-export of imported goods found defective, goods imported from foreign supplies on loan basis etc., without G.R. Waiver under intimation to the Development Commissioner.
- "Write-off" of unrealised export bills up to 5 per cent.
- Commodity hedging by SEZ units permitted.
- Capitalization of import payables.
- Profits allowed to be repatriated freely without any dividend balancing requirement.
- No fixed wastage norms.
- Full freedom for subcontracting including subcontracting abroad.
- Subcontracting facility available to jewellery units.
- Duty free goods to be utilized in 5 years.

Administrative Set up

Special Economic zones in India have a three-tier management structure.

At the apex level is the SEZ section within the Ministry of Commerce headed by the Commerce Secretary, which considers policy issues and periodically reviews the working of zones. At the next level is the Board of Approval, which is responsible for examining proposals for setting up enterprises in the sectors. It is headed by a person of the Additional Secretary level.

At the third tier is the: Development Commissioner who is the chief executive of the SEZ. He is responsible for the day-to-day administration, approves investment proposals under the automatic route and enforces various regulatory provisions. Recently, powers of Labour Commissioners are also delegated to him. He is assisted by a Joint Development Commissioner, four Deputy Development Commissioners, two Assistant Commissioners of Customs, security officer and other ministerial staff. Furthermore, Government delegated more powers to Development Commissioners of the Special Economic Zones (SEZs). Development Commissioners (DCs) of Special Economic Zones were now authorised to exercise the administrative powers in capacity expansion, broad banding and export import permissions5.

Besides, DCs were also allowed to authorise the change in name of the company or the implementing agency, to permit change of location from the place mentioned in the Letter of Approval/ Letter of Intent to another, to extend the validity period of Letter of Intent/Letter of Permission/Letter of Approval, to revise the Value Addition upward or downward upto the minimum Value Addition percentage as prescribed for the item of manufacture under the Policy and to permit disposal of obsolete capital goods, in DTA, on payment of applicable duties, without any restrictions.

Procedures for sourcing indigenous capital goods and raw materials were simplified. Multiple bonds for import clearance were replaced by a single bond. In 1998, custom procedures were further simplified when a common bond for imports, exports, job work and repair was introduced. It was in 2000 that path breaking reforms were introduced in the zone governance. Conditions for automatic approvals are relaxed considerably.

Now the Development Commissioners (DCs) may accord automatic approval to all projects where the activity proposed does not attract compulsory licensing. All proposals which do not meet any or all of the parameters for automatic approval are considered and approved by the Board of Approval of SEZ set up in the Department of Commerce. These include all services related proposals. The Board of Approval now is a larger body and quite broadbased to provide a single interface to those keen on setting up units. It has representatives of various Ministries like Small-Scale Industries, Environment and Forests, Science & Technology as members of the board. It has been broad based to include a representative of the Central Board of Direct Taxes and state government representatives also.

All proposals for FDI/NRI/OCB investments in EPZ units qualify for approval through automatic route subject to sectoral norms. Proposals not covered under the automatic route are considered and approved by FIPB.

Thus the process of approval has been relaxed considerably and important powers have been delegated to the Development Commissioners only after 2000. The approval process now takes 7-10 days. The other formalities that need to be completed however include, Legal undertaking, Custom bonding, Factory registration, Building approval, Sales tax registration, Labour and environment certifications.

Our survey of the SEZ units revealed that units have to deal with as many as 15 authorities at the time of entry. These include, DC, municipal body, ESI, PF, Income tax, sales tax, factory registration, labour, pollution and excise. They have to deal with many of them in day-to-day operations as well. The zone acts as a facilitator in providing many of these services. The role of the administration here is to invite the government officials from various departments and arrange meetings with entrepreneurs.

However, around 40% of the respondents felt that the zones are not effective in providing single window services. Besides, most entrepreneurs complained that there were delays in decision making by the Ministry of Commerce and that there was lack of flexibility and sensitivity. Most of the firms located in SEZ is of the opinion that in order to improve the quality of governance, more powers should be delegated to Development Commissioners.

INFRASTRUCTURE

One of the basic elements critical for any export activity is adequate infrastructure especially physical infrastructure (transport system such as port, airport, water, electricity and communication facilities). Infrastructure within SEZs is generally considered superior to that available in the wider economy.

Foreign Investment

Foreign investment is the key to success of EPZs/ SEZs. With substantially liberalized EXIM policies, most of the East Asian countries attracted huge foreign investment in the initial stages of their opening up. EPZs in India have been largely dominated by domestically owned enterprises or joint ventures.

Table. Types of Investments in Indian Epzs (as on 31st March 1998) (rs. Crore)

Zone	Nri	Foreign	Domestic	Total
KAFTZ	2.6	0.6	82.4	85.6
SEEPZ	13.8	21.7	222.9	258.4
MEPZ	6.6	45.3	68.2	120.2
CEPZ	18	25	217	260
FEPZ	5	5.7	178.3	189.1
NEPZ	34.5	54	341	429.5
TOTL	80.6	152.4	1,109.9	1,342.9

Low level of foreign investment in Indian SEZs is attributed to regulatory policies, excessive controls and unattractive package of incentives for FDI. As a result of this situation, Indian advantage in terms of low labour cost, availability of trained manpower and existence of vast domestic market remained unexploited. Until July 1991, out of 325 operating units in EPZs, 70 were joint ventures and 26 fully foreign owned.

These two categories represented 30 per cent of the total units in EPZs. Between July 1991 and March 1998, 200 units were added to the EPZs. Of these units, 74 were joint ventures and 15 were fully foreign owned. After the liberalization of Indian economy, the proportion of joint ventures/ foreign owned units in the EPZs has gone up to 45 per cent. This reflected comparatively larger involvement of joint ventures in Indian EPZs/ SEZs. With overall restructuring of trade related policies and continuation of economic reforms, investment climate in the Indian SEZs will improve further.

Offshore Banking

Offshore banking units (OBUs) are permitted in the SEZs. These banks virtually are the foreign branches of banks, but located in India. OBUs are exempted from Cash Reserve Ratio (CRR) and statutory liquidity ratio (SLR) and make available finance to SEZ units and SEZ developers at international rates.

Technology Transfer

Transfer of foreign technology in the Indian SEZs has been insignificant. This is mainly due to excessive involvement of domestic units in the SEZs and their greater pre-occupation in the manufacture of low technology items like garments and electronics which do not require great skill. Nearly 60 per cent of exports from SEZs comprise gems and jewellery which are based on local skill and indigenous know-how.

Unless foreign investment in Indian SEZs increases, the transfer of technology in these clusters will remain low. So far the transfer of skills and know-how in the SEZs has been confined to study tours and training of workers for production of simple and labour intensive items. Transfer of product and process technology in the SEZs is limited.

Employment

Unlike smaller countries, employment is not a major objective for establishment of SEZs in India. An ILO study has pointed out that while the impact of MNCs on generation of employment in the SEZs has been very high in Singapore and Malaysia and significant in Korea and Hong Kong, it is negligible in India. Considering the level of activities in SEZs, the incremental effect of foreign units on employment generation in Indian SEZs is satisfactory.

Total employment increased constantly from 70 workers in 1966 to nearly 88,977 workers in 2002. Employment per zone also spurted from 70 to over

12,000 during the period. The average annual growth rate in employment, however, declined continuously despite setting up of 5 additional zones – 4 in the late 1980s and VSEZ in 1995. This shows that Indian SEZs could not maintain the rate of growth after the initial phase of rapid expansion. Among Indian SEZs, SEEPZ is the largest followed by MSEZ. Though variations exist, overall male/ female sex ratio is 57:43 and lowest in NSEZ at 25 per cent. Female workers are mainly involved in electronics and garments.

Linkages

Linkages of SEZs with the domestic economy are governed by the policies/ procedures for sale and sub-contracting in DTA. Due to high rate of duty, domestic sale of SEZ item has been very small (3% of production in 1997-98). Sourcing of raw material is limited as inputs for garments, electronics and gems and jewellery are imported. Sub-contracting was marginal due to restrictive policies and cumbersome procedures.

Net Foreign Exchange

NFE earning of EPZs have been quite significant: Exports from Indian SEZs were to the extent of Rs. 18,655 crore (US$ 4.14 bn) in the year 2004-05. however, with the establishment of new SEZs, exports, employment, FDI and value addition in the country in the expected to increase phenomenally in the coming years. SEZ is certainly going to become a main instrument in export promotion and employment generation.

Exports

Staring with a few lakh in 1966, exports of EPZs/ SEZs have touched Rs. 18,655 crore (US$ 4.14 bn) in 2004 –05. Although exports of EPZs/ SEZs have registered a spectacular growth over the years, their share in all India exports has remained insignificant.

This is largely attributed to smaller number of these zones and their limited size of operation in relation to huge Indian economy. Zone-specific problems in terms of location, infrastructure, etc., have also affected export performance of EPZs/ SEZs. Further, no EPZ was established after 1991. Interest for setting up these Zones has revived after introduction of SEZ policy in 2000. Post SEZ policy announcement, three SEZs set up at Manikanchan, Jaipur and Indore showed an export performance of Rs.156.23 crore during 2004-05. This development gives a positive signal for future growth of exports of EPZs/ SEZs.

Of the traditionally operating SEZs, only three enclaves – SEEPZ SEZ, NOIDA SEZ and MSEZ – have faired well and their forex earnings account for nearly û th of the total exports of SEZs. Variations existing in the export performance of these zones are directly related to their internal problems and order bookings of individual units. SEEPZ SEZ which accounts for over 50 per cent of export of these zones is ideally located, infrastructurally well developed and have pioneering entrepreneurs.

This zone picked up substantial growth with the addition of Gems & Jewellery complex in 1986 and liberalization of EXIM Policy after 1991. Gems & Jewellery accounts for more than 50 per cent of SEEPZ SEZ exports. Area of this zone is small and it has no scope for further expansion. Location of NSEZ and MSEZ is equally good. NSEZ is closer to national capital and international airport. MSEZ has the advantage of being nearer to a port as well as airport.

Both these zones provide relatively developed infrastructure and have easy access to skilled and unskilled workers. KASEZ was set up 40 years ago and has not yet been fully occupied. Falta SEZ is far away from Kolkata and Haldia ports. Falta also lacks in markets, housing colonies and vending facilities. Transport facilities are inadequate and the approach road is in a bad shape. As pointed out earlier, major problem of the Indian SEZs is their small sized operations. Excepting a few large units, most of the operators in SEZs are small and lack financial muscle and managerial strength to withstand competition.

This is evident by the fact that a small number of units have a highly disproportionate share in exports and employment. Nearly û th of exports from the EPZs/ SEZs are confined to items like gems & jewellery, computer software, textiles, electronics and pharmaceuticals. Barring electronics and gems & jewellery, export of most of the items from EPZs fluctuated significantly over the years.

This is followed by 11.9 to 20.0 per cent by engineering and software, 11.2 to 19.7 per cent by engineering and hardware, 7.3 to 10.1 per cent by textiles, 3.6 to 5.6 per cent by engineering goods, 4.9 to 6.3 per cent by pharmaceuticals & chemicals and the balance by plastics & leather products, food and agro products and trading.

Table. Sectoral Performance of Zones of Indian Sez In Selected Years

Year	Drug	Electronics	Engineer	Gems	Textiles	Others
1985	24.1	19.3	39	0	14.2	3.4
1990	26.4	24.6	27.4	10.6	8.8	2.1
1995	5.2	30.3	27.9	25.1	6.8	4.7
2000	5.0	39.8	5.6	35.2	8.2	6.2
2001	6.2	33.6	4.7	35.2	10.2	10.1
2002	6.2	33.6	4.8	42.3	7.2	5.9

Expansion in Zone Investment and Employment

India had a very slow expansion in the initial phases of EPZ policy. Expansion in the zones started picking up in the 1980s in terms of employment but total investment remained abysmally small till the late 1980s. In the 1990s, investment also started increasing. Growth rates in employment slowed down considerably in the late 1990s but in terms of investment growth rate India outperformed Sri Lanka. Thus, while India started the EPZ programme in the mid sixties, expansion in EPZs started taking place in the 1980s.

In contrast, SEZs in India continue to be dominated by domestic investment. This was despite its edge in terms of labour costs, availability of trained manpower and a stable macroeconomic environment. The share of FDI in total investment increased slowly from 12% in 1989 to slightly over 18% in 2000. During 2000-2003, however, FDI inflows increased faster. By 2003, its share in total investment had increased to 25%. Under the SEZ plan, therefore, FDI is expected to assume a much larger role.

Of the three South Asian countries, zone investment and employment levels remain the lowest in India. Though Kandla, is the biggest zone in South Asia having the size of 700 acres, it ranks the lowest in terms of investment. Vizag and Noida have comparable size as Dhaka but in terms of investment and employment they cannot be compared with the latter. Santacruz which is the smallest in size (104 acres) in India has the highest employment. Chennai and Noida are the other zones that have employment exceeding 10,000. All other zones, Cochin (103 acres), Falta (280 acres), Vizag (360 acres) have very small employment and investment. Surat which became operational in the late 1990s also appears to be amongst the slowest growing new zones of South Asia.

It shows that FDI accounts for substantial investment in Chennai and Vizag EPZs in India. Cochin and Noida follow them with FDI accounting for around one-fifth of their total. Though Santacruz has expanded very fast, FDI participation is very small in the zone. Kandla and Falta also continue to perform poorly in attracting FDI. Indian zones exhibited the lowest growth rates in employment and investment for a long period of time. It was in the late 1990s that investment levels increased rapidly in the zones. India thus could not take advantage of being an early mover.

EXPORT PERFORMANCE

The share of SEZs in a country's exports is an index of their relative role amongst various other instruments of export promotion. In India, the share of SEZs in total manufactured exports was 0.14% in 1973. In the next 5 years, by 1979, the share of SEZs in manufactured exports increased to 0.59%. It moved slowly to touch the figure of slightly over 5% by 2002-03 i.e. in 23 years.

In the mid 1980s, engineering sector accounted for the largest share of exports followed by drugs, electronics and textiles in that order. By the late 1980s, the share of engineering goods started declining. Currently it is around 5% of total exports. The share of drugs also started declining in 1989 and fell from over 25% in the mid 1980s to around 5% by 1991. Decline in textile had been slow but steady. It declined from 15% in 1984 steadily to about 7% in

2002. In contrast, exports of gems and jewellery rose rapidly. In 2002, they accounted for 42% of the total EPZ exports. Electronics exports also grew faster than the overall zone exports. As a consequence, their share almost doubled from 20% in 1984 to 40% in 1997. Thereafter, it fluctuated and in 2002 stood at 33%. Exports of other products, including leather products did not show any perceptible rise. Currently, only two sectors, electronics and gems and jewellery account for three fourths of the total zone exports. In the electronics sector, over 50% of total exports are currently accounted for by software.

Zone-wise sectoral distribution of exports shows unmistakable trends of increasing specialisation. Cochin tends to specialise in electronics (in particular hardware), Falta in textiles, Kandla in pharmaceuticals and Vizag in gems and jewellery. Santacruz is allowed to have only electronics and gems and jewellery units. The share of the latter has been increasing in the zones. Noida is also specializing in gems and jewellery while Chennai has electronics, engineering and textile units.

Variation in the Zone Performance

SEZs are benefited usually from better location, modern and efficient infrastructure, general fiscal and non fiscal concessions to firms and single window facilities to ensure corruption and red tape free business environment. These factors ensure good investment climate. This in turn helps in reducing the costs of exporting and, hence enhances competitive advantages of firms in the zones.

Good investment climate may also be crucial for attracting FDI in the zones. In practice, export oriented FDI in developing countries is cost efficiency seeking and remains essentially labour/resource intensive. Export oriented FDI in these countries may also take the form of relocation of some of the production facilities. MNCs seek locations where they can combine their mobile resources most efficiently with the immobile resources they need to produce goods and services The location of investment then becomes more responsive to the factors that ensure lower costs of production and the availability of complimentary factors of production. Since zones provide the platform for low cost production, they are expected to be successful in attracting FDI.

Securing lower production base was the most important motive for their investing in the zones. Thus, the zones' performance in attracting investment and promoting export competitiveness seems to be directly related with the location, infrastructure facilities, quality of governance and the incentive package. Zone specific characteristics such as the size and level of diversification may also affect the performance of the individual zones.

Five sets of determinants are known for zones' success:

- Location specific factors
- Quality of infrastructure

- Quality of governance
- Incentive package
- Zone specific characteristics.

Location Specific Factors

Early proponents of EPZs considered them as potential hubs for non urban, decentralized industrial development. They favoured placing SEZs away from urban and industrial centres. International experience however suggests that if SEZs are located in backward areas with poor social and economic infrastructure and lack of industrial culture their performance is likely to be below expectation. For instance, it is argued that the growth in Hainan SEZ in China was rather slow due to its location in backwardness region. Bataan zone in Phillipines, Puertio Limone zone in Costa Rica and Franche d'Inga zone in Zaire and Dakar EPZ are also examples of poor location. All these zones failed to achieve success. Locating SEZs near or in industrial/urban areas is also likely to be an important factor critical to their success. This satisfies the labour needs of the zone firms, ensures more accessible and uninterrupted utilities, better services and allows for more spillover effects. Furthermore, if EPZs are located near ports or airports they are expected to be more attractive than other industrial sites and are likely to show better export performance.

Finally, country specific factors such as the level of development of the country, availability of cheap labour and raw materials and overall policy regime also confer locational advantages on producing firms. The level of development reflects the investment climate in a country and may be crucial in determining the success of the zone. Efficiency seeking or export oriented investments may be influenced by the availability of cheap labour also.

- *Region specific location factors:* Development of the region in which zone is located and Industrial culture in the region.
- *Strategic Location specific factors:* Proximity of the zone to ports, and airports and proximity to a bigger city.
- *Country specific location factors*: development of the country, Labour cost, availability of raw materials, Policy Regime.

Quality of Infrastructure

The term 'infrastructure' includes physical infrastructure within the zone, physical infrastructure external to the zone and social infrastructure within the zone.

Physical infrastructure within the zone includes: water, electricity, warehousing, transport within the zone, telecommunication, police station, fire station and banks while physical infrastructure external to the zone includes: transport facilities for the zones, roads leading to the zones and port facilities. Social infrastructure within the zone comprises of residential complexes, schools, hospitals and recreation facilities.

Availability of good quality infrastructure improves the business climate by reducing the costs of operations and hence raising rates of returns. The effect of physical infrastructure on the zone's ability to attract FDI and export performance would be positive. The presence of housing, schools, hospital and recreation facilities are also likely to influence the level of investment and economic performance of the zone's performance significantly. Variables representing three types of infrastructure namely, economic infrastructure within the zone, infrastructure external to the zone in the rest of the economy, and social infrastructure.

Quality of Governance

A streamlined, prompt and efficient bureaucracy and custom controls in all stages of the creation and running of an SEZ is crucial to its performance. It greatly influences the attractiveness of a zone to foreign investors and its eventual performance.

The provision of efficient bureaucratic and economic services, a clear and transparent legal and regulatory structure and an unfettered and stable policy framework ensure the success of the zones. The units need to interact not only with the zone administration but also with the government departments outside the zones.

Policy Concessions

A major preferential treatment is given to SEZ units by granting them the government policy concessions. Governments offer a multitude of fiscal and non fiscal concessions. Fiscal concessions include duty free imports of raw and intermediate inputs and capital goods and income tax exemptions. Non fiscal incentives vary widely across countries. These include, relaxation from industrial laws including labour laws. The theory behind these incentives is that liberalising the rules and tax commitments lowers direct and indirect costs.

Fiscal incentives have direct bearing on the cost. These incentives may help in directly reducing the costs of producing and exporting. Non fiscal incentives affect costs indirectly. These concessions expedite the decision making, and streamline day to day operations. Investor friendly custom regime for instance implies that the entrepreneurs are free from routine inspections of import- export cargo. Relaxations in labour market help in reducing labour market rigidities and may affect the labour productivity. In a distorted economy these concessions are used to offset anti export bias. Zones are termed 'international laboratories' in which developing countries liberalising their economies can experiment with highly liberal trade and industrial policies while changes in national policies may be slow. Governments can therefore play a crucial role in putting into place an export-friendly 'enabling environment'. Therefore the more attractive is the incentive package, the better will be the performance of the zones.

Zone Specific Characteristics

Size: Generally, it is believed that only a large sized zone can generate economic activity on some reasonable scale. In a small zone, the requisite infrastructure and services cannot be provided nor can multiple economic activities be promoted. Size of the zone therefore is expected to be positively related with the performance of the zone.

Concentration of economic activities: Cluster approach suggests that highly concentrated zones are more likely to succeed. External economies of scale and other advantages of the cluster help the operating firms in reducing costs and acquiring competitive advantages. Thus the lower the extent of diversification of the zones in a country, the greater may be the advantages that firms reap from the clusters. However, there is also another view, which suggests that diversification of economic activities in a zone may act as a hedge against the risk of fall in the international demand for a specific product. Furthermore, it also implies diversification of countries to which exports may be directed.

Capital intensity of the zone: In labour- abundant South Asian countries, zones are likely to attract labour intensive investment. Sectoral decomposition of zones' exports suggests that these countries have been attracting labour intensive production in the zones. In such a scenario, capital intensity may vary largely due to different techniques of production or the scale of production. High capital intensity may imply the use of relatively more sophisticated technology, better quality control (Wells 1973, Keddie 1976) or larger scales of production. Capital intensity may, therefore, be related positively with the export performance of zones.

Infrastructure

Of the three categories of infrastructure, physical infrastructure within the zone and that external to the zone are equally important. It is not the internal infrastructure only that needs to be taken care of but rather; infrastructure connecting the zone to the wider economy should also be developed for the export competitiveness. Social infrastructure on the other hand such as schools, hospitals, recreation centres etc also plays a vital role.

Location

Location of the zones along with the effect of the country specific factors influences the attractiveness of the zones. Zones should be close to bigger cities. It is not important that they should be located in developed region. It was argued for instance that Chittagong was located in an underdeveloped region near a well Noida was also located in a backward region but its proximity with Delhi benefited the zone. The presence of government offices, better residential and banking facilities and cosmopolitan nature of the city attract foreign investors to the zones near bigger cities. Presence of other industrial clusters within the regions is also likely to benefit the zone units in terms of support services and labour availability. Thus the spill over effects of the bigger city is stated to have a significant impact on the zone attractiveness.

While the strategic location of the zones and proximity to the ports and airports is also equally important. If ports/ airports are not in the proximity of the zone, then roads and transport facilities linking the zones with the ports and airports should be developed. This is simply because much of the trade is routed through ports. Availability of cheap raw material is an important location specific factor. Availability of cheap labour and lower real estate and overhead costs are also some of the most important factors among factor availability factors. Availability of cheap raw materials was considered desirable but not very/most important. This because many units were importing raw materials. Better law and order conditions are stated to be very important for better zone performance. The prevalence of industrial peace influences the investment climate adversely. The zones provide them secured business environment.

Sometimes it is argued that companies are not attracted by incentives per se and that good infrastructure and cheap labour availability are important. However, it has been found that fiscal incentives are considered very important in determining the attractiveness of the zones. For many of the units tax benefits are much more important than subsidies or grants. In India, on the contrary, a highly restrictive package was offered to zone units at the time when tax rates and protective barriers were very high in the rest of the country. Even FDI norms were also not relaxed for the zones. This perhaps contributed to the failure of the zones in attracting FDI. Later, when policy barriers were relaxed in the rest of the economy, zones were also given benefits of liberalization but this might not have ensured higher relative advantage to the zone units vis-â-vis the rest of the economy. Exemption from other industrial laws is also considered very important However; exemption from labour laws was considered a very crucial factor.

Governance

Good quality governance is another factor that emerged crucial in determining the success of the zones. Single window clearances (pre entry, and post entry) and custom clearance facilities, attitude of the officials, work culture of the department etc.Among other governance related matters such as simple rules and accessibility to rules are most important. Two things may be observed. One, all the four sets of factors namely better location, infrastructure, governance and an attractive incentive package are rated almost equally important in determining the attractiveness of the zones. It is the package of all these complementary services that ensures success of the zones. Two, various aspects of location, facilities and incentives are rated differently.

The study can be summarized as follows:

- Traditionally, EPZs/ SEZs were created as open market within an economy that was dominated by distortionary trade, macro and exchange regulation and other regulatory governmental controls. However, new theories developed since the 1980s posit that EPZs/ SEZs play a crucial initiating role in the development of national industrial capacity by creating an environment conducive to promote investment and exports. As a result, many developing countries have been reverting to them in the early stages of their industrial development with the expectation that they provide the engine of growth to propel their economies into industrialization.
- Evolution of EPZs/ SEZs in India is associated with the traditional view to develop a platform for building industrial and export capabilities at the early stages of industrial development. However, promoting SEZs/ EPZs programme are much more vigourously done now than in the initial phases of their evolution.
- Bangladesh and Sri Lanka both created an elaborate institutional framework to govern the EPZs in the initial stages. Their vision was clear and resolutely pro-business. They enacted legislation, created a focused administrative infrastructure to govern EPZs, offered highly attractive incentives and located zones in the best possible locations. In India on the other hand, EPZs policy suffered from a lack of vision. The first zone was established as early as in1965 with multiple objectives in a highly backward region. The second zone was set up in Santacruz with a different set of objectives. The management and operation of the zone was affected by the overall policy regime. Wide-ranging measures were initiated by the government for revamping and restructuring EPZs as late as in the 1990s. The SEZ policy announced in 2000 is the most significant thrust towards ensuring the success of export processing zones in India.
- Zone units in Bangladesh are enjoying huge relative benefits compared to the domestic units in terms of incentive package, infrastructure facilities and the quality of governance. Sri Lanka also offers a highly focused administrative set up for the development of the zones and highly developed infrastructure facilities like Bangladesh. Besides, Sri Lanka also offered several incentives to the units in the initial phase of the evolution of the zones. However, since the late 1990s, the government is cutting down the incentives offered to the units. In India, EPZs/ SEZs are managed by the government department till recently. At the zone level, there is no fine tuning of the division of responsibilities along the lines that is

seen in other two countries. However, one distinguishing feature of the Indian system is with regard to the custom services. In India, these services are directly under the jurisprudence of the zone administration. In Sri Lanka and Bangladesh, on the contrary, custom departments are controlled by the government. The incentive package had been highly restrictive till recently but now the government has announced a substantially improved set of incentives and facilities. Infrastructure facilities provided by the zones in India are comparable with Sri Lanka. However Bangladesh appears to have an edge here also due to direct interference of the EPZ authorities in providing major infrastructure facilities (water, electricity and telecommunication) to the zone units.

- Clarity in vision and concerted efforts finally reflected in the expansion of the zones and participation by FDI in Sri Lanka and Bangladesh. In terms of over all export growth also the two countries scored over India. However, in terms of productive efficiency (Exports per unit of labour) India appears to have excelled. Even after controlling the effect of capital intensity, India's productive efficiency turned out to be the highest in the 1990s. During 2000- 2003 however, Sri Lanka out performed India.
- Countries wishing to take advantage of the opportunities provided by zones will have to put together a co-ordinated package of incentives, infrastructure and good governance. Some aspects of location, facilities and incentives are more important than the others. Tax benefits are more sought after than subsidies, relaxation in labour laws is stated to be more important than relaxation in other laws, locating the zones near bigger cities/ports is considered more important.
- Our empirical analysis reveals that the relative advantages enjoyed by the EPZs/ SEZs units (in terms of incentives, infrastructure and governance) vis-â-vis the rest of the economy attract investment in the zones while overall governance and infrastructure facilities in a country determine the export competitiveness of its zones. Furthermore, location of a zone in a development region and/ or near strategic positions such as bigger cities, ports and airports affect both the investment and export competitiveness. Composition of economic activities in the zones such as clustering and capital intensity also affects the export competitiveness.

Four major policy implications are:

- The establishment of a successful EPZ/ SEZ programme does not require removing one or two obstacle; it requires removing all of them simultaneously. This is because EPZs offer a package of services simultane-ously. In short, EPZs/ SEZs have a much higher probability of success when there is vision in the design, establishment and operations of the EPZ.

- Overall investment climate (infrastructure, governance) in a country matters in the success of its zones in terms of competitiveness. Generally, it is argued that the EPZs/ SEZs concept is attractive because it is much easier to resolve the problems of infrastructure and governance on a limited geographical area than it is to resolve them countrywide. Zones may attract investment due to relative advantages that the units enjoy here but they may not be efficient in terms of productivity. Zones cannot be insulated from the broader institutional and economic context of the country and that they cannot be treated as an economy within the economy. Zones are a part of the economy and require overall improvement in the investment climate to ensure success in the long run. They should not therefore be viewed as alternative to the overall development model. This is perhaps the reason why EPZs failed to fulfill the role of engines of industrialization in most countries on a sustainable basis.
- Zones tend to specialise in terms of economic activities depending on the availability of human capital, resources and infrastructure in the region. They thus tend to transform into horizontally-integrated industrial clusters, which includes industries that might share a common market for the end products, use a common technology or labour force skills, or require similar natural resources. It seems therefore that it would be desirable to develop zones as industrial clusters of specific products. This may encourage downstream industries also.
- Finally, zones in the long run, need to give way to industrial clusters of horizontally and vertically integrated industries in general, high tech industries in particular. This would not only help in jump-start the manufacturing processes but would also improve export competitiveness with greater return.

SEZ BILL AND ESSENCE

The EXIM policy, 1997-2002, effective 1-4-2000 had seen the announcement of a plan of Special Economic Zones (SEZs). The EXIM Policy, 2002-2007 made effective from 1-4-2003 gives a stimulus to the plan by providing more incentives and procedural relaxation. It also serves to emphasize that the SEZs plan is visualized by the Government as its most important export incentive plan. The SEZ has been defined as a specifically delineated area wherein units may be set up for specified purposes for export. The units are eligible for duty free import/procurement of required raw materials, inputs etc. The idea is that the incentives granted, fiscal and non-fiscal, attract investment, both foreign and domestic, and the export will be facilitated. At first look it may appear that there does little or no difference between the then exist EPZs and the new SEZ. Both are enclaved duty free areas wherein the units avail hose of fiscal and other concessions with the objective of facilitating their exports. However, a closer look reveals the critical differences between the two.

The essential underlying principle governing the policy on SEZs is the two. The essential underlying principle governing the policy on SEZs is that these are treated as foreign territories... much more that tin the case of the EOUs/ EPZs. Thus, whereas the fiscal incentives in terms of duty exemptions are available both to SEZ and EOUs, additionally other legislation such as Labour Law is sought to be relaxed to a large extent in the case of the former. It is also the intention that the units shall avail 'single window' clearance, whether the matter releases to the Central or the State Government. As regards the operationalization of the SEZ plan, with effect from 1-11-2000 the FTZs/ EPZs at Kandla, Kochi, Surat and Mumbai stand converted to SEZs. The EPZs at Noida, Falta, Vishakapatnam and Chennai were likewise converted to SEZs with effect from 1-1-2003. Thus, as on date there are no EPZs. Further, the policy is t o set up only SEZs shall be done by the State Governments or Private Sector or as joint Sector venture between these two.

Exim Policy Provisions for Sezs

The EXIM Policy, 2002-2007 detail the SEZ plan. As provided therein, the SEZs are envisaged as duty free enclaves deemed to be foreign territories for the purposes of trade operations, duties and tariffs. In other worlds, all activities within the SEZs will be as if being done outside India. Naturally, the units therein may import/ procure the required raw materials, inputs, capital goods etc. duty free. Also, their clearances to the DTA will be treated as imports into India.

The said Policy provisions are briefly summed up, as follows:

- SEZ units are permitted to be set up fro the purpose of manufacture of goods and rendering of services. The SEZ itself may have areas demarcated as processing areas wherein units will be set up and non-processing areas wherein other facilities may be provided.
- SEZs may be set up in the public, joint sector or by State Governments, as notified by the Ministry of Commerce and Industry.
- SEZ units are allowed to import. procure free of duty (including from bonded warehouses in the DTA and from International Exhibitions held in India) all their requirement of inputs, raw materials, capital goods (including second had capital goods) etc. Goods may also be got free of cost or on loan from the clients. Goods required for making capital goods for use in the unit may be imported. However, good which are prohibited items of import in the ITC (HS) are not allowed.
- The Unit Approval Committee is the competent authority for approval of units under the plan, if they satisfy the specified conditions. IF not, approval will be given by Development

Commissioner after clearance of BOA. Any change in approved activity or undertaking of any new activity is to be intimated to the Development Commissioner.

- A SEZ unit is required to execute a legal undertaking with the Development Commissioner to fulfil its obligation to achieve positive NFE.
- A SEZ unit is required to be a positive Net Foreign Exchange Earner (NFE), calculated cumulatively over a five year period.
- DTA sale facility is available to SEZ units, including service/ trading units, subject to payment of full duty (not concessional duty, as in the case of EOUs) and meeting the requirement of the EXIM policy.
- The units including gem and jewellery units may sub-contract a part of their product or production process in the DTA or through other SEZ/ EOU/ EHTP/ STP units with permission of customs. Further, the units, other than gem and jewellery units are allowed to undertake job work on behalf of the DTA units for direct export. Sub-contracting of part of their production process may also be got done abroad, with approval of BOA.
- The transfer of goods imported. Procured or manufactured by a SEZ unit to another SEZ/ EOU/ EHTP/ STP unit is allowed subject to maintenance of proper records.
- The units may carry out all activities, unless otherwise specified, on the basis of self-certification, subject to monitoring by a Committee headed by the Development Commissioner and including the customs.
- Gems and Jewellery units may participate in exhibitions in India and abroad.
- Specified supplies by SEZ unit in DTA such as supplies to other SEZ/EOU/EHTP/STP units; supplies to bonded warehouses in DTA; supplies against special entitlement of duty free import of goods; supplies to defence and internal security forces, foreign missions/ diplomats of (if exempted from duty) etc., will be counted towards fulfilment of its NFE.
- A SEZ unit is allowed to export through merchant exporter/ status holder or other SEZ/ EOU/ EHTP/ STP unit.
- A SEZ unit may supply/ sell samples in DTA for display/ market promotion and also transfer the goods to DTA for repair/ replacement, testing or calibration, quality testing and R & D purposes, on the basis of records maintained and on prior intimation to the customs authorities.
- Supplies by DTA units to SEZ units will qualify as 'deemed exports', eligible for the specified benefits.
- Duty free imported/ procured goods may be disposed in DTA on payment of duty and subject to import license, as applicable or exported or destroyed.

- Imported/procured goods or parts thereof found defective maybe brought back for repair/ replacement.
- A SEZ unit may replace the goods or parts therefore found defective or otherwise unfit for use or which become damaged or defective may be returned or destroyed and replacement thereof or the same goods after repairs thereof may be imported or procured from the authorized suppliers in India/ domestic suppliers.
- A SEZ unit may exit from the plan after approval of the Development Commissioner as per the specified conditions including payment of applicable customs and central excise duties. Such unit may also be permitted, as a one-time option, to debond and enter the EPCG plan.
- Developer of SEZs in Private/ Joint/ State sector may import/ procure the specified goods without payment of duty for the development, operation and maintenance of SEZs.

Therefore, the policy provisions in respect of the SEZ units are similar to those for the EOU/ EHTP/ STP units.

This is to be expected since, as in the case of the erstwhile EPZ units, the SEZ plan also envisages like duty free enclave for the units along with necessary fiscal and other incentives such as the duty free procurement/ import of goods. Yet there are certain critical differences, which make the SEZ plan an improvement.

Eligibility And Approval Under The Plan

The EXIM policy defines a SEZ as a delineated duty free enclave deemed to be a foreign territory for purposes of trade operations and duties and tariffs. Further, goods and services going to SEZ are treated as exports and the reverse is treated as imports. The areas of activity for which the SEZ units may avail the facility of duty free import/ procurement of goods are the manufacture of goods and rendering of services. This is an exhaustive list and practically every activity is covered. Thus, units undertaking the said activities are eligible under the plan.

Whereas the eligibility for units under the SEZ plan is seen in the context of the proposed activity, other important eligibility criterion are the viability of the project, the projected turnover, and whether it would satisfy the condition of positive NFE. The EXIM policy read the Hand book of Procedures 3 copies of the application in the prescribed proforma are to be submitted to the Development Commissioner of the SEZ concerned.

Completed application entitled ' Application Form for setting up units in SEZ must be accompanied by a crossed bank draft for Rs.5000/- in favour of the Pay and Accounts officer, Department of industrial Policy and Promotion, Ministry of Industry, payable at Central Bank of India, Udyog Bhawan Branch, New Delhi. The Development Commissioner will acknowledge the receipt of the application and a reference number will be given.

With few exceptions the Unit Approval Committee is the competent authority for approval of units under the SEZ plan. It is also provided that the units shall inform the Committee/ Development Commissioner in case of any change in approved activity or undertaking of any new activity. This shall specify the conditions/ parameters and also obligations and conditions under which the unit shall work. If the application does not satisfy the conditions of automatic approval (it requires an industrial licence or is in service sector (other than software, IT, trading etc.) or it is a case of conversion of EOUT into SEZ unit) it shall be remitted to the SEZ, BOA, and Department of Industrial Policy and Promotion and after its clearance the Development Commissioner will grant the approval within 45 days.

Once the application for setting up a unit under the SEZ plan is approved/ rejected, the Letters of Permission/ Intent (LOP/ LOI) or letters of concerned. The LOP/LOI shall specify the item(s) of manufacture/ service activity; annual capacity; projected annual export performance for the first five years in dollar terms; Net foreign exchange earnings as a percentage of exports (NFE) to be achieved; limitation, if any, regarding sale of finished goods, by-products and rejects in the DTA; and such other matter as necessary.

It shall also impose such conditions as necessary. Further, in case of any change in the approved activity, or if the unit undertakes a new activity, the Development Commissioner is required to issue an amended LOP within 6 days of the receipt of intimation. The LOP shall be construed as a license for all purposes under the plan, including for the procurement of raw materials and consumables either directly or through designated canalising agency. It is valid for 3 years from its date of issue during which the time the unit should commence commercial production.

The LOP shall automatically lapse if an application for the extension of its validity is not make before the end of the said period. Each LOP/ LOI shall have separate earmarked premises. The LOP/ LOI is valid for 5 years once the unit commences production. The approval may be further renewed for another 5 years.

It is also provided that the Importer-Exporter code numbers for SEZ unit's hall is allotted by the Development Commissioner concerned. This is issued after the execution of the legal undertaking.

Note:

- As a policy it has been decided not to allow polluting industrial units (agro-chemicals, dyes, solvents etc) and socially obnoxious items (liquor etc.) and strategically important items of defence in the SEZ. Units engaged in re-cycling of ferrous and non-ferrous metals will not allowed under they make ingots.
- In terms of the Handbook of Procedures failure to abide by any of the conditions of the LOP/ LOI shall render the unit liable to penal action under the Foreign Trade (Development and Regulation) Act, 1992 and the Rules and Orders made thereunder without prejudice

to any other action under any other law/ rules and cancellations or revocation of LOP/ LOI/ IL]

The registering authority for the SEZ unit will be the Development Commissioner concerned. A separate registration cum membership certificate shall not be required, as provided for the EXIM Policy. It is also provided that the Importer-Exporter code numbers for SEZ units shall be allotted by the Development Commissioner concerned.

The SEZ units are also entitled to automatic issue of the Green Card by the Development Commissioner after the execution of the legal undertaking.

The identified criteria for approval of SEZ units by Unit Approval Committee are:

- The project is not included in Schedule I or II of the Notification No. 447 (E), dated 25-7-1991 issued under the Industries (Development and Regulation) Act, 1951. In other words, the item of manufacture does not require an Industrial Licence under the said Act.
- The project is located in area within a SEZ for which availability of space and conformity with environmental and other standards is satisfied.
- The project undertakes to achieve positive NFE.
- The foreign technology agreement, if any entered into by the unit, is as per the RBI regulations i.e. restricted to a lump sum payment of US $ 2 million or 8% royalty (net of taxes), over the period of 5 years from the commencement of production.

General Conditions of Approval of Units

The several terms and conditions of governing a unit approved under the SEZ plan are summed up, as follows:

- The approval period shall be 5 years, renewable for further 5 years at a time.
- The LOP will be valid for 3 years from the date of its issue within which period the unit shall implement the project and commence commercial production.
- Unit shall export its production of goods and services as per the EXIM Policy for the approval period of 5 years with option to bedond thereafter or continue further under the plan. Export of Special Chemicals, Organisms, Materials, Equipment and Technologies (SCOMET) shall be subject to fulfilment of conditions in the ITC (HS).
- Possession of allotted plot/SDF is to be taken within 3 months of issue of LOA and construction/ implementation of project started within next 6 months.
- The unit is required to confirm the acceptance of the terms and conditions mentioned in the LOP within a period of 45 days to the Development Commissioner.

- The start of commercial production/ business is to be intimated to the Development Commissioner.
- The entire operations shall be in a customs bonded premises.
- The unit shall be required to execute a legal undertaking with the Development Commissioner for meeting the conditions of approval including the export obligation.
- The achievement of positive NFE shall be necessary. Duty free raw materials procured from an EOU/SEZ/EHTP/STP unit shall be treated as imports for the purpose of computing the net foreign exchange earnings.
- Duty free import of capital goods, components, raw materials and consumables, spares, material handling equipment etc. shall be permitted. Items in the Prohibited list of imports in the ITC (HS) will not be allowed. Services may be procured from DTA free of Service Tax.
- Indigenous available capital goods, components, raw materials etc. will be allowed without payment of central excise duty.
- If an industrial enterprise is operating both as domestic unit and as SEZ unit, it shall have two distinct identities with separate accounts including separate bank accounts. It is however not necessary for them to be two separate legal entity. It should be possible to distinguish the import or export or supplies effected by the SEZ unit from those made by the other (domestic) units of the enterprise.
- Normally raw material tie-ups will not be insisted upon.
- No export benefits like cash assistance, replenishment licenses would be admissible on the exports.
- The exit of the unit from the plan upon completion of the export obligation shall mean the physical vacation of the premises in the SEZ. Thereafter, the permission to the unit to produce the domestic market (when located in DTA) shall be decided in the light of the industrial policy in force at that time in relation to production of the items reserved for small scale sector.
- On exit from the plan duties of customs and central excise, as applicable shall be levied on the finished goods, raw materials capital goods etc.
- An application for industrial license to the SIA shall be treated as an application under the MRTP Act, 1969.
- If an approved unit fails to fulfil its export obligation, the future course of action will be decided by the Monitoring Committee.
- There shall be exemption from taxes on finished products, when exported. Export duties shall be leviable unless specifically exempted.
- Supplies to SEZ units by domestic units will be treated as deemed exports with accompanying benefits.

Note: Finance Act, 2002-2003 has amended the Central Excise Act, 1944 and Customs Act, 1962 with the objective that the good sent from the DTA to the SEZ would be treated as exports with all attendant benefits.

- SEZ unit can sell its products to domestic projects under Global Tender conditions.
- Adequate steps shall be taken to prevent air, water and soil pollution and the standards of the State Pollution Board in this regard must be satisfied. Further, adequate steps will be taken to the satisfaction o the State Government in regard to the process hazards for ensuring safety in plants for manufacture of chemicals, fertilizer and pharmaceuticals.
- The external commercial borrowing, if any, shall be subject to approval of RBI in terms of Foreign Exchange Management Act, 1999 as per guidelines of the ECB Division, Department of Economic Affairs, Ministry of Finance. Generally, loan agreements may be entered into for raising fresh ECB with average maturity of not less than 3 years for an mount of US$ 50 million and for refinancing an existing ECB without prior approval.
- Repatriation of dividend/ profits and foreign travel expense etc. is freely allowed.
- 100% NRI holding in the undertaking is allowed.
- Foreign collaboration would be permitted. Engagement of foreign technicians and payment thereof shall be as per Government policy in force.
- The condition of foreign equity as stipulated in the Department of Economic Affairs Press Note of 19-2-1972 will not be enforced.
- Royalty will be calculated on the basis of the net ex-factory sale price of the product, exclusive of the excise duty minus the cost of the standard bought out components and the landed cost of the imported components, irrespective of the source of procurement, including ocean freight, insurance, customs duty etc.

SEZ POLICY

The Government of India through the SEZ Policy has made available a basket of Incentives, Exemptions, Concessions and Privileges (IECP) to the SEZ. Developers and the SEZ Units. Some of the major IECPs available to the Developer and Unit are:

The benefits available under the SEZ Policy essentially translate into:

- Reduced Cost of Infrastructure
- Reduced Cost of Utilities
- Reduced Cost of Raw Material
- Reduced Cost of Capital
- Reduced Cost of Manpower
- Operational Ease

These Baskets of Benefits available to the Developer and the Units are aimed at enabling Global competitiveness

BENEFITS – SEZ DEVELOPER

The Developer is an entity who develops, operates and maintains any infrastructure facility in an SEZ. The benefits available to the Developer have now been made available to Co Developers of the SEZ as well.

Some of the benefits available to SEZ Developer are:

- Developer of a SEZ may import/procure goods from DTA without payment of duty for the development, operation and maintenance of any Infrastructure, Utility, Facility or Service.
- Income tax exemption for a block of 10 years in 15 years from the date of operations at the option of developer
- Income Tax exemption to Investors in SEZs.
- Investment made by individuals etc. in the SEZ Company is also eligible for exemption u/s 88 of IT Act.
- Exemption from Service Tax
- Exemption from Central Sales Tax on Sales made from Domestic Area to SEZ Developer
- Full authority to provide services like water, electricity, security, restaurants, recreation centres etc. on commercial lines.
- Generation, Transmission and Distribution of Power in SEZs allowed.
- Foreign investment permitted to develop township within the SEZ with residential areas, markets, play grounds, clubs, recreation centres etc.
- Freedom in allocation of developed plots to approved SEZ units on purely commercial basis

Benefits – Sez Unit

The Policy provides a basket of Incentives, Exemptions, Concessions & Privileges to the SEZ Unit. It is aimed at making SEZ Exports more competitive and gives an advantage to SEZ Exporters.

Some of the benefits available to the SEZ Units are:

Customs and Excise:

- SEZ units may import or procure from the domestic sources, all their requirements of capital goods, raw materials, consumables, spares, packing materials, office equipment, DG sets etc. in the Zone without any license or specific approval.
- Exemption from Customs duty on import of capital goods, raw materials, consumables, spares etc.
- Exemption from Central Excise duty on procurement of capital goods, raw materials, consumables, spares etc. from the Domestic Market

- Goods imported/procured locally duty free could be utilized over a period of 5 years.
- Domestic Sales on payment of applicable duty.

Taxes:

- 100% Income Tax exemption (Sec. 10A) for first 5 years and 50% for 5 years thereafter. Reinvestment allowance to the extent of 50% of ploughed back profits for the next 5 years.
- Exemption from Service Tax
- Physical export benefit to DTA units for goods supplied to SEZ units

Foreign Direct Investment:

- 100% foreign direct investment under the automatic route is allowed in manufacturing sector in SEZ units.
- No cap on foreign investments for SSI reserved items.

Banking & Finance:

- Setting up Off-shore Banking Units (OBUs) allowed in SEZs. Thus SEZ units can avail of financing at International rates.
- OBU's allowed 100% Income Tax exemption on profit for 5 years and 50% for next 5 years.
- External commercial borrowings by units up to $ 500 million a year allowed without any maturity restrictions.
- Flexibility to keep 100% of export proceeds in EEFC account with freedom to make overseas investment from it.
- Commodity hedging permitted.
- Exemption from interest rate surcharge on import finance.
- Facility to realise and repatriate export proceeds within 12 months.
- SEZ units allowed to 'write-off' unrealised export bills up to 5%.

Operational:

- Performance Monitoring on Self Certification basis.
- No routine examination by Customs of export and Import cargo

Gujarat SEZ Act, 2004

In addition to the benefits made available by the Central Government, the Government of Gujarat has committed to make available the following benefits by passing the Gujarat SEZ Act.

Fiscal Benefits:

- All sales and transactions within the processing area of the Zone shall be exempt from all taxes, cess, duties, fees or any other levies under any State law to the extent specified below:
  - Stamp duty and registration fees payable on transfer of land
  - Levy of Stamp duty and registration fees on loan agreement, credit deeds and mortgages.
  - Sales Tax, Purchase Tax, Motor Spirit Tax, Luxury Tax, Entertainment Tax and other taxes and cess payable on sales and transactions.

- Exemption from electricity duty under the Bombay Electricity Duty Act, 1958 for a period of 10 years from the date of production or supply of services as the case may be.
- Inputs (goods and services) made to Zone Units from Domestic Tariff Area shall be exempted from sales tax and other taxes under the State laws.

Relaxations in Labour Laws:

- The power, duties and functions conferred on the Commissioner of Labour shall vest with the Development Commissioner of the SEZ.
- The Units in the Zone to furnish Consolidated Annual Report to the Development Commissioner instead of periodical returns under the following *Acts, namely*:
  - The Workmen's Compensation Act, 1923;
  - The Payment of Wages Act, 1936;
  - The Factories Act, 1948;
  - The Minimum Wages Act, 1948;
  - The Maternity Bene fit Act, 1961;
  - The Payment of Bonus Act, 1965;
  - The Contract Labour (Regulation and Abolition) Act, 1970;

Modifications in various labour laws:

- The provisions of Bombay Industrial Relations Act, 1946 shall not apply to units set up in the SEZ
- The State Government authorized to vary the time limit laid down in section 66(1)(b) of the Factories Act, 1948 (pertaining to work timings of women worker).
- Industry or establishment set up in the special economic zone granted the status of Public Utility under Industrial Disputes Act, 1947.
- SEZs excluded from the definition of establishment under The Contract Labour (Regulation and Abolition) Act, 1970.
- All the office bearers of the registered trade unions of the industrial establishments situated in the SEZ shall be persons actually engaged or employed in an industry with which trade union is connected – benefit granted under Trade Unions Act, 1926.

All requisite approvals and permissions will be through "Single Window Mechanism" ensuring "hassle free operations".

Cost advantage of sez units compared to dtas:

- Land Acquisition Stage
- No Stamp duty & Registration Fee
- Land through Mundra SEZ Ltd.
- Project Planning Stage
- No Service Tax on Consultancy Services availed
- Financing Stage
- Various exemptions bring down the project cost by about 15-20%

- Foreign Currency funding through OBUs
- Rupee funding at lower rates – no CRR, SLR & Priority lending.
- Construction Stage
- No duties on imports or goods sourced locally for capital goods.
- No State & Local levies like Sales Tax, Turnover tax, Purchase Tax, Mandi Tax etc.
- Operations & Maintenance Stage
- No duties on consumables & spares.
- Development commissioner "Single Window" for all approvals and clearances
- "Single Window" for all infrastructure, Utilities, Facilities & Services
- Reduced Transportation Cost & Reduced Transit Time.

INDIAN SEZS- ARE WE REPLICATING THE CHINESE SEZS

SEZs in China have been extremely successful with a 40% share of exports, compared to the 4% of Indian SEZs. SEZs were the key drivers of the growth of the Chinese economy in the last two decades. India has much to learn from the Chinese SEZ model. The SEZ bill, which is a part of the foreign trade policy 2004-2009, is poised to make India a favourable destination for investment.

SEZs have been the growth engines for exports, FDI and Industrial growth across many countries in Asia. SEZs have become laboratories for the economic reforms in the past two decades. In the late 1970s, the Indian and Chinese economies were comparable. But, in the 1980s and 1990s China cruised ahead of India, and today it finds itself at the top in all sectors against India except in software and knowledge-based products. This growth in the Chinese economy is mainly due to the fact that the Special Economic Zones (SEZs) were a part of their open door policy.

In India, SEZs were first planned in the Exim Policy in 2001 to boost exports. The Indian Government has converted all in the 1990s, into SEZs because they failed to increase the exports. EPZs are small industrial estates, whereas the SEZs are industrial townships offering more facilities and incentives. The intentions of the SEZs are much larger than mere endorsement of export processing zones. After studying the Chinese SEZ model, the Indian authorities have decided to start the SEZs in strategic locations close to port cities and economic centres. The developments of Greenfield SEZs have already started in the country. The incentives offered by the Indian SEZs are more or less the same as those offered by the Chinese SEZs, but they are failing to attract both the FDI and the domestic investments.

Lessons From Chiense Sezs

China started four SEZs in 1979 and the fifth one was set up in 1988. Cities along the sea coast, including Shanghai, were 'opened up' for foreign investments and given a status comparable to SEZs. In the late 1980s, almost every city in China had its own science and technology development zone, where conditions were more or less similar to the SEZs. There are many distinctive features that have contributed to the success of Chinese SEZs. The include large size, FDI from the non-resident Chinese, attractive incentives, flexible laws, liberal customs procedures and decentralization of power to the local authorities.

The SEZs in China are located on the coasting near Hong Kong and Taiwan which are major economic centres in the region. A large chunk of the FDI was contributed by the non-resident Chinese from Hong Kong and Taiwan. They invested in the labour intensive industries. Later, the MNCs also started investing in technology-oriented industries by bring modern technology to China. If we ignore the phenomenon of non-resident Chinese for a while, and assume that they were not there then reality is that the SEZs in China did not see much success for a long time. FDI received during 1979-2004 was about $ 400 billion, which are primarily capital intensive. Almost 80-90% of FDI in China has gone into SEZs located on the eastern coast, particularly in southern china's Hainan and Guangdong provinces and in the greater Shanghai and Beijing areas.

The size of the SEZs has been an important factor in the success of China's reforms process. China has now declared the entire region or province as an SEZ. The area occupied by the Chinese SEZs is very large; these townships provide almost every facility like housing, transportation, telecommunication, power generation etc. Every SEZ in China is spread over thousands of square kilometres. For foreign investors, it is the labour policy in China's SEZs that is the biggest attraction. The hire and fire policy has attracted foreing investors to invest in China's SEZs. All the jobs are on a contract, which can either be meant for one particular job or be flexible enough for all kinds of jobs.

Decentralization of power to the local authorities is another major reason for the success of SEZs in China. Local authorities have the necessary powers to frame their own policies to improve the SEZs and attract foreign and domestic investors. They can approve FDI proposals up to $ 30 million. Most foreign investments can be approved locally and require virtually no central clearance.

A strong domestic market has played an important role in the success of China's SEZs. SEZs in China benefited from linkages with domestic economy. This promoted local purchases and technology transfers. China focuses on unsophisticated labour intensive products such as clothing and footwear.

Marketing has another factor in attracting foreign investment to the SEZs. The thrust of the SEZs in China was to attract FDI and technology. The SEZ authorities in China persuaded investors aggressively and provinces and local authorities competed with each other to attract FDI.

ADVOCACY FOR INDIA

Indian, receiving $ 4 billion a year as FDI in skill-intensive. Most of the

FDI in India is concentrated in the IT sector and only a small portion of it is invested in SEZs. India's SEZs are lacking in NRI investments, which was not the case with China. "But they have their distinct roles in terms of transfer of knowledge, skill, software and experiences.

India cannot compete with China in the unsophisticated, labour intensive products such as clothing and footwear. Alternatively, India has got strength in biotechnology, electronics and knowledge-based products with the assistance of NRIs. Concentrating on those industries in which we expertise and management skills will help benefit the Indian SEZs. So, the thrust should be on sector-specific SEZs. Indian SEZs are small in size and these zones are built in very limited space. In India, the average size of a SEZ is 1 – 3 sq. km. It is a difficult to develop, the requisite infrastructure in such small areas. Multiple economic activities are also difficult to perform. Acquiring land in the proposed SEZ locations region is the key to building large SEZs.

Indian SEZs are small in size and these zones are built in very limited is 1-3 sq. km. It is difficult to develop the requisite infrastructure in such small areas. Multiple economic activities are also difficult to perform. Acquiring land in the proposed SEZ locations region is the key to building large SEZs. Labour laws are very inflexible and trade unions seem to be strong in India. This can impact productivity and delay exports. Flexibility in labour laws is one important step for improving the exports from the SEZs.

The state governments or public/ private/ joint sector can set up SEZs. The power of approving the FDI proposals is with the development commissioner appointed by the Central Government. This causes the delay in the approvals. Decentralize the powers to the local authorities and state governments for the quicker approvals of the investment proposals. A single window clearance perhaps is the best policy for attracting investments.

India has big domestic market like China, but the SEZs, even after paying high import duties, are not allowed to sell more than 50% of the exports. These are policy barriers to sales in domestic market. The objectives of the SEZs in China and India also differ. While China concentrates on FDI and technology, India concentrates only on the exports. India needs to update the skills level over time to match biotechnology, electronics and knowledge-based industries.

Proper balance needs to be maintained among the following investors: 100% foreign owned, joint ventures with foreign companies, and 100% domestic companies. This will encourage the private profit to be spent in India for re-investment. The higher the linkages of SEZs higher will be the benefits to the economy. Indian SEZs policy allows sales in the domestic market on the payment of current indirect taxes and not on the existing high import duties. India, like China should also concentrate on FDI and technology for the SEZs. India should send its officials and development commissioners for SEZs for foreign countries to attract prospective investors. If India wants foreign investments, then it should market and promote its SEZs.

Manufacturing bases are shifting from the developed countries to the developing countries primarily due to cheap labour prices and proximity to new markets. The potential for attracting FDI is the SEZs in manufacturing is high, if India provides a hassle free environment for the investors and all necessary fiscal incentives. Linking the SEZs and domestic markets will also be beneficial for the economy. Once the obstacles of investing in the SEZs are removed, then India can replicate China's success.

MERITS AND DEMERITS OF SPECIAL ECONOMIC ZONE

Limitation of sezs:

(A) *Sezs as panoply against poverty*:

- *Women*: It is argued that Special Economic Zones would provide gainful employment to large numbers of people who hitherto would not be able to find jobs. The bogey of poverty removal through employment is therefore bandied about with much aplomb by the proponents of SEZs.

As in other countries, where Special Economic Zones attract a large number of women workers, India too has many women workers in the SEZs and in future, more women are likely to be employed in them. While women workers usually earn salaries that they would not be able to earn outside the zone and also, the difference between men and women workers' wage would not be too different, a number of problems are endemic to the SEZ cause:

Multinational corporations that set up their factories in these special zones employ thousands of women but their work is mostly repetitive in nature like knitting, sewing or fixing small parts. As a result, women often suffer from chronic illnesses because of the monotony and repetitive nature of their jobs and the highly restricted spaces in which they are confined to during work hours. They suffer from various problems related to night shifts and close monitoring by tyrannical supervisors. They are also not given proper contracts and are hired and fired easily. No health benefits are usually given to women workers and with marriage or pregnancy, their contracts are often terminated.

- *Infrastructure*: For India to attract anywhere near the quanta of investment from multi-national corporations that China does it would have to beef up its infrastructure. In general the state of India's infrastructure is nowhere near China's. While Special Economic Zones are meant to be export generation zones the grim fact remains that the majority of the SEZs in India lack international connectivity. Indeed, SEZs at Kandla, Mundra, Indore and Jaipur have no international airports and do not have maritime access.
- *Competition*: Most countries in South Asia-Nepal, Bangladesh, Sri Lanka and Pakistan have all tried to promote their exports

and also create employment by establishing these special economic zones. Since all are highly populous countries, they are heavily into exports of goods requiring cheap labour. In fact they are all competing with each other in almost the same products-garments, sports goods, knitted garments, textiles, gems and jewellery. Bangladesh and Sri Lanka have really done well in garment exports and 90 per cent of the workers in Bangladesh's garment sector, are women. Employment of women in SEZs in Bangladesh is epitomized by the fact that women are paid considerably lower than men.

- *Precipitous Movement of Multinational Corporations*: One of the major predicaments that face SEZs is the fact that multi-national corporations that are being wooed with a missionary zeal by India and her neighbouring countries would jump ship the moment they realise they'll get a better deal in other countries.

At the moment, multinational companies are being offered opportunities on terms that are on par with those existing in all of India's neighbouring countries. China has by far the most attractive terms and conditions. In this intense competition, there has been a tendency for the multinational companies to keep changing their locations whenever they see a slight cost advantage. This can result in sudden closure of factories and resulting unemployment.

- Do the Numbers stack up: An estimated only 50,000 additional jobs can be created in the Special Economic Zones as compared to the big monetary and fiscal concessions given to them, the best course would be to have a few really well functioning special economic zones that are properly and efficiently run.
- *Bandwagon Effect*: Copying the Chinese model entirely may not be beneficial to India as Chinese SEZs are much larger in magnitude, and in addition to export processing they promote activities such as commerce, tourism, housing, agriculture and industrial production. The scope of Indian SEZs is limited

(B) SEZs and India's Energy Security: Tax arbitrage possibilities in special economic zones and excessive protection for refining are combining to harm India's energy security. Global oil majors are keen to set up shop in India's special economic zones in order to take advantages of the reduced duties on petroleum products which guarantee steep, world-beating refinery margins.

Even domestic oil majors such as upstream crude oil specialist ONGC have chalked out big plans to foray downstream, into refining. The issue that arises is that oil companies would tend to take advantage of the duty differential and would give the prospect of investing in oil exploration a goby. Given that India is already one of the largest consumers of crude oil, upstream investment is a crucial facet in India's energy security.

Value adds-The Lack of it: Value added in refining is modest, normally in the single digits. India's very high duty differential between crude and products translates as effective protection of almost 50%. This is the reason why gross refinery margins (GRMs) in India have traditionally been way above global levels and gives rise to the fact that India has a thoroughly high-cost oil economy, now a big and fast-growing chunk of its GDP.

ONGC, India's most valuable company, does need to become wholly integrated oil major, as is standard practice abroad. But its investment intentions belie a balanced approach. The plan is for ONGC to boost its crude output by just about 10% to 30 million tonnes by 2009-10, but shore up refining capacity to over 40 million tonnes well beforehand.

ONGC is of the opinion that its reserves and assets are best leveraged by increasing refining capability, and the assured cash-flow that goes with it. However, there is no reason for policy to encourage such a trend, given that refinery projects are hugely capital-intensive but result in minimal value addition. And the fact is that there are huge tax benefits and outright write-offs on offer for refining projects in the SEZs, where ONGC plans much of its downstream investments. Such generous tax breaks would thoroughly distort resource allocation.

The logic behind propping capital-intensive refinery projects with a smorgasbord of tax breaks seems farfetched. Limited tax benefits and other incentives might be justified for labour-intensive textile projects with much scope for value addition. Besides, the steeply higher import duty on refined products compared to that on crude further distorts the investment regime.

It makes it worth the while to rev up refining capacity and simply cash in on the almost 50% effective tariff protection on hand. Meanwhile, for 2004-05, ONGC has failed to make a single oil discovery although it reportedly drilled nine wells and invested $416 million. It may well be that its planned cash-flows downstream would ultimately help ONGC step up high-risk upstream investments. But it's clearly all the more reason to eschew tax breaks for refinery SEZs and high relative oil duties.

(C) *An idea whose time has lapsed*: The idea of SEZ came to value addition, employment generation and all such remnants of the control regime. Now, the sole purpose of the SEZs is to export goods and services and earn foreign exchange. And to make it easier, an SEZ developer and enterprise can export goods or services or, simply, trade. The word 'processing' that bound 'export' and 'zone' is now unnecessary. Small wonder then, the Commerce ministry is flooded with applications from domestic and foreign companies.

So what do blue chip Indian and foreign companies hope to get when they apply to the Commerce Ministry for an SEZ? The SEZ Act provides tax exemptions to SEZ units and SEZ developers from all indirect taxes including basic customs duty, countervailing duty education cess and, direct taxes. As the Act lays emphasis on providing good infrastructure at low cost for SEZ units and developers, basic inputs needed to achieve that end will attract lower duties.

The act is also mindful of the need for uninterrupted and cheap power. So power plants can be imported or procured from domestic producers without attracting any duty. Transaction costs, the nightmare of every enterprise, will also be minimised for the SEZ participants by the single window clearance at the zone level via the good offices of the Development Commissioner.

SEZs, like the EPZs before them, are supposed to develop backward and forward linkages. Presumably, the means ripple effects on job work and technology transfer of non-SEZs areas, the hinterland. But one of the prominently highlighted attractions is the complete freedom to subcontract, even abroad. An unlike the EPZs of the caution and control era, SEZs today can engage in manufacturing, trading or service activities. Foreign investors will be permitted to develop townships within the SEZs with residential areas, markets play-grounds, clubs, recreation spaces and the like. In China, the idea was a runaway success, though only parts of it – the SEZs reaped benefits. The rest of the country became all the more poor in comparison with the self-perpetuating wealth creators of the eastern provinces. Will it work for India? In 2000 when the SEZ took roots, India was being liberalised with goal being to make economic activity more efficient, cost effective and profitable. Data on economic growth bear testimony to the success of policy, half-baked, reluctant or even accidental at it may have been.

With two successive quarters posting 8 per cent growth in GDP, and a strong export growth despite sluggish G7 growth rates, what magic can the SEZs pull off that the rest of the economy, without those special order privileges? A look at the share of EPZs/ SEZs exports in total manufactured exports presents a different picture. The average annual growth rates of SEZ exports declined continuously over the years, falling steeply over the period from 77 per cent in the first phase (1966-1980) to 7 per cent by 2001- 2003, the fourth phase.

Employment, as a measure of expansion, grew absolutely. But the average annual growth rate shrank continuously. This was despite the fact that four new EPZs became operational in the late 1980s and another EPZ at Vizag came up in 1994" So, after an initial expansion the momentum slowed. Foreign exchange earnings – the most important benefits to be expected from SEZs. In absolute terms the export earnings look very impressive.

It is when you look at the rate of growth that the picture gets bleaker with the figure actually declining. But the true picture is that the value addition, the ratio of net foreign exchange to exports, did not record any appreciable increase.

The rest of the country has always done better than EPZs/ SEZs without the privileges that the zones enjoyed.

(D) *SEZs – A Problem Of Plenty*: It may become a problem of plenty.

Too many SEZs in the state have left the state government worrying about the implications it might have on the state revenue collections, especially sales tax.

The centre cleared nine SEZs in Gujarat in addition to the two in Kandla and Surat, which had already got the nod. Two more proposals by Adani's in Dholera and Essar in Hazira are taking the tally of approved and proposed SEZs in the state to 13.Officials in the sales tax department as well as the finance and industries departments have been discussing the issue of quite some time now. It came up as a major issue when Reliance' Jamnagar SEZ was taken up for clearance but the revenue department's observations were overruled. Experts believe that if the sales are not integrated with DTA properly, it can spell huge losses for the state government.

While transactions within the SEZ shall be exempted from all states taxes including sales tax, VAT, motor spirit tax, luxury tax and entertainment tax, purchase tax and other state taxes " inputs (goods and services) made to SEZ units from Domestic Tariff Area (DTA) will be exempt from sales tax and other state taxes.

Virtues or Reasons To Promote Sez

(A) SEZs enhance competitive efficiency

- Liberalisation forced industry into a drive for internal efficiency thereby stimulating exports and GDP; but domestic external inefficiency has to be tackled for further sharpening export competitiveness. The special economic zone (SEZ) is the strategic answer both to overcome transactional inefficiencies and to take advantage of globally reduced tariff levels under the WTO.
- The SEZ would be specially earmarked geographical zones, which can be developed by private sector or public sector developer or in a PPP mode. Approved industrial units, banks, insurance, etc, can be located here. A state can have more than one SEZ with freedom to the manufacturing unit to establish in any SEZ in any state. State governments will have to attract industry by framing bold policies and providing world-class external infrastructure to the zone.
- Cost of the infrastructure has been reduced by about 20% by exempting all materials and services, purchased by the SEZ developer, from Customs, excise duty, service tax, central sales tax and many states already have a policy of exemption from state taxes. The services provided by the developer are free from services tax and income tax. The dividend payment by the developer or service provider would also be free in the hands of payer and payee. Stamp duty exemption has been provided for the SEZ estate transactions.

- Power plants can be set up within the SEZ for supply to SEZ approved units with the above duty exemptions on capital equipment as well as raw materials and will become a source of efficient, quality power at competitive prices. As there is no customs duty on power imported from abroad these units can perhaps supply power to units in the domestic area (DTA) outside the SEZ also very competitively without high countervailing duties.
- A strategy for reducing cost of finance has also been developed. Offshore banking units (OBU), international financing centres (IFC) and insurance units can be set up in SEZ. Such OBU and IFC will be exempted from tax deducted at source from NRIs. SLR investments or SLR deposits with the RBI will not be required thereby increasing the proportion of deployable funds and reducing cross subsidisation by borrowers. The profits of the OBU relating to SEZ units financing would also be exempted from tax for 10 years. These measures would sharply reduce the OBU's cost of credit for the SEZ approved units. OBUs should be authorised to fund export activities of export units wherever they may be located, i.e. within or outside the SEZ. OBUs would be under RBI rules.
- The SEZ Act (2005) Second schedule ushers in a wide-ranging tax holiday plan. No excise duty, customs, service or sales tax or state taxes (subject to specific state legislation) would be payable on inputs of raw materials, components or services; also on capital equipment.
- The SEZ Act has adopted a one window approach to cut down on time consumed by bureaucratic processes. The Act envisages a board of approvals at the central level. Application for approvals of SEZs has to be made either directly to the board; or through the state government. In the former case, after the board approval, it has to be submitted to the state government. A development commissioner (DC) is to be appointed by Central Government for each SEZ. All powers for approval under 21 laws as per Schedule 1 of SEZ are delegated to this DC except those of approvals by the RBI. The state government are also expected to similarly delegate powers to him and to grant exemption from some laws.
- A proposed business unit in the SEZ has to apply for approval to the board of approvals initially and with appointment of DC, only to the DC. All formalities of customs, excise and other taxes would thereafter be complied with on a self-certification and self-regulation basis by the approved unit, with all filings to the DC office. These measures will hugely

simplify compliances and cut down on time. The State Government can consider giving flexibility in some of the labour laws as in IT industry; but large-scale exemption has not been provided for.

- The approved unit must have positive net foreign earnings in five years. For this purpose Forex cost of asset is to be recovered as per Schedule of Depreciation over five years. Forex cost of know-how, plant depreciation, royalty, and production inputs must be so covered by forex sales earnings. SEZ units are allowed to sell to DTA units on payment of relevant customs duty; and sale to other SEZ units or units under EPCG, EOU, etc, are counted on export. The Act also provides for transfer of ownership of financially weak units with the DC approval and for the tax holiday for the balance period to be available to the new owner.

- To enable existing export activity to get a fillip, EOUs & EPCG units are allowed to move to SEZ; however, their profits would be tax free only for the remaining period of their tax holiday under the currently applicable tax holiday. Industry now has a challenging opportunity to stimulate export based units in a conducive environment without abusing the system.

(B) *Ways to make sezs privately run cities*: SEZs should be viewed as a vehicle for introducing policy and institutional reform that are difficult to introduce more generally but could be feasible in these limited areas. Thus, Indian SEZs have been successful in streamlining the customs procedures and keeping corruption levels low. Lack of single window clearance facilities, centralized governance, stringent labour laws and poor investment climate in SEZs.

The incomplete success of SEZs can been seen from the fact that the share of these zones in the total exports is just around 4.5% when compared to 64% for Mauritius, 40% for Mexico and 20% each for Bangladesh and Sri Lanka. India could introduce laws allowing private companies to own and manage SEZs as a possible solution. With say 10 such zones focusing on exports, India could aim to double its exports every five years. SEZs can become privately run cities. China's Shenzen, for example, has become a city with 10 million people in two decades. If India were to start with 10 new privately run SEZs they could perhaps accommodate 100 million people in two decades.

Indian SEZs have so far seen a lopsided growth in exports, with gems and jewellery being the single largest contributor (as high as 49.87% of the total exports from Noida SEZ), followed by electronics and software. Heavy manufacturing is absent, given that Indian SEZs have a focus on "low volume high value" products. Heavy manufacturing industries are not encouraged to set up their plant in these SEZs because of the relatively small size o these zones.

The large size of the Chinese SEZs is critically important for bringing greater economies of scale, a diversified activity mix and social infrastructure other zone, and attracting private entrepreneurs to China. Indian SEZs need to spread to larger areas. Industrial Dispute Act and Factory Act should be reviewed for the zones. In China, labour contracts are signed between the employer and employees, which regulate the labour relationships. This system provides flexibility to SEZs in labour relationships. This system provides flexibility to SEZs in labour retrenchment during a business downturn.

Providing export credit at cheaper interest rates will also help. Chinese SEZs get export credit at about 4%.

(C) Endorse modern sezs in india: Indian authorities should promote the modern version of SEZs - free ports, and encourage setting up of growth poles and clusters. This is what countries like Korea, Japan, Malayasia, Hong Kong, Taiwan and Singapore did. China has also moved in that direction to promote a Freeport in Pudong, and growth poles and clusters in the Shanghai-Suzhou region. In both versions of SEZs, and growth poles and clusters, an important role was played by the diasporas. The first four Chnese zones were in close proximity to Hong Kong and Taiwan, and were thus able to attract investment and technology from overseas Chinese. The diaspora's role in the development of growth ples and clusters in Eat Asia is also acknowledged. This aspect will probably be ignored in the SEZ legislation.

The traditional version of SEZs cannot succeed in India because there will be too much government control. The commerce ministry will decide who heads the zones, and the same customs officials with a control mindset will operate there. Not to speak of a host of public authorities involved with the implementation of SEZ policies, adding to the confusion. Bureaucratic approval will be time consuming, especially if tax incentives and other sops are to be provided.

We should move towards the modern version of SEZs- free ports. It is a much broader concept than the earlier Chinese SEZs and appropriate for an economy moving towards becoming a developed country. It replicates a First World environment with minimal restrictions, streamlined procedures, sound infrastructure and easy access through world class ports and airports. All activities are eligible, with no export requirements. Sales to domestic tariff areas are allowed, subject to payment of national duties. Permanent Visas are allowed to qualified investors. The process should be demand-driven, with a bulk of investments coming from the private sector - domestic and foreign. Singapore, Hong Kong, Gibraltar and Jebel Ali in Dubai are well known free ports.

(D) *The SEZ bounty*: Among the developers of the approved zones are such prominent corporate names as Reliance, Bajaj Auto, Mahindra

& Mahindra, TCS, Wipro and Ranbaxy, as well as others known for their strategic orientation and long term commitments. Their participation provides a great deal of credibility of the process and reinforces the expectations of proponents of the whole programme.

Before going into the merits of those expectations, one would have to concede that both history and the current policy regime run somewhat counter to them. Over the years that we have had various generations of the concept in place - free trade zones or export processing zones or any other their collective share of the country's total exports has not risen above 5 per cent. This sluggishness was evident even while the growth rate of aggregate exports was quite buoyant, leading to the inescapable cease that these mechanisms simply did not offer a large enough advantage for exporters to locate their facilities in them.

What ever impeded the competitiveness of domestic producers outside the zones apparently had an influence inside them as well. The direct fiscal incentives were obviously not strong enough to offset those advantages. The developer: Private or in partnership with a public agency - will have enough control over the infrastructure and services within the zone to provide his clients with a high degree of assurance with respect to their quality and reliability. The zones tht we have had so far have been managed by public agencies, who, as we all know, cannot usually offer that kind of comfort.

What the developers are essentially banking on is a huge pent up demand for high-quality facilities, the absence of which is deterring a range of investment activity. There is a perception that a lot of investment that would otherwise take place isn't because the infrastructure situation is a huge deterrent. If this problem is solved within the frame work of the SEZ, a substantial part of this potential would be realised.

The commercial interest in SEZ development, is this interest aligned with the country's economic objectives? From the macroeconomic standpoint, it would be a tragedy if the performance of the economy did not stimulate a high level of investment, which would then complete the virtuous circle by itself reinforcing the growth momentum. To the extent that the zones bring about an improvement in the investment climate and thereby contribute to increasing levels of investment in the economy, their impact will be unambiguously positive.

Given the average size of the bigger zones, the developers should be able to offer extremely attractive prices for high-quality services, sweetened by the fiscal benefits they will receive. Although the policy objective is oriented towards exports, it does not prohibit producers from selling in the domestic market, provided they pay all the duties that exports are exempt from, including customs duties on imports to the country. The critical question is: are the zones "investment creating" – attracting investment that wouldn't otherwise take place or "investment –diverting" – inducing relocation from existing facilities? Either way, the business proposition remains intact, but, quite obviously, the macroeconomic interest is best served by the former. Which way will the pendulum swing?

Two factors will determine the direction. The first is the signal that state governments send on allowing de facto labour market flexibility. If they fight shy, producers who already have workers on their rolls will shift in order to take advantage of the infrastructure, while losing nothing on the labour front. However, new business will continue to have a problem with the prospect of a permanent labour force. The second is the degree of dependence on infrastructure outside the zone, which will, almost be definition, not match up to its counterpart within. Again, the logic of relocation is clear, while the logic of start-ups is not.

In short, in the current policy framework the zones undoubtedly offer a great business proposition to the developers. Their overall economic impact, however, depends not only on the zone policy itself but also on the situation with respect to several other issues.

A broad brush picture of epzs/ sezs experiences:

- Under propitious circumstances and good management, EPZs generally achieve the two basic goals of creating employment (especially non-traditional employment and income opportunities for women) and increasing foreign earnings. For instance, Mauritius EPZs boasted 71 per cent of the nation's gross exports in 1994 and employed 16.6 per cent of the work force.
- However, some argue that the net foreign earnings may not constitute a large enough sum to warrant the investments undertaken by the country to accommodate a zone. The opportunity costs of such public investments should be considered more closely.
- Furthermore, there are potential revenue losses from concessions on income taxes and tariffs.
- EPZs/ SEZs are sensitive to the national economic environment. They will perform better when the country pursues sound macroeconomic and realistic exchange rate policies.
- Zones may contribute to the building of national human capital in two ways. Previously unskilled workers have benefited from EPZ presence. Their productivity has increased via job training and learning by doing. The benefits of this skill acquisition is limited however, as most production processes are low-skill and low-tech. The most valuable aspect of this type of employment, aside from the income earned, may be the workers' learning of industrial work discipline and routine.
- Training has also occurred at the supervisory and managerial level, with local employees becoming privy to new organizational and managerial methods, negotiation and marketing skills, general business know-how, foreign contacts and entrepreneurship.
- In addition, a successful zone, per se, is an efficient and competitive industrial infrastructure. As such it provides the country in which

it operates an industrial set-up which it may lack. Most African nations would fit this profile.

- There are many cases of catalyst and demonstration effects on the host economy. These effects, together with the labour training, may be the zone's lasting contributions to the country in which it operates.
- Creation of backward linkages seems largely conditional on the industrial base of the nation. In countries which did not already enjoy a solid industrial base and which adopted EPZs/ SEZs to encourage these linkages and foster a domestic industrial base, some linkage occurred, though it was spotty and inconsistent, with firm zones complaining of the poor quality or the incompatibility of local inputs.
- In countries where a solid industrial base existed prior to the establishment of the EPZs/ SEZs e.g. Taiwan and S. Korea- linkages have occurred. The transfer of know-how and technology was facilitated by the existing technological sophistication and highly educated labour force. In these cases, EPZs/ SEZs fostered economic growth through export promotion. Even at the height of their influence, EPZs/ SEZs never acquired a prominent role either in terms of exports value or employment creation in S. Korea or Taiwan.
- Wages in most EPZs/ SEZs are equal or higher than average wages outside the zones. Labour work safety and health laws in many zones have raised concerns with regards to workers' welfare. The size, nationality and corporate policy of the firm, the type of industrial production, labour market conditions and the country's institutions and regulations play a determining role in establishing the wage rate, workers' rights and work environment in EPZs/ SEZs.
- Overall, the EPZs/ SEZs did not universally fulfill the role of "engines of industrialization and growth" as some proponents had anticipated. They have been an engine —among others – in the economy, when they have been given their proper place as a policy tool, and where proper perspective is taken as to the ultimate achievements and costs. EPZs/ SEZs' greatest contribution seems to be job creation and income generation. Their lasting legacy can be three fold. They can contribute to building human capital, and through their demonstration and catalyst effects on the country entrepreneur pool. Also, an efficient, competitive zone is an industrial infrastructure that many countries lack.
- EPZs/ SEZs face new challenges in the increasingly global economy. Rapid changes in consumption preferences and the resulting competitive pressures to meet this demand can affect the locational

choices of investors. Furthermore, increased product sharing is changing the reducing the need for country specific technical expertise. This phenomenon has a differential impact on industries as a function of their technical sophistication.

- Exclusion of a country from a preferential trade/ integration arrangement seems to impact EPZ/ SEZ firms which operate there. These firms may or may not flourish from the membership of their host country in preferential trade arrangements. The EPZs/ SEZs firms' initial product mix, market orientation, technological sophistication, strategic business planning and adaptability to the new competitive conditions will have influence on their continued success and contributions to the country in which they operate.

SEZ DRIVE IN GUJARAT

What is clear however is that the successful development strategies of some countries/regions cannot produce the same salubrious results when implemented in other national settings? When China opened some coastal pockets for foreign direct investment, these SEZs quickly blossomed into vibrant export platforms and created backward linkages with the immediate hinterland. Whereas, when landlocked Mongolia turned the entire country into a free trade and investment zone in the late 1990s, the inflow of foreign capital was a mere trickle compared to China's experience. This case is that the time-tested effective growth policy package for a coastal economy, and minor modifications of it, are unlikely to work for an interior economy. Gujarat being a coastal state where a number of prerequisites for attaining and sustaining high growth are already in place is a very strong candidate for following an outward-oriented growth strategy.

China's boom has come in three main ways:

- First, agriculture boomed as soon as the commune system was dismantled, and peasant farming resumed on the basis of household plots of land.
- Second, rural industry was greatly liberalized after 1978, especially in the form of TVEs (Township & Village Enterprises)
- Third, urban export-oriented enterprises were encouraged by the designation of a growing number of SEZs, coastal open cities, and economic and technological development zones (EDTZs), all designed to encourage manufacturing exports.

These special areas received various kinds of favourable tax and regulatory treatment, such as tax holidays, duty-free access to imported inputs and capital goods needed for export production. Thus, the SEZs and other special areas were akin to the export processing zones that had been used in other parts of Asia as part of their initial export-led growth.

SEZs in the manufacturing sector can play a major role in the overall growth strategy of the state. Virtually all of the East Asian countries have utilized SEZs to help attract foreign investment and to initiate the process of manufacturing export-led growth. SEZs have attempted to carve out a geographical zone in which export businesses can conduct profitable export-oriented activities, exempt from costly regulations, tax laws, and labour standards that apply more generally within the country. In general, the relatively successful industrial policies have had a few common characteristics:

- They have aimed to promote exports, rather than to protect the domestic market;
- They have provided subsidies on the basis of successful performance (e.g. the growth of exports) rather than to cover losses;
- They have given temporary rather than permanent subsidies (e.g. a five-year tax holiday for new export firms).

At the centre of China's export strategy were the special economic zones in which favourable export conditions were assured. These SEZs, along China's coastline, were designed to give foreign investors and domestic enterprises favourable conditions for rapid export promotion. All key aspects of the export environment were secured. Exporters, for example, were allowed to import intermediate products and capital goods duty free. They were given generous tax holidays. The exporters were assured decent physical infrastructure, often through the provision of land, power, physical security, and transport to the ports, within specially created industrial parks.

The Open Door Policy had five major goals:

- Import of foreign Capital
- Import of advanced technology
- Import of western management know-how
- Export promotion and import substitution.
- Employment generation and improvement of skills for the Chinese labour force

FDI inflows did not respond immediately in large volumes to the establishment of the SEZs in southern China (1979 in Guangdong, and 1980 in Fujian), partly because out of caution and partly because the liberal regulatory framework began to be introduced only in 1982. FDI flows started pouring in only from 1984 onward (when it doubled from US$0.6 billion in 1983 to US$1.3 billion in 1984). This jump in total FDI in 1984 was not simply due to the opening of 14 Open Coastal Cities and 10 Economic and Technological Development Zones that year, but because there was an enormous rise in FDI into the existing SEZs. FDI into Guangdong increased from US$245 million in 1983 to US$ 542 million in 1984.

As far as FDI is concerned, Gujarat is not rated as one of the most attractive destinations for FDI in India, perhaps ranked around 5th or 6th out of total States and Union Territories. It is interesting to note that while Gujarat is perhaps next only to Maharashtra as far as attracting domestic private investment is concerned; it does not score as well when it comes to foreign direct investment. This issue needs to be looked at from several different angles, for instance is the State doing enough on the marketing front, not just in the U.S., but also in other parts of the westerns world; have there been any exercises undertaken to understand what could be the issues and concerns of MNCs when it comes to investing in Gujarat; are the investment incentives offered by the State in line with others, such as Maharashtra or Tamil Nadu? Perhaps, a strategy focusing on the comparative advantages of Gujarat, relative to its other competitor states in India needs to be put in place that highlights for MNCs why they should consider Gujarat ONLY if investments are planned in X, Y, or Z sectors.

Coastal, urban-based industry can serve both the internal market and the international market, and can more readily make logistical links with foreign suppliers and customers than can interior-based enterprises. New export-oriented units are therefore heavily concentrated on the coast. As China's experience demonstrates, trade liberalization in a low-wage, surplus-labour environment permits a rapid expansion of export-oriented industry, which can absorb large numbers of workers to provide goods for the world market in real, significant foreign exchange earning private sector activity.

The concentration of FDI in the coastal provinces of China and especially in five of them has been increasing over time: from 1992 to 2002, coastal provinces received 80 per cent of FDI (against 70% in 1979-1991). Foreign trade was even more concentrated in coastal provinces which were responsible for more than 90 per cent of foreign trade (88% in 1992). Thus these coastal provinces showed a close relationship between FDI and foreign trade and this relationship has strongly influenced the economic openness of the coastal Chinese regions vis-â-vis the inward regions.

At the end of the nineties, non-coastal provinces were still closed economies, as evidenced by the ratio of foreign trade and FDI in GDP, whereas several areas of Eastern China were becoming internationalized economies (Guangdong, Fujian, Tianjin, and Shanghai). The rapid expansion of export oriented industries based on imported inputs had accelerated the integration of coastal economies in international trade and production networks, but this had possibly been achieved at the expense of backward and forward linkages with the rest of the economy and especially at the expenses of inland economies. Regional breakdown of FDI shows a dividing line between coastal provinces and inland provinces in attracting foreign capital. Since 1992, four fifths of FDI have been concentrated in coastal provinces and more precisely in five of them; Guangdong, Jiangsu, Fujian, Shanghai municipality and Shandong received more than 60 per cent of total FDI. The private money inland has moved to the coast, with net capital flows moving from the lagging West to the prosperous Eastern belt, where earnings are much higher.

Thus the coastal regions have grown extraordinarily rich and other regions do not have a share in their growth. Unemployment in other regions is rising and includes those leaving farms and others retrenched by state-owned enterprises (SOEs). To make matters worse, the inland region has suffered a brain drain, as skilled and entrepreneurial youth migrate east for higher salaries and better living conditions. Some 115 million migrant workers are seeking jobs as migrants in booming cities along the coast.

As most of FDI in China is export-motivated, FDI would prefer provinces that provide easier access to sea transportation. Unlike policy, however, geography has another key growth mechanism beside FDI, and that second growth mechanism (which is more important) is rural enterprises. Since a large (and growing) proportion of China's exports are produced by rural enterprises, it has been natural for these export-oriented rural enterprises to be established in the coastal provinces. Our view is that these rural enterprises had generated agglomeration effects that induced new rural enterprises (not necessarily export-oriented) to locate themselves in the same localities.

The prediction of this agglomeration effects hypothesis is that the positive impulse from export would create a vibrant rural industrial sector that would make the coastal region a major growth pole. The SEZs have allowed for the transfer of management know-how from abroad. This is important to India/ Gujarat as it expands its experiment with market based economic policies and tries to compete in the global marketplace. There is enough evidence to show that the SEZs have resulted in true export creation, not just diversion. Restrictions on exports and imports have also been liberalized, compared with pre-1979 levels.

The domestic resource cost ratio, a measure of the financial benefit that an enterprise can generate from its exports, is significantly lower in the market oriented cities in China than elsewhere in the country. This shows also that these enterprises are operating as profit maximizers and are not being state-subsidized. Designation as an SEZ contributes significantly to developing infrastructure in the province in question. A case in point is Guangdong which lagged behind Shanghai significantly in terms of infrastructure. Now it has become one of the foremost developed areas in this respect.

Enterprises in the SEZs are offered preferential treatment in terms of taxation, import licensing, and tariffs. The most important difference between the SEZs and the rest of China is that investment decisions are made autonomously, not subject to central planning. Local authorities can implement policies to attract investment and to develop local infrastructure as long as they can raise the funds to do so. This has created a climate that is very conducive to foreign investment. Enterprises in the zones are both state-owned and non-state owned. Non-state owned enterprises can be fully foreign-funded and owned, equity joint ventures, or contractual joint ventures.

Additionally, SEZs enjoy considerable autonomy in investment, pricing, housing, and labour and land management policies. There has been a dramatic impact on employment generation in the SEZ provinces, and this has had favourable spillover effects on the rest of the country. Much of this is employment generation, not simply diversion. There is some concern that the jobs are primarily low-skill and low-paying.

However, there is no question that labour is being released from the less productive agricultural sector to a more 'modern' sector with higher returns. This has stimulated the growth of light industry and service activities. The open door policies further helped because small-scale enterprises set up initially to meet domestic demand can expand by exporting labour intensive manufactured goods. Thus the huge potential gains from specialization and trade have been effectively exploited, and significant amounts of employment have been generated through the zones.

Consistent with the experience of other East Asian countries such as the Republic of Korea, Singapore, Taiwan, and Thailand – is that exports are key to high GDP growth rates. Successful export expansion in turn depends on a policy package which conveys a clear message that the country will give priority to export-oriented firms rather than sheltering import-competing industries. China has benefited greatly from the clear direction its reforms have taken, in spite of occasional bumps along the way.

Focussed sectors in gujarat sez for competitive advantages:

Kandla:

- Engineering
- Chemical and allied products
- RMG
- Plastic Units
- Packaging industries
- Trading Units

Mundra:

- Light & Heavy Engineering.
- Auto & Component
- Textile & Apparel
- Agro & Food Processing
- Drugs & Pharma
- Chemical & Fertilizer

Surat:

- Diamond
- Gems & Jewellery
- Pharmaceuticals

- Chemicals
- RMG
- Light Engineering
- IT Hardware
- Tobacco

SEZ IN GUJARAT – ENTREPRENEURS' PERSPECTIVE

(A) *Quality of Governance*: We attempted to analyse the entrepreneurs' perspective on the quality of governance across the selected zones in Gujarat through the units to understand and analyse.

- First, the quality of governance in general is above the average in almost all the cases.
- Second, the factor of 'simplified rules' suggesting that the rules in these zones are complex and that this leads to increase in delays in bureaucratic decisions, holds true for Kandla Zone.
- Third, custom clearance powers are delegated to the zonal authorities. Moreover the government has implemented the plan of self certification. This might have helped in reducing the level of rent seeking.

Note: If provision of amenities such as on-site canteens, day cares and health services enhances the employees' work and living standard and improves their productivity while reducing absenteeism and labour turn-over. Privately run, high-end zones tend to fulfill these services better than public SEZs. The government should apply uniform regulations to all zones.

(B) *Incentives*: Sometimes it is argued that companies are not attracted by incentives per se and that good infrastructure and cheap labour availability are important (ICIR, 1992). To understand more, we checked with the units in these zones to know: 'how important it is to offer fiscal incentives for attracting investment in the zones?' The fiscal incentives are considered very important in determining the attractiveness of the zones. Over 85 per cent of the respondents in India regarded them as very important. It is therefore important to analyse the incentive package offered by these zones to the zone units.

Prior to 1981, income tax concession plans were not given to the zone units. Tax holidays of 5 years were extended to the units only in 1981. Besides, there were no standardized procedures for exemption from excise duties. In Kandla, on the other hand, all inputs were entitled to excise exemptions. There was no state sales tax exemption for Kandla until 1974. Central sales tax was not exempted until 1978. Domestic tariff area sale was permitted only against import licenses and the rates of duty were exorbitant. Subcontracting of production was not allowed.

Some favourable policy changes were introduced in the incentive package during the 1980s. The condition of import license for DTA sale was waived in 1987. Subcontracting for job work in DTA was allowed with the approval of Assistant Commissioner of customs. Sub contracting procedures relating to indemnity bonds and revolving bank guarantees were simplified and in 1986, reimbursement of CST was granted to EPZ units. There were no significant changes in other laws and procedures pertaining to EPZs.

During the 1990s, when the government undertook to simplify and rationalize the tax structure and major tax cuts were being introduced in the rest of the economy, incentive package was made more attractive for the zone units also. Though there was no change in the tax holiday, duty on DTA sales was reduced to 50% of custom duty in 1991 and the rate of duty on sale of rejects was reduced to 50% of the applicable duty. Besides, DTA sales entitlement for agro based EPZ units was raised in 1992 to 50% of production.

EPZ units were given option in 1995 to switch over to export promotion capital goods (EPCG) plan. In the EXIM policy for 1997-02, additional DTA sale was allowed to units based on indigenous raw materials, provided they fulfilled the export obligation. Electronic hardware units were allowed to sell upto 50% of production in the domestic market on payment of applicable duties. Software units were permitted to effect online DTA sales. An attractive package of incentives was offered to SEZ units in 2000 and thereafter both in Fiscal and Non Fiscal.

Note: Unless domestic firms benefit from such tax (income, trade) privileges, bestowing them on SEZ firms discriminate against the domestic firms excluded from the zone. The special treatment acts as a barrier to connect with the host economy. More specifically, if domestic firms do not benefit from functional drawback policies, the tariff free inputs for the firms in the zone acts as import subsidies competing against domestic input production and discouraging creation of backward linkages. If countries do not allow domestic sales of SEZ products, the potential for forward linkages vanishes as well.

(C) *Infrastructure Facilities by the Zones*: The analysis of the infrastructure facilities directly provided by the zone authorities in the three zones. No exclusive arrangements have been made for water, electricity or telecommunications by the zone authorities in Gujarat except Mundra which plans to have its own thermal power plant and water supply in the near future. The units have to depend on the state boards for electricity supply. Units may arrange water from outside the zones. Zones are providing, financial infrastructure such as banks, ATMs and post offices but the units can use banks outside the zones also. Some of the zones are providing other trade related infrastructure such as warehousing facilities, ICD, transport facilities and other physical infrastructure such as water purifiers and effluent treatment plant etc.

The firms or units in the SEZ, were asked to comment about the quality of infrastructure and found that water and electricity are two most important aspects of infrastructure. The satisfaction level of entrepreneurs in respect of these infrastructures facilities available/ provided in SEZ. Water is not equally important for all the firms but essential in Pharmaceuticals, FMCG, Dyeing and Bleaching industries but in rest of the industries, it is required primarily for the drinking purpose. Some of the units in Kandla had shown their concern on the quality of water provided in the SEZ, as they have to depend on water tankers and further water treatment required for their usage. This results in more wastage of their resources and adds to their cost.

Table. Evaluation of the Factor Availability and Factor Cost

Sr. No.	Factors
1	Lower real estate cost
2	Lower wages
3	Availability of skilled labour
4	Domestically manufactured parts and components
5	Availability of concessional finance
6	Availability of cheap raw materials

Evalutaion of governance:

1	Single window clearance
2	Custom clearance
3	Easy information on zones
4	Accessibilty to rules
5	Simplified rules

Evaluation of the factors crucial for the success of the zones: Investor's perspective in descending order.

Sr. No.	Factors
1	Tax Concessions
2	Physical Infrastructure within zone
3	Infrastructure external to the zone
4	Proximity to port, airport and bigger cities
5	Governance of the Zone
6	Exemption from other industrial laws
7	Regional development
8	Availability of raw materials
9	Social Infrastructure
10	Subsidies

- *Power*: Power availability is rated satisfactory in major zones. Power cuts are very frequent outside the zones especially in Kutch. Many firms however have installed their own power generators. This was mainly due to fluctuation in power supply or to meet power failures. The major concern for the units in these zones is cost of power available to them than the rest of the country. The charges are the highest in the country. Drastic steps to reduce the power cost are taken by the SEZs to make these units more competitive. For e.g. In Mundra SEZ, apart from the power supply from State Board, Adani Group is planning to set up its own thermal power plant in the SEZ. This will not only ensure continuous power supply but also will bring down the cost from Rs. 4.5 per unit to Rs. 2/- per unit.

Transport: Transport facilities are also considered important and vital as it relates not only to the prosperity of the region but also plays a vital role in their logistics cost and time duration. Transport facilities within the zones are almost non existent in all the three zones and hence are below average. From Gandhidham to Mundra transport for the zones and road conditions are considered to be below average and pathetic.

In most of the zones except Surat, transport facilities for the zones are average. Poor and congested roads sharply increase the time for transporting the containers as well as movement of people to and from the Port/ SEZ. This also results in time loss for the labours working in these zones. If these zones provide company buses to carry labour to the zones it will be of great help in saving time and availability of perennial labour supply and also to avoid heavy rush and traffic jams in the morning and evening hours. Rail transport system is not well developed either in Kandla or Mundra except for containers. Thus the outside road infrastructure connecting the zones with port, airport and other social utilities is poor in these zones. Port facilities are rated best at Mundra and Kandla when compared with the rest of the ports of the country but it has to travel a long way to match the standards of some its immediate neighbours such as Colombo or Singapore.

- *Port*: The port in Western part of Gujarat has the deepest draft of the country and is sufficiently deep for large international vessels. Feeder ships connect the country with Singapore or other countries from where these are loaded in larger vessels. This increases time and cost of transportation. Besides, cargo handling facilities are also stated to be poor when compared to Hong Kong or Singapore but far better than available in some of the Indian ports. Non availability of port near Surat SEZ has proven to be a great disadvantage as it has to depend on JNPT or Navi Mumbai for transportation of goods and generally these ports remain congested all through out the year. Indian ports are also stated to be characterized by delays and inefficiencies. Cost of Indian goods can be brought down if proper and timely handlings of goods are carried out at ports.
- *Airport*: Lack of international airports at Surat or Kandla/ Mundra may also have an adverse effect on the progress of these SEZs. For

instance, Gems and Jewellery business being a high value added item requires air connectivity. This can be one of the main reasons for SEEPZ benefiting from the Gem and Jewellery industry irrespective of Surat being the major centre for processing, due to its proximity to both port and international airport. The same can be said for Kandla/ Mundra, as foreign investors find it difficult to reach these places as it requires 4 to 5 hours of road travel, which can be taxing on these investors.

Note: Early proponents of EPZs considered them as potential hubs for non-urban, decentralized industrial development. They favoured placing EPZs away from urban and populated centres to encourage job creation and economic development in rural areas and to reduce the rural-urban migration. It soon became clear that EPZs would not flourish in such an environment unless they were fitted with easy access to sea ports or airports, energy and water sources, good roads, above average (by country standards) communication facilities and available and adequately skilled workers. The Bataan Zone in the Philippines, located in a mountainous area some 160 km from Manila, is a prime example of a poor locational choice.

Despite the government spending nearly $200 million in 1973 on building the zone (Warr, 1985), it failed to reach its goals due to it isolation from the country's industrial centre and poor infrastructure. The same occurred to the Puerto Limon zone on Costa Rica's Atlantic/Caribbean cost (Ryan, et. al., 1993).

The Zone Franche d'Inga in Zaire is a third example of this miscalculation. It was located in a remote area of the country, with poor infrastructure to service it and few workers with adequate skills to satisfy its labour demands. The new philosophy highlights the importance of locating EPZs near or in industrial/urban areas. This satisfies the labour needs of the zone firms and allows for more spillover effects. Such a locational choice also ensures more accessible and uninterrupted utilities, better infrastructure and services, and proximity to airports and sea ports.

- *Communication*: Communication facilities are considered to be the most satisfactory of all the infrastructure facilities. Given the information revolution taking place these zones, have benefited a lot. But still more can be done by providing facilities such as broadband connectivity etc.

Apparently, overall quality of infrastructure in the zones is considered above average when compared to rest of the zones in the country. However, infrastructure external to the zones such as roads and ports are not found to be adequate in general. When compared to the zones of South East Asian countries or Middle East infrastructure needs a major thrust.

(D) *State-run sezs lose out to private competitors*: Despite the hype generated by the Government over its Special Economic Zone (SEZ) lack of infrastructure are turning many big business houses away from the state SEZ.

Though the government is of the opinion that SEZ policy would lead employment generation, the lack of enough land required for setting up huge units, lack of clarity over the labour laws in a SEZ are turning big entrepreneurs away from the se SEZs.

Many point that out that state SEZ lack social infrastructure, such as educational institutions, entertainment centres, accommodation for employees etc. Even the tax sops are not acting in impetus. But when the state SEZ lack these, private players such as Adani Group under the banner of Mundra SEZ Ltd., Reliance Industries Ltd., and Seaking Infrastructure Ltd., are planning to take the state-run SEZs head-on by offering the social infrastructure within their proposed SEZs along with hughe lands devoted to the industries with the offer for providing them flexibility to expand their units in future if required.

While the Adanis have already initiated civil work for its mega-SEZ project to be spread over 10,000 hectares of land at Mundra in Kutch and have finalized plans for setting up health facilities with Apollo Group, discussions are on between Adanis and various educational institutions to set up schools/ colleges within the proposed SEZ. Reliance also finalized its plan to setup its port-based SEZ in the Jamnagar coast with an investment ranging between Rs. 12,000-15,000 crore which according to sources also would be armed with various facilities for the family members of the employees working in the industrial units to be setup in the SEZ. Reliance is also planning to setup a technical and management school within its proposed SEZ and a school till 12th Standard on the line of its Kokilaben Ambani School at Vadianar may be setup within the SEZ campus or adjoining areas.

Reliance like the Ambanis is expected to spread its SEZ on over 10,000 hectares of land thus offering flexibility for future expansion for the industries to operate from within its SEZ. However, the state run SEZs such as Kandla feel that they could have hiked up their business in several multiplications provided they could have offered required infrastructure and social infrastructure to the industries which are already in and these SEZs could have also attracted bigger industry players. As far as Kandla Special Economic Zone (KASEZ) is concerned, it is the most spacious of all the Special Economic Zone Export Processing Zones of India.

Though authorities have termed it as "The Paradise for free enterprise" industry representatives are not happy with the infrastructure at Kandla. Lack of flights discourages foreigners and high power and water charges push up input costs. Lack of servicing globally had caused despair to international customers. There are no flights to Kandla and clients have to drive from Bhuj to the unit in the Kandla SEZ.

While power was available at Rs. 2 per unit in Indore, Madhya Pradesh SEZ, at Kandla SEZ it cost Rs. 5 per unit. Also water supplies are irregular, for which the units had to buy water tankers at huge cost.

In the current global scenario, it is possible for Gujarat to achieve very dynamic growth based upon labour-intensive manufacturing that combines the vast supply of its labour, including skilled managerial and engineering labour, with foreign capital, technology, and markets. On this basis, the East Asian economies have achieved growth rates consistently above 6 per cent per year up until their financial crisis, and China has managed growth in excess of 10 per cent per year in the 1990s.

Traditional textiles and apparel, electronics and other labour-intensive operations remains an area where India in general and Gujarat in particular could do a lot more than in the past. Gujarat has the resource base, it has the entrepre-neurship, has the access to the sea coast, a vast labour force, it has everything that coastal China has had except the interest of the bureaucrats which neglected this for a long time and which even today underemphasizes the role of industrial facilities, underemphasizes the role of infrastructure, of land area, of effective port facilities that one needs to sustain high rates of growth.

But it is, a place where one could find tens of millions of jobs over the next few years in real, significant foreign exchange earning private sector activity. This would require a change of attitude, a real promotion of these sectors both at the state and central government levels. The reform process in India has so far mainly concentrated at the federal level. India has yet to free up its state governments sufficiently so that they can add much greater dynamism to the reforms. Greater freedom to the states will help foster greater competition among themselves.

The state governments in India need to be viewed as potential agents of rapid and salutary change. While some healthy competition is evident in India among the three southern states of Andhra Pradesh, Karnataka, and Tamil Nadu, and the two western states of Gujarat and Maharashtra, however, much of the rest of Indian states are yet to begin competing with each other. Brazil, China, and Russia are examples where regional governments have taken the lead in pushing reforms and prompting further actions by the central government.

Decentralization has been crucial in making the SEZs attractive to investment. Special policies that allow a greater portion of firms' profits to be retained instead of being transferred to the Centre are notable. China's economic system is highly decentralized and policy implementation is now largely under the control of provincial authorities. Hence in fast growing provinces, provincial and local officials have been deeply involved in the development process in general and export promotion in particular. Besides their role in facilitating foreign investment, there are a number of ways in which local governments promote exports.

The central government sets mandatory targets or export quotas for only a limited number of items or by volume. But in some provinces, like Jiangsu, the export quota system is far more elaborate. Moreover, taking advantage of their monophony power, TCs are able to buy goods at prices well below domestic prices, making their output competitive in the world market. Operating within central government guidelines, provincial governments have been expanding Direct Export Rights to enterprises, but the criteria for doing so are very stringent. As a result only 5 per cent of China's exports are produced by enterprises with Direct Export Rights. Also within central government guidelines, local authorities decide the allocation of imported raw materials by sharing locally retained foreign exchange earnings among enterprises, collectives, and town and village enterprises in different sectors.

Provinces and cities also indirectly subsidize exports by providing critical inputs like electric power to export-oriented enterprises. Additional incentives are provided in the form of higher bonuses for managers and employees awarded on the basis of export performance. Finally, local authorities establish joint ventures between FTCs and enterprises to promote exports.

The success of Gujarat lies in the factor that export growth should be diversified away from traditional sectors, especially raw materials, into non-traditional sectors, especially manufactured goods. Gujarat may lack in the technology by itself to be competitive in manufactured goods. Therefore, it has to invite foreign direct investors to provide the capital and the expertise to achieve export competitiveness in a wide range of sectors, including electronics, apparel, plastic goods, ceramics, and many other labour-intensive sectors.

In each sector, the key is to link foreign investor capital and expertise with a large and low-cost labour force. The foreign investors should bring in the product design, specialized machine tools and capital goods, key intermediate products, and knowledge of world marketing channels. The State Government should assure these foreign investors certain key conditions for profitability, such as low taxes, reliable infrastructure, physical security, adequate power, decent logistics for the import and export of goods, and so forth.

At the centre of State's export strategy should be SEZs in which favourable export conditions should be assured. These SEZs, along Gujarat's coastline, should be designed to give foreign investors and domestic enterprises favourable conditions for rapid export promotion. All key aspects of the export environment should be secured. Exporters, apart from being allowed to import intermediate products and capital goods duty free along with generous tax holidays should also be provided with decent physical infrastructure, often through the provision of land, power, physical security, and transport to the ports, within specially created industrial parks.

State's export environment suffers from several institutional weaknesses. Vast majority of India's employment is informal, in small, tax-evading, inefficient enterprises. Equally remarkably, India's legislation continues to restrict the entry of large firms, or the growth of small firms into large firms, in several areas of potential comparative advantage. Thus, garments, toys, shoes and leather products continue to be reserved, to a varying extent, for small-scale producers. Such restrictions virtually assure China's dominance in these sectors compared with India. India's tax and tariff structures similarly remain anti-export biased. India's high overall tariff rates, especially tariffs on intermediate products that are used by exporters, impose a heavy indirect tax on export competitiveness.

Deregulation of the private sector is perhaps one of the most critical areas in the context of India's reforms. Since almost 90-plus per cent of the workforce is in the informal sector, it is of utmost importance to deregulate the private sector so as to get the unorganized sector workforce in the mainstream. Workers in large firms in the formal sector have a virtual guarantee of continued employment according to the Industrial Disputes Act. For firms of 100 employees or more, reductions in the workforce must be upon the permission of state government, which is almost never granted. Remarkably, loss-making firms are also not allowed to close their operations without government consent.

Indeed with a more open and deregulated economy, and a positive and prompt decision making State Government, Gujarat may well be in a position to perform as China has done over the last two decades. The proper elements of a revised growth strategy - rapid export-growth- should now be clear. Both the hardware and software of export-led growth need revamping. On the hardware side, the development of industrial parks for exports should be greatly intensified and enhanced. Private developers need the freedom to acquire urban and peri-urban land and to develop privately financed infrastructure in support of exports.

The government must take urgent measures to reduce export costs, including private-sector provision of port services; zero tariff ratings on capital and intermediate goods imports used for export (based on an effective duty exemption plan); enhanced export-oriented infrastructure, especially roads to the ports and airports, reliable power supply, and telecommunications facilities to support export zones. Labour legislation should be revised to allow managerial flexibility in the hire and dismissal of workers in export-oriented sectors.

The reservation of labour intensive sectors to small-scale enterprises should simply be scrapped. The government should actively encourage inward investment in export-oriented sectors, allowing 100 per cent foreign ownership without administrative interference, and with the provision of generous tax holidays as necessary to attract internationally mobile capital from other locations.

As a general matter, Gujarat has an advantage over other states. Fortunately, there is a vast amount of economic reform that can be carried out to improve conditions in rural Gujarat. There is no reason for expensive and counter-productive charity for these parts of the state, and still less any case for holding back the fast-growing coastal regions. Perhaps the key step is to improve the most basic infrastructure so that the vast rural populations can take part in more rapid state economic growth. They will do so through increased exports to coastal regions, and greatly improved productivity for local production.

Rural Gujarat needs a new social contract, in which there will be a reliable infrastructure supplied at commercial prices rather than given for free. The Government's commitment, at the state level should be that every village will be assured at least minimal telephone service, clean water, a road to the regional market, and reliable power; but that every village will be responsible for covering the commercial costs of those services on a normal user-fee basis. Technological changes in each of these areas (telephony, water, road building and maintenance, and power) allow these key sectors to be organized, at least in part, on the basis of competitive, private-sector producers, who will provide the initial financing of the investments in return for a reliable stream of user charges over time. The availability of infrastructure services, such as power, telecom, and roads in rural Gujarat can significantly help develop rural industry in Gujarat.

The Township and Village Enterprises operate outside of the state plan, and largely without funds from state banks. Therefore, they are subject to quite rigorous market competition and hard budget constraints. TVEs should be linked with the urban areas for development. This will facilitate the transportation of goods between rural and urban areas, and rising income and productivity in rural areas. As for urban enterprises, this link would open up a bigger market and help in diversification or restructuring which is currently under constraint due to area limitations.

Rural enterprises can also compete in the cities with their products having the advantage of relatively low labour costs. In this way, they will help absorb surplus labour locally, thereby resulting in less rural-to-urban migration (population in urban areas have reached levels far above what the urban cities can efficiently accommodate given their capacity to provide urban infrastructure services). Urban enterprises will also provide more employment opportunities since they would have a larger market. In addition, the linkage will benefit the rural industries via flow of technology and information.

SEZ - LESSONS FOR GUJARAT

- To attain and sustain high rates of economic growth, follow a two-pronged growth strategy, wherein the first prong is export-led growth, and the second prong is rural improvement. For the first prong, lessons from the Chinese coastal provinces are particularly instructive, since the Chinese provinces achieved in the past twenty years the kind of export-led growth that Indian states could have achieved, but have so far failed to achieve because of poor public policies. With regard to the second prong, Gujarat needs a specific strategy to bring modern economic growth to rural Gujarat, through a concerted campaign of infrastructure upgrading and appropriate re-design of state policy.

- Establish SEZs all along the Gujarat coast on an expedited time table. This is critical in view of the fact that several Indian states are in the process of setting-up such SEZs and the sooner Gujarat's SEZs are up and running, the better it will be for attracting both potential domestic and foreign investors. These SEZ companies of Gujarat should not be bound by minimum export performance requirements. Companies need to balance or have positive net foreign exchange earnings. Put briefly, when benchmarked against Chinese SEZs, broadly, the Indian SEZs are by and large at par with them.
- Identify key sectors where Gujarat offers comparative advantage for investors relative to other Indian states;
- Working with the federal government move expeditiously to reform labour laws, especially with respect to the SEZs. Labour laws in Chinese SEZs are more favourable, allowing labour contracts to be modified or rescinded through consultations between both parties.
- An exit policy needs to be formulated such that firms can exit from the market freely. While it would be incorrect to ignore the need for, and potential merit of, certain safeguards while designing an exit policy, it is also important to recognize that safeguards, if wrongly designed and/or poorly enforced would turn into barriers which may adversely affect the health of the firms. Exit policy needs to be designed in a way that it removes exit barriers and at the same time protects the necessary internal order in the firms.
- Make investments on a much higher level to upgrade existing major port facilities and to use minor ports more efficiently.
- Make the necessary changes to align Gujarat's incentives structures in line with other competitor Indian states.
- The State Government should develop networks with Gujarati Non-resident Indians for them to invest in Gujarat. As a follow-up of the Global Investors Summit, quick and timely follow-up action is critical
- The State Government should explore if Township and Village enterprises (TVEs) can be set-up in rural Gujarat. The TVEs have huge potential to fuel growth in rural Gujarat.

(B) *Good governance results in better performance*: The governments' role can be outlined as follows. They provide the necessary legal framework and potentially, the initial bureaucratic effort such as launching a feasibility study, encouraging domestic private sector involvement and marketing the zone abroad.

In drawing up the legal and administrative framework for a zone, the government should be fully appraised of the nature of incentives offered and the type of industries they might attract (light or heavy industry, long or short-term investments, etc) to ensure that they match the government's general policy framework and expectations.

In a majority of cases the governments invest in the creation or upgrading of the infrastructure necessary for the zone. These include improvement of roads, ports, and airports near the designated zone location. Generally, governments have to secure a steady supply of electricity and water (building of new power plant/dam), and expanding the country's international communication capacity.

Once the initial legal, bureaucratic and physical framework has taken shape, the government provides (and shoulder the cost of) the ongoing services such as customs, regulatory and supervisory duties, leaving the running of the business to a private corporation or managerial group.

SEZs in Gujarat should be streamlined, prompt and efficient bureaucracy and customs control in all stages of the creation and running of an EPZ is crucial to its success. It greatly influences the attractiveness of the zone to foreign and domestic investors and the eventual performance and success of the firms established in it.

All points to the fact that, regardless of whether the zones are private or public, governance is key to the success of EPZs. The provision of efficient bureaucratic and economic services, a clear and transparent legal and regulatory structure, an unfettered and stable policy framework, and non-preferential treatment of economic actors allow an arena prone to success.

(C) *Government holds the key*: *Industrial Policy*: While the policies announced by the State govt. is quite dynamic and pragmatic and is basically growth driven yet the implementation of policy is halting and hesitant. It leaves much to be desired in respect of promotion of Industries large, medium and small, infrastructure development, employment intensive parks, Hi-tech parks, investment parks, trade centres as well as backward area development, environmental protection, and export promotion. Tardy progress made in these directions so far indicates poor and weak follow up and lack of publicity of the incentives and facilities available to industries. Corrective measures are therefore required to be taken to sustain and accelerate industrial growth in Gujarat so that with maximisation of larger manufacturing capacities and productivity, enhanced employment opportunities could be generated and enlargement of exports could be achieved.

Leads and Lags in Industrial Growth

It has to be realised that Gujarat's inherent advantages of low labour cost, intelligent man power, highly qualified and trained man power in the form of pool of scientists, prolonged period of industrial peace, entrepreneurial edge of the people, good grasp of technology and proactive govt. attitude and approach and supportive bureaucracy etc. should have taken it right to the top of the league on the industrial firmament of the country. This potential has not been realised reflects that there are still problem areas on which govt. needs to pay special attention to enhance competitiveness of our products both in the domestic and international market. This is the crux of the matter which should not be ignored while evolving and implementing

Power Availability and Rates

Periodical inadequate and irregular supply of power and high cost thereof obstructs industrial growth and hampers competitiveness. The power cost to total expenditure in major industrial units in Gujarat works out to 4.3% to 11.77% whereas in chemical industry units it comes to 13.15% to 37.3%. Power cost works out to about 7.5% to 8% of the sales which is very high. Besides high cost of power, the quality and reliability of power supply leaves much to be desired due to periodical interruptions, failure, voltage fluctuation and power cut and staggering. What is worse, because of restriction on sale of captive power and private sector investment in IPP's is not coming despite the fact that power is cheaper.

While on the one hand there is heavy shortage of power, the industries and agriculture are facing many problems due to shortage of power in the peak of the summer. The net result is that excess capacity in captive power units is not fully utilised. Even power is not available to exporting units at international price of Rs.2 per unit/kw as is being done in China. Concrete actions are needed for augmenting power supply and for reducing cost there of including duties and it is apprehended that large number of chemical and other units will face closure.

Infrastructural Constraints

Infrastructure bottlenecks and costs thereof are prohibitive and hamper competitiveness of our industries and exports. Inadequate facilities and congestion at ports, condition of roads being far from satisfactory, ineffective working of railways and antiquated facilities at airport etc. operate as impediments and add to the cost of the transaction and ultimately make goods uncompetitive both in the domestic and international market. Since this makes it difficult to ensure timely delivery and honour commitments, the exporters have to permanently lose the buyer. Rapid improvement of infrastructure with the help and assistance of funds both domestic and FDI and effective and efficient maintenance thereof is essential for promotion in capturing market share for our industries and trade in India and abroad. When Hyderabad is already promoting itself as the hub of chemical and pharma industry in the country and is willing to take all possible steps, it is high time that this issue be given priority it deserves so that existing or new units do not migrate over there from Gujarat.

Tax Structure

The old economy industries viz. Textiles, chemicals and petro-chemicals, mineral based industries and others have already started losing their competitive edge. Despite the predominance of chemical and petro-chemical industries in the industrial structure of Gujarat, it is facing serious problems of multiple taxation.

Technology

It is now universally acknowledged that success and survival of industries in the new millennium largely depends on the advances made on the technology innovation front and upgradation of technology in the existing industries both large and small so that they can achieve productivity and competitiveness at the earliest. Meagre measures like strengthening of R&D institutions or linkage with industry or setting up of incubation centre at IIM or encouragement to product development are not enough.

The emerging challenges in the context of globalisation, liberalisation and privatisation all over the world in post WTO era warrant that Gujarat which has all the wherewithal to make rapid advances in the IT and bio-technology is languishing in this vital field. If we do not leapfrog in this direction then it is apprehended that as suggested, be left out and will be relegated in the background vis-â-vis some of the southern states viz. Andhra:Pradesh, Karnataka and Tamilnadu Surprisingly, there issues have not been addressed in the approach paper which is the crying need of the day.

Finance

It is distressing to note that out of 2.65 lakh SSI units registered in Gujarat at present, about 76% are working and about 20% are closed.

The percentage of disbursement to SSI via-a-vis total disbursement for priority sector had dropped from 49.19% to 32.24%. The same situation of deceleration had continued in 2000 and 2001 and still continuing. The major constraint is non availability of working capital. Despite the fact that banks are flush with funds and credit policy advocates liberalisation of finance for SSI, the picture in reality is otherwise and SSI units are starving for want of funds.

While interest rates have shown signs of softening and prime lending rate has been revised down ward to 11%, the actual lending rates which SSI units have to pay varies from 12% to 16% which are still way above international bench mark. It is therefore reasonable and necessary that interest costs for SSI be reduced by making available finance between 8 to 10%. Even the bank charges and guarantee cost for sanctioned limit works out to about 2% which are required to be reduced. Pressure to be brought on nationalised banks, not only to augment credit deposit ratio from 45% to 65% but also finance for SSI be augmented at highly concessional rate.

If SSI units are encouraged, then lot of backward integration can be carried out for the SEZ units rather than importing it directly. Moreover, NRI investment is minimal and they need to be attracted to invest in the SEZs, for which Government should think of various attractive plans.

Cluster Development

Although Gujarat has developed 73 product clusters which include clusters like brass parts industry in Jamnagar, oil engine in Rajkot, ceramic tiles industry in Morbi, Ship breaking industry at Alang, rerolling mills in Sihor, cotton powerloom industry in Ahmedabad artsilk powerloom industry in Surat and, diamond cutting and polishing industry in Surat and Ahmedabad, yet none of them have been declared as centres of economic and export excellence in the New Exim policy such as Tirupur, for hosiery, woollen blanket in Panipat, woollen knitwear in Ludhiana. These latter centres have been provided various advantages by GOI viz. facility of EPCG plan for common service, market access funds, central assistance for infrastructural gap and entitlement of export house status at Rs.5 crores instead of Rs.15 crores for others which should be sought for main Gujarat clusters also in the Tenth plan. Despite better performance, Gujarat clusters woefully lack the aforesaid facilities for organic growth and export development.

Exports

Even though Gujarat accounts for about 17% of the total exports of the country, a lot more needs to be done to diversify and consolidate manufacturing capacity, enhance productivity and competitiveness and increase market access to newer markets which are opening up due to globalisation and liberalisation.

What is more distressing is the fact although govt. of India had approved 20 agri -export zones for various local commodities of export in various states in the country out of which 4 are in Maharashtra, 3 in U.P. and 2 in West Bengal whereas Gujarat has been granted approval for Agro export zone only recently. This is the position despite the fact that Gujarat has enough to offer in terms of processed fruits and vegetables. Out of above, work on 15 agro export zones has already started while Gujarat has lagged far behind in this regard. Govt. of Gujarat will have to reinvent and reinforce export strategy for Gujarat so that industries and trade of Gujarat achieve enhanced productivity and competitiveness in the export market. Govt. will have to move fast locally by taking prompt remedial measures particularly keeping in view international vision. This implies for a comprehensive policy for promotion of exports, to attract investments both domestic and foreign and to enhance employment on an urgent basis.

Labour Reforms

Despite the talk of India/Gujarat having lower wages, the labour productivity in India/Gujarat compares very unfavourably with many other countries like Pakistan, China, Fiji, Japan, Malaysia etc. as also compared to many leading states in the country. It is understood that out of 12 countries for which comparison of productivity indices are available, India is at the 8th position. Even compared to China we are lagging behind in labour productivity in all most all industrial sectors to the extent of 7% to 180%.

It is high time to introduce hire and fire policy and link wages with productivity and efficiency so as to enhance competitiveness of our products both in domestic market and international markets. Even pragmatic exit policy also needs to be implemented with social concern in view.

Priority Areas for Action

- Since the Indian economy and Gujarat are rapidly moving from shortages to surpluses, it is in the fitness of things that SEZ and Agro export zones approved in the state should not only be established expeditiously but also requisite incentives and facilities be provided to export industries so as to enable them to be competitive in the international market. Urgent steps are required to be taken in this direction so as to speed up recovery of Gujarat's economy and achieve target for enhancement of exports and employment in Gujarat. In short level playing field is ensured to the industries of Gujarat.
- Water intensive industries are not developing in Gujarat and are not given proper encouragement due to shortage and high cost of water. When 31% of the chemical industries of India are located in Gujarat, it is in the fitness of things to make water rates cost competitive. Paper making units located in Southern Gujarat are facing closure due to scarcity of water. For water intensive industries urgent steps be taken to augment water supply through establishment of desalination plants.

Looking ahead and beyond warrant that both state and central govt. together should resolve to buck the global slowdown and bring about rapid resurgence of Gujarat in this turbulent times and show to the world that Gujarat State and India as a nation can overcome all odds. Adversity can not be cause for despair as tough times do not last long. Rather, it is a summon and a stimulus for action - indeed for bold but constructive and aggressive action to forge ahead on the path of progress and prosperity trouble free and struggle free. Such positive and pragmatic actions will produce visible recovery for Gujarat in the times ahead. The business community of Gujarat is totally dedicated, devoted and determined to be partner with govt. in a joint and complementary action to revive the Gujarat's economy and to take it on high growth path.

SEZ promoters underline that thanks to such zones foreign investors have been encouraged to invest and create employment in countries that would not be the natural choice for direct foreign investment if it were not for the incentives offered. But will these investors remain in such countries if the financial incentives are with- drawn, if the cost of labour increases or the quota-based trading system for garments comes to an end?

The host governments devote considerable funds to the infrastructure and operations of these zones without collecting any taxes for a given period. In return, they manage to attract investment, sometimes receive employers. Contributions to pensions, generate foreign currency earnings, and create jobs.

Yet the benefits are limited in the following ways:

- The investors usually limit their activities in the EPZs to simple processing operations, thus limiting the transfer of technologies and skills
- Most jobs are poorly paid, low quality and involve few skills
- A very small share of the foreign currency earnings generated remain in the country; the foreign investments are not secure and can be withdrawn from the country with relative ease, as seen with the numerous companies that have left the EPZs of various countries to relocate in China, where there is particularly little respect for workers rights
- The investors often import all they need and source very little from the local market.

With the SEZ ACT coming into existence and permission given to establish as many as 45 new zones in the private and joint sector, it is quite apparent that the future industrialization of the country will be closely interlinked to and concentrated in the Special Economic Zones. At present foreign exchange earned by all the 811 units in the 8 Zones put together came to Rs 18,309 crores, (4.08 billion dollars) a mere 5% of India's exports during the fiscal 2004-05.But a lot of costs are associated with this revenue: As much as two-thirds of this is used by them for imports of raw materials and components. Add to that the profits transferred from the country by wholly owned foreign companies, the revenue loss from tax concessions, and the hidden costs of the natural resources used up by the Zones - and the SEZs actually appear to be a net drain on the economy.

On the face of it SEZs do not seem to be driving export growth and coupled with the fact that a lot of worker related issues are bogging it in a mire, the future of SEZs in India seems uncertain. All in all, SEZs have the potential to script the China success story and for this reason alone they are worth the bet. By the incorporation of Redressal mechanisms, improving investment climate, improving infrastructural facilities and ensuring better working conditions, the future of SEZs in India doesn't seem anywhere bleak as it is perhaps made out to be.

5

Foreign Direct Investment and International Business Cycle

INTRODUCTION

Business cycle behaviour has been relatively synchronised since the mid-nineties. In 2001, the dispersion of economic growth rates across the industrialised economies even fell to its lowest level in over 30 years, as the global economy experienced a downturn that was unusually wide-spread across countries. Broadly speaking, the observed degree of output comovement reflects both the nature of the shocks that have occurred and the degree of economic interdependence. Output developments will be more correlated if common shocks happen to be predominant, while they will be more asymmetric if idiosyncratic shocks are most important. Because of economic relations among economies, country specific shocks may get transmitted to other countries, enhancing output comovement indirectly.

The higher degree of output comovement in recent years has partly been driven by common shocks, such as large changes in crude oil prices, the rise and fall of the information technology boom and restrictive monetary policies. However, it is widely felt that common shocks are not the whole story, raising the question to what extent deeper economic linkages, and what kind of linkages, may have contributed to the more synchronised nature of economic fluctuations. The rise in international economic interdependence has occurred along three dimensions. The first is international trade in goods and services, which is the 'traditional' channel through which economies may affect each other. Although imports and exports as a share of GDP have in general increased, there has been no marked across-the board acceleration of this trend recently.

It is therefore unlikely that deeper trade interdependencies have contributed significantly to the recent rise in output correlations. The second type of link is provided by international trade in financial assets, such as equity and bonds, and cross-border credit relations. Cross-border holdings of portfolio assets have mushroomed in recent years. For example, foreign holdings of

US long-term securities amounted to 42 per cent of US GDP in March 2000, having tripled in less than 2½ years. Correlations between stock markets of the major countries have greatly increased over the last twenty years, with the exception of Japan.

Financial markets have thus gained importance as a channel for the international transmission of shocks. The third dimension of interdependence is the internationalisation of production through foreign direct investment (FDI). Foreign direct investment has grown at rates far beyond those of international trade or output since the late 1980s. Especially in the second half of the 1990s, firms were exceptionally active in cross-border mergers and acquisitions (M&A). The outstanding global stock of FDI more than doubled in ten years time from 8.3 per cent of world GDP in 1990 to 17.5 per cent in 2000. At present, about 11 per cent of world output is produced by foreign affiliates. It is conceivable that the larger presence of FDI is partly responsible for the observed increase in cross-country business cycle comovement. The empirical literature on the effects of FDI is often based on firm-level data and mainly deals with supply-side effects on host economies in the longer run, focusing on the transfer of technology, management techniques and business models. This stage focuses on another aspect of FDI, namely the possible role FDI may play in the transmisssion of economic shocks across borders. Using aggregate data, we examine to what extent the rapid expansion of FDI and the internationalisation of production can be related to the phenomenon of more synchronised business cycles. Our basic empirical question is: Do countries that have comparatively intensive FDI ties tend to have more synchronous business cycles? To our knowledge we are the first to investigate this issue. To preview the results, we find that before 1995 there is no strong evidence in favour of an independent role of FDI (next to foreign trade) in explaining cross-country business cycle correlation patterns. But after 1995, FDI linkages are much better able to explain the pattern of international business cycle linkages than foreign trade relations. Moreover, FDI is associated with the vulnerability to foreign output spillovers that occur with a lag, but international trade is not. This result holds for the complete sample as well as the more recent years.

FOREIGN DIRECT INVESTMENT AS A CHANNEL FOR INTERNATIONAL TRANSMISSION OF DISTURBANCES

Foreign direct investments are investments made by a resident of one economy with the objective of establishing a lasting interest in a company located in another economy (host economy). With 'lasting interest' we mean both the existence of a long-term relationship and a significant degree of influence by the direct investor on the management of the foreign firm. In statistics, ownership of at least ten percent of the ordinary shares or voting stock is the criterion for the existence of a direct investment relationship.

Ownership of less than ten percent is considered a portfolio investment. FDI comprises not only mergers and takeovers/acquisitions (brownfield investments) and new investments (greenfield investments), but also reinvested earnings and loans and similar capital transfers between parents and affiliates. Industrial countries typically act both as host to FDI projects in their own country and as participant in investment projects in other countries. A country's inward FDI position is made up of the hosted FDI projects, while the outward FDI position consists of the FDI projects owned abroad. Both larger inward and outward FDI positions may make the domestic economy more sensitive to economic disturbances abroad in the short run. As the inward position represents imported capital, the host country always runs the risk that foreign investors, for whatever reason, may want to withdraw their money.

More generally, a deterioration of the economic conditions in the foreign investor's home country may weaken the financial health of the parent company, which in turn may lead to cutbacks in employment, wages and investment in the host countries. International rent sharing within multinational companies may be at the root of this type of vulnerability. Within a multinational corporation, firm-specific assets are a joint input, giving economics of scale at the company level rather than at the level of the individual plant. Global profits may be shared (with a lag) with affiliates and their workers. Due to the trend towards internationalisation of production, domestic wages and employment may thus increasingly reflect international factors in addition to local economic conditions.

Budd and Slaughter provide evidence of cross-border profit sharing between American and Canadian firms. Budd, Konings and Slaughter found that foreign-affiliate wages were positively related to parent profit per worker for a sample of European firms. The macroeconomic risks related to the outward FDI position have to do with the consequences that disturbances abroad may have for the financial position of the investing firms. Unfavourable developments in the host countries may reduce the value of the investment projects abroad, and thus the value of domestic firms. This reduction of net worth may lead to lower stock prices and greater difficulties for domestic firms in securing external finance for planned domestic investment projects, both in the capital market and with banks. Domestic investment may thus be hurt via the balance sheet channel and the stock market channel. The fall in stock prices, at home and abroad, may adversely affect domestic consumption via wealth effects, balance sheet effects and confidence effects. In addition the type of FDI (horizontal or vertical) may be relevant. Horizontal FDI is motivated by the desire to be close to customer markets due to high trade costs.

The firm then runs similar operations at different locations, producing and selling in the same country (or nearby countries). This type of FDI is thus a substitute for international trade relations. Vertical FDI arises when firms want to take advantage of international differences in factor prices. The firm then splits up the production process, allocating the parts over different countries on the basis of cost efficiency. The firm services its markets by exporting from a single location. Hence, this type of FDI creates trade, both of intermediate and final goods. The FDI transmission channel applies to horizontal FDI. In case of vertical FDI, the transmission channel becomes even stronger, because some production decisions become directly linked across countries. If the parent company decides to cut output, output in affiliates producing intermediate goods and parts will also be reduced. Most empirical work tends to conclude that most real-world FDI is horizontal. As we focus on FDI relations among highly industrialised countries, this is likely to be true for our data as well.

SOME FACTS ON FDI AND ITS SIGNIFICANCE FOR THE HOST ECONOMIES

Stocks and flows of FDI have grown rapidly across the OECD area since the mid-1980s, with a marked acceleration since 1995. FDI has also increased faster than international trade. The outward FDI position of Germany and France is currently around 25 per cent of GDP, four to five times the level of 1985. For traditional investor countries like the UK and the Netherlands, positions are much larger, 55 per cent and 80 per cent respectively. The outward investment position of the US increased from 5 per cent of GDP in 1985 to 13 per cent in 2000. As outward and inward FDI positions tend to move in tandem over time, gross positions have grown much faster than net positions. The increase in FDI ties among the industrialised countries can thus be characterised as a process of diversification. The Japanese experience does not fit in with the general picture. Japanese corporations even reduced their presence abroad in the second half of the 1990s, while Japan's stock of inward FDI is very small. To gain some insight into where countries undertake FDI projects, Table presents data on the geographical distribution of the stocks of inward and outward FDI for Canada, France, Germany, the Netherlands, the UK and the US for the years 1985 and 2000.

Table. Bilateral FDI Positions, 1985 and 2000

	1985					
	Canada	France	Germany	N'lands	U.K.	U.S.
	Inward Foreign Direct Investment Position (% of total)					
Australia	0.1	0.0	0.1	0.0	4.7	1.8
Belgium	0.4	9.5	2.2	5.4	1.7	1.4
Canada		0.5	0.9	0.2	2.9	9.3
France	1.7		6.1	4.4	4.4	3.6
Germany	2.9	13.5		7.7	2.4	8.0
Italy	0.0	4.3	1.4	0.1	0.5	0.7
Japan	2.5	0.5	5.8	2.6	2.2	10.5

	Canada	France	Germany	N'lands	U.K.	U.S.
Netherlands	2.2	17.1	12.7		18.0	20.1
Sweden	0.4	1.0	2.1	2.1	1.5	1.3
Switzerland	1.7	10.3	14.0	11.2	6.3	5.7
U.K.	9.6	13.7	8.9	14.1		23.6
U.S.	75.1	23.1	37.6	34.3	51.2	
Total (% of GDP)	18.6	5.6	4.6	15.1	12.1	4.4

	2000					
	Canada	France	Germany	N'lands	U.K.	U.S.
	Inward Foreign Direct Investment Position (% of total)					
Australia	0.5	0.0	0.0	0.2	3.4	1.7
Belgium	1.2	15.5	33.1	18.7	1.4	5.6
Canada		0.5	0.3	0.2	3.2	9.4
France	9.9		7.2	5.2	16.7	10.8
Germany	2.4	11.4		13.8	8.9	10.3
Italy	0.3	4.0	1.2	0.4	0.8	0.5
Japan	2.6	1.9	1.8	3.5	3.6	13.5
Netherlands	4.7	19.2	19.7		14.1	12.1
Sweden	0.8	2.3	1.7	2.5	1.3	1.8
Switzerland	2.0	7.9	4.9	4.8	3.1	5.7
U.K.	7.3	13.7	7.1	15.7		17.6
U.S.	63.2	15.0	17.5	21.6	34.4	
Total (% of GDP)	28.4	19.5	23.8	64.6	30.9	12.4

	1985					
	Canada	France	Germany	N'lands	U.K.	U.S.
	Outward Foreign Direct Investment Position (% of total)					
Australia	0.1	0.0	0.1	0.0	4.7	1.8
Australia	2.1	0.5	1.3	0.7	9.6	3.8
Belgium	0.2	11.9	9.2	7.0	1.7	2.5
Canada		2.0	3.8	3.3	6.8	20.4
France	0.3		8.3	5.6	2.9	3.3
Germany	1.1	8.9		9.3	4.2	7.3
Italy	0.3	4.2	3.8	1.4	0.9	2.6
Japan	0.5	0.9	1.5	1.0	1.0	4.0
Netherlands	0.9	7.0	6.1		5.2	3.1
Sweden	0.0	0.1	0.5	0.3	0.6	0.4
Switzerland	1.0	16.3	7.4	5.6	1.3	6.8
U.K.	7.7	6.5	4.9	5.8		14.3
U.S.	69.2	24.2	29.7	41.3	35.2	
Total	11.8	4.6	6.6	29.6	21.7	5.5

(% of GDP)							
Correlation	1.00	0.82	0.91	0.94	0.94	0.47	in-out
same, excl U.S.	0.90	0.69	0.44	0.67	0.32		

	2000					
	Canada	**France**	**Germany**	**N'lands**	**U.K.**	**U.S.**
	Outward Foreign Direct Investment Position (% of total)					
Australia	1.3	0.6	0.6	0.8	1.3	2.7
Belgium	1.0	13.8	7.7	12.1	9.9	3.5
Canada		7.0	1.1	1.8	1.7	10.0
France	1.3		5.0	6.1	3.6	3.0
Germany	1.1	5.6		10.5	3.9	3.9
Itlay	0.9	3.2	3.4	1.8	0.6	1.7
Japan	1.6	1.7	1.7	0.4	0.8	4.6
Netherlands	2.3		9.0	13.2	30.4	9.1
Sweden	0.3	0.6	1.4	0.8	3.2	1.8
Switzerland	1.5	4.0	3.1	4.9	1.1	4.3
U.K.	10.4	12.7	10.4	10.7		18.7
U.S.	48.3	25.4	28.0	25.7	23.5	
Total (% of GDP)	32.0	32.8	24.9	79.8	63.3	13.2
Correlation in-out	0.98	0.71	0.57	0.91	0.68	0.75
same, excl U.S.	0.51	0.78	0.68	0.95	0.52	

The most intensive FDI link is that between Canada and the US. In 1985 75 per cent of total Canadian inward FDI originated from the US, while in 2000 this was still 63 per cent. In general, the US is a major source and destination of FDI. In 2000, the UK was the largest direct investor in the US (17.6 per cent of the US total), followed by Japan (13.5 per cent) and the Netherlands (12.1 per cent). The UK, Canada and the Netherlands received the largest amounts of American FDI. France, Germany and the Netherlands have established intensive FDI relations with EU countries, both as investors and as hosts.

The overall trend towards diversification is also visible in the geographical distributions of the FDI positions, which have become more even over time. Finally, shares in the inward FDI portfolio and shares in the outward FDI portfolio are positively correlated. Inward and outward FDI move together, not only at the aggregate level, but also bilaterally. This observation confirms that the FDI process between two countries typically involves capital flows of comparable size in both directions, through which countries swap claims on their capital stocks. The presence of foreign investors means that part of domestic output is produced by firms controlled by foreigners.

Comprehensive data on the share of output accounted for by foreign affiliates are scarce.

Table. The Role of Foreign Affiliates in Host Economies

	Share in Host Country GDP of Affiliates (%)		Estimated Share in Host Country GDP of all Foreign Affiliates (%)		Share in Host Country Man Employment of all for , Affiliates (%)	P.M. US Share in Host Country Inward FDI stock (%)	
	1989	1999	1989	1999	1998	1989	1999
Australia	4.9	4.7	18.7	10.8		26.3	43.6
Belgium	5.6	5.1					
Canada	9.5	10.0	14.5	14.4		65.6	69.5
France	2.3	2.6	12.0	15.0	27.8	19.1	17.3
Germany	3.0	2.9	9.3	12.0	7.2	32.4	24.2
Ireland	12.4	16.8			36.8		
Italy	1.9	2.0	12.7	15.0	14.0	15.0	13.3
Japan	0.5	0.7	1.0	1.7	1.8	50.5	40.5
Netherlands	5.8	4.5	21.4	17.7	21.9	27.1	25.4
Sweden	1.2	2.6	12.2	19.6	26.8	9.9	13.2
Switzerland	2.9	3.3	12.3	10.3		23.6	32.0
UK	6.2	7.0	14.7	14.9	27.3	42.1	47.0
US			4.1	5.6	13.4		

We have collected some data, taken from several sources, that may give an impression of the weight of foreign-owned companies in the manufacturing sector and the total economy in 13 host countries in 1989 and 1998-1999. The output produced by majority-owned foreign affiliates (MOFA) of US companies as a percentage of host country GDP in 12 countries. In 1999, US MOFAs alone were responsible for 17 per cent of Irish GDP, 10 per cent of Canadian GDP and 7 per cent of UK GDP. In Australia, Belgium and the Netherlands their output share was around 5 per cent. We combine this information with the share of the US in the host country's inward FDI position, if available, to arrive at a back-of-the-envelope estimate of the output share of all foreign affiliates taken together.

Our, admittedly rough, estimates indicate that between 10 and 20 per cent of GDP could be accounted for by foreign-owned firms, pointing to a potentially substantial role for foreign affiliates in the domestic economy. Because the US economy is so large, foreign affiliates still account for a relatively small part of US GDP: 5.6 per cent in 1999 and 6.0 per cent in 2000. Still, this represents a substantial increase from the level ten years ago. Finally, depending on availability, the share in employment in the manufacturing sector accounted for by foreign affiliates in 1998. These data too are suggestive of an important role of foreign firms in their host economies.

FDI RELATIONS AND INTERNATIONAL BUSINESS CYCLE LINKAGES

We investigate whether there is a positive relationship between the size of bilateral foreign direct investment positions and the degree of business cycle comovement among countries. If two countries have invested a lot in each other, do their output cycles tend to move in a more synchronised way? In addition we examine whether this relationship has changed over time. Taking a bilateral perspective, we focus on the experience in the past 20 years of Canada, France, Germany, the Netherlands, the UK and the US. For these countries bilateral FDI positions (both inward and outward) that are consistently measured across time are available for a long period, including estimates for the year 2001.

As suggested, refer to these six countries as the reporting countries, since the FDI positions are measured from their perspective. We look at the bilateral linkages of the six reporting countries among themselves and with six other countries (Australia, Belgium, Italy, Japan, Sweden and Switzerland). These latter six countries are selected because of their size and their importance as an importer and exporter of FDI. Taken together, our 12 countries represent 70 per cent of the outstanding stock of FDI at the end of 2000. For each reporting country we thus distinguish bilateral links with 11 countries, which as suggested, refer to as its partner countries.

The data on the FDI positions are available on an annual basis and reflect the state at the end of the year. We define the bilateral FDI position of country R versus country P as the sum of R's stock of direct investments in P and P's stock of direct investments in R, as reported by country R (in R's currency). We take the sum of both the inward and the outward position as our measure of the bilateral FDI link, as disturbances in country P may affect economic conditions in country R via both types of exposure. For instance, an unfavourable shock in country P may reduce the value of domestic firms' investment projects located in P, depressing their stock prices. This in turn may negatively affect domestic consumption and investment via wealth effects, confidence effects and balance sheet effects. Alternatively, companies in P may react to the worsening situation in their home country by reducing their presence abroad, cutting back employment and/or reducing investment at their affiliates in country R and other countries. In the absence of a well-established definition of international output comovement, we distinguish five measures of the degree of output comovement.

The first measure is the correlation of the quarterly growth rates of real GDP. The second measure is the correlation of the quarterly output gaps, the log difference between actual real GDP and its trend level (estimated by the Hodrick-Prescott filter). The third measure is the business cycle coherence on a quarterly basis, which is based on a business cycle dating by the IMF. It equals the fraction of time that two countries are in the same business cycle phase (expansion or recession). The fourth and fifth comovement measures are the correlation of the annual growth rates of real GDP and the correlation of the annual output gaps respectively. The correlations derived from annual data may also pick up spillover effects that occur with a delay of one or more quarters.

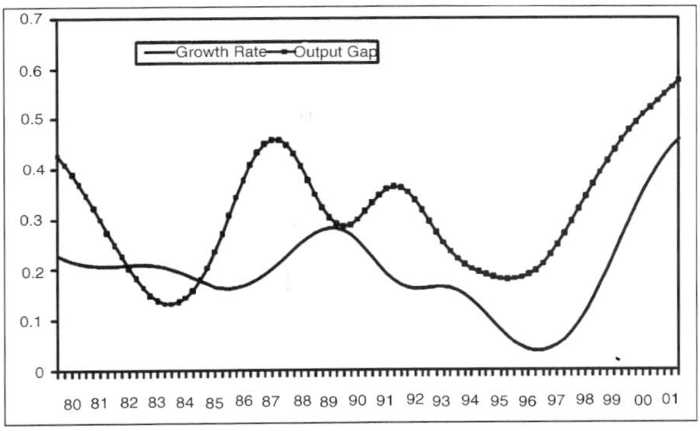

Fig. *Average Output Comovement among G7 Countries*

Figure offers an impression of the average degree of business cycle comovement among the G7 countries (the United States, Japan, the United Kingdom, Germany, France, Italy and Canada) in the years 1980-2001, based on our first two measures. The graph first of all shows that the degree of output comovement has been high by historical standards in recent years. Moreover, its behaviour over time differs from period to period. In the 1980s the average correlation of real GDP growth rates was fairly constant, in the first half of the 1990s it substantially declined, while in recent years it sharply increased. This non-monotonic time profile underscores the importance of time-variation in the mixture of common and idiosyncratic shocks. Given that the time profile of FDI linkages (and other measures of interdependence) is strictly increasing, Figure makes clear that any link between FDI and business cycle comovement must be hidden in the cross-section of countries. Our estimation method has to take into account that time variation in the mix and size of disturbances may obscure the relationship between FDI positions and output correlations. For this reason, crosssection regressions for each reporting country are the natural estimation design. Due to the limited number of observations per country, we have pooled the cross-section regressions for the six reporting countries into a single one. To find out whether more intensive FDI linkages are associated with a greater degree of output comovement, we estimate the following regression equation

$$\rho(\iota,j) = \alpha_0 + \alpha_1 D_1 + \alpha_2 D_2 + \alpha_3 D_3 + \alpha_4 D_4 + \alpha_5 D_5 + \beta FDIP(\iota,j)$$

where Di indicate country-specific dummies, which are one if the observation refers to reporting country *i*, and zero otherwise. $\rho(i,j)$ denotes the measure of business cycle comovement between reporting country i and partner country *j* over a certain time-span, while FDIP(i,j) is the average strength of the corresponding FDI link. Equation assumes that the intercept differs across countries, but that β is the same for each country. Differences in intercepts take into account fixed differences across countries and may also correct for methodological differences between national FDI statistics. The parameter β measures the sensitivity of output comovement to variations in the intensity of FDI relations. We conduct diagnostic tests whether the data support the implied restriction that all countries have the same β. If the sample period for which we compute output comovement measures and FDI exposures happens to be characterised by a preponderance of common shocks, all $\rho(i,j)$ will tend to be large, which will translate into high estimates of the intercepts $\alpha 0+\alpha i$ in equation By contrast, if the sample period is dominated by idiosyncratic shocks, all $\rho(i,j)$ will tend to be small, resulting in low estimates of $\alpha 0+\alpha i$. However, conditional on the mixture of shocks, differences in $\rho(i,j)$ for a given country i vis-à-vis its partners could still be explained by differences in the intensity of the bilateral economic relations. The coefficient β can thus be interpreted as the effect of a unit increase in FDI exposure given the mixture and size of shocks in the years over which output comovement and FDI positions have been measured.

The average vulnerability through bilateral FDI linkages —denoted by FDIP(i,j)—over a certain timespan is calculated as follows. Since both inward and outward FDI make a country more sensitive to outside developments, we first compute, for each year, the total FDI position (both inward and outward) of country i vis-à-vis country j, as recorded by country i (in the currency of country i). To calculate the vulnerability of reporting country i and partner country j that is associated with this amount, we express it as a percentage of GDP of country i and j, respectively. Since a correlation is a symmetric concept, we take the simple average of both vulnerability measures as our annual observation of the exposure associated with the bilateral FDI link. FDIP(i,j) is the average of the annual observations over the time-span under consideration. Simple pooling of six cross-section regressions into a single one renders 66 observations, which implies some sort of double counting of the observations relating to the links among the six reporting countries. Although there are 66 independent observations on FDI exposures, there are only 51 unique observations on the correlations. Observations relating to links among the six reporting countries thus get double weight in the sum of squares, once with FDIP(i,j) according to country i's statistics and once with FDIP(i,j) according to country j's statistics. Note that estimation of six separate crosssection equations would implicitly involve the same double counting. For this reason we always report two sets of estimation results: the first one is based on OLS (66 observations), the second one on weighted least squares (WLS). Observations relating to links among the six reporting countries are assigned a weight of ½, all other observations a weight of 1, so that all observations on $\rho(i,j)$ receive equal weight in the sum of squares. The effective number of observations in case of estimation by WLS is 51.

Table. Pooled Cross-section Regression of Output Comovement on FDI Positions

	OLS-Estimates				WLS-Estimates			
			P-Value	P-Value			P-Value	P-Value
	Estimate		Test	Test			Test	Test
	Beta	t(Beta)	A(i)=a	B(i)=b	Beta	t(Beta)	a(i)=a	B(i)=b
(a) Quarterly Growth Rate of Real GDP					(a) Quarterly Growth Rate of Real GDP			
1982-2001	0.014	2.83	0.321	0.165	0.020	4.01	0.135	0.331
1982-1989	0.018	2.10	0.367	0.393	0.023	2.62	0.257	0.356
1990-1994	0.025	2.32	0.664	0.504	0.030	2.78	0.393	0.486
1995-2001	0.019	5.36	0.088	0.612	0.023	6.30	0.011	0.721
(b) Quartarly Output gap (HP Filter)					(b) Quartarly Output gap (HP Filter)			
1982-2001	0.021	2.93	0.331	0.328	0.022	2.97	0.224	0.428
1982-1989	0.026	2.44	0.028	0.503	0.018	1.66	0.007	0.394
1990-1994	0.027	2.08	0.242	0.651	0.027	2.17	0.046	0.887
1995-2001	0.016	2.71	0.125	0.476	0.025	3.83	0.150	0.657
(c)Business Cycle Indicator (coherence)					(c)Business Cycle Indicator (coherence)			
1982-2001	0.448	2.97	0.225	0.843	0.361	2.01	0.373	0.847
1982-1989	0.083	0.43	0.942	0.286	0.063	0.28	0.932	0.047
1990-1994	1.319	2.48	0.274	0.842	0.874	1.49	0.359	0.658
1995-2001	0.325	1.85	0.054	0.998	0.365	1.70	0.086	0.990
(d)Annual Growth Rate of Real GDP					(d)Annual Growth Rate of Real GDP			
1982-2001	0.023	3.10	0.184	0.367	0.024	3.12	0.159	0.475
1982-1989	0.021	2.06	0.000	0.594	0.017	1.69	0.000	0.407
1990-1994	0.048	2.64	0.245	0.727	0.043	2.30	0.078	0.783
1995-2001	0.017	3.06	0.102	0.982	0.020	3.23	0.158	0.907
(e)Annual output Gap (HPFilter)					(e)Annual output Gap (HPFilter)			
1982-	0.024	2.79	0.226	0.643	0.022	2.36	0.205	0.494

Table reports the empirical results for the complete sample period 1982-2001 and three subperiods, 1982-1989, 1990-1994 and 1995-2001. This particular split-up of the sample is based on the work by Helbling and Bayoumi, who studied business cycles in the period 1973-2002 for the G7 countries. They found that the years 1990-1994 were characterised by an atypical pattern of business cycle linkages, probably because of the aftermath of German reunification and the collapse of the Japanese asset market bubble. Moreover, FDI grew very rapidly in the period 1995-2001. The empirical results provide supportive evidence for a link between bilateral FDI patterns and output comovement patterns. Contemporaneous correlations of quarterly growth rates are significantly higher for economies that have intensive investment relations than for countries that have less intensive investment relations. Moreover, the positive association of FDI and output comovement is more apparent in the most recent years, as evidenced by the larger point estimate and t-statistic of the slope coefficient β for the subperiod 1995-2001, compared to that for the complete sample.

The estimate of β indicates that a difference in FDI exposure of 1 percentage point is associated with an 0.02 percentage point higher output correlation in recent years. Panel 4b shows that there is also a statistically significant positive association between the intensity of FDI relations and the correlation of output gaps for all subperiods considered. This holds for both the OLS and the WLS estimates. However, the relationship does not appear to have gained in strength in recent years. Measuring output comovement by business cycle coherence, we find a positive and significant β-estimate for the complete sample but for the eighties there seems to be no connection between FDI relations and output co movement. Finally, the results for correlations derived from annual data also point to a positive association of FDI exposures and business cycle linkages. Lastly, parameter tests show that the pooled regression design is appropriate, as the hypothesis of equal slope coefficients across reporting countries cannot be rejected at conventional significance levels, while the hypothesis of equal intercepts is rejected in a number of cases.

THE ROLE OF INTERNATIONAL TRADE

The evidence presented thus far only focuses on FDI links between countries. Economies are also linked by international trade ties, however, which is an alternative explanation of international business cycle comovement. Moreover, it is likely that countries that invest a lot in each other will also tend to trade a lot with each other. The countries of the European Union, or the U.S., and Canada, are a case in point. Investment ties and trade ties may also vastly differ, however. For example, the share of the U.S., in the foreign trade of the Netherlands is only 4 per cent, whereas its share in Dutch FDI capital is more than 20 per cent.

The fact that geographical distributions of FDI exposures and foreign trade relations are correlated, implies that the estimates in Table may partly reflect the effects of trade relations (or economic relations in general). To shed light on this issue, this section examines the role of bilateral trade ties in explaining output comovement patterns. We first look into the relationship between international trade and output comovement along the same lines as the analysis for FDI.

$$\rho(\iota,j) = \alpha_0 + \alpha_1 D_1 + \alpha_2 D_2 + \alpha_3 D_3 + \alpha_4 D_4 + \alpha_5 D_5 + \gamma TRADE(\iota,j)$$

Table. Pooled Cross-section Regression of Output Comovement on Foreign Trade Flows

	OLS-estimates				WLS-estimates			
	estimate		p-value test	p-value test	estimate		p-value test	p-value test
	beta	t(beta)	a(i)=a	b(i)=b	beta	t(beta)	a(i)=a	b(i)=b
	(a) quarterly growth rate of real GDP				(a) quarterly growth rate of real GDP			
1982-2001	0.030	3.65	0.182	0.068	0.033	3.26	0.209	0.327
1982-1989	0.027	2.18	0.359	0.176	0.024	1.78	0.302	0.743
1990-1994	0.061	3.90	0.623	0.124	0.055	3.12	0.756	0.223
1995-2001	0.027	3.04	0.433	0.670	0.046	3.92	0.183	0.382
	(b) quarterly output gap (HP filter)				(b) quarterly output gap (HP filter)			
1982-2001	0.043	3.46	0.397	0.068	0.043	3.01	0.338	0.258
1982-1989	0.021	1.33	0.011	0.477	0.015	0.88	0.007	0.811
1990-1994	0.068	3.59	0.269	0.325	0.053	2.62	0.128	0.811
1995-2001	0.032	2.46	0.381	0.289	0.062	3.38	0.523	0.121
	(c) business cycle indicator (coherence)				(c) business cycle indicator (coherence)			
1982-2001	0.839	3.21	0.143	0.423	0.961	2.84	0.187	0.584
1982-1989	0.174	0.63	0.954	0.952	0.091	0.27	0.937	0.997
1990-1994	2.580	3.18	0.366	0.164	2.466	2.62	0.446	0.325
1995-2001	0.384	0.95	0.054	0.962	0.806	1.34	0.072	0.810
	(d) annual growth rate of real GDP				(d) annual growth rate of real GDP			
1982-2001	0.044	3.35	0.157	0.110	0.044	3.02	0.150	0.353
1982-1989	0.034	2.36	0.000	0.475	0.026	1.74	0.000	0.557
1990-1994	0.095	3.48	0.365	0.276	0.083	2.71	0.196	0.665
1995-2001	0.022	1.68	0.316	0.828	0.039	2.18	0.398	0.672
	(e) annual output gap (HP filter)				(e) annual output gap (HP filter)			
1982-2001	0.043	2.88	0.197	0.199	0.044	2.46	0.196	0.441
1982-1989	0.020	1.64	0.172	0.485	0.012	0.82	0.321	0.531
1990-1994	0.044	3.17	0.106	0.267	0.039	2.60	0.083	0.689
1995-2001	0.021	1.19	0.763	0.575	0.052	1.99	0.808	0.398

TRADE(*i,j*) measures the average vulnerability associated with the bilateral trade link between reporting country *i* and partner country *j* over a certain time-span. As in the case of the FDIP variable, the source of the data is country *i*'s statistics. The basic data are the (annual) exports and imports of country *i* relating to country *j*, as recorded by country *i* (in the currency of country *i*). We assume that only exports are a source of vulnerability. Recording country *i's* vulnerability is therefore calculated as its exports to partner country j, expressed as a percentage of country *i*'s GDP. Reporting country *j*'s vulnerability is calculated as country *i*'s imports from *j*, expressed as a percentage of country *j*'s GDP.

We take the simple average of these two as our annual observation of the exposure associated with bilateral trade link. Finally, TRADE(*i,j*) is the average of the annual observations over the time-span under consideration. We find that, in general, the estimates of γ are statistically significant from zero for all measures of output comovement and both estimation methods. Hence, more intensive foreign trade relations go hand in hand with more synchronised business cycles. Judged by both the estimates and the t-statistics, international trade linkages had their weakest effects in the 1980s.

During the years 199—1994 — when Germany ran current account deficits in the aftermath of reunification and Japan adjusted to collapse of the stock market and real estate bubbles— trade linkages are strongly linked to the correlation pattern of GDP growth rates. For the most recent subperiod 199—2001 the influence of trade ties, although significant in most cases, is more muted compared to that measured over the whole sample period, especially for correlations based on annual data. Like for FDI, the results are weakest for the coherence measure. FDI relations as well as trade relations are important determinants of the degree of business cycle comovement. So the next natural step in the analysis is to incude both linkages into the regression equation,

$$\rho(i,j)=\alpha_0+\alpha_1 D_1+\alpha_2 D_2+\alpha_3 D_3+\alpha_4 D_4+\alpha_5 D_5+\beta FDI\,P(i,j)+\gamma TRADE(i,j)$$

If multicollinearity is a problem the estimates of both β and γ will be insignificant. In this case we can conclude that economic relationships do matter for business cycle comovement, but we cannot statistically distinguish between the contribution of international trade and that of FDI.

Table. Pooled Cross-section Regression of Output Comovement on FDI Positions and Foreign Trade Flows

	OLS-estimates				WLS-estimates			
	beta FDI	t(beta)	beta Trade	b(i)=b	beta FDI	t(beta)	beta Trade	b(i)=b
	(a) quarterly growth rate of real GDP				(a) quarterly growth rate of real GDP			
1982-2001	0.006	1.13	0.024	2.44	0.015	2.47	0.015	1.23
1982-1989	0.012	1.23	0.019	1.36	0.020	2.02	0.011	0.77
1990-1994	0.006	0.49	0.056	3.02	0.016	1.29	0.039	1.85
1995-2001	0.017	4.17	0.007	0.80	0.021	4.46	0.010	0.80
	(b) quarterly output gap (HP filter)				(b) quarterly output gap (HP filter)			
1982-2001	0.011	1.33	0.032	2.18	0.014	1.47	0.028	1.54
1982-1989	0.025	2.01	0.005	0.27	0.017	1.40	0.004	0.19
1990-1994	0.005	0.36	0.064	2.82	0.013	0.88	0.041	1.66
1995-2001	0.011	1.68	0.019	1.27	0.018	2.17	0.032	1.41
	(c) business cycle indicator (coherence)				(c) business cycle indicator (coherence)			
1982-2001	0.265	1.50	0.585	1.89	0.099	0.45	0.845	1.98
1982-1989	0.034	0.15	0.151	0.48	0.045	0.18	0.062	0.16
1990-1994	0.621	1.02	2.062	2.15	0.048	0.07	2.420	2.10
1995-2001	0.324	1.56	0.008	0.02	0.299	1.09	0.297	0.39
	(d) annual growth rate of real GDP				(d) annual growth rate of real GDP			
1982-2001	0.014	1.57	0.030	1.98	0.015	1.63	0.027	1.46
1982-1989	0.013	1.11	0.026	1.57	0.012	1.04	0.019	1.11
1990-1994	0.022	1.06	0.077	2.38	0.022	0.98	0.063	1.68
1995-2001	0.016	2.49	0.003	0.22	0.018	2.31	0.008	0.37
	(e) annual output gap (HP filter)				(e) annual output gap (HP filter)			
1982-2001	0.015	1.47	0.029	1.63	0.013	1.12	0.029	1.29
1982-1989	0.024	2.51	0.005	0.34	0.019	1.85	-0.001	-0.05
1990-1994	0.009	0.87	0.036	2.21	0.010	0.92	0.029	1.62
1995-2001	0.022	2.51	-0.004	-0.22	0.024	2.08	0.011	0.33

Table presents the results of equation. For the years 1982—2001 the OLS-results indicate that bilateral trade ties are mostly significant while bilateral

FDI ties are not, although the t-statistic is always greater than one. However, this finding is not robust with respect to the estimation method. In particular, correlations of real GDP growth rates are found to be closer related to FDI relations than trade relations. In addition, for three of the four other comovement measures the coefficient estimates for both linkages are not significantly differently from zero, while their t-statistics are similar in magnitude. This is an indication that multicollinearity between trade and FDI relationships is significantly affecting the estimation problem. Consequently, there is strong and robust evidence for a link between bilateral economic relationships and bilateral business cycle correlations. However, it is difficult to disentangle the effects of FDI relations and those of foreign trade relations.

The results for the various subperiods suggest, however, that a remarkable change has occurred over the past 20 years. Bilateral FDI relations are far more closely linked to bilateral output comovement patterns than trade relations in the most recent period 1995-2001. This holds in particular for correlations of real GDP growth rates, but the same pattern emerges for the output gap and the other comovement measures. By contrast, the years 1990-1994 appear to have been characterised by a more dominant influence of foreign trade relations. For the early years of the sample the picture is mixed. In most cases the estimates of both β and γ are insignificant, implying that it is difficult to disentangle the roles of trade and FDI as transmission channels of disturbances. For the output gap correlations we find a significant effect of FDI relations, but not of trade relations when estimating by OLS. We get a similar pattern using WLS for correlations of real GDP growth rates.

LAGGED SPILLOVERS

The discussion so far has concentrated on cross-country variations in contemporaneous correlations. This offers an incomplete picture as international spillovers may occur with some lags as well. For this reason, we next analyse the link between FDI exposures and the extent to which economies are affected with a lag by developments in other countries. Our measure of the lagged spillover is based on the concept of Granger causality. For each country pair *(i,j)* — 66 in total — we first estimate the following regression equation for various time-spans where y denotes the quarterly growth rate of real GDP or the output gap, and m stands for the maximum lag with which *y(j)* affects *y(i)*. Granger causality from *y(j)* to *y(i)* obtains if some of the λl's are non-zero.

$$y(i,t)=\alpha+\sum_{l=1}^{m}\gamma l y(i,t-l)+\sum_{l=1}^{m}\lambda l y(j,t-l)$$

In that case, conditions in partner country *j* influence those in reporting country *i* with a lag. We take the sum of the coefficients λl as our measure of the lagged spillover from country *j* to country *i*. Preliminary tests indicate that the maximum lag length m in equation for most country pairs equals 1 for output growth rates and equals 2 for output gaps. We therefore restrict our analysis to lagged spillover measures derived from equation with *m* set to either 1 or 2. The left-hand side variable is now the lagged spillover measure. As the focus is now on the vulnerability to lagged spillovers from partner countries, the bilateral FDI position is expressed as a percentage of reporting country GDP.

Table. Pooled Cross-section Regression of Lagged Output Spillovers on FDI Positions or Foreign Trade Flows

	Foreign direct investment				Foreign trade			
	Over 1 quarter		Over 2quarter		Over 1 quarter		Over 2 quarter	
	beta	t(beta)	beta	T(beta)	beta	t(beta)	beta	t(beta)
Quarterly growth rate of real GDP								
1982-2001	0.0135	2.60	0.0171	3.02	0.0113	1.51	0.0159	1.93
1982-1989	0.0208	2.35	0.0306	3.10	0.0109	0.86	0.0255	1.78
1990-1994	0.0126	1.18	0.0102	0.64	0.0116	0.80	0.0083	0.38
1995-2001	0.0110	2.47	0.0130	2.08	0.0097	1.48	0.0087	0.94
(b) output gap (HP filter)								
1982-2001	0.0144	4.58	0.0090	3.53	0.0171	3.71	0.0076	2.02
1982-1989	0.0212	3.16	0.0149	2.57	0.0210	2.18	0.0142	1.71
1990-1994	0.0132	1.76	0.0057	0.73	0.0070	0.68	-0.0056	-0.53
1995-2001	0.0115	3.14	0.0080	2.08	0.0131	2.42	0.0063	1.11

Tables reports the estimation results of suitably modified versions of equations We find that a country's vulnerability to past disturbances in partner economies is positively related to the size of its bilateral FDI exposure. This holds for both the full sample period and the period 1995—2001. The relevance of FDI linkages for the cross-country pattern of lagged output spillovers is more apparent for the output gap, as indicated by the generally larger t-statistics.

Once again, the period of German reunification emerges as an atypical episode. For foreign trade relations we mostly find weaker effects than for FDI linkages, notably in the case of lagged spillovers of real GDP growth rates. This contrasts with our findings about contemporaneous comovement patterns, where FDI linkages mattered most in the most recent period only.

Table. Pooled Cross-section Regression of Lagged Output Spillovers on FDI Positions and Foreign Trade Flows

	1lag				2lag			
	beta FDI	T(beta)	beta Trade	T(bera)	beta FDI	T(beta)	beta Trade	T(beta)
(a) Quarterly growth rate of real GDP								
1982-2001	0.015	2.07	-0.003	-.026	0.017	2.24	-0.001	-0.05
1982-1989	0.026	2.28	-0.011	-0.70	0.031	2.45	-0.001	-0.05
1990-1994	0.012	0.86	0.000	0.01	0.011	0.51	-0.002	-0.06
1995-2001	0.012	1.94	-0.002	-0.21	0.017	1.93	-0.007	-0.61
(b) Output gap (HP filter)								
1982-2001	0.011	2.65	0.006	1.07	0.010	2.79	-0.002	-0.32
1982-1989	0.019	2.23	0.005	0.41	0.014	1.87	0.002	0.23
1990-1994	0.018	1.73	-0.009	-0.65	0.015	1.47	-0.019	-1.38
1995-2001	0.012	1.90	0.001	0.14	0.009	1.78	-0.003	-0.38

Table presents the empirical results for the case in which both FDI and trade relations enter the regression equation. These findings show that FDI patterns dominate the explanation of cross-country lagged spillover patterns, both for the complete sample and all subperiods. In all cases, the estimated coefficient of the bilateral trade position is insignificant and often wrongly signed. This particular result suggests that the FDI channel of transmission may be working for a longer time than the international trade channel. In case of a shock in a certain country, the trade channel quickly transmits the shock to the other economies, but then shuts down. The presence of an FDI channel implies that this shock may affect the other economies not only contemporaneously, but also in the next two quarters.

SUMMARY AND CONCLUSIONS

This examines to what extent the rapid expansion of foreign direct investment (FDI) and the internationalisation of production can be related to the phenomenon of more synchronised business cycles. Both larger inward and outward investment positions may make the domestic economy more susceptible to economic disturbances abroad. We focus on the relationship between bilateral FDI positions and cross-country business cycle patterns. Do countries that have comparatively intensive FDI ties also exhibit a relatively large degree of business cycle comovement? We analyse the experience in the years 1982—2001 of Canada, France, Germany, the Netherlands, the UK and the US, looking at the bilateral linkages of these six countries among themselves and with six other countries (Australia, Belgium, Italy, Japan, Sweden and Switzerland), employing five measures of international output comovement.

In addition, we investigate the ability of international trade patterns to explain business cycle linkages. Taking into account both FDI relations and foreign trade relations, we conclude that before 1995 there is no strong evidence in favour of an independent role of FDI in explaining cross-country business cycle patterns. Although the degree of output comovement tends to be higher for economies that have relatively intensive investment relations, we find the same to be true for international trade relations.

We thus find strong and robust evidence for a link between bilateral economic relationships and bilateral business cycle correlations, but multicollinearity problems prevent a precise assessment of the respective contributions of trade and FDI. Trade patterns tend to explain the pattern of output comovement better than FDI linkages in the years immediately following German reunification and the collapse of the Japanese asset market bubble. The strong growth of FDI since 1995 appears to have changed this picture. FDI linkages are much better able to explain the pattern of international business cycle linkages than foreign trade relations in the years 1995—2001. Regarding the vulnerability to foreign output spillovers that occur with a lag, we find that FDI exposures are relevant, but international trade relations are not. In contrast to the case of contemporaneous linkages, this result is also obtained for the complete sample, not just the most recent period.

The empirical results of this stage are supportive evidence for the view that apart from the foreign trade channel, FDI now constitutes a separate channel through which economies may affect each other in an economically significant fashion. Moreover, foreign disturbances may influence the domestic economy for a longer time-span when relayed through the FDI channel than through the trade channel, which mainly operates contemporaneously. Our research has two policy implications.

The first one is that the trend towards greater economic interdependence through FDI implies an underlying tendency for business cycles to display a more synchronised behaviour than in the past. This is not to say that as suggested, actually observe greater output comovement in the future all the time, however. As the experience of the 1990s teaches, the effects of large asymmetric shocks may overshadow the upward influence on account of increasing interdependence. The second lesson for policy makers is that FDI appears to have become an important channel for the international transmission of disturbances.

This aspect of global linkages should be incorporated into the macroeconomic models that are used for making forecasts, evaluating scenarios and conducting policy analyses by national policy makers and international organisations, such as the IMF and the OECD. Up until now, international trade and financial asset prices serve as the main linkages among individual economies in these models. Finding out how the FDI channel exactly operates constitutes an interesting research agenda. In related research, we present evidence for several countries that domestic labour market conditions (wages and/or employment) are partly determined by the profitability of firms abroad. International rent sharing may thus be an important aspect of global economic linkages at the macro-level. Adding a variable measuring foreign profitability to the specification of wage or employment equations could be a useful first step towards the incorporation of the FDI channel into (large-scale) econometric models.

6

The Buying Function

In every transaction someone engages in buying. Goods or services may be purchased for industrial or commercial use, for resale, or for ultimate consumption. The buyer may be one who specializes in performing this function, one who does buying along with many other business activities, or an ultimate consumer satisfying a personal want. In any event, there is no better indication of the importance and pervasive nature of the buying function than the fact that someone buys every time a sale is made. Buying is significant not only as a differentiated specific function but also as an economic activity, the understanding of which is basic to modern concepts of customer-oriented marketing management.

BUYING—AN ACTIVE MARKETING FUNCTION

While buying is a basic marketing function, it is often improperly relegated to an unimportant position. It is sometimes erroneously assumed that it is of a *passive character*—merely the opposite of selling. Quite to the contrary, buying does not take care of itself, but is indeed an *active* function.

The skill used in buying has an important influence in determining the relative value of what is purchased by the consumer. The constant increase in the variety of products offered to him, the growing tendency to procure more goods and services in the market rather than to produce them in the home, the multiplicity of brands, the frequency of relatively small quality differentials, and the widely differing services offered by stores, all combine to add to the difficulty of the consumer's choice and to stress the importance of his being able to buy with intelligence. The active character of buying is especially conspicuous in the case of the consumer. Traditionally, he has taken the initiative in the exchange process. When wants are recognized and the consumer is ready to act upon them, it is customary for him to seek out a seller or sellers. When a salesperson comes into contact with the consumer-buyer, the process of exchange is often nearly completed. This is dramatically emphasized by the small proportion of retail business which is accounted for by house-to-house canvassers or other sellers who take the initiative in seeking out prospective consumer-buyers, and, by way of contrast, by the predominant proportion which is accounted for by regular retail establishments that are visited by a purchasing-minded public. Developments in simplified selling or self-service merchandising accentuate the importance of consumer buying activity.

The more the retail selling and service functions are curtailed, the greater becomes the task and responsibility of the consumer as a buyer. While there is a substantial amount of pre-buying stimulation in the form of aggressive retailer and manufacturer advertising and sales promotion activity, the number of items competing for consumer attention is so vast and diverse that the ordinary person must play an extremely active role in making the purchases that satisfy his wants. It may be observed, however, that buying is often as active when examined from the standpoint of the firm as it is in the case of the ultimate consumer.

Unless buying of raw materials, semimanufactures, and the many items of equipment and supplies needed for the production process is effectively accomplished, manufacturers handicap themselves in their ability to compete with those who may be more skillful in the performance of this function. Ability to select from many offerings just what will sell best and to determine the most economic quantities to be bought at a given time is one of the prime tests of the efficiency of both wholesaler and retailer. Moreover, buying is closely related to other marketing functions. Its practices and policies are often determined, in part at least, by the financial position of the purchaser, the availability of adequate and economical transportation and storage facilities, and the degree to which standardization has been accomplished. Risk is often reduced by the adoption of proper buying policies. Skillful buyers make use of reliable and pertinent market information from a variety of sources. Goods purchased for resale must be selected primarily with reference to what the market will absorb. In short, this marketing function is closely related to the functioning of almost every part of our marketing system.

SPECIALIZATION IN BUYING

That buying is a very active and quantitatively significant function cannot be questioned when it is considered that manufacturing companies and middlemen ordinarily employ specialists to perform this activ-ity. In manufacturing establishments a key employee, generally known as the purchasing agent, sometimes bearing the title of Vice President in Charge of Procurement, is responsible for the function. All wholesale merchants have buyers who generally occupy the position of executives, the number depending upon the size of the business and the number of different merchandise departments involved. Larger retail stores employ buyers who are also usually the managers of merchandise departments. Quite a number of large department stores have more than 100 buyers each. In the chain store field the buying function is either centralized or divided between the central office and the individual retail store unit. Among smaller independent stores, the buying function is usually the responsibility of the proprietor or one of the partners, but it is almost invariably one of the most important of their activities.

WHAT BUYING INVOLVES

Like the other marketing functions, buying may be subdivided into a number of important elements or responsi-bilities. The most important of these are:

- The selection of kinds of goods,
- The determination of quality or suitability,
- The determination of quantities,
- The selection of sources of supply.

Selection of Kinds of Goods

Freedom in determining the kinds of goods to be purchased varies from one type of business to another. In many lines of manufacturing the materials to be bought are fixed automatically by the nature of the product manufactured. The manufacturer of cotton textiles must buy cotton yarn or raw cotton, and the butter manufacturer must have cream. Installations and industrial equipment are determined largely by the nature of the manufacturing process, with the result that there is sometimes rather limited freedom in their purchase. For most merchants, on the other hand, the determination of kinds of goods to be purchased is a real problem, since the firm may not constantly handle exactly the same merchandise.

While within certain limits most wholesalers and retailers find their choice of merchandise circumscribed by their clientele and competition, nevertheless it is a rare mercantile business which does not have some latitude. This problem has been aggravated considerably by a pronounced tendency for many types of stores to expand or diversify their merchandise lines. Self-service grocery stores, for example, have sought to handle any type of merchandise that is suitable for sale by self-service methods. In seeking new items to purchase, they have been attracted by the higher margins obtainable on numerous items normally handled by drug-, de-partment, or hardware stores. As a result, numerous advertised brands of proprietary remedies, toilet preparations, cosmetics, housewares, magazines, and alcoholic beverages have been successfully added to the lines carried by many supermarkets.

Drugstores, hardware stores, and other kinds of business, feeling the pressure of this competition, have also sought to expand their offerings by invading fields hitherto foreign to them. Similarly, most variety chains have abandoned their limited-price position, and some have become in essence junior department stores. Department stores, in turn, have expanded their sales volume by the addition of departments for sporting goods, cameras and photographic equipment, and other kinds of merchandise that have been sold traditionally in specialized types of establishments. Many marketing establishments have made costly mistakes in experimental attempts to diversify their merchandise offerings. For most small establishments, experience has indicated that new items cannot ordinarily be added successfully *unless*

- they are in keeping with the general character of the business as reflected by firm name, atmosphere, location, and advertising and promotion policies;
- They can be sold according to the present method of sale and by present employees;
- Sufficient space and capital investment can be devoted to the new merchandise to offer customers a reasonable range of choice within the classification to which it belongs. Obviously, these rules have not been important limiting factors for very large wholesale or retail firms where it is more feasible to add specialized personnel or facilities to handle the merchandising of items not closely related to those previously sold.

Determination of Quality

A second major buying responsibility relates to the determination of the suitability of goods for business use or for resale. This is a matter of quality, which involves consideration of materials, workmanship, grades, sizes, designs, colors, and patterns.

To a large degree manufacturers determine the quality of goods purchased by the characteristics of the products they make. For example, furniture sold in the highest price ranges demands materials far different from those used in making furniture to sell on a price basis. Although the final product depends greatly upon the skill of craftsmen assigned to its manufacture, minimum qualities of materials must be established. In many lines of manufacturing, however, there is an opportunity to exercise choice in selecting qualities for purchase. Sometimes additional labour may be applied to cheaper materials with resulting equal end results and a net cost reduction. While the specifications for materials are usually dictated by the requirements of the product being manufactured, final product design is often determined, at least in part, by the prices at which materials of varying qualities can be purchased.

Determination of quality is of especial interest in the purchase of business supplies. Good purchasing practice involves obtaining the *right quality for a particular purpose*—not the highest obtainable quality. This may be illustrated with respect to paper which is available over a wide range of quality. To purchase such a product which is either not good enough or better than necessary involves potential waste. Take the case of a large insurance company that has substantial paper requirements. For inter-office communications that are promptly read and quickly discarded, only minimum quality standards need be observed. For documents which will be kept a long time and handled often, however, much attention must be given to various quality factors which are relevant to preservation.

Retailers and wholesalers have a somewhat similar problem. Their market must be analyzed to determine the quality of merchandise which will appeal to prospective buyers. Often such a study reveals that a considerable part of the community desires either higher or lower qualities than are being supplied by stores. Not only must quality be determined, but merchants must give careful consideration to the salability of various sizes, materials, patterns, colors, and designs before entering the buying market.

Consumer demand is not, however, the sole consideration in determining just what qualities to buy. This may be illustrated with respect to the marketing of fresh peaches. Generally speaking, the consumer wants peaches which are ready to eat when purchased and prefers those that are picked from trees in a near ripe state. In the very early part of the season, however, peaches are usually quite expensive and sell rather slowly on both wholesale and retail levels of distribution. At this time, produce jobbers and retailers wish to buy peaches which are picked green because they will keep longer and can be handled with less risk of damage or spoilage. Thus, quality considerations are dictated by cost and handling factors rather than by consumer preference. Later, as supplies become more abundant, prices decline, and the volume of sales increases markedly. Both wholesalers and retailers are then more willing to handle peaches which have been picked in a more mature state and which are more satisfactory to the ultimate consumer.

A somewhat similar situation exists in ready-to-wear apparel establishments and other stores selling style merchandise. Consumer demand may dictate quality decisions for the most part, but in some instances there are other reasons for purchasing a given quality. Some retailers will buy a few items of more expensive quality than can be readily sold to their clientele. Their reason may be that the highest priced items make the next higher priced items in the line appear less expensive by comparison. Another motive may be to use the higher quality items chiefly for prestige purposes—that is, for display to give the store more of an atmosphere of elegance and fashion leadership than it would have if it confined its offerings solely to qualities that it can merchandise profitably. All of this suggests the wisdom of not confining motivation research to consumerbuyers or to industrial users, but of extending it to buyers of consumer goods on both the retail and wholesale levels of distribution.

Measuring Quality

While it is important to determine the desirable quality before buying, it is equally important to ascertain just what quality has actually been supplied by a seller. When quality factors are related to consideration such as flavour, visual appeal, or fashion, tests of quality are confined substantially to the judgment of the purchaser. Many aspects of quality are, however, precisely measurable. The process of analysis is used to determine the composition of an alloy or the purity of a chemical substance. Physical tests are employed to obtain the tensile strength of metal or the bursting strength of paper cartons. Precision measurements are used to find out whether the thread count of woven fibers or the thickness of sheet steel are within stated tolerances. Tests of performance are appropriate to determine how well paint will wear on a surface or how well automobile tires will last in use.

Many manufacturers utilize their own testing facilities for this purpose; others employ commercial testing laboratories. In some cases the test is made to determine the effective price, which may depend on the quality actually delivered. More often the test is made to prevent acceptance of products the quality of which is lower than was ordered. Many large retailers have installed testing laboratories for similar reasons, realizing that they must know the quality of merchandise which they sell if they are to serve their customers well. Certain trade associations perform a similar service for their members.

Determination of Quantities

A third important buying responsibility is ascertaining the proper quantities to be purchased. In wholesaling and retailing concerns this is based upon planned sales, and in manufacturing enterprises it is based upon manufacturing schedules which are ultimately dependent upon the sales volume anticipated. In some factories scheduling is altogether or largely based on orders already received and little or no manufacturing for stock takes place. In such instances, the manufacturer may defer the purchase of materials until he has orders for his product. Most manufacturers, however, cannot defer the purchase of all materials until they have orders in hand, since to do so would mean undue delays in delivery. All merchants are forced to carry some stock, and most merchants must carry substantial inventories. For them quantitative considerations in purchasing must rest upon estimates of future sales.

The sales estimate may be made directly in terms of numbers of units of merchandise to be sold, i.e., dozens, hundreds, pounds, barrels, tons, etc., or first in terms of dollars and cents. Expressing planned sales in money is a convenient common denominator for indicating total potential sales of a diverse and varied line of merchandise. The sales estimate or plan in terms of dollars becomes a valuable "yardstick" for measuring actual sales against planned sales. Obviously, where the manufacturer or merchant begins with a sales estimate in terms of value he must convert the dollar-and-cents figures into merchandise units.

In retail stores that handle fashion merchandise, careful sales plans are made twice a year, once for the spring and summer season and again for the fall and winter season. Planned purchases are derived from such estimates. For example, a shoe retailer may anticipate sales of $150,000 for the fall and winter season. If the merchant expects to realise a gross margin of 30 per cent of sales, then 70 per cent of sales or $105,000 may be spent to purchase shoes for this season. It would ordinarily be very bad judgment to spend the entire

$105,000 before the season of retail sales arrived, since that would greatly increase the expense of operating the business through higher costs in obsolescence, deterioration, interest, rent, and taxes.

It is necessary, therefore, to decide just how the $105,000 in purchases is to be distributed over the period. That is, the buyer must decide how much merchandise shall be purchased or delivered before autumn and how much shall be spent for merchandise to be received during each of the autumn and winter months. If actual sales fall below the planned total, it will be necessary to curtail purchases. If actual sales exceed planned sales, then additions must be made to the sum allotted for the season's purchases.

Most retail and wholesale establishments that deal in staple commodities do not find it necessary to formulate such sales plans in order to buy intelligently. The typical grocery, hardware, or drugstore is supplied by wholesale firms in the vicinity and can obtain immediate replenishment for most items. Similarly, tobacco wholesalers reorder from manufac-turers of cigarettes who maintain inventories in most major cities. Such merchants need anticipate their requirements only a short time ahead to determine quantities to be bought.

Quantity Versus Small-lot Buying

While the total quantity to be purchased *over a period of time* is derived from anticipated sales volume, most manufacturers and merchants have considerable latitude in determining the quantity of specific products to be ordered *at a given time*. Such decisions are often a matter of policy, determined after consideration of the advantages of placing large orders and the disadvantages of such a practice.

Among the various *advantages of quantity buying*, the ability to obtain merchandise at lower cost is a foremost consideration. Many sellers quote special prices on large orders because the costs of selling and shipping are relatively less than on small orders. Price concessions may take the form of lower list price quotations, extra discounts from list prices, or "free deals" involving, for example, an offer of one dozen units of free merchandise if a merchant orders a full gross at one time rather than a mere one or two dozen. Substantial transportation economies are often associated with large orders. This is especially true if a full carload or truckload is purchased instead of an ordinary freight shipment, or if a freight shipment of 100 pounds or more is purchased instead of a considerably smaller amount. When large quantities are purchased, fewer orders are placed, which means that less time and effort may be required to perform the buying function, fewer incoming shipments need be received and checked, and a small number of invoices is to be accounted for and paid. Quantity buying is often stimulated by speculative desires. This is especially true when market prices are rising, and buyers wish to profit thereby, or when conditions of scarcity are anticipated, as in a national emergency.

While it offers many inducements, a number of *disadvantages also result from quantity buying*. The practice may lead to a decreased stockturn rate through a larger average stock on hand without a corresponding increase in sales volume. This, in turn, tends to accelerate depreciation both from physical deterioration and from style obsolescence. As against the possible speculative gains of quantity buying there must be offset the possible losses due to declining prices. Buying in smaller quantities gives more flexibility to the merchandising programme, since the smaller inventories make it possible for the merchant to change his stock to bring it into conformity with changes in demand. Buying in larger quantities sometimes results in an inability to take advantage of late season bargains and other special opportunities. Furthermore, the larger stocks of goods which result from quantity buying practices spell higher costs of owning or carrying a merchandise inventory. Illustrative are greater interest costs on capital invested in inventory, larger requirements for storage space, greater insurance needs, and higher taxes on inventories, as well as greater depreciation or obsolescence losses.

Selection of Sources of Supply

A fourth major buying responsibility is determining the firms from which purchases are to be made. If it be assumed that decisions regarding kinds, qualities, and quantities of goods have been made, and if buying decisions were altogether objective and impersonal, it would appear that suppliers would be chosen on the sole consideration of price. The lowest price, it might be argued, would point inevitably to one particular vendor as the most logical source of supply, except where the same price is quoted by several suppliers which may be the case under conditions of either oligopoly or extremely keen competition. This sometimes holds true when an inflexible purchasing system is prescribed, as in the case of many government agencies where the purchasing agent must accept the lowest of a number of competitive bids. In business practice generally, many factors enter into the picture, often with the result of making this facet of buying very complex.

Factors Governing the Choice of Suppliers

Price is obviously a very important consideration, for different vendors often quote different prices on goods of varying quality. The vendor's price quotation must be considered in relation to transportation costs, if these are to be paid by the buyer, especially if suppliers are located at a considerable distance or if the goods are heavy or economically bulky. The ability of a supplier to make *prompt delivery* is often most important. In some cases, this may be a prime consideration, as when repair parts are needed to keep from shutting down a factory. Retailers of fashion merchandise are willing to pay premiums for immediate delivery when the demand for a specific fashion is great and stocks are depleted.

Terms of sale sometimes vary among vendors and are considered in the selection of suppliers. Cash discounts, which are offered to encourage the payment of bills before the expiration of a regular credit period, are often an important inducement, especially to firms that are in a healthy financial condition. The length of the credit period is important to many buyers, particularly those in weak financial condition.

The vendor's general reputation for *reliability* is often a patronagedetermining factor. This may relate to integrity in observing the terms of contracts, making deliveries on schedule, or supplying goods that conform with samples or contract grades.

Buyers are often influenced by the *distribution policies* of vendors. If a manufacturer sells direct to some retailers, some wholesalers may refuse to consider him as a source of supply. If a manufacturer operates some retail stores of his own, this may cause ill will among retailers, especially in shopping areas where the manufacturer's stores are located. Some manufac-turers select only a few outlets for their products in each community, and many have only one exclusive representative. When a retailer or wholesaler is so selected, he is likely to be more favorably inclined toward the seller than in a case where a seller distributes his product widely through a large number of competing establishments.

Sales promotion policies of vendors also influence their selection as sources of supply. A maker of women's dresses may purchase the fabric of a particular cloth manufacturer because the latter's consumer advertising will help in the sale of the dresses made from it. Some manufacturers win the favor of retailers because of assistance provided in local cooperative advertising, point-of-sale display materials, demonstrations, direct mail advertising, or sales training programs for the buyers' employees. The ability of a vendor to provide *continuity of supply* is often very important. Retailers do not like to patronize wholesalers who are often out-of-stock on important items and have to "back-order" them. In industrial purchasing, this factor is especially significant in connection with raw materials and supplies which are used regularly.

The selection of vendors is sometimes resolved on the basis of *reciprocity*. This is especially true in the industrial marketing field where large quantities are usually involved in a single transaction. Although this is not a scientific way of selecting suppliers, it is often rationalized by the attitude of "buying from those who buy from us, and thus we help each other." Just because a possible supplier is a customer does not mean that he is a good supplier on the basis of more rational considerations explained above. Some companies carry a policy of reciprocity to the extreme. A manufacturing company, for example, analyzes its sales to oil companies and distributes its purchases of supplies such as lubricating oil to each company in relation to the approximate volume of each oil company's purchases from it.

When a number of different potential suppliers are all satisfactory on the basis of the factors herein considered, the actual selection of sources is likely to hinge on the human equation. The personality, character, and technical proficiency of the *vendor's salesman* is frequently the factor that swings the balance of decision from some alternatives to others.

Concentration of Purchases

The practice of buying from one source or a small number of suppliers is known as concentration of purchases. Although often a phase of quantity buying, a policy which limits the number of suppliers is practiced because of certain special advantages. Price concessions other than regular quantity discounts, better terms of credit, special help from the whole-saler or manufacturer in solving merchandising problems, and an opportunity for prior selection of desirable merchandise are often of enough importance to justify a policy of concen-tration. Moreover, such a policy tends to minimize the chance of overstocking, largely through a reduction in the number of brands, styles, patterns, designs, or price lines. Some retailers and wholesalers concentrate their purchases in order to secure an exclusive agency or in order to become affiliated with a voluntary chain organization.

Rigid limitations on the number of resources is not, however, always a wise policy. Some wholesalers and retailers find it necessary to buy from many sources to secure the best assortment of style goods. Good buying strategy calls for alertness for special offers which often preclude concentration, because such offerings may come from suppliers not normally patronized or from newly established sources. Many industrial purchasing agents make it a policy to develop a number of supply sources for important materials to insure continuity of procurement under circumstances that might jeopardize normal operations.

Scientific Developments in Buying

The performance of the various sub functions or elements of buying has been considerably modified by the growing use of sophisticated techniques or practices, including value analysis, vendor rating programs, determination of optimum order quantities, and automatic reordering. Such techniques are highly technical in application; hence, it is essential to limit the present discussion to an indication of their nature and significance to marketing.

Value Analysis

Value analysis as consisting of formal analytical procedures used to relate design and function of purchased products to cost, with a view to reducing cost substantially through modification of design, change in specifications, different method of manufacture, change in source of supply, possible elimination of an item, or incorporation of a new item. Value analysis differs from former buying methods in two ways—first, in the wide scope of its activities which involve participation by all departments of a business concerned with the use of resale of products being purchased and, second, in the carefully planned, methodical approach to the problem of getting the most *ultimate value* from money spent.

It tends to take the emphasis away from the net cost of the item being purchased and focuses attention on eventual total costs. For example, one manufacturer had been satisfied for years with a lacquer the cost of which was substantially lower than competitive makes. One gallon covered 250 square feet. Through value analysis techniques, the purchasing department identified a much superior but higher-priced lacquer which covered nearly twice the area per gallon. While the invoice price of this lacquer was substantially greater, the ultimate cost of using it, per unit of finished product, was reduced by 30 per cent.

Vendor Rating

Closely akin to and often considered as a part of, or a supplement to, a value analysis programme are formal procedures for evaluating vendors. Traditionally, vendors have been evaluated on the basis of relatively few factors, with high priority often attached to the criteria of lowest purchase price and convenience and reliability of supply. Many business firms have developed elaborate check lists, often comprising 30 to 50 specific rating criteria, which are used periodically to evaluate alternative suppliers, with a view to identifying those who best serve the total needs of the purchaser on an overall basis. While value analysis is concerned largely with functional attributes of a physical product, vendor analysis goes beyond, to consider the other values available from suppliers and which, therefore, are an important aspect of productive purchasing.

Optimum Order Quantities

From the preceding discussion of quantity versus small-lot buying, it is evident that the optimum quantity to purchase of a given item depends upon a wide range of complex variable factors including the following: risk of losses from deterio-ration and obsolescence; costs of storing or warehousing inventories; financial costs of carrying inventory, such as interest on investment, insurance, and taxes; risk of lost sales or interrupted manufacturing operations owing to a lack of availability; transportation costs which may vary on a per unit basis with quantity purchased; discounts or price concessions related to quantity bought; and acquisition costs such as those of processing purchase orders and handling accounts payable transactions.

The number of such variables is so large, their applicability varies so much from one product class to another, and the number of items to be purchased by most businesses is so great that traditionally the determination of purchase quantities has necessarily been largely a matter of subjective judgment, often taking into account only the most obvious of such variables, such as quantity discounts and transportation economies. However, under modern conditions of automatic data processing by means of high-capacity electronic computers, it is relatively easy to use mathematical formulas which relate all of the variable factors listed above, for the purpose of determining the optimum quantity to purchase for each one of thousands of items which are *regularly* bought in substantial amounts. It is, moreover, feasible to do this as frequently as changes occur in any of the variable factors included in the formulas.

Automatic Reordering

In many large organizations, electronic computers are used to reduce the amount of human judgment involved in routine reordering of staple items continually maintained in stock. This necessitates the prior determination of minimum stock levels for individual items, based on factors such as historical rates of sale, optimum reorder quantities (as discussed in the preceding section), normal stockrepleni- shment time, and safety factors (stock "cushion") to allow for random or unpredictable needs (e.g., delays in transit or occasional sales in unusually large quantities). Once a minimum stock quantity for an item is determined, computers can be used to reduce reordering to a semiautomatic or completely automatic basis. All information about changes in stock levels is fed into the computer. New purchases or receipts are added to previous balances, and all sales or use information is deducted, with the result that data are constantly available within the computer to reveal the current inventory figure for each item.

A computer can be programmed so that it prepares daily a list of all items for which the amount of stock on hand, plus the stock on order, is less than the previously determined minimum. The computer can also indicate the number of units that should be ordered to bring the inventory (plus commitments) up to desired levels. This results in semia-utomatic reordering, since the buyer need give attention only to computer determined replenishment requirements of those items listed on such special reports.

In some cases reordering is completely automatic in the sense that the computer is programmed to prepare an actual purchase order for a predetermined optimum purchase quantity whenever the stock on hand and on order falls below specified minimums. The buyer then needs only to signify approval of the computer-prepared purchase order by signing it.

Marketing Significance

While the various scientific or analytical procedures discussed above have been growing in importance, their application has been confined mainly to large-scale buyers and even then principally in connection with goods which are purchased regularly. Extensive use of such procedures involves two prerequisites—specialization of a fairly high order in the buying organization and volume of sales sufficient to warrant the use of expensive data processing equipment. Such procedures are of rather limited value for new items for which there is no historical information on use or resale, for items the sale of which is relatively unpredictable owing to changing consumer tastes or fashion, and for items needed only occasionally. Nevertheless, their application has been widespread in industrial purchasing, particularly for materials used in manufacture and for supply items with a high consumption rate. It has also been extensive in wholesale distribution warehouses (whether operated by manufacturers, chain store companies, or regular wholesalers), particularly those dealing in numerous items continuously maintained in stock as, for example, groceries, hardware, drugs, and automotive supplies.

The impact of such procedures has been to place buying on a more scientific plane, with the result that the buying function is controlled more rigidly by predetermined criteria. As a consequence many sellers have been forced to adapt their marketing operations more closely to the requirements of customers who have committed themselves to any or all of the buying procedures here discussed. This has made it much more difficult for the seller, in appropriate cases, to count upon his own selling effort to bring about changes in buying practices. Such procedures have also had an important bearing upon more scientific approaches to the physical distribution of goods.

BUYING PRACTICES

Various practices are followed in contacting resources, appraising their selections, and making purchases. Buying may be accomplished through central market visits, by negotiating with salesmen who visit the purchaser's premises, by means of trade registers and directories, in cooperation with other buyers who have similar needs, or by delegating the authority for purchases to a central agency.

Visiting the Market

In a number of lines of business, leading central markets have developed, and these are regularly visited by merchants or store buyers who wish to make purchases. New York City, for example, is both an important manufacturing and buying centre for women's clothing. Other cities such as Chicago, Miami, St. Louis, Dallas, San Francisco, and Los Angeles are of importance as centers of supply for the same merchandise and are visited annually by merchants.

The major market for furniture and home furnishings is in Chicago. Hundreds of exhibitors have offices and show-rooms in this city in, or in the vicinity of, the Merchandise Mart, which is a famous market centre with 93 acres of floor space. Other major furniture markets include New York, Dallas, Atlanta, Los Angeles, and High Point, North Carolina. A general trend in both apparel and home furnishings markets has been for the number of centers to increase with more emphasis upon regionalism. This has made it possible for larger numbers of buyers from all parts of the country to visit at least one market centre, but it has also created problems for many manufacturers who now find it necessary to display merchandise in a greater variety of market centers.

A number of considerations affect the frequency of market visits. Buyers from stores located in communities remote from central or regional markets, even though interested in style merchandise, may go to market but once or twice a year or not at all, while those near at hand make frequent visits. Buyers from large firms usually visit markets more often than do representatives of the smaller houses. Retail stores which feature special sales at short intervals make frequent market trips to procure merchandise for these sales.

Trade Shows

A great deal of buying activity takes place at special trade shows which are held periodically, usually annually or semiannually, in many lines of business—for example, toys, house wares, hardware, office equipment, scientific instruments, packaging materials, and materials-handling equipment. Such shows are usually held in a major city with hundreds or thousands of exhibitors displaying their wares in temporary booths established for the duration of the show in hotels or exhibition halls. Some of the well-known shows of this type are held in connection with national, regional, or state trade association conventions so that buyers can combine buying trips with attendance at business meetings of their association. Trade shows are of such outstanding interest in lines in which they are common that considerable attention is devoted to them in trade magazines.

Buying on the Purchaser's Premises

All kinds of business firms do a large part of their buying on their own premises, either by mail orders or through suppliers' salesmen. Mail orders sent to suppliers are the least important for most organizations. They are usually based on catalogs furnished by vendors or information contained in trade registers and directories. Many retail stores and wholesalers use the mails for fill-in orders which are placed in the interval between salesmen's calls or visits to market centers. This method is also commonly used in industrial purchasing, especially for routine or occasional buying of supplies, tools, and stocks of repair parts.

Buying from salesmen is the second form of purchasing on the buyer's premises and is doubtless the most important single form of buying. Most independent dealers in convenience goods buy a large part of their stock from wholesalers' salesmen who visit the store. Much style merchandise, even that sold in the very largest department stores, is purchased from manufacturers' salesmen who visit the store with samples of ready-to-wear items supplied by New York garment houses and other similar resources. Buyers for wholesale establishments, factories, and governmental units also spend a considerable amount of time with suppliers' salesmen who call at their offices, and a large proportion of their requirements is bought in this manner.

Group Buying

The practice of *cooperative combination of orders from a number of buyers* so that relatively large purchases can be made at attractive prices is known as group buying. This practice is used occasionally by some wholesale and retail merchants in a wide variety of trades but is especially important among groups of department, dry goods, and apparel stores that have combined orders of many articles to the mutual advantage of participants. Arrangements for group buying are often made by resident buying offices. These arrangements include plans for group participants to visit the central market at the same time. Samples of the type of merchandise under consideration are collected and examined by the attending buyers who express their preferences by voting upon various offerings. Quantities desired by the participants are then pooled into a combined order and a price is negotiated with the resource.

The principal advantages of group buying lie in the lower prices usually secured from vendors, the fact that the merchandise may be produced to specifications of the group and packaged or labeled with the group's brand name, and the use of the combined judgment of a group of qualified experts in selecting merchandise. Group buying has, however, met with only limited success. For this there are several reasons. First, some lines of goods must be selected with the particular needs of each store's clientele in mind.

The pooled judgment of a group of buyers from different stores does not always result in the selection of just the type or style of goods which a given store needs. Second, many buyers have failed to cooperate fully in such purchases because of the tendency of the plan, if successful, to minimize the value of their individual buying skill. Third, some manufacturers refuse to make offerings to cooperative groups because sales can be effected only at such low prices as to make the business economically unattractive or impossible to justify under the price discrimination provisions of the Robinson-Patman Act.

Central Buying

An important buying practice, limited substantially to large multi-unit organizations, is that of central buying. Its distinguishing feature is that *authority and responsibility for purchasing are vested in a central office rather than in the individual operating units* involved. This practice is widely used by almost all types of large retailing chains, to a limited degree by independent retailers of fashion merchandise through arrangement with resident buying offices, to a considerable extent by multi-unit wholesaling and manufacturing companies, also by various governmental units that have a central purchasing organization for different divisions or departments. In some shoe or apparel chain stores, for example, there are no buyers in the individual stores. Local store managers are chiefly responsible for sales and have responsibility for buying only to the extent of providing the central office with daily or other frequent stock control information that indicates the sales of various items and changes in the inventory situation. The central office buyer makes all market contacts, handles negotiations with suppliers, and makes actual purchases. On the basis of individual store stock and sales reports, merchandise shipments are made to them as directed by central office personnel, either direct from factories or from a central warehouse operated by the chain. In the grocery, variety, and drug fields the practice varies from this pattern. Store managers or other key employees check the stock periodically and requisition or order merchandise as needed, but from warehouse stocks or catalog listings that have been made available through central office negotiations.

Similar practices are sometimes followed in industrial or governmental purchasing. A large manufacturer of automotive equipment may operate a number of different factories, widely scattered geographically. If each of them requires similar equipment, materials, or supplies, the individual requirements are sometimes consolidated and purchased centrally.

Specific procedures used in central buying vary from one type of industry to another and often among different firms within a particular industry or trade. Regardless of variations in detail, central buying is generally adopted to obtain specific advantages which include the following: greater skill and specialization in the buying function than would be possible if each unit did its own purchasing; lower merchandise costs through the negotiating power which comes from consolidating the requirements of the various units; ability to take advantage of favorable market opportunities through continual contacts with suppliers; and economies in purchasing and accounting obtained by combining what would otherwise be a large number of individual transactions, each entailing the same unit costs for office procedures.

Specification Buying by Contract

When a firm exercises rigid control over the quantitative and qualitative characteristics of an item being purchased, the practice is known as specification buying. This type of buying is quite frequently accompanied by a contractual arrangement in which the buyer agrees to purchase stipulated quantities of goods for delivery at periodic intervals or as requisitioned, and at prices which either are set forth in the contract or are to be established in terms of some formula which is incorporated in the agreement. Contracts sometimes involve commitments for a substantial proportion of the seller's total output and may cover all or a major part of the purchaser's requirements for a period of many months or even a year or more.

Because of the rather substantial character of many such contracts, they are often negotiated through high-level executives of both parties. This buying practice is encountered in various segments of business, including retail chain and mail order companies which sell products under their own brand names, wholesaling companies that feature private brands, manufacturing companies that require materials of certain specifications for further processing or for incorporation in their end product, and governmental purchasing units, especially the military organizations.

Various considerations underlie such contractual arrangements. In the case of manufacturers, the assurance of a continuing supply of raw materials at a predetermined price is often the dominant motive. On the part of some purchasers, contracts for periodic delivery of instalments may be dictated by a desire to secure quantity prices without assuming the burdens incident to carrying heavy average inventories.

Many merchants have also attempted to secure the advantages of quantity buying without assuming the disadvantages through placing contracts for the periodic future delivery of large orders. Some large retailing concerns, for example, enter into contracts calling for the delivery of a certain number of pairs of hosiery each month for a period of months. Such contracts involve careful manufacturing specifications. Colors and shades are usually not determined at the time when the original contract is made but are furnished by the buyer from time to time during the life of the contract.

The manufacturer finds such an agreement advantageous in that it enables him to plan a production programme and to buy raw materials more intelligently. At the same time the purchaser profits by securing a quantity price and an assured supply without increasing his average inventory and, by supplying currently a schedule of colors and shades, he is enabled to adjust his stock to shifting consumer preferences in colour and shade.

Buying Committees

Owing to the proliferation of new product offerings in the post-World War II era, many merchandising organizations have removed ultimate responsibility for adding or eliminating new products from an individual departmental buyer and have assigned authority for final judgment and decision on such matters to a buying committee. While such committees are used in many kinds of retailing and wholesaling establishments, they are most common in the supermarket industry where about 90 per cent of the larger organizations report their use. Under the buying committee arrangement, a departmental buyer handles all purchasing responsibilities for items regularly stocked. He also sees salesmen for new products and collects all relevant information about new items which are presented. He may reject a new item, but if it meets with his approval he still does not have the authority to buy it. Instead, it must be presented to the buying committee which considers not only matters of departmental significance, but also reviews proposed new items in terms of corporate objectives. Each new item presents certain problems relating to limited shelf space, capital investment in inventory, promotional requirements, ware-house storage and handling, and competitive significance. It is largely due to these over-all problems that buying responsibility for new items is often assigned to buying or merchandising committees.

Specialized Buying Agencies

The dynamics of marketing is vividly illustrated by a number of agencies which have emerged as specialized buying institutions. Their economic justification rests upon ability to render a unique service at a low cost to a group of firms with common buying problems.

Resident Buying Offices

A well-established segment of our buying structure is the resident buying office. Principally serving department, general merchandise, and apparel stores, these offices have largely supplanted private central market offices which were formerly maintained by some larger independent stores. Resident buying offices developed for the purpose of supplying central market representation for merchants and of relieving them from the necessity of making frequent trips to central markets. Such offices represent many retailers in the same line of business, and because of this fact they are able to render many services at a relatively small cost.

By means of a staff of experts constantly in touch with market developments, the resident buying office is able to keep its client stores in touch with the best sources of supply. The office becomes the headquarters of visiting buyers who are guided in their purchases by office buyers of comparable lines. Style bulletins and other market information are sent to member stores at regular intervals and, in general, the office acts as their representative in the market. Some group buying and central buying is sponsored by resident buying offices, and many fill-ins are selected by its buyers for member stores.

Payment for the resident buyer's services by a fixed yearly fee is a common practice in this field, the amount being fixed by the estimated sales of the store during the period of the contract. Smaller stores are often served by resident buyers who may receive payment in the form of commissions on sales made for certain manufacturers. Resident buyers are an increasingly important factor in the distribution of ready-to-wear and certain dry goods lines. Distance from the market and the importance of style merchandise to the individual merchant are the principal factors determining the extent to which they are used.

Several hundred resident buying organizations are located in New York City in the so-called "garment district" in midtown Manhattan. Many of the larger organizations have branches in other principal markets for fashion merchandise, including Chicago, Los Angeles, San Francisco, and certain foreign countries.

Independent Purchasing Agents

Several independent business firms, known as purchasing agents or purchasing companies, provide a buying and market information service for wholesalers of consumer goods and for industrial distributors. Typical is an organization in the wholesale hardware and mill supply trade which serves many wholesalers by locating sources of new, superior, imported, or scarce merchandise and in other cases by securing attractive price quotations for them. Descriptions of thousands of items are supplied to the wholesalers in the form of a loose-leaf price book. Whenever the client believes that he can do so advantageously, he places orders with the purchasing agent, who in turn transmits them to the proper supplier for shipment. Each client pays a monthly membership fee for the services thus rendered. Similar organizations serve hundreds of wholesale grocers.

Purchasing agents of this type render an important service and constitute an important element in the distribution of certain lines of goods. Their freedom to develop and operate was somewhat curtailed by the Robinson-Patman Act, for this law forbade collection of brokerage fees from sellers except for services rendered to such sellers rather than to buyers. It had been the practice of the purchasing agent to collect brokerage fees from sellers and to remit at least part to their clients, a fact which gave the clients a price advantage as compared with their competitors who bought directly from the same supplier or through the regular broker who kept his entire brokerage fee.

Prevention of this and other types of price discrimination was one of the primary objects of the law. The result has therefore been that membership fees must be large enough to cover the cost of the purchasing agent's service, a fact which has somewhat reduced his importance as an agent for placing orders but which has in no way lessened the value of the market information provided.

In many trades brokers are sometimes employed by buyers to locate advantageous sources of supply, particularly for seasonal commodities or for items in short supply. When so utilized, the broker performs some of the functions of the independent purchasing agent.

Commissioners

In purchasing goods in foreign markets buyers are frequently under the disadvantage of a lack of knowledge of good sources of supply and are further handicapped by a lack of knowledge of the language. To assist such buyers, individuals known as commissioners or commissionaires are found in foreign markets. It is the function of the commissioner to bring the buyer into contact with proper vendors and to function as an interpreter. When the American buyer is not abroad, the commissioner keeps in communication with him, furnishing him with samples and information about goods. The commissioner represents the buyer and receives his compensation from him.

Buying and the Law

Owing to its significance as one of the two exchange functions of marketing, buying comes within the purview of certain public policy regulations. Since the whole subject of government and marketing is dealt with at a later point, it is sufficient here merely to note some of the more important legal implications.

Under the Sherman Antitrust Act, a buyer is prohibited from conspiring with other buyers whereby as a group they agree not to make purchases from certain sources of supply, when the agreement would be in restraint of trade, thus foreclosing a market or channel of distribution to one or several potential suppliers whose policies do not meet with the favor of the buyers who are in collusive agreement. Such an agreement is in violation of the law *per se,* regardless of actual effect. A buyer may also be guilty of unfair methods of competition in trade or commerce, under the Federal Trade Commission Act, if he joins with others in formulating lists or directories of buyers, where the purpose or intent of such lists is to cause suppliers to sell only to those whose names appear thereon. Under the Robinson-Patman Act it is unlawful for a buyer operating as a wholesaler (or retailer) also to presume to act as a broker and thus receive a brokerage fee on merchandise purchased for resale as a merchant.

The Act limits the payment of brokerage fees to parties that are acting on behalf of, or are controlled by, the party making the payment. Also under the Robinson-Patman Act it is unlawful for a buyer knowingly to induce or to receive a discrimination in price which is prohibited by the law. As this matter has been viewed by the courts, it pertains primarily to cases in which a buyer, knowing full well that there was little likelihood of a cost saving or other legal defence by the seller for a price discrimination, nevertheless received or proceeded to exert pressure for lower prices than could be legally justified by the seller. These few illustrations are sufficient to indicate that regulations exist which, to some extent, limit the buyer as well as the seller in situations involving monopolistic, trade restraining, or unfair competitive practices.

7

Knowledge Management in HRD

The economy is rapidly being transformed into a knowledge economy. Therefore, individuals, teams and companies need to develop the necessary competencies to be able to participate in a working life that is mainly based on knowledge productivity. Traditional approaches to management, training and development will not provide the learning environment that is required for knowledge work. Therefore, each company needs to design a corporate curriculum that turns the day to day work environment into a powerful learning environment.

The knowledge economy offers the possibility of prosperity to those who can join the new elite of knowledge workers. It also inherently creates new imbalances. The learning environment should help individuals to develop their talents and take part in various forms of knowledge work. The concepts of knowledge productivity and the corporate curriculum raise also the question of how far knowledge productivity can be managed. These concepts may even question the role of managers in a knowledge economy.

Perceptions of the role of human intervention in economic transactions have changed. The emphasis upon individual physical labour and ability to regulate and coordinate transactions has given way to an emphasis upon the potential human contribution to the production and application of knowledge. Of the products manufactured and services rendered by organizations, material items (such as commodities), capital and physical labour, are now less significant than the combination of knowledge embodied in the product or service. It is widely accepted that we are moving away from an industrial economy to a knowledge economy. Of course, traditional economic aspects such as labour and materials are still important, but it is now critical to be able to add value to products and services through knowledge. Economic success requires the ability to improve and innovate.

This slow but dramatic change in the economy will have a tremendous impact on organizing work and the meaning of learning. As a consequence, professionals in the domain of human resource development will have to reconsider their role and their potential contribution to a 'knowledge productive' work environment.

One of the views underlying the knowledge economy is that the application of knowledge adds more value than the traditional economic factors like capital, raw materials and labour. Many writers have commented on such an economy, using a variety of synonymous terms including: the 'information society', the 'learning society', the 'network society', the 'learning economy' and 'economies of expertise'. In all these concepts learning and collabouration are key aspects.

Organizations must learn quickly, drawing on information from many external as well as internal sources, in order to be able to repeatedly improve and innovate. Sustained competitive advantage depends on the rapid generation and application of 'dynamic capabilities', defined as the firm's ability to integrate, build and reconfigure uniquely valuable competencies. Venkatraman and Subramaniam (2002) argue that the key resources that drive value creation are knowledge and expertise. In economies of expertise strategic capability emerges from knowledge, which is embodied in people. Therefore the authors suggest that we may find a direct and significant link between the talent pool of the employees and the performance of the firm. Here the need for collabouration and networking of employees becomes crucial for the development of an organization.

The Organization for Economic Cooperation and Development (OECD) adopted the idea of an emerging knowledge economy and developed supporting policies in its reports Lifelong Learning for All (1996), Literacy Skills for the Knowledge Society (1997) and Knowledge Management in the Learning Society (2000). In 2001 two OECD publications, The Well-being of Nations: The Role of Human and Social Capital (2001a) and The New Economy: Beyond the Hype - The OECD Growth Project (2001b), contained a strong plea for major investment in education, training and lifelong learning to enhance economic growth.

Economic Necessity for Individual Learning

In the current timeframe, it is challenging to investigate the characteristics and requirements of an emerging knowledge economy and its implications for individual development in the context of work-related learning. Such analysis might lead to the fresh hypothesis that externally imposed performance goals, power-based managerial positions and the concept of ownership of knowledge-intensive companies in the hands of anonymous shareholders could well inhibit knowledge productivity.

The defence of such propositions resides in the economic necessity for an individual-centred perspective on HRD, with a strong emphasis on the emancipated and autonomous professional. Such a perspective is not restricted to the highly educated service worker: even manual workers must be cooperative, responsible, creative and autonomous. It could be argued that the cultural shift from social solidarity and collectivity to individual lifestyles and independent membership might hamper the socially embedded process of knowing.

However, the social context of an organization should counterbalance the potential risk of individual self-centeredness, and should foster networks that find their cohesion through the mutual attractiveness, reciprocal appeal, shared interest and the passion of their members. Traditional virtues like obedience and loyalty do not propel improvement and innovation. Human capital as a resource for organizational performance will not be enough. It needs to be supported by social capital, based on shared responsibility, integrity, trust, respect for human dignity and environmental awareness. All these elements require high levels of critical individual learning.

Human resource development is not an exclusive corporate interest. More than ever before, individuals want to master their own lives and expect to contribute to the economy and society. The International Labour Organization (2002) places the individual at the centre of the knowledge and skills-based society and reports impressive growth results in Danish enterprises that combined learning activities and innovation. In Sweden, the Adult Education Initiative (AEI) is the largest adult education investment initiative ever undertaken in the country and explicitly puts the focus on the individual. In Europe, the development of individuals as active citizens of society is given a central place in statements of learning and education objectives.

Learning opportunities and decent work underpin individuals' independence, self-respect and well-being, and, therefore, are the key to overall quality of life. The European Council held a special meeting on 23-24 March 2000 in Lisbon to agree a new strategic goal for the European Union in order to strengthen employment, economic reform and social cohesion as part of the knowledge-based economy. Investing in people is the focal point in the European Union's policies, not only to play an important role in the knowledge economy, but also to resolve existing social problems of unemployment, social exclusion and poverty.

Economic growth, innovation, social cohesion and lifelong learning are considered as inseparable. More recently, the 2002 European Council in Barcelona stressed the importance of education and training in the achievement of the Lisbon ambitions, by setting a new overall goal 'to make Europe's education and training systems a world quality reference by 2010'. These policies put HRD at the core of a learning society and a knowledge economy.

Knowledge Management

The managerial tendency since the 1920s has been based upon routine work and mass production, an approach characterized by standardization with a focus upon efficient procedures and regulations controlled by the 'brains' at the top of the organization, who set the strategy. The problem with this is that in the knowledge economy, where the complexity of work increases and the role of knowledge creation is gaining importance, (top) management is no longer equipped to direct and control the organization in a traditional way. Management now has to be done at every level, and it also requires a contribution of knowledge from all employees at all levels. As a consequence an entirely new approach to employing and managing workers is called for.

The old work contract was based upon obedience and loyalty, in return for a decent salary and the company taking care of you and managing your performance. As soon as employees offer an entirely different input to the company, in terms of contributing ideas and proposals to improve and radically innovate, they become part of the collective ambitions of the organization. This is already happening in consultancy businesses and small, knowledge intensive networks.

When capital is displaced by the capability to create knowledge, the legitimate base for a company shifts from ownership by anonymous shareholders to knowledge workers. This leaves managers in an insecure position: the traditional role of the middle person between capital and labour becomes obsolete, and controlling brainwork is hardly possible any more. Many recognize the importance of organizational knowledge and the capability to develop new knowledge, but they often apply the traditional management principles to exploit this potential resource. From a classical business perspective it was inevitable that 'knowledge management' entered the organizational area.

Yet, the move to the knowledge economy has been accompanied by an engineering approach to knowledge management, based upon building knowledge systems, extracting knowledge and making it explicit - which is far from knowledge sharing. When in the new economy knowledge comes to be regarded as an individual capability that cannot be directed, handled, controlled and assessed in a manner familiar to managing financial capital, commodities and physical labour, then knowledge management will appear to be an anachronism, using an outdated term to facilitate a new phenomenon.

However, the concepts of knowledge productivity and the corporate curriculum do raise the question of how far knowledge productivity can be managed. These concepts may even question the role of managers in a knowledge economy. Managerial ability to develop strategies, procedures and control work processes turned top management into the ruling business class of the twentieth century, a position that they inherited from the company owners. In exchange for security and material support employees carried out their jobs in a disciplined and obedient fashion. As knowledge productivity becomes the driving force in the twenty-first century and, as this knowledge production will be found at every level of economic activity, knowledge workers and autonomous professionals will take charge. The corporate curriculum, as a collective learning space, might become the binding force of knowledge networks, and smart communities that heavily depend on shared intrinsic motivation and personal affinity with the content of the job.

Knowledge Productivity and HRD

Although the capability of knowledge creation already plays an important role in the new economy, the breakthrough of the knowledge revolution will occur as soon as we are able to apply knowledge systematically to the production of knowledge. Understanding the processes of knowledge productivity, organizing a knowledge productive work environment and supporting employees in their ongoing work-related learning will probably become one of the main challenges for HRD.

Where knowledge is dominant - not just among upper management but at all levels of organizations - daily operations should be designed to support knowledge productivity. This process entails signalling, identifying, gathering, absorbing and interpreting relevant information, using this information to develop new capabilities and applying these capabilities to incremental improvement and radical innovation of operating procedures, products and services.

Most of the elements in the description of the concept of knowledge productivity are supported by learning processes. In fact the process of knowledge productivity is a way of facilitated individual, team and organizational learning. These notions on the development of knowledge and making it productive are closely related to human resource development if not at the core of it. In the years ahead, knowledge productivity will become an increasingly critical economic factor. Understanding how knowledge productivity arises and the competence to promote knowledge productivity are becoming critical capacities for participation and survival in a knowledge economy.

The knowledge productivity concept is based on the view that knowledge is a personal competence. More specifically when 'knowledge' is defined in terms of a personal, individual capability, capacity, craftsmanship or expertise, it involves a subjective skill that is inextricably linked with the individual(s) concerned. The objective is not merely to apply rules and procedures in dealing with standard problems but also to improve on such rules, analyse new situations, devise new concepts and improve understanding of the mental and learning processes underlying the capabilities stated. Thus, knowledge development is seen as a combination of individual knowledge application within teams and the company's coordination capabilities in providing the direction and resources for these teams. As Tomassini concludes: 'the firm is a mechanism for the governance of economic activities, coordinating processes that integrate the knowledge of different individuals for the production of goods and services'.

For organizations, knowledge becomes productive when the creation and application of knowledge results in gradual improvements and radical innovations of operating procedures, products and services. These processes take place in collabourative work relationships. Knowledge work and learning cannot be enforced on the basis of power, control or contract. It requires a shared ambition that is attractive, comprehensible and meaningful for both employees and the organization. New ways of organizing work for knowledge production need to be developed. The idea that management does not set the goals nor determines the direction of employee development, is central to the concept of knowledge production and the supporting learning. Knowledge workers and autonomous professionals take charge of their own development.

The main principles for this concept are self-control and self-organization, integration of working and learning, coaching, leadership and collabouration. Such learning processes take place among staff members and clients in the course of their work. In addition, people are becoming increasingly aware that learning for knowledge work may be stimulated and supported through a variety of means other than formal training programs. Options include issuing special assignments, changing positions or seconding staff members, and actively participating in quality teams and discussion groups. Alternative possibilities entail organizing the work through project management and equipping the workplace with electronic performance support systems.

Given the vital importance of the learning processes involved, leaving the necessary learning to random opportunity would be imprudent. A systematic approach with a clear purpose therefore appears necessary. Yet the feasibility of managing such learning processes is open to question and is hardly possible in the manner in which we are accustomed to running other industrial processes. Ascertaining knowledge creation appears far from simple, as the necessary learning processes will not appear on command. Alternatives have been presented by Tjepkema (2003) when she studied the learning infrastructure of self-managing work teams. In fact her research introduced a different language to describe the nature and quality of a work-related learning environment.

Adopting a socio-constructivist approach, she uses terms such as a 'rich landscape for learning' where learners become motivated, not on the basis of hierarchy and power, but through relevant, authentic and meaningful work, in collabouration with colleagues. Instead of 'managing' the required learning processes, nurturing and supporting the learning ecological system is advised.

Knowledge work probably requires a transformation of work processes. Tapscott (1999) describes this transformation as follows:

When knowledge is the basis of value creation, work and learning are the same. Knowledge workers, whose 'products' often don't exist in the physical world, have a different relationship to their work and their employers, and different expectations about their professional growth.

Similarly one of the main conclusions of Stewart and Tansley's (2002) research on training in the knowledge economy is that this transformation has major implications for HRD:

Informal and work-based learning is of increasing importance in the knowledge economy. Highly developed learning skills are necessary to maximise the potential offered by conscious and deliberate learning through work. Her research at Harvard on behavioural interaction with technology led her ultimately to a powerful conclusion on enthusiasm for the knowledge content of every activity, that could easily form the core of modern HRD theory:

This love of learning is woven throughout the organisation, whether the activity be problem solving across internal boundaries, creating knowledge through experimentation, importing from outside, or transferring it to other sites and nations. People who are knowingly engaged in building core technological capabilities are curious: they are information seekers. There is a sense of enjoyment in the work - the lightness of step that suggests that building knowledge not only makes good business sense but is fun.

These statements, findings and conclusions reinforce the main point that in a knowledge economy the characteristics of work processes can best be described in terms of learning processes, and that these do not appear on command, and require a mutual interest of employee, team and organization.

Learning in a Knowledge Economy

The traditional approaches to management, training and development will not provide the learning environment that is required for knowledge work. Therefore, each company should consciously develop an integrated plan for learning, 'a corporate curriculum' that turns the day-to-day work environment into a powerful learning environment. On the basis of the argument made in the previous sections, participants in a knowledge economy who wish to integrate the necessary learning in their actual work, need to adopt a number of learning strategies, that involve reflecting on the meaning of their actual work in relationship to their talents and capabilities.

These learning strategies also include regular discussions on how to turn the work environment into a rich and interesting setting. As teamwork is so important, members need to confer on how to improve their collabouration and make it more appealing. Individual professionals will search for the hidden factors that inhibit and support their motivation, involvement and commitment. In fact, these strategies aim at enhancing the learning infrastructure of knowledge work.

These considerations and strategies lead to three development principles for knowledge work that refer to the social context, the personal affinity with domain specific content, and deliberate interventions to support the learning culture.

Enhancing Reciprocal Appeal

Knowledge-productive workplaces are rich learning environments in which the social context fosters collabourative efforts. No single manager, instructor or trainer is exclusively responsible. Participants work hard to maintain their reciprocal appeal, which means that they do their best to provide each other with a fruitful learning environment. Important characteristics of this social context for learning seem to be: reciprocal respect, appreciation and integrity, ample security and openness for constructive feedback and confrontations. The communicative and interactive skills of the participants are required to meet high standards. The need for reciprocal appeal is a keenly understood self-interest. Knowledge workers who are dissatisfied with the current learning environment cannot hold others responsible for improving it. If they are unable to improve the interactive setting, they have no choice but to seek out more appropriate surroundings. Teams may lose valuable colleagues this way, while overly eager 'jobhoppers' fail to cultivate their own appeal for others.

Searching for a Passion

People are clever only if they want to be. Nobody can talk somebody else into curiosity, motivation, interest and ambition. People cannot be 'smart against their will'. Discipline, loyalty and obedience may be welcome and valuable support systems for overcoming a temporary hurdle or an impasse. Without any substantive drive, however, they are likely to lead to mediocrity at best.

Knowledge-productive environments encourage cultivation of a personal, substantive theme. Such an individual theme and passion for work inspires curiosity and enables information to be traced more quickly. It facilitates establishing connections with attractive, professional networks and stimulates exceptional achievements where others might give up. Knowledge workers need to become competent to navigate through the diffuse arena of affinity, motivation, passion and ambition to be able to develop and apply their capabilities in a productive way.

Enticement Towards Knowledge Productivity

Cultivating reciprocal appeal serves primarily to create a favourable social context and a rich learning infrastructure, while searching for a passion establishes the foundation for substance and subject matter expertise. However, promoting knowledge productivity also requires the competence to work deliberately and systematically on the quality of the social context and the substantive component. The desire to manage, control and monitor in these matters is becoming increasingly difficult to fulfill. The growing interest in self-guidance is apparent in both work and learning contexts. If we touch here on issues that cannot be managed in the traditional way this raises the question of how we can tempt or entice each other towards knowledge productivity. The main objective is to develop the capability to design a work environment that fosters the development of capacities like learning to learn, organizing reflection, increasing reflexivity and basically applying knowledge to knowledge development.

These three principles for knowledge development directly support the learning infrastructures needed for the successful establishment of communities of practice as described by Wenger (1998) and Wenger and Snyder (2000), the ethical, social and psychological attributes of the social relationships in networks as identified by Lundvall and Borrás (1997) and the development of social capital marked by trust, cooperation and mutual sharing as explained by Putnam (1993) and Nahapiet and Goshal (1998).

In a knowledge economy, where improvement and innovation are required for long-term survival, standardization is not the goal, but rather the extraordinary, the surprising, the artistic.

This assumption not only affects managerial thinking, but also influences our perception of the characteristics of almost every employee and knowledge worker. As a result, one of the arguments in the upcoming debate is that the required knowledge for improvement and innovation is basically an individual, subjective competence. Team learning and organizational learning provide the context for individual knowing. The knowledge economy will probably require the autonomous, independent individual to undertake learning for personal growth. However, this will happen in a context of communicative rationality: a process of reaching understanding through the cooperative negotiation of common definitions of a situation. Here the paradox of emancipation comes into play. Howell observed that when workers become active participants in process improvement, they also take on more and more responsibility. Doing so, they inevitably start questioning whether their interests match the interests of the organization.

Knowledge development, improvement and innovation require a high level of personal involvement from employees. This capability cannot exist without critical reflection and emancipation. Emancipated employees will critically examine the corporate goals, the ethics of governance and shareholder property of their knowledge work. In a knowledge economy, corporate success and individual emancipation will be difficult to separate. Are top managers and shareholders able and prepared to pay this price for sustainable economic growth?

The Basis of Knowledge Productivity

From such a perspective it is evident that the focus in HRD should shift to the individual, to individual learning, objectives, motivation and conditions. This means that work-related learning will inevitably comprise reflection, learning from mistakes, critical opinion sharing, challenging groupthink, asking for feedback, experimenting, knowledge sharing and career awareness. These characteristics of critical reflective work behaviour are identified in the research of Van Woerkom (2003) and point towards an emancipated, autonomous professional as the main protagonist in a knowledge intensive work environment.

Such work environments should encourage employees to become self-directed learners:

To pursue their interests, to find personal meaning, and to adapt to and change their life circumstances ... adult learners are assumed to be capable of framing their own choices, reflecting on their options, and making responsible, informed decisions that serve their interest.

When the knowledge economy thrives on the basis of individual learning and critical knowing, this has major implications for organizing work, establishing knowledge networks and promoting professional development. The deliberate choice of incorporating personal meaning, the social context and ethical values within the concept of knowledge productivity supports the prevalence of tacit knowledge. However, its inherent social embedding and implicit character rather than the formal scientific knowledge expressed in peer reviewed research and protected patents, will be central to organization-based knowledge development.

Implications for HRD

Research on knowledge development in the context of organizations is making it increasingly clear that far more attention needs to be focused on how to bring workplace communities of practice together in a shared organizational purpose, without, however, destroying the unique self-regulating properties that make them so attractive to individuals and so powerful in driving the knowledge process. This realization lends further weight to earlier conclusions that the emphasis in knowledge-creating organizations should be less on devising management systems to 'control' learning or to 'manage' knowledge, and more on encouraging people to think creatively and provide the skills and support systems to share and apply their findings to benefit the organization.

The concept of the corporate curriculum requires the HRD function to produce and promote processes and initiatives to support the acquisition of subject matter expertise, learning to identify and deal with new problems, cultivating reflective skills, acquiring communication and social skills, supporting self-regulation of motivation, affinities and emotions, promoting peace and stability, and stimulating creative turmoil.

It is quite widely agreed that HRD professionals need to become learning facilitators, and learning architects who can promote strategically valuable knowledge. The move away from training and the view that HRD is an organization-based process is widely recognized. McGoldrick et al. conclude: 'HRD will be increasingly concerned with facilitating the learning of individuals, teams and organisations through the design, structuring and organisation of work itself.'

The concept of the knowledge productive work environment focuses not only on the social aspects of a favourable learning climate, but also on the need for individuals to explore and invest in their personal domains of interest, and to create meaningful work.

To do so HRD is not an objective science of 'social engineering' but has a strong philosophical dimension which needs to be made explicit? When exploring knowledge as a social process of 'knowing' the key issue will become rather the emancipation of the knowledge worker - engendering a new freedom for knowledge workers, as it is they who are at the centre of knowledge development. Qualities of social capital, trust, respect, integrity, ethics, meaningful work, affective involvement and practical wisdom assume key significance, in order to generate knowledge that will bring benefits to all parties, whether in the board room or in the workplace.

This way of reasoning brings us back to the roots of adult education focusing on individual learning experiences, critical consciousness and liberation, interventions for promoting well-being, emancipatory learning and critical theory, critical, reflective thinking and analysis, the direct facilitation of the development of individuals through improving the educative quality of their environment and lifelong learning and the new educational order.

This case for a critical and individual development perspective, leading to the emancipation of knowledge workers, may engender a strong reminiscence of the radical and politically engaged adult educators of the 1970s. However, the argument developed here is not a naive U-turn to a socialist, communist or anarchistic past, in a period of economic crises, following the collapse of an over-enthusiastic free market play.

Promoting the development in organizations of an appropriate learning culture does not only require critical thinking and emancipatory learning. When the focus shifts from the external and internal transfer of explicit knowledge to the social construction of tacit knowledge among members of informal networks, more emphasis has to be placed on creating favourable conditions for learning in the workplace than on organizing the provision of formal training. The new literature on technological change, improvement and innovation emphasizes an evolutionary process, which takes the form of the steady accumulation of a tacit capability through work-related learning processes. Thus, public knowledge can be effectively exploited only by firms that develop learning processes embodied in a form of social organization. Even economists start to acknowledge that successful linkage between science, research and technology requires face-to-face contacts in communicating the results of complex learning processes which embody a tacit element.

Improvement and innovation require individual learning in a favourable social context.

First, it should contribute to an understanding of the process of knowledge productivity, improvement and innovation, and the support of learning. Second, it should develop interventions to facilitate the learning functions of the corporate curriculum for knowledge work, and with an emphasis upon the learning infrastructure and critical reflective work behaviour. Third, it should start a dialogue on the need for emancipation as a prerequisite for sustainable growth. Finally, it should promote the development of social capital in which knowledge networks are embedded.

8

Documentation and Preparation of Vouchers

DEFINITION OF DOCUMENT

A document is a bounded physical or digital representation of a body of information designed with the capacity to communicate. A document may manifest symbolic, diagrammatic or sensory-representational information. To document is to produce a document artifact by collecting and representing information. In prototypical usage, a document is understood as a paper artifact, containing information in the form of ink marks. Increasingly documents are also understood as digital artifacts. Colloquial usage is revealed by the connotations and denotations that appear in a Web search for document.

From these usages, one can infer the following typical connotations:

- Writing that provides information person's thinking by means of symbolic marks.
- A written account of ownership or obligation.
- To record in detail; "The parents documented every step of their child's development".
- A digital file in a particular format.
- To support or supply with references; "Can you document your claims?".
- An artifact that meets a legal notion of document for purposes of discovery in litigation.
- Document is the practical construct for describing matter in different forms which retain information for a reasonable period of time wherein it can be perceived by a sentient observing entity.

The variety usage reveals that the notion of document has rich social and cultural aspects besides the physical, functional and operational aspects:

- Document is just a practical concept which presently would be defined narrowly based on human understanding and perception of the external world.

- Document in its wider connotation could include matter in all its forms, even a universe could be perceived as a document on a wider scale.
- The practical construct requires the retention of information but the relevance of the information
- The information must also be with reference to the observing entity be retained for a reasonable period of time wherein it can be observed. Fleeting images which cannot be seen are almost as if never observed.

CONCEPTUALIZATION IN ANALYTICAL PHILOSOPHY

The notion of document admits both an empirical and analytical characterization. The analytical characterization hinges on the semantic character of the word document, as well as the use of a primitive notion of document in accounts of larger communication constructs such as discourses, or related constructs such as language games. The nominal 'document', like other nominals, exhibits familiar patterns of polysemy.

For example, "document" might be used on an occasion to denote a certain body of information independently of how that information is physically rendered, or it might be used to denote a particular physical instantiation of a body of information. This kind of polysemy bears some similarity to what Nunberg, 1979 termed "container/contents polysemy". These patterns of polysemy exhibited by 'document' matter for the following reason.

A certain document qua body of information will have different properties than a document qua physical rendering of a body of information. Importantly, the latter would have the property of being a static, physically bounded thing.

The former would have the properties of being able to evolve over time, being susceptible of certain changes to information content, and being capable of supporting multiple physical instantiations that have allowable differences in information content. This distinction is relevant to the discussion of aspects and history of documents below.

EMPIRICAL CHARACTERIZATION

In light of the polysemy of the core concept of document, it is useful to note a number of examples ranging from instances commonly understood as prototypical documents, to instances that are understood as documents only in specialized or rare situations.

- *Prototypical Documents*: Letters, memos, legal forms, owners manual
- *Documents of Record*: Newspapers, magazines
- *Books*: Textbooks, novels, cookbooks, encyclopedias, comic books
- *Canonical Documents*: Code of law, statute, constitution, religious text
- *Transactional Documents*: Cheques, contracts, medical prescriptions, receipt, forms, Postage stamps

- *Functional Documents*: Portable Document Format files, PostScript files, XML files, e-mail
- *Non–Prototypical Documents*: Post-it notes, fortune cookie strips, maps, paintings, milk cartons, cereal boxes
- *Non–Classical Digital Documents*: Web pages, blogs, wikis
- *Boundary Examples*: The Pioneer plaque on the Pioneer 11 spacecraft, designed by astronomer Carl Sagan, and using information assumed to be universal is an extreme example of a document that is intended to communicate with aliens. Conversely, the recorded and printed signals of the SETI project would constitute documents if they were discovered to contain alien communication.

SOCIAL ASPECTS OF DOCUMENTS

Documents play a key role in the construction of social reality and therefore play a part in accounts of every important aspect of human society and culture. An example of this type of account is in the seminal account of the role of print in political evolution, Imagined Communities. More direct examples include the works of Marshall McLuhan.

Many key social aspects of documents arise from their historically unchanging character. This aspect leads to a definition of a document as a talking thing, whose strengths and weaknesses both arise from its relative immutability with respect to oral forms of communication.

The relative immutability of documents has thus historically been important for establishing a record of transient events, or for preserving information whose precise linguistic form is of ritual or practical importance. Note though, that historically many societies have accorded greater authority to disciplined oral traditions as more reliable than parallel written ones.

With this caveat in mind, the following social aspects of information may be noted:

- *Social Value*: The information in documents as well as documents themselves are often valuable; the information because of the influence represented, and the document itself when it is believed to be a rare or unique and authentic representation of the information it contains.
- *Manifestation of authority*: Documents are often produced to provide a record that will be considered authoritative in the future, particularly with respect to government. Consider receipts, titles, and deeds as examples of proof of ownership, and passports or driver's licenses as proof of identity.
- *Conventional*: Documents inherit a key feature of language-based communication in general: they are denoted as documents by convention. Virtually any medium can constitute a document provided the people involved can agree on the meaning represented. Hence cave drawings, hieroglyphics, scrolls of sheepskin, sheets of papyrus, ink on

paper, magnetic tape and electronic files are all documents under certain accounts.

- *Manifestation of economic labour*: Historically, the effort required to produce a document has been significant, so only the most important documents were created. The Illuminated manuscript of the pre-Gutenberg era demonstrates the cost have become richer.
- *Manifestation of business processes*: Documents play many roles in the internal management of a business as well in the interfaces between businesses and their suppliers, employees, and customers. Current trends towards longer value chains and increased regulation increase the number of documents that must be generated and processed.
- *Instruments of Governance and Law*: The unchanging aspect of documents is crucial to the consistent communication of policy and administration of law to citizens. Documents that play such roles include constitutions, corporate annual reports and religious texts.
- *Analytical philosophical character*: The notion of document plays a role in political philosophy, as well as in the philosophy of law
- *Role in Religion*: Documents play a key role in religion, and constitute canonical content. Document-related terms such as dogma and doctrine have today acquired pejorative connotations primarily due to historical events associated with religious documents.
- *Cultural Significance*: Documents play a central role in art of all varieties. In the movie Office Space for instance, central plot elements are frustration with bureaucratic process involving the fictional "TPS reports" and a malfunctioning printer.
- *Metaphoric Significance*: Metaphors based on documents permeate our thinking, ranging from the obvious to the highly allegorical.

FUNCTIONAL CHARACTERISTICS

Documents also manifest several, more localized characteristics that determine how we use them in everyday life:

- *Manifest nature*: Information is physical, *i.e.* it always must exist in a tangible form, even when digital. IBM computer scientist Rolf Landauer is credited with this observation and working out its implications. By virtue of being realizations of chunks of information, documents are necessarily physical in all their forms.
- *Contextuality and Situatedness*: All communication takes place in a context, which includes at least the shared understanding of the parties communicating. Explicit and implicit references to the context can convey a large amount of meaning by building on the shared understanding, but that meaning is lost to another party that does not share that context. For example, Shakespeare in the original would be incomprehensible to modern readers simply because of the evolution of language and spelling since the seventeenth century,

and modern readers normally read modernized versions. Similarly, hypertext documents exist in a context which is lost if printed, leading to a different offline reading context.

- *Evolvability*: When we think of a document as a definitive source containing the best known information about a topic there is need to change that information as more is learned. This is frequently done by revising the document into a new version or edition. Typically, older versions are archived to facilitate understanding how the document has changed. In modern contexts, when technologies such as wikis or software source code are under discussion, this evolvability can require very sophisticated version control technologies.
- *Renderability*: Every abstract entity that is understood to be a document in some context can be rendered, often in more than one way. A rendition of a document refers to a particular physical or electronic representation of the information from the document. For example, a portable document format representation and a web page may contain the same information but have substantially different properties and appearances. We think of them as different renditions of the same document. We might similarly consider different translations of a document to be the same document although differences in language context and structure may make it impossible to express precisely the same meaning in both languages.
- *Affordances*: Documents in digital and physical forms manifest various "affordances". The affordances of a particular rendition of a document determine its uses. For example, paper has the affordances of allowing flipping and easy tactile manipulation, while digital forms are easier to edit.

CLASSICAL ROLES AND WORKFLOWS IN DOCUMENT PRODUCTION

There are a number of roles in which people are involved in the creation and distribution of traditional paper documents; some, but not all documents are processed by people acting in each role, each of which may be performed by an individual or a group. Books are a well known example of documents that require an extensive publication process, but many other documents undergo similar processes to at least some of those from book publication.

Each of these roles is considered to improve or add value to a document. These roles are generally understood as being clustered in various phases in the production of a classical document, including authorship, editing and prepress.

Roles and workflows in the production of modern digital documents are more variable and are discussed in the part on future documents:

- An author selects the content to be communicated and performs the initial organization and recording of the content. A document in this state is often called a manuscript.

- A reviewer reads the content and evaluates it with respect to the intended audience. Reviewers often recommend only the best documents to be published. Documented reviews are frequently published as guidelines for document consumers as well.
- An editor helps to organize and express the content so that the meaning is clear and understandable, and follows the conventions of the symbolic representation such as spelling and grammar.
- A publisher orchestrates the process of producing a document, often decides whether a document is worth the effort of publishing, and collects and disseminates the profits from sales of a produced document.
- A printer formats the document into a comfortable form such as a bound book. Printing can be a very complex and elaborate process, including
  - *Pagination:* function performed by an individual who takes on the tasks of organizing text, fonts, images, headings, footnotes, chapters and parts to accommodate the physical constraints of a printed page aesthetically.
  - *Pre–Press*: function performed by print shops in preparing paper documents for production.
  - *Imposition*: organizing desired pages on a larger media such that when folded and trimmed the pages will be upright and in order.
  - *Printing*: marking paper with ink or toner
  - Folding pages into parts
  - Binding pages together and covering
  - Trimming
  - Packaging
- A distributor manages inventory and physical distribution of printed documents to retailers.
- A retailer manages a local inventory and sales to consumers, and often is familiar with the content and can make appropriate recommendations.
- A librarian organizes, tracks borrowing of, and archives documents.

A publication process enables a consumer to purchase or borrow, read and learn from documents. Consumers are often the intended audience of the publication process.

DOCUMENT PRODUCTION TECHNOLOGY

Document production technology has evolved significantly through history. While a great deal can be said about ancient production technologies including papyrus, palm leaves, stone tablets and marking devices ranging from quills to chisels, the modern form of the document has evolved largely under the influence of printing technologies.

The Illuminated manuscript of Europe is a useful prototypical instance of the document at the end of its evolution before the widespread use of printing. The associated technology was largely a human one. Other cultures at this stage used other forms of pre-print era documents.

The history of printing can be traced as follows:

- Bronze Age civilizations made extensive use of seals for commercial and transactional purposes. The particular case of the signet ring was of particular importance, and is still in use in place of signatures in East Asian countries like Korea, where it is common for individuals to carry a seal.
- Chinese Woodblock printing was the first widespread technology that automated important parts of the document production process.

The Gutenberg Printing Press enabled the mass production of faithful copies of documents, and hence the widespread dissemination of information. The widespread access to information enabled fundamental changes to society in religion, government, law, business, and entertainment. Prior to the press the huge effort required to faithfully hand-copy severely limited the number of documents available, and hence access to the information contained therein.

The effort to set type and prepare a document for reproduction was still high, but many high fidelity copies could be produced.The development of Lithography constituted the next great advance in document production technology and continues today to dominate the economic landscape of document production, an economic sector estimated to be of the order of $1 trillion. Lithography brought economies of scale and extremely high quality and low cost to documents. The typewriter improved the accessibility of document production technologies and enabled it to enter mainstream workplaces. Carbon paper enabled a modest number of copies to be produced concurrently with the original. A brief era of photography-based technologies flourished in parallel with the age of typewriters.

The Xerox Copier became a major milestone in document production by eliminating the typesetting effort required by a printing press. The Xerographic technology could produce durable and economical copies of a paper document easily and quickly. Modern digital printers from Xerox and other companies such as HP, Canon and Ricoh, can produce more than 240 black and white or 170 copies of a page each minute, and work with up to 6 colours and dry and wet inks.

This technology supports a $100 billion market in digital printing, particularly in domains where lithography has clear limitations. Computers enabled information to be stored electronically in databases and electronic files on magnetic tapes, drums, and disks. This led to a radical disruption of all document production technologies. Initially most of this information was printed onto paper by teletypes, but computer printers rapidly became faster and more sophisticated. Computers, by controlling lasers in xerography, micro-nozzles in inkjet systems, and tiny solenoids in mechanical systems, became capable of being serially embedded in the document production process. Computers are also critical to modern lithography. A whole interaction style with computers was developed around the metaphor of working with documents and folders on a desktop, to the point that the word document is now commonly associated with the information stored in a computer file according to the metaphor. Today, electronic paper is viewed as one potential future evolutionary physical form of the prototypical document, as it can present the electronic document with the readability of printed paper.

DOCUMENT LIFE CYCLE MANAGEMENT TECHNOLOGY

Technology to manage documents has evolved in parallel with documents themselves. Of particular importance are practices concerning the preservation, archival, destruction and management of documents.

These constitute what is known as the "document life cycle":

- *Physical preservation*: Documents in both traditional physical forms and in digital physical forms such as magnetic media must be physically preserved. This aspect of document management deals with such issues as the aging of paper and obsolescence of magnetic media.
- *Storage*: This aspect includes management of scarce resources such as shelf space and disk space, and associated technologies such as optimal space utilization. Modern libraries such as the University of Nevada and the University of Michigan often use complex space-saving technologies such as robotic retrieval systems for stacks and moving bookshelves. In the digital realm, the entire discipline of compression technologies can be viewed as concerned with the storage of documents.
- *Cultural Preservation*: This function, traditionally ascribed to librarians involves the selection, arrangement and storage of documents in safe places. The importance of this part of document life cycle management can be seen in the impact of historical events such as the destruction of books in ancient China and the burning of the library at Alexandria. Today, library and information science has evolved into an important academic discipline.
- *Bibliometrics*: This aspect of document management involves functions of indexing, generating statistics and taxonomies, and improving the usability of large collections of documents. The modern history of this management technology dates back to Melvil Dewey and the Dewey Decimal System. Today, the science of bibliometrics is largely concerned with managing the impact of electronic technologies. This aspect must also deal with ISBN numbers, Library of Congress data and other standards.
- *Digital Content Management*: The explosion of digital content has resulted in technologies to manage large collections of digital

information generated by organizations. Such systems must manage access control and privileges, multiple electronic format, interface with printing infrastructures and enable collaborative work flows around documents.

- *Digital–Physical Interaction Management*: As long as both paper and digital documents continue to have value, the modern management technologies to manage their interaction will continue. Key to this management is the management of large scale and systematic scanning of physical documents.
- *Destruction*: With the increased cost of identity theft, corporate scandals and privacy concerns, the destruction of both paper and electronic documents has become increasingly important to manage. Technologies such as shredders play a role, as do verifiable processes of destruction of electronic documents to ensure compliance with privacy laws.
- *Security*: Shannon's information theory has led to an entire discipline that concerns itself with the security of documents, and associated technologies such as encryption, as well as more physical security features such as watermarks and making currency documents safe from counterfeiting.
- *Transportation*: The entire postal system, as well as modern courier systems, is largely built on the need to move documents physically from one location to the other.

THE DOCUMENT ECONOMY

The economics of the production and management of documents indirectly impacts every economic sector. While the total economic value of the document economy is hard to estimate, the economic sectors with business models directly dependent on documents include:

- *Document Authoring Technology*: This sector supports a huge variety of digital and physical production technologies, ranging from Microsoft Word to LaTeX to advanced layout software.
- *Education*: The production and processing of documents is so critical that entire educational disciplines have evolved around writing, editing, layout and design of documents. The information sciences are also part of the document economy.
- *Electronic Document Management*: Managing documents within organizations and in public and personal contexts supports a huge industry in content management systems, ranging from free public infrastructure such as wikipedia to proprietary enterprise applications such as Docushare and Documentum.
- *Physical Document Management*: Large manufacturing sectors producing everything from 3-ring binders to filing cabinets and office desks exist largely due to the need to process documents.

- *Media*: The paper industry exists to support the document economy.
- *Print equipment*: From lithography and xerography to pencils and crayons, an extraordinarily diverse set of equipment industries depend on documents.
- *Document Services*: In large organizations, the life of documents in the work flows and processes of daily activity represent an enormous locus of value addition and cost reduction, which has led to a burgeoning industry in managed document services, ranging from specialized niches to managed office printing.
- *Retail Production*: From large chains such as Kinko's in the United States to small copy shops and offset print shops, documents support a large production sector for the end user.
- *Publishing*: All publishing, ranging from offset-based newspaper and magazine printing, to highly customised modern publishing using publish-on-demand digital print technology, is part of the document economy. The publishing industry includes major sub-areas such as the writer's market, small, medium and large publishing houses, small and large distributors and a vast network of independent and chain bookstores, online retailers, a large used-documents market and subscription-based markets.
- *Document Transportation*: The international postal system, as well as the commercial package transportation systems represented by companies such as DHL and UPS have economic models based largely on the demand for document transportation.

FUTURE OF DOCUMENTS

Since the advent of the digital era, documents have been rapidly evolving, and may require fundamental reconcept-ualization. Efforts at this reconceptualization include Vannevar Bush's initial conceptualization of hypertext.

The impact of digital technology can be understood in terms of several key aspects:

- *Blurring the notion of document boundary*: Hypertext and Web content make it hard to determine what is being denoted by the term document. While the early days of the Web resulted in documents that mimicked their physical ancestors, Web content rapidly took on new characteristics. Reconceptualization of the notion of "boundary" is a key intellectual challenge.
- *Increasing structure and openness*: The document is going from an opaque container of information to a much more open, structured document. XML is underlying most document formats today. In the future, it will become even more queriable, with the actual elements of this document being tagged—*e.g.* HR-XML.
- *Dynamic nature*: Web analogs of traditional paper documents like a newspaper column have taken on a dynamic character due to the

impact of technology enabling the addition of comments from readers. The document will increasingly become "virtual", bringing up-to-date information from various sources in one container—as such,it will be kept evergreen.

- *Paper and electronic are reconciling*: Paper has traditionally been a gap in document processing workflows. Technologies such as OCR, OMR, 2D Barcodes and Anoto pattern technology are helping get its content back into the electronic world. In the future however, Not only will that transition be seamless, but it will also be possible to track it while in the "physical" world through RFID and MemorySpot.
- *Hybrid automated/human authorship*: authorship workflows for digital documents have evolved to include the computer in a key role. Dynamic Web pages may be viewed as the joint output of a human author and a software system. Sophisticated examples of this phenomenon can be found in recent evolutions in paper documents as well. Variable data technology, for instance, allows creators of direct mail marketing documents to vary the content of every piece in a print run using technologies such as DesignMerge or Xmpie.
- *Prosumer workflows*: Content repositories such as Wikipedia radically alter traditional document production workflows by blurring roles such as author and editor.
- *Customizability*: Digital technology allows users to actively participate in the construction of documents they see, realizing the postmodern notion of construction of meaning in an unexpectedly literal way.
- *Long Tail Economics*: Technologies such as blogs have allowed document production economics to operate with such radically cheap cost structures that single individuals can derive an income from a global audience with low capital expenses. This has led to an explosion of niche content.
- *Blurring of Documents and Interfaces*: Technologies such as Ajax or Apollo blur the distinction between documents and user interfaces to "intelligent" technologies, leading to a whole class of smart documents that can go beyond the passive nature of traditional documents.
- *Fluidity and Dynamic Microstructure*: Distinct from the impact of hypertext on the notion of document is the fluid potential of modern documents at the microlevel, which allows an enormous variety of word and sentence level dynamic phenonomenology.

DOCUMENT MANAGEMENT SYSTEM

A document management system is a computer system used to track and store electronic documents and/or images of paper documents. The term has some overlap with the concepts of content management systems. It is often viewed as a component of enterprise content management systems and related to digital asset management, document imaging, workflow systems and records management systems. Beginning in the 1980s, a number of vendors began developing systems to manage paper-based documents.

These systems managed paper documents, which included not only printed and published documents, but also photos, prints, etc. Later, a second style of system was developed, to manage electronic documents, *i.e.*, all those documents, or files, created on computers, and often stored on local user file systems.

The earliest electronic document management systems were either developed to manage proprietary file types, or a limited number of file formats. Many of these systems were later referred to as document imaging systems, because the main capabilities were capture, storage, indexing and retrieval of image file formats. These systems enabled an organization to capture faxes and forms, save copies of the documents as images, and store the image files in the repository for security and quick retrieval. EDM systems evolved to where the system was able to manage any type of file format that could be stored on the network. The applications grew to encompass electronic documents, collaboration tools, security, and auditing capabilities.

COMPONENTS

Document management systems commonly provide storage, versioning, metadata, security, as well as indexing and retrieval capabilities.

Here is a description of these components:

- *Metadata*: Metadata is typically stored for each document. Metadata may, for example, include the date the document was stored and the identity of the user storing it. The DMS may also extract metadata from the document automatically or prompt the user to add metadata. Some systems also use optical character recognition on scanned images, or perform text extraction on electronic documents. The resulting extracted text can be used to assist users in locating documents by identifying probable keywords or providing for full text search capability, or can be used on its own. Extracted text can also be stored as a component of metadata, stored with the image, or separately as a source for searching document collections.
- *Integration*: Many document management systems attempt to integrate document management directly into other applications, so that users may retrieve existing documents directly from the document management system repository, make changes, and save the changed document back to the repository as a new version, all without leaving the application. Such integration is commonly available for office suites and e-mail or collaboration/groupware software. Integration often uses open standards such as ODMA, LDAP, WebDAV and SOAP to allow integration with other software and compliance with internal controls.

- *Capture*: Capture primarily involves accepting and processing images of paper documents from scanners or multifunction printers. Optical character recognition software is often used, whether integrated into the hardware or as stand-alone software, in order to convert digital images into machine readable text. Optical mark recognition software is sometimes used to extract values of check-boxes or bubbles. Capture may also involve accepting electronic documents and other computer-based files.
- *Indexing*: Track electronic documents. Indexing may be as simple as keeping track of unique document identifiers; but often it takes a more complex form, providing classification through the documents' metadata or even through word indexes extracted from the documents' contents. Indexing exists mainly to support retrieval. One area of critical importance for rapid retrieval is the creation of an index topology.
- *Storage*: Store electronic documents. Storage of the documents often includes management of those same documents; where they are stored, for how long, migration of the documents from one storage media to another and eventual document destruction.
- *Retrieval*: Retrieve the electronic documents from the storage. Although the notion of retrieving a particular document is simple, retrieval in the electronic context can be quite complex and powerful. Simple retrieval of individual documents can be supported by allowing the user to specify the unique document identifier, and having the system use the basic index to retrieve the document. More flexible retrieval allows the user to specify partial search terms involving the document identifier and/or parts of the expected metadata. This would typically return a list of documents which match the user's search terms. Some systems provide the capability to specify a Boolean expression containing multiple keywords or example phrases expected to exist within the documents' contents. The retrieval for this kind of query may be supported by previously-built indexes, or may perform more time-consuming searches through the documents' contents to return a list of the potentially relevant documents.
- *Distribution*: A published document for distribution has to be in a format that can not be easily altered. As a common practice in law regulated industries, an original master copy of the document is usually never used for distribution other than archiving. If a document is to be distributed electronically in a regulatory environment, then the equipment tasking the job has to be quality endorsed AND validated. Similarly quality endorsed electronic distribution carriers have to be used. This approach applies to both of the systems by which the document is to be inter-exchanged, if the integrity of the document is highly in demand.

- *Security*: Document security is vital in many document management applications. Compliance requirements for certain documents can be quite complex depending on the type of documents. For instance, in the United States, the Health Insurance Portability and Accountability Act requirements dictate that medical documents have certain security requirements. Some document management systems have a rights management module that allows an administrator to give access to documents based on type to only certain people or groups of people. Document marking at the time of printing or PDF-creation is an essential element to preclude alteration or unintended use.
- *Workflow*: Workflow is a complex problem and some document management systems have a built-in workflow module. There are different types of workflow. Usage depends on the environment the electronic document management system is applied to. Manual workflow requires a user to view the document and decide who to send it to. Rules-based workflow allows an administrator to create a rule that dictates the flow of the document through an organization: for instance, an invoice passes through an approval process and then is routed to the accounts payable department. Dynamic rules allow for branches to be created in a workflow process. A simple example would be to enter an invoice amount and if the amount is lower than a certain set amount, it follows different routes through the organization. Advanced workflow mechanisms can manipulate content or signal external processes while these rules are in effect.
- *Collaboration*: Collaboration should be inherent in an EDMS. In its basic form, a collaborative EDMS should allow documents to be retrieved and worked on by an authorized user. Access should be blocked to other users while work is being performed on the document. Other advanced forms of collaboration allow multiple users to view and modify a document at the same time in a collaboration session. The resulting document should be viewable in its final shape, while also storing the markups done by each individual user during the collaboration session.
- *Versioning*: Versioning is a process by which documents are checked in or out of the document management system, allowing users to retrieve previous versions and to continue work from a selected point. Versioning is useful for documents that change over time and require updating, but it may be necessary to go back to or reference a previous copy.
- *Searching*: Finds documents and folders using template attributes or full text search. Documents can be searched using various attributes and document content

- *Publishing*: Publishing a document is sometimes tedious and involves the procedures of proofreading, peer or public reviewing, authorizing, printing and approving etc. Those steps ensure prudence and logic thinking. Any careless handling may result in the inaccuracy of the document and therefore mislead or upset its users and readers. In law regulated industries, some of the procedures have to be completed as evidenced by their corresponding signatures and the date(s) on which the document was signed. Refer to the ISO divisions of ICS 01.140.40 and 35.240.30 for further information. The published document should be in a format that is not easily altered without a specific knowledge or tools, and yet it is read-only or portable.

STANDARDIZATION

Many industry associations publish their own lists of particular document control standards that are used in their particular field. The following is the list of some of the relevant ISO documents. Divisions ICS 01.140.10 and 01.140.20.

The ISO has also published a series of standards regarding the technical documentation, covered by the division of 01.110:

- ISO 2709: 1996 Information and documentation—Format for information exchange
- ISO 15836: 2009 which replaces ISO 15836:2003 Information and documentation—The Dublin Core metadata element set
- ISO 15489: 2001 Information and documentation—Records management
- ISO 21127: 2006 Information and documentation—A reference ontology for the interchange of cultural heritage information
- ISO 23950: 1998 Information and documentation—Information retrieval—Application service definition and protocol specification.
- ISO/CD 10244 Document management—Business process/workflow baselining and analysis associated with EDMS technologies
- ISO 32000—portable document format

DOCUMENTATION

Documentation may refer to the process of providing evidence or to the communicable material used to provide such documentation. Documentation may also refer to tools aiming at identifying documents or to the field of study devoted to the study of documents and bibliographies.

Subfields of documentation include:

- Medical documentation
- Technical documentation
- Legal documentation
- Administrative documentation

- Historical documentation

Documentation In Computer Science:

The following are different types of documentations usually seen in the Computer Science field:

- Architectural and Design documentation.
- Technical Documentation.
- User Documentation.
- System Documentation.
- Marketing Documentation.

There are various types of Documentation Tools which are available for this purpose.Documentation understood as document is any communicable material used to explain some attributes of an object, system or procedure. It is often used to mean engineering documentation or software documentation, which is usually paper books or computer readable files that describe the structure and components, or on the other hand, operation, of a system/ product.

A professional whose field and work is documentation used to be termed a documentalist. Normally, documentalists are trained or have a background in both a specific subject and in the field of documentation. A person who more or less exclusively writes technical documentation is called a technical writer.

Technical writers are similarly trained or have a background in technical writing, along with some knowledge of the subject(s) they are documenting. Often, though, they collaborate with subject matter experts, such as engineers. Common types of computer hardware/software documentation include online help, FAQs, how-tos, and user guides.

The term RTFM is often used colloquially in regard to such documentation, especially to computer hardware and software user guides. A common type of software document frequently written by software engineers in the simulation industry is the SDF. While developing the software for a simulator, which can range from embedded avionics devices to 3D terrain databases by way of full motion control systems, the engineer keeps a notebook detailing the development lifecycle of the project.

The notebook can contain a requirements part, an interface part detailing the communication interface of the software, a notes part to detail the proof of concept attempts to track what worked or didn't work in solving certain problems, and a testing part to detail how the software will be tested to prove conformance to the requirements of the contract.

The end result is a detailed description of how the software is designed, how to build and install the software on the target device, and any known weaknesses in the design of the software. This document will allow future developers and maintainers of the trainer to come up to speed on the software design in as short a time as possible and have a documented reference when modifying code or searching for bugs.

PRINCIPLES

While associated ISO standards are not easily available publicly, a guide from other sources for this topic may serve the purpose. David Berger has provided several principles of document writing, regarding the terms used, procedure numbering and even lengths of sentences, etc.

The following is a list of guides dealing with each specific field and type:

- Documentation in health care
- Thesis writing
- Papers for academic journal publishing

PROCEDURES AND TECHNIQUES

The procedures of documentation vary from one sector, or one type, to another. In general, these may involve document drafting, formatting, submitting, reviewing, approving, distributing, repositing and tracking, etc., and are convened by associated SOPs in a regulatory industry.

JOURNAL VOUCHER PREPARATION AND APPROVAL

INTRODUCTION

Adequate support for Journal Vouchers (JV) is important to ensure JVs accurately record financial events and detailed audit trail documentation exists. Proper preparation and adequate support for JVs is the joint responsibility of Agency Office of the Chief Financial Officer (OCFO), and Centers' OCFO personnel. The accurate and timely preparation of financial statements and other financial reports is often dependent upon accurate, timely and fully supported JVs.

NASA Agency OCFO and each of the Centers shall take due care and diligence to fully comply with each of the following requirements:

- Internal controls;
- Use of JVs;
- Supporting documentation;
- Approval thresholds; and
- Management oversight and review.

Applicability. The requirements in this stage are applicable to all NASA organizational elements that prepare and approve JVs.

For the purposes of this NPR, a transaction is considered to be a journal voucher when:

- The General Ledger accounts to be debited and credited are selected and entered by the user;
- A transaction is corrected with a regular SAP document;
- Embedded system logic is not used to determine the general ledger accounts to be posted, or;
- When transactions meeting the criteria in 1.1.3.1.a to 1.1.3.1.c above are reversed or when a reversing document is a correction.

Automated distributions of summary amounts such as the distribution of payroll charges provided by the Department of Interior (DOI) based on the automated labour distribution information are not within the scope of this stage.

AGENCY REQUIREMENTS

Operational Controls. Operational internal controls shall be in place to ensure the proper recording of JVs. JVs may be prepared at the NASA Center level or at the Agency level. The Center CFO and the Director of the NASA Shared Services Center (NSSC) are responsible for developing center level operating procedures that ensure full compliance with the requirements of this stage.

General Requirements. All JVs shall be:

- Sequentially numbered in the Center's JV log and systematically numbered by the core financial system when posted by the reporting unit.
- Classified as a correction entry or a source entry based on user ID. Each SAP user has a duplicate user ID that starts with ER. These are to be used when recording transactions to identify those JVs and transactions that are correcting errors. Normal user IDs should be used on source JVs. Additional types of JVs may be added by the Agency OCFO in order to ensure greater management control and oversight of the JV process.
- Adequately documented to support the validity and amount of the JV transaction.
- Reviewed, and approved before posting at the appropriate level of management by the appropriate Agency or Center CFO or designee to ensure proper recording of entries at the posting account, appropriation, and fund levels.
- Annotated with the name, title, date, office symbol, and signature of both the preparer and the approver. In an electronic environment, the name, title, and office symbol may be represented by a user identification. A separate table shall be maintained to correlate user ID to identifying information.
- Maintained in sequential order in a central location in either hard copy, electronic form or both. The Center OCFO and the Agency OCFO must each maintain a summary log of all JVs that identifies the JV numbers and dollar amounts. The log must also reference the SAP document number that was recorded for the JV, the SAP document that was corrected and the source document information supporting the entry.

Segregation of Duties. In order to maintain the proper segregation of duties, the functions of preparation and approval of JVs must be performed by different individuals. Once the JV is prepared, the preparer submits the JV together with the supporting documentation to the approving official for approval. When the approver has approved and initialed the JV, the preparer enters the JV into the core financial system.

The preparer must then give the approving official a copy of the system printout showing how the JV was posted. Centers must have adequate internal controls in place to ensure that JVs are posted exactly as they were approved. This should be accomplished as part of the periodic monitoring and control processes.

ROLES AND RESPONSIBILITIES

Director for Financial Management, Agency OCFO shall:

- Review and, if appropriate, approve Center JVs exceeding $50 Million that are submitted by Center CFOs.
- Review and, if appropriate, discuss with the Agency DCFO and approve all prior period adjustment JVs.

Financial Management Division Branch Chief, Agency OCFO shall:

- As needed, request Agency level JVs and supporting documentation from the Center CFOs.
- Review the Agency level JVs and supporting documentation submitted by the Center CFOs for completeness and accuracy.

Center CFO shall:

- Together with the Center DCFO review and, if appropriate, approve Center JVs with dollar amounts greater than $25 Million and equal to or less than $50 Million
- Review Center JVs with amounts greater than $50 million and, if appropriate, forward to The Director for Financial Management, Agency OCFO for approval.
- Prepare Agency level JVs and supporting documentation as requested by the Financial Management Division Branch Chief, Agency OCFO.

Center Deputy Chief Financial Officer shall:

- Together with the Center CFO review and, if appropriate, recommend approval of Center JVs with dollar amounts greater than $25 Million and equal to or less than $50 Million.
- Together with the Center Reporting Branch Chief review and, if appropriate, approve Center JVs with dollar amounts greater than $10 Million and equal to or less than $25 Million.

Center Reporting Branch Chief shall:

- Together with the Center Reporting Branch Chief review and, if appropriate, recommend approval of Center JVs with dollar amounts greater than $10 Million and equal to or less than $25 Million.
- Review and, if appropriate, approve Center JV equal to or less than $10 Million.

USE OF JOURNAL VOUCHERS

JV Groupings. NASA has two primary types of JVs:

1. Correcting entries, and
2. Source entries.Correcting Entries.

Correcting entry JVs adjust for errors detected subsequent to posting including errors identified during the financial statement reporting and review process. This type of accounting entry includes specific amounts, accounts, and/or transactions related to the required correction. In some cases, correcting entries are required to adjust for errors on previously prepared JVs. In those instances, correcting entries should both reverse the incorrect entries and record the correct amount. In some cases, both entries can be made with one JV properly documented by a single set of supporting documentation. Regardless of whether a single JV is prepared, or multiple JVs are prepared, the correcting JV shall include a copy of the original JV, documentation supporting the correct amount and a narrative explanation detailing the reason why the original entry is incorrect and why the correcting entry is necessaryAll error corrections shall be recorded in SAP using ER user IDs so they can be identified by the Agency OCFO on a NASA-wide basis.

This applies when transactional corrections or other document types are used for error correction. Where feasible, error correction JV transactions shall be linked to the original transactions that were corrected. In cases where corrections are processed through interfaces and an ER user ID cannot be used, the Center shall still employ the approval process and will log the transactions in a manner that will allow them to be identified and sent to the Agency OCFO on a monthly basis.JVs record those accounting entries that, due to system limitations or timing differences have not been otherwise recorded.

By nature, source-entry JVs are usually summarized at the entity level by general ledger account. The source-entry accounting transaction shall be supported by documentation for the summarized amounts and identify the location of the transaction-level supporting detail. These documents shall be recorded in SAP using normal user IDs. Source entry JVs generally are used for month-end closing and year-end processing and closing purposes.

Source-entry JVs also may include postings of information provided through data calls, such as those required to record values for property, plant, and equipment recognition; if so, such JVs must be supported by documentation for the summarized amounts and identify the location of the transaction-level supporting detail. Presentation.

Both correcting and source entry JVs normally will be summarized amounts for which documentation is required. In these situations, the summarized accounting entry represents the amount to record the sum of the detailed transactions.

In all such cases, the summarized accounting entry shall include documentation of the effect of the detailed transactions and identify the location of the transaction-level supporting detail. JV Reversal Transactions. When JVs are reversed, the transactions must be prepared, approved, recorded, and documented in accordance with all of the requirements applicable to the original JV except when the JVs are reversed automatically as part of the routine JV reversal process.

In those instances, documentation and approval for the original JVs will be considered as the documentation and approval for the reversing entry.Sub-groupings. Both correcting and source entry JVs are further subdivided into audit-recommended JVs and customer-requested JVs. Audit-Recommended JVs. If, as a result of their audit, auditors recommend a JV adjustment be made, the auditors shall be asked to provide copies of the appropriate work papers or relevant information from the work papers to support the recommended JV adjustment.

The JV approving official shall perform an analysis of the recommendation using the auditors' work papers and other relevant information to determine if the recommended adjustments should be made. If the JV approving official identified determines that the auditors' recommended adjustments are required, a correcting JV shall be prepared. If the JV approving official determines that the audit recommended adjustments are not required, no adjustment shall be made. All auditor recommended adjustments must be approved by the Center CFO or DCFO and the Director Financial Management, Agency OCFO.

Any determination regarding JV preparation shall:

- Document why the adjustment is, or is not, required;
- Indicate how the JV approving official determined the audit recommendation should, or should not, be followed;
- Identify the audit recommendation serving as the basis for the actions taken;
- Include documentation of the decision to prepare or not prepare a JV, along with other pertinent information as the documentation for that voucher.

Customer-Requested JVs. When NASA personnel prepare proposed JVs to enter adjustments or corrections, the approving officials at NASA Centers or Headquarters must determine that they comply with this JV preparation guidance.

Evidence to support the adjustment must include, at a minimum, supporting documentation which has been reviewed and approved by the JV approving official and any related analysis performed by the JV approving official to ascertain that the adjustment is fully supported and in accordance with this JV preparation and approval guidance.

SUPPORTING DOCUMENTATION

Documentation. Proper documentation, in either hard copy, electronic form or both is necessary to support all JV entries. This documentation must be sufficient for the approving official and auditors to clearly understand the reason for preparing the JV and to be able to determine that it is proper and accurate. A request for a JV entry not supported by accurate or proper documentation shall be denied with a demand for additional information required to process the JV, along with any applicable authoritative guidance to support the need for the JV.

The supporting documentation, whenever practical, should be attached to a copy of the JV. In some cases, however, due to the large number of detailed transactions summarized in the voucher, it may not be practical to attach all of the documentation. In those cases, specific and detailed information summarizing the content and identifying the location of the supporting documentation shall be attached to the voucher.

The specific types of JV and the explanations of what is considered sufficient documentation. Note: Regardless of what method of documentation is used for any category of JV, *i.e.*, whether it is a detailed listing, a narrative explanation, or a calculation supporting the amount, the dollar amount(s) on the JV shall be clearly and readily identifiable in the supporting documentation.

Identified Errors and Reasonableness Checks/Timing Differences due to Monthly/Annual Closing. When the JV approving official has identified errors through analysis, reasonableness checks, quality control procedures, subsequent activity occurring after a period closes, or other means, a correcting JV shall be prepared. In the event an auditor identified an apparent error or omission and provided the documentation for the JV, the JV approving official will be a management official at the appropriate authorizing level, consistent with the entity internal control structure.

Evidence to support either an "authorized official" or "auditor identified" correcting JV shall include a detailed listing of identified errors, narrative explaining why the original entry is incorrect, why the correcting entry is necessary, a related analysis documenting the calculation of the correct amount, and the sources of the data used in the analysis. Reconciliation of Trial Balance and Budget Execution Reports.

When the JV approving official has determined during a reconciliation of data between two or more sources that a discrepancy exists, a correcting JV may be necessary. JV entries included in this category often are made to reconcile trial balances or other source data reported by NASA Headquarters or Centers to NASA's budget execution reports. Evidence to support this type of JV includes reference to specific documents, other source data, and a complete analysis that supports the correct amount.

If a JV is necessary, the voucher shall document why the discrepancy exists in the data, it shall contain evidence to support the proposed correction, and a description of the methodology used to validate the entries on the JV.Reversing Entries for Prior Reporting Period. When monthly or yearly accruals or correcting entries have been made for reporting purposes, they may need to be reversed in the following reporting period. The JV reversing entries shall include documentation regarding the original accrual or correcting entry and an explicit statement that the JV is a reversing entry. Data Call Entry.

Frequently, during the financial statement preparation process, source-entry information is provided by data calls where data are not recorded on a detailed transaction basis. For example, transactions at the detail levels from sources external to the OCFO may not be available in the core financial systems or information required from external Government agencies to prepare the financial statements are available only in summarized forms.

If this occurs, JVs shall be prepared to record the summarized data call amounts, so these amounts can be recorded in the general ledger trial balance. The data call entry shall be supported by documentation for the summarized amount and shall identify the source or location of the transaction-level supporting detail and/or information for the entry. Data call information, in most cases is not contained in the core financial systems and is provided by sources outside of the CFO's office.

Examples of an independent source include the NASA logistics data calls, environmental liability data calls, and accrual information from the Department of Labour and the Office of Personnel Management. Evidence to support the JV includes the transmission record of the data.

Examples of data call entries include:

- Property, plant and equipment;
- Operating materials and supplies;
- Environmental liabilities;
- Contingent liabilities; and
- Employee benefits data, Federal Employees Compensation Act data, and other information from other Federal sources.

Other Accruals. A number of typical month-end and year-end adjusting entries are made, and subsequently may be reversed at the beginning of the next period to accrue amounts for payroll, workers compensation, judgment fund liabilities, unfunded leave, and other transactions. The supporting documentation for these other accrual JVs shall include a narrative explaining the basis for the accrual, a worksheet documenting the calculation of the amounts being recorded, and the basis for any subsequent reversal.

Prior Period Adjustments. All JVs that adjust amounts reported in audited financial statements issued for a previous fiscal year, regardless of amount and type, must be approved by the Center CFO and the Director Financial Management, Agency OCFO.

APPROVAL THRESHOLDS

Journal Vouchers Prepared and Posted at the Center Level. Approval of the JV also constitutes acceptance of the supporting documentation. The organizational level within the Center or NSSC, at which JVs must be approved, varies by the dollar amount of the voucher as shown by the following table.

Table. Approval Thresholds for Center Generated JVs

JV Dollar Amount	JV Approving Official
0 to $10 Million	Center Reporting Branch Chief
Over $10 Million to $25 Million	Center Reporting Branch Chief and Center DCFO
Over $25 Million to $50 Million	Center DCFO and Center CFO
Over $50 Million	Center CFO and Director for
Financial Management, Agency	OCFO

Prior period adjustments - JVs that are adjusting beginning balances Center CFO and Director for Financial Management, Agency OCFO All JVs regardless of the type or amount that adjust amounts reported in audited financial statements issued for a previous fiscal year must be approved by the Director for Financial Management, Agency OCFO.

All auditor recommended adjustments must be approved by the Center CFO or DCFO and the Director for Financial Management, Agency OCFO. Within each of the foregoing thresholds, other approval thresholds with lower dollar values than those specified may be established to accommodate the organizational level of those preparing the JV.

The Center CFO shall designate in writing the approval threshold structure—dollar thresholds and position of approving officials within the Center. In the event that the approval authorities must be delegated to an individual other than the one identified, that delegation must also be documented in writing and signed by the Center CFO.

Journal Vouchers Posted at the Agency Level. The Agency OCFO, Financial Management Division, Data Analysis Branch Chief in coordination with the External Reporting Branch Chief will, as needed, request Centers CFOs submit JVs that will be posted at the Agency Level. These JVs must be submitted with all applicable supporting documentation and approvals.

Upon receipt of the requested JV the FMD, Data Analysis Branch Chief in coordination with the External Reporting Branch Chief will review the supporting documentation for completeness and the JV for accuracy. When the JV is determined to be accurate and all required documentation is present the Branch Chiefs will forward the JV to the FMD Director or his/her designee for approval. If the JV is over $100 million, the FMD Director will discuss the JV with the Agency DCFO prior to posting in SAP.

MANAGEMENT OVERSIGHT AND REVIEW

Managerial Controls. Adequate managerial internal controls shall be maintained at each level of management to ensure proper oversight of JV preparation. The Center CFO's and the Director of the NSSC must ensure the validity and accuracy of the JVs processed as part of their normal monthly financial management monitoring process by ensuring that adequate documentation exists to support the JV entry before it is recorded.

All corrections made by the Competency Center or by the Agency OCFO on behalf of the Centers or Agency OCFO are subject to this process. The Competency Center and/or the Agency OCFO will only make corrections/adjustments once this documentation is received. Copies of the documentation of the corrections will be attached to the Service Request and originals maintained in the Centers' logs and records. Service requests shall be established for activities performed either by the Competency Center or the Agency OCFO.

COMMERCIAL PAYMENT VOUCHERS AND SUPPORTING DOCUMENTS

AN OVERVIEW

Purpose

This stage prescribes the policy for the preparation of commercial payment vouchers and the supporting documentation. It highlights the forms most often used for contracts, receiving reports, and vouchers. It provides guidance on their usage, certification, and distribution to the paying office.

Scope

A properly certified voucher is the authority for Disbursing Officers to make payments of government obligations. The certifying officer must review evidence sufficient to support a determination that the payment is proper. Preparation and certification of a payment voucher by the entitleme1nt office advises the disbursing office that the contractual conditions for payment have been met.

9

Recording of Transfer Pricing and Taxation Transfer Pricing and Taxation

INTRODUCTION

A small operation managed by a few individuals was the typical beginning of a large corporation with a hundred operating affiliates dispersed around the world. Decision making was highly centralized and lines of communication were short. As the company grew, the founding management team found it more difficult to keep matters under control.

This problem was greatly exacerbated when operations within the company became physically separated. Centers of activity in different locations called for a different style of management. Funneling of all decisions from diverse locations through a small group of individuals, who no longer possess the necessary intimate awareness of the circumstances surrounding each decision, is a surefire prescription for stifling growth.

Growth is the name of the game for modern corporations. Growth entails individual operating affiliates taking appropriate action to enhance productivity, market share, and the scope of a company's product line. It has been found that operating affiliates physically separated from the parent organization can best achieve these objectives under a decentralized style of management. Responsibility now falls on the shoulders of the manager of an operating affiliate to make the necessary decisions that will lead to improved financial results, the universal measure of performance. The parent organization takes on a new role as coordinator and monitor of activities now that responsibility for operations has been transferred to the operating units.

Far from playing a passive role, the parent organization focuses its attention on optimizing the performance of its semiautonomous operating affiliates. To do this, the parent organization must establish, and articulate, a set of strategic goals and allocate limited corporate resources to the various operating affiliates to best achieve these goals. It must ensure that the short–term action plans of the operating affiliates are in accord with its long–term plans.

Top management positions in the operating affiliates must be filled with individuals capable of leading their affiliates in the right direction and an incentive system must be set up to induce managers to orient their thinking to the goals of the company. Finally, the parent organization must set up a financial reporting and control system to monitor its global operations, to provide necessary information for the making of decisions and to evaluate the performance of the affiliate managers.

Although operating affiliates appear to be semiauton-omous units in that they are given a wide spectrum of decision–making responsibility in managing their local operations, they are not independent centers of corporate activity. They are often united in manufacturing and marketing a common product line, in the course of which they routinely buy and sell finished goods, components, or raw materials from one another.

These intra company exchanges of goods, components, and raw materials require a transfer price. The parent organization sets the transfer price after considering various factors with an eye on optimizing corporate performance as a whole. Transfer prices are often not negotiated and agreed on by the actual buyers and sellers of the goods and components being shipped between operating affiliates. Yet transfer prices directly affect the revenue and cost of goods sold, and therefore, the profitability of the operating affiliates. Because the affiliate managers are monitored by a financial reporting and control system that scrutinizes their financial results, one can expect that affiliate managers have an entirely different perspective on transfer pricing than the executives of the parent organization. Transfer pricing can easily embroil executives of the parent organization and the managers of operating affiliates in endless disputes. Some firms have even established an administrative panel for reviewing transfer prices to resolve sharp differences of opinion between those responsible for managing operating affiliates and those responsible for setting transfer prices.

TRANSFER PRICES AND TAXES

A global company with operations in many nations must deal with a new dimension of complexity in establishing transfer prices, which is not present when a company operates solely within the confines of a single nation. A company whose operations are within a single nation pays the same taxes on profits regardless of the transfer pricing policy.

The consolidation process, whether for financial or tax accounting purposes, eliminates intra company transactions to arrive at either a book profit or a before-tax profit. When a company transacts business through affiliate companies in different nations, however, transfer pricing provides a mechanism for shifting taxable profits between tax jurisdictions.

Tax authorities in various nations are concerned with the notion that transfer pricing, often set by parent organizations outside their jurisdiction, is based on minimizing taxes paid in their jurisdictions. There certainly is an element of truth in this contention, but there are other considerations in administering transfer prices than minimizing taxes. The setting of transfer prices provides a way of moving funds internationally for a variety of purposes, of circumventing currency exchange controls that threaten to choke the operations of a company, of minimizing the deleterious impact of other artificial barriers to trade such as duties and tariffs, and of reducing currency risk exposure. A transfer pricing policy attempts to satisfy a multiple set of objectives. Some of these objectives call for high transfer prices, whereas others require low transfer prices. A company must select what it considers to be an optimal transfer price, which is a compromise price for best achieving divergent objectives.

This optimal transfer price may not be the one that minimizes taxes on profits. The selected transfer price may not be satisfactory both to the local tax authority and to the manager of an affiliate if it reduces the reported profitability of the affiliate. However, setting the transfer price is critical to optimizing the financial performance of the corporation as a whole, given the conditions that prevail at a point in time.

MINIMIZING TAXES

Tax authorities of most countries have guidelines or controls that are expected to be complied with in setting transfer prices. Management is not free to arbitrarily select transfer prices without having to substantiate their transfer price decisions. Nevertheless, there is still an element of choice where a selected transfer price may reduce the tax burden of a company. Suppose that a company consists of a parent organization and two operating affiliates—one in nation A, where the tax rate on profits is 30 per cent, and one in nation B, where the tax rate on profits is 40 per cent. The tax is applied to each affiliate's gross margin for illustrative purposes. The affiliate in nation A makes a product that is entirely sold through the affiliate in nation B. Two cases are considered—a low and a high transfer price.

Case I-Low Transfer Price

	Nation A Tax 30%	Nation B Tax 40%	Consolidated
Sales	$2000	$3200	$3200
Cost of Goods Sold	1500	2000	1500
Gross Margin	500	1200	1700
Tax	150	480	630
Net Income	$350	$720	$1070

Everything made in a factory in nation A is sold through a marketing organization in nation B. Therefore, total sales in nation A, calculated on the basis of an administered transfer price, is also the cost of goods sold in nation B. Sales in nation B of $3,200 is the net consolidated sales for the company, because all goods produced in nation A are sold in nation B.

The actual cost of manufacturing the goods in nation A is $1,500. Because nation B does not add value to the goods, the consolidated cost of goods sold for the company is also $1,500. The consolidated tax is the sum of the $150 and the $480 paid to the tax authorities of nations A and B, respectively.

The consolidated net income is $1,070, the sum of the net incomes of the two affiliates. Suppose that the transfer price is increased from $2,000 to $2,500 for goods shipped between the two affiliates. Consolidated sales, cost of goods sold, and gross margin are unaffected by the change in the transfer price, because it is netted out in the consolidation process. Taxes paid in each nation are no longer the same because of the change in the transfer price.

In case II, the increase in the transfer price shifts the profit to Nation A, which has the lower tax rate. The affiliate in nation A earns more taxable income and pays more in taxes than in case I. The affiliate in nation B earns less taxable income and pays less in taxes in case II than in case I. The net effect, as seen by comparing case II with case I, is that the company as a whole is paying less in taxes, which increases its consolidated net income.

It is true that had the two nations the same tax rate, the total taxes paid by the company, and the consolidated net income, would not be affected by changes in the transfer price. Even so, transfer prices determine what portion of total taxes are to be paid to the tax authority in nation A and to the tax authority in Nation B. Although the parent organization may be relatively insensitive concerning to whom it pays taxes, needless to say, the tax authorities are very much concerned as to which is collecting taxes.

The problem is compounded, from the point of view of a tax authority, because the transfer price is probably set by a parent organization not under its jurisdiction. The importance of transfer pricing to both managers and tax authorities can be appreciated when it is realized that between 40 per cent and 60 per cent of international trade involves goods moving between affiliates of the same company.

Corporate decisions on transfer prices do have a meaningful impact on what a tax jurisdiction collects. There are nations, islands, and localities where tax authorities exhibit little interest in transfer prices. Ireland, Puerto Rico, and other nations or areas designated as free trade zones or having special tax privileges may not tax corporate profits, or have a very low tax rate.

These nations or locales are interested in companies building plants on their soil for the social benefits that accrue from employment of individuals who might otherwise be unemployed. Companies operating in such nations or locales can substantially decrease their overall tax rate. The effective reduction in tax rates depends on the transfer prices of imported components and semi finished goods and the transfer prices of exported finished goods.

Granting tax concessions is one way for a nation to attract companies. At this time, eastern European nations offer tax incentives but do not have a prescribed accounting methodology to calculate profits, which makes it impossible to quantify the tax benefit. More than one company has set up an operation in eastern Europe to later discover that the government had a much different version in mind of the nature of the tax benefits than the investors anticipated.

Such shortsightedness by government officials has a deleterious impact on attracting other companies. Many nations are discovering that viewing business solely as a way to fill the public coffers may not be in their long-term best interests. Within the United States, states with high corporate tax rates have experienced companies moving to states with low corporate tax rates.

The higher they raise their corporate tax rates, the less they collect in taxes. As once companies moved from one state to another, now they move from one nation to another. In selecting a potential site, a businessman considers many factors, of which taxes are but one.

Some of these are social and political stability; a system of commercial law to resolve disputes; a set of acceptable accounting practices (both to assess tax liabilities and evaluate tax incentives); a labour force with the requisite skills and will to work; and an infrastructure of transportation, communication, and utility and social (education, medical care) services.

There are more locations that offer good potential sites for factories than before. Managers no longer feel that their factories must be anchored to one nation and have learned to manage far–flung operations. Nations must now compete for factories. Tax authorities in developed nations are beginning to realise that they may end up collecting less tax revenue in their eagerness to collect more tax revenue by raising tax rates.

The United States was forced to repeal a luxury tax on pleasure boats because pleasure boat construction virtually ceased with the passage of the new tax. New Jersey was forced to repeal a sales tax on trucks when truck selling companies moved their operations to nearby Pennsylvania. In both cases, tax revenues fell when tax rates were raised, and the tax authorities were forced to rescind tax increases. In a global economy, companies are mobile and will relocate to avoid especially burdensome taxes.

INTERNATIONAL FUNDING

Businesses operating in hard currency nations have the advantage of being able to transfer and convert currencies as necessary. Many nations, however, have currencies that lack convertibility, the so-called soft currencies. Transfer pricing provides a means of moving funds from one country to another, when direct currency convertibility is not possible.

If a nation has an affiliate that completes the manufacturing process and sells its output within that nation, funds can be moved out of that nation by increasing the transfer price for goods imported by the affiliate. The same objective can be accomplished by increasing the charges for services rendered by the parent organization to the affiliate, such as selling and administrative (S&A) fees, research and development (R&D) expenses, financial charges on transferred assets, and royalties for rights to patents and dividends.

Sometimes currency exchange controls focus on the amount of dividends that can be paid by an affiliate to its parent. A quasi–dividend can be paid by raising the transfer price of goods moving into the nation or by increasing corporate fees, financial charges, and royalty payments. Some nations with severe restrictions on dividend outflows will permit increases in transfer prices and service fees. These quasi–dividend payments are allowed because the local government recognizes that few companies can afford the luxury of investing in a nation that prohibits the company from earning a return on its investment.

However, actions such as these that drain funds out of a soft currency nation eventually result in some sort of currency exchange restriction. This often results in affiliate profits accumulating in a currency that may not be particularly desirable. Sometimes currency exchange restrictions can be bypassed by the affiliate making an investment, or lending funds, to an affiliate in another nation.

CONTROLLING REPORTED PROFITS

Shifts in transfer prices, corporate administrative fees, and other parent company charges to an affiliate are means of managing the affiliate's reported profitability. It may be in the interest of a parent organization to lower the reported profitability of an affiliate for reasons other than tax minimization. These include deflecting union demands for higher wages, reducing political pressure to nationalize or expropriate a profitable affiliate, and dissuading potential competitors from entering the market.

Lowering profitability is also a way to counter price controls that limit profitability. If a government has set price controls based on the cost of production plus a limited markup for profits, increases in the transfer price of goods sent to the affiliate lowers the profit margin of goods sold in that nation. This may permit goods to be sold at government decreed profit margins with the company as a whole still able to earn its normal profits.

A few nations have tax rates that are linked to profitability. The greater the profitability, the higher the tax rate. The logic behind this taxation policy is that there is a level of profits on investment that seems "excessive" to the government. Such excessive profitability should be punished by the government, and there is no greater punishment than taking away the excess profits through a higher tax rate.

By increasing the transfer price of goods being imported into the nation, the degree of profitability is decreased, lowering the tax rate and, presumably, restoring respectability in the eyes of the government. Alternatively, it may be in the interests of the parent organization to enhance the profitability of an affiliate. This may be done by lowering the transfer price of imported goods.

One reason for enhancing the profitability of an affiliate is to provide sufficient financial resources to the affiliate for it to withstand price cutting by competitive companies. Improving an affiliate's profitability, even at the cost of paying more in taxes, may allow the affiliate to borrow needed funds for operation from local banks and other financial institutions, to improve its credit rating to qualify for lower interest loans and to fund capital outlays from its own resources.

CIRCUMVENTING EXCHANGE CONTROLS

Governments with soft currencies often limit the amount of their currency that companies operating in their nations can exchange for other currencies. Their motivation is to discourage the selling of the domestic soft currency and the buying of a hard currency, which would exert downward pressure on the value of the local currency. In other words, exchange controls are set up to keep a soft currency from becoming softer.

From the point of view of a parent organization, restricting hard currency outflows inhibits an affiliate's ability to pay for imported components or other items necessary for its operations. Transfer prices for the needed components can be kept artificially low to expand the volume of goods that are being imported into a soft currency nation.

This sustains an affiliate's manufacturing operation without exceeding government decreed restrictions on converting soft currency to hard currency. But there is an adverse consequence because such a course of action results in a parent corporation accumulating even larger amounts of soft currency. These holdings of soft currency are constantly losing purchasing power through inflation.

The soft currency cannot be converted to a more desirable currency because of currency exchange restrictions and the soft currency, which has little value within the nation, has no value outside the nation. One of the knottiest problems associated with an operating affiliate in a soft currency nation is funding of hard currency imports necessary for its operation and obtaining a hard currency return on a hard currency investment.

Some companies will not set up an operation in a soft currency nation unless there is a prearranged means to earn hard currency to pay for hard currency imports and to provide a hard currency return on a hard currency investment. Pepsi Cola struck a barter deal for producing its soft drink in the former Soviet Union. Its soft ruble revenue, net of soft ruble expenses, is exchanged for Russian built tankers, which are then sold for hard currencies.

Oil companies will not set up operations in the Commonwealth of Independent States, and other soft currency nations, unless they receive a share of the output, which is shipped out of the nation and sold for hard currency. The easiest way for a company to earn hard currency in a soft currency nation would be to export a portion of its output to hard currency nations. However, most soft currency nations do not permit the hard currency revenue to remain with the company.

The hard currency revenue is exchanged for an equivalent amount of soft currency, which is then credited to the exporter's bank account. In essence, the national government receives the hard currency revenue from exports and pays soft currency to the exporter.

Sometimes international banks are at fault for imposing this condition on a nation as a means to guarantee repayment of international debt. Regardless of whether the nation or the international banks impose this condition, it is self-defeating because the economic development of a developing nation is held back by the inability of companies to earn sufficient hard currency to justify their investments.

MINIMIZING DUTIES AND TARIFFS

Duties and tariffs imposed on goods imported into a nation can be reduced by lowering the transfer price. This is the exact opposite of reducing taxes on profits by increasing the transfer price. Because the tariff rate is usually less than the tax rate on profits, lowering transfer prices to reduce import tariffs often results in a higher tax on profits. In some nations, however, tariffs on certain imported goods and commodities are not set by a corporate-determined transfer price but by an internationally posted price.

This can be done only for generic goods (steel) or commodities (oil), where there is an active market with published and verifiable prices. Sometimes tax authorities will reference costs not to a "transfer price" cost but to an internationally agreed standard. One example of this is tanker rates in the oil business. An oil company can manage the profitability, and therefore, the tax liability, of a refinery by the transfer price associated with international tanker transportation for moving oil to and from a refinery.

The tax authorities of many nations and the oil companies have agreed to a panel of experts determining a fair and representative tanker rate that is used for the computation of taxes independent of the transfer price, or internal cost, that oil companies charge for shipping oil among their affiliates. This eliminates arguments between tax authorities and oil companies concerning the appropriate shipping charge.

Determining the optimal transfer-pricing policy is further complicated when a nation in which an affiliate operates has an export subsidy programme or provides a tax credit on the value of exports. It may be advantageous to lower transfer prices to an affiliate whose output is exported to third parties or other affiliates in other nations to take advantage of these tax incentives.

The optimal transfer price depends on the nature of the export subsidy or tax credit, the volume of the affiliate's output that is exported from the nation, the relationship between taxes on profits and the generation of tax credits and on the capacity of the affiliate to utilize the tax credit or export subsidy. The nature of the taxes paid in a nation in the form of income taxes, duties and tariffs on imported goods, and export subsidies or tax credits on exported goods influence the setting of transfer prices.

There is no hard and fast rule on whether a high or a low transfer-pricing policy is best for a company. The particular circumstances of a company's operations in a nation and the nature of taxes and subsidies determine the best transfer-pricing policy. A transferpricing system integrated into a financial reporting and control system should be capable of analyzing "what" if scenarios to evaluate the effect of different transfer-pricing policies.

REDUCING CURRENCY EXCHANGE RISK

Changes in currency exchange rates result in transaction and translation gains and losses. More importantly, they affect the competitive position of an affiliate. If an affiliate manufactures and markets its goods in a nation, and imports components from another nation, a revaluation of the currency where the finished goods are being sold relative to the currency of its purchased components reduces manufacturing costs.

This makes the affiliate more competitive and profitable. A devaluation, on the other hand, increases the cost of imported components, making the affiliate less competitive and less profitable. Reality is much more complex than this simple example because affiliates may export and import components and finished goods to and from a variety of nations.

Changes in exchange rates benefit some affiliates and hurt others, and it may not be obvious because of the nature of buying and selling of goods and services. It is possible that a change in currency exchange rates that is adverse to a particular affiliate may be beneficial to the company as a whole because of the nature of the net exposure of the company to the affected currencies. Adjustments to transfer prices may affect currency holdings before an anticipated change in exchange rates takes place and may be able to restore a company's competitive position after the change has taken place.

Therefore, a financial reporting and control system should have the capacity to assess changes to both transfer prices and currency exchange rates to enable the parent organization to respond both to anticipated changes in currency exchange rates and to subsequent shifts in its competitive position.

TRANSFER PRICING AND JOINT VENTURES

A joint venture partner, a local partner owning a portion of an affiliate, and a minority shareholder are going to be as interested in transfer pricing as the local tax authority. Less often, a partnership is structured on the basis of a claim, or royalty, on revenue. More often, it is a claim on profits. If one party to a venture or partnership can influence revenue, costs, and profitability through transfer pricing, then the other party or partner, or a minority shareholder, will be deservedly concerned.

One way to manage transfer pricing with regard to having partners or minority shareholders is to formalize the setting of transfer prices in some verifiable manner such as a set markup above costs, another is to reference transfer prices to an observable market transaction. Either way minimizes the opportunity for one party to a partnership or joint venture to manipulate transfer prices to its advantage.

If the partners, participants, and minority shareholders feel that their interests are vulnerable by virtue of the other party to a business venture controlling transfer prices, then they may not contribute to the venture that which was expected of them. Avoiding these problems can be more easily said than done. Some years ago, Ford Motor Company purchased the minority shares of its partially owned subsidiaries because the company felt that it could not administer transfer pricing in a way that was fair to all concerned.

Some managements have made the strategic decision not to enter into joint ventures, or have local partners or minority shareholdings in corporate affiliates, where they can manage the profitability of the venture through transfer prices. Sometimes, the solution for a problem is to avoid the problem.

TRANSFER PRICING AND MANAGERIAL PERFORMANCE EVALUATION

It may be in the interest of the corporation as a whole to transfer in components that are more highly priced than those an affiliate can purchase from other sources. It may be in the interest of the corporation as a whole to transfer goods made in one affiliate to another affiliate for less than what the affiliate can sell them for to third parties. Although the corporation may gain by such a set of transfer prices for goods moving among affiliates, it does not serve the interests of the affiliate managers if they are subsequently judged on profitability.

This dichotomy of purpose in establishing a transfer-pricing policy for the good of the whole company, yet holding managers of affiliates accountable for profits that are contaminated, so to speak, by transfer prices has not been successfully addressed when transfer prices are different from market prices. In fact, this is one potent argument in favour of companies having transfer pricing policies based on the market price for comparable goods.

If transfer prices are set at the price for goods exchanged between unrelated parties, then there is no dichotomy of purpose in setting transfer prices and measuring performance. Managers of affiliates can be judged in an unbiased fashion on the profitability of their operations because they are buying and selling at market prices—the same prices that would prevail if they were independent companies.

The disadvantage of letting the market set transfer prices is that the parent corporation can no longer utilize transfer pricing as a means to pursue the overall optimization of the financial performance of the corporation. One possible approach to the dysfunctional aspects of setting transfer prices at other than market prices and measuring management performance of affiliates is to isolate and separately state the amount of inter company "profit" or "loss" that each affiliate is experiencing in its transactions with other affiliates.

This approach provides the parent organization with information on whether an affiliate is suffering from unwarranted decreased profitability or enjoying unwarranted increased profitability because of transfer pricing.

SETTING TRANSFER PRICES BY COST OF PRODUCTION

There are two general approaches for setting transfer prices: the cost of production and market prices associated with third party, or unrelated, transactions. The cost-of-production approach bases the price of goods to be transferred between affiliates on the variable cost of production, an allowance for fixed costs that are general in nature and are apportioned over the entire product line, and an allowance for fixed costs that can be apportioned among the individual products.

This latter category usually includes research and development costs and selling and administrative costs. The remaining components may include financial fees and royalties associated with tangible and intangible assets to be apportioned to individual products and the selection of an appropriate profit margin. The variable cost of production includes labour, material, and other direct costs that are consumed in the production of an item.

If the policy of the company is to hire and fire (lay off) factory workers as production rises and falls, then labour is a variable cost. If a company is reluctant to let go of their workers when sales decline, then factory labour should be considered part of fixed costs. Factory labour costs are usually part variable and part fixed.

Other variable costs can be the unit financing and utility costs associated with machinery and processes used in the manufacture of a particular product and unit shipping costs. These costs can also be treated as fixed costs depending on how the company's cost accounting system is set up. Fixed costs are all costs not included in variable costs. Fixed costs are the financing or depreciation costs of the factory; the overhead costs of marketing, accounting, and supervision; the cost of inventories, warehouses, insurance, utilities, communication, property taxes, and other non-variable cost items.

Fixed costs may not be entirely fixed in that there is some variation as production levels change. For instance, bonuses, which would be considered part of the fixed costs of having an executive suite, rise and fall with profits, which are related to production levels. The number of staff personnel in marketing, accounting, engineering, and other overhead functions can vary with the production level.

Some elements of fixed costs are allocated in the transfer price setting mechanism in a way that fairly apportions the fixed cost burden among the various products. Other elements of fixed costs can be apportioned more on the basis of the benefit derived by an individual product. One of these is research and development, where the allocation can be made over a product line in proportion to the degree of R&D expenditures associated with the development of an individual product.

Although there is general agreement that this is a fair way to apportion R&D expenses of successful undertakings, there is lack of agreement on how to apportion R&D expenses for failed projects. Some maintain that the allocation of expenses associated with failed R&D projects should be apportioned to all products on the basis that every product should bear the risk of failed R&D efforts.

Others object on the grounds that had the R&D effort succeeded, a particular product might not have benefited. Therefore, it makes no sense for the transfer price to contain the cost of a failed R&D effort, which, had it succeeded, would not be part of the transfer price of the product. The question as to the proper treatment of failed R&D projects is not an internal accounting matter.

Tax authorities are interested in who takes the write off of a failed R&D project. In the United States, the Internal Revenue Service (IRS) is concerned whether a transfer price contains a provision for failed R&D expenditures. If a transfer price contains only that portion of R&D expenditures that were successful with regard to a particular product, then failed R&D projects of a U.S. corporation are being written off solely against U.S. income. A portion of the tax loss write-off is passed on to the tax authority of another nation by including an element of failed R&D expenditures in the transfer price. Another fixed cost element that can be separated and apportioned in a different manner than general fixed costs are services provided to an individual product.

These may be coordination and control expenses associated with a product; costs for enhancing the efficiency of operations for manufacturing the product or expanding the scope of its market; and the costs of recruiting and training of management and operations personnel associated with manufacturing, marketing, and repairing or servicing the product. The allocation of these service costs to individual products provides another element in deriving their transfer prices.

The derivation of the transfer price also includes elements for tangibles and intangibles associated with a product. Tangibles are the plant, equipment, and other physical assets dedicated to the manufacture of the product. Part of the transfer price provides a financial return for tangibles based on their value. Intangibles represent the technical knowledge and expertise and applicable patents that can be allocated to a particular product.

The transfer price also contains an element that provides a company with a return on intangibles. Intangible costs within a transfer price cannot be capriciously determined by management because intangible costs affect taxable profits. For this reason, the IRS has established guidelines for determining the intangible cost element in a transfer price.

An intangible cost element must be present if there are intangible costs associated with the manufacture or marketing of a product and must be so identified. Intangible costs can be proportioned in relation to the income attributable to the intangibles by units of production, sales, net or gross profits, or other reasonable methods. The fee for intangible property incorporated in a transfer price must be similar to what would have been arranged with an independent third party.

The last part of the cost approach in setting transfer prices is determining the proper profit margin on the goods made by one affiliate and shipped to another. This may be the average profit margin for the company as a whole or a profit margin associated with a specific product line. Regardless, the stipulated profit margin must be reconciled in some manner with the profitability of the company or a product line to satisfy the tax authorities.

The need for reconciliation of the profit and the various cost elements of the transfer price with the tax authorities sometimes results in the tax group within the finance department of a company being responsible for administering transfer prices. However, this choice may hinder general management from using transfer prices as a means to achieve corporate objectives.

The chief advantage of the cost of production approach for setting transfer prices is that the costs are available and are subject to quantification. For this reason, the production cost approach has been more common in the past than the market price approach. The chief disadvantage is that there is no real incentive for an affiliate to improve its manufacturing process, to enhance its efficiency, or to take steps to lower costs.

Mistakes, errors, inefficiencies in manning or machinery, management inattention to detail, worker carelessness, and excessive remuneration of white and blue collar workers alike may all be incorporated in the determination of costs and passed on to the affiliates in the transfer price. Another disadvantage is that both the tax authority and the affiliates may object to the nature of the apportionment of R&D, S&A, tangibles, and intangibles among the various products and the assigned profit margin.

SETTING TRANSFER PRICES BY MARKET PRICES

The disadvantages associated with the cost-of-production method of setting transfer prices can be mostly avoided by referencing transfer prices to third party transactions for identical, or nearly identical, products. If an affiliate can obtain the item being purchased from a third party for a certain price, then that price can be the basis for setting the transfer price.

The proponents of market-oriented transfer prices maintain that letting the market set the transfer price is inherently more fair than a production-cost-based system because one affiliate is not supporting the inefficiencies of another. If an affiliate receives only the global competitive price for its products, then there is an incentive for it to take whatever actions are needed to correct the inefficiencies in its operations that are resulting in higher costs.

In a truly decentralized operation, managers are expected to make their decisions on an independent basis, and unrelated companies are permitted to compete for the business of an affiliate, along with other affiliates. The parent organization does not set transfer prices and has little or no influence over the decisions made by the managers of the affiliates. No favour or special consideration is shown to fellow affiliates in the competitive process of selecting suppliers for components and goods. The hope, of course, is that everyone is kept on his or her competitive toes to produce salable goods at the lowest possible cost. This managerial philosophy, where each affiliate is treated as an independent company, is sometimes referred to as the small business unit (SBU) management philosophy.

The disadvantage is that, although each affiliate is focused on optimizing its operations, the end result may be suboptimal performance of the corporation as a whole. Suppose that affiliate X produces all of a component (part X) for a number of widget manufacturing affiliates. Total demand for part X is 2 million per year. Affiliate X has $10 million in fixed annual costs, which include a profit margin on the investment in manufacturing facilities plus a return on the R&D investment for the development of part X. The variable costs for manufacturing part X is $5. The transfer price based on the fixed and variable costs of affiliate X supplying all other affiliates with part X is $10.

Volume of Sales: 2,000,000

Fixed Costs	$10,000,000
Variable Costs at $5 per Unit	10,000,000
Total Costs	$20,000,000
Transfer Price Based on Cost of Making 2,000,000	$10.00

Affiliate A is free to cut its best deal and obtains a quote of $9.50 from another company. Affiliate A does what is best for maximizing its profits and purchases 200,000 part X's from a third party for $9.50 rather than pay $10 to affiliate X. Affiliate X has lost a contract for 200,000 part X's and now operates on a basis of a sales volume of 1,800,000 per year.

Volume of Sales: 1,800,000

Fixed Costs	$10,000,000
Variable Costs at $5 per Unit	9,000,000
Total Costs	$19,000,000
Transfer Price Based on Cost of Making 1,800,000	$10.56

The remaining affiliates must pay a higher price because there is less sales volume to cover the fixed costs of affiliate X. The increase in transfer price to cover the fixed and variable costs is essentially equivalent to treating fixed costs as a component of variable costs, which it is not. Nevertheless, affiliate X must cover all its costs. When affiliate X announces the increase in price, affiliate B concludes a deal with a third party at $9.75 causing another loss of 200,000 for affiliate X.

Volume of Sales: 1,600.000

Fixed Costs	$10,000,000
Variable Costs at $5 per Unit	8,000,000
Total Costs	$18,000,000
Transfer Price Based on cost of Making 1,600,000	$11.25

Now it's time for affiliate C to say goodbye to affiliate X, as it maximizes its profit by reducing the cost of part X by paying $10.50 to another outside source. This is higher than the $10 price that applied when all the affiliates received part X from affiliate X. It is clear from the continuation of this exercise that, as each affiliate maximizes its profits by cutting costs, the corporation as a whole is being sub optimized.

Even if the various affiliates do not pay more than an average price of $10 per unit for part X in purchasing all part X's from outside sources, the global company is stuck with an affiliate with no sales and a fixed annual cost of $10 million that represents, in large measure, financing costs on plant and equipment. It is highly likely that the fixed costs in affiliate X contain an allowance for R&D expenses and product development that have to be recouped in the operation of a company, but do not have to be recouped by another company if it is essentially manufacturing a copy of part X.

Copying is fairly common in global commerce because patent protection is limited to the nation issuing the patent. Global companies often obtain patents in a number of nations, but this may not be possible for all nations. A company may manufacture a copy of a product in one of these nations. Although it is true that affiliate X is free to pursue patent infringement action against sales in a particular nation where it has patent protection, the time involved in enforcement proceedings and the legal expenses may make such protection prohibitively expensive.

Furthermore, there is no internationally recognized legal structure to handle patent infringements. In addition to R&D expenses, the fixed costs of affiliate X may also contain a service element for the benefit of the affiliates purchasing its output that may not be provided by third parties. By each affiliate "doing its own thing," the R&D and service costs cannot be covered.

One principal problem associated with using market reference points for transfer pricing is that the affiliates may be shipping components and parts that are not readily available from other firms. Most components and parts are specifically designed for a company's product line and are not available from third parties unless contracted for by an affiliate. Market prices for similarly designed components that cannot be actually used in the company's product line may not be relevant.

Moreover, the quality inherent in third-party quotes for similar parts may not be up to the standards imposed on products made within a global corporate family. There is no easy answer as to which approach for determining transfer prices should be followed. Both have their adherents and detractors. Either approach restricts transfer prices to something related to third-party, or market, transactions or to the cost of manufacture.

Surveys have shown that nations seem to exhibit cultural preferences as to which approach to follow and as to what motivates companies in setting transfer prices. Companies in some countries favour costbased transfer prices, whereas companies in other nations favour market-based transfer prices.

U.S. based corporations have historically preferred setting transfer prices by the cost approach because the necessary data is available, whereas the necessary data for setting transfer prices on the basis of market transactions may not be available.

Oftentimes, market quotes for uniquely designed parts and components may have to be derived rather than observed because there are no market transactions for the precise item. Should General Motors set its transfer price on carburetors being shipped to Europe based on its cost of production or on what Toyota charges its U.S. transplants? The two carburetors are not the same and do not have the same cost of production. Furthermore, there may not be a data base available for prices for carburetors sold between related and unrelated parties from which to derive a market price. Preferences change with time.

Surveys done in the 1970s indicated that the preponderance of U.S. companies were motivated by tax minimization in setting transfer prices. More recent surveys indicate that companies are more interested in setting transfer prices on the basis of measuring the performance of affiliate managers and of providing reliable and unbiased information for the making of decisions. This change in attitude in U.S. companies may be the result of the United States becoming a relative tax haven compared to other nations.

Its corporate tax rate of 34 per cent, plus state taxes, is less than in many other industrialized nations, where tax rates range between 40 per cent and 55 per cent. A U.S. company's total tax bill may, in fact, be reduced by allocating more profits to the United States.

Regardless of changes in attitudes as to what is important in setting transfer prices, the essential point is that there is no unanimity on which approach to use and on what motivates companies in setting transfer prices.

Up to this point, an important assumption has been that the parent company has real control over transfer prices to manage corporate cash flows and the profits reported by affiliates and to overcome artificial barriers to trade in the form of custom duties, currency exchange, and price controls. Some recent surveys suggest that competitive forces and market conditions within a nation seem to be more important in setting transfer prices than decisions made by a parent organization.

If transfer prices are being set by exogenous commercial forces, then the presumption that a parent organization is able to achieve optimal financial performance of a global family of affiliates through the careful orchestration of transfer pricing is being challenged.

TAX CONSIDERATIONS

Taxation and transfer pricing are intimately entwined, because transfer pricing of goods, parts, and components moving in and out of a nation has a direct impact on taxes on profits and on the amount of duties and tariffs paid to the tax authority. The discussion on transfer pricing based on the cost-of-production approach shows an intimate involvement with the tax authority in the methodology for calculating various elements of the transfer price. There is little uniformity on taxation among nations. Taxes range from taxation of a corporation's activities to the "water's edge" or on its global earnings, the so-called "unitary tax." The state of California invented the unitary tax in the 1930s when movie companies in California began moving out of the state to avoid state taxes.

A unitary tax was applied against the global earnings of a company and the tax was determined by the proportion of a company's sales, property, and payroll within the state to its global sales, property, and payroll. The resulting tax had no relation to the degree of profitability of a company's operation in California. A company could operate at a loss in California and still pay a tax based on its global profits.

Needless to say, both foreign governments and multinational companies have vigorously fought the unitary tax. A number of court decisions confirmed or restricted unitary taxation over the years. Ultimately, opposition to the unitary tax succeeded. In November 1991, Alaska was the last state to abandon having a company's state tax liability based on the global earnings of the company.

The unitary tax still exists in a truncated form, where earnings are restricted to the "water's edge." The state tax is calculated on the portion of a company's activities within a state as compared to its activities within the United States. Although most other countries limit their assessment on what is to be taxed to the operations of a company within their jurisdiction, there is no universal agreement as to what constitutes revenue and expenses in the calculation of taxable income and no uniformity on tax rates.

Every nation decides what is subject to taxation and the applicable tax rates. The complexity of tax regulations, in general, and the diversity of tax laws among nations are such that it is necessary for an affiliate to retain the technical expertise necessary to understand and comply with local tax regulations.

The parent organization must retain the technical knowledge for its own tax jurisdiction and have sufficient knowledge of tax matters elsewhere to coordinate tax planning among the various affiliates. The vigour with which tax payments are enforced varies among nations.

Some countries with seemingly high tax rates permit an underground economy to flourish without much in the way of enforcing tax payments. The other side of the coin is the willingness of companies to adhere to tax laws. In some nations, a businessman who scrupulously follows the tax laws and pays what is owed to the tax authority will find himself at a competitive disadvantage.

NATURE OF TAXES

Taxes can be direct or indirect. The United States relies more on direct taxation, which is applied to each taxable entity. A U.S. corporation is taxed at 34 per cent on its profits. If a corporation pays a dividend to its shareholders, then the next taxable entity, the individual, pays a tax, which may be 28 per cent or more. This is double taxation.

Some nations, such as Germany, have two corporate tax rates on profits—one for retained profits and the other for distributed profits in the form of dividends. A lesser tax rate applies to profits that are distributed to shareholders to reduce the degree of double taxation.

Europe relies more on indirect taxes—particularly, the value added tax (VAT). The VAT is basically a tax applied to each stage of the production process and is not directly associated with the degree of profitability. Indeed, only a small portion of a VAT is associated with profits. Suppose that a company's manufacturing operations has the following financial results.

Wages, rents, interest, profit	$400,000
Outside purchases of goods and services for which VAT has already been paid	600,000
Total sales	$1,000,000

The additive method is to apply the VAT rate, say 10 per cent, to all costs associated with the production of goods, including profit and excluding purchases of goods and services from third parties for which the VAT has already been paid. In this case, $400,000 of a company's activities falls into this category resulting in a VAT of $40,000. A simpler method of calculation is to take the gross sales of the company ($1,000,000), subtract all purchases of goods and services for which VAT has already been paid ($600,000), and apply the VAT rate to the balance ($400,000).

Either method yields the same result. The VAT is essentially equivalent to a national sales tax, because every company associated with the production and marketing of goods and providing services pays a tax on whatever value it adds to the goods or services. The value added tax, like a sales tax, is a tax on consumption, whereas U.S. taxes are on income and profits.

Value added tax rates vary widely from country to country and according to the nature of the business. Certain European countries have low VAT rates (5 per cent) for business transactions associated with food and high VAT rates (40 per cent) for luxury products. Others attempt to have one rate that applies to most forms of commerce.

Because the VAT is not paid on items that have already been exposed to a value added tax, and with the European economy becoming more integrated, there is a powerful incentive for the European Community to harmonize VAT rates and coordinate the handling of VAT payments for products or components shipped between members of the European Community.

The amounts of value added by a company are frequently disclosed in European financial statements. In the excerpt from the British company, the company had gross revenues of 3,213 million pounds in 1987 of which 919.1 million pounds represents added value by the company. Of the total of 919.1 million pounds of added value, 496.8 million pounds was paid to the company's employees, 157.1 million pounds was paid in taxes to government tax authorities, and the remainder was paid to the internal and external providers of capital.

U.S. TAXATION OF GLOBAL COMPANIES

Nations have different ways of taxing global companies domiciled within their jurisdiction. If a parent corporation is domiciled in the United States, it does not pay taxes in the United States on profits earned by incorporated affiliates in other nations, unless the nation is considered a tax haven. This, in the United States, is known as Subpart F income, which will be discussed later under rein voicing centers.

Unlike an incorporated affiliate, a branch of a U.S. company located in a foreign nation is taxed directly on its earnings regardless of whether the earnings are remitted to the home office or not. The taxes paid on remitted and unremitted earnings are not the same, in that unremitted earnings have to be translated to U.S. dollars before a tax liability can be assessed, and therefore, are influenced by changes in currency exchange rates.

Taxes can also be calculated on the basis of the increase in the net worth of the branch, which can also be affected by changes in currency exchange rates. Sometimes a U.S. company will first open a branch operation in another country to permit startup losses to flow back to the parent organization.

When the branch becomes profitable, it may be reorganized as a wholly owned subsidiary, reducing the company's overall tax liability. U.S. based companies usually operate in the global market through operating affiliates whose stock is owned by the parent corporation. The parent corporation pays U.S. taxes only on the profits generated from dividends, royalties, and other service payments and fees paid by a non-U.S. domiciled affiliate to the parent organization.

Taxes paid on profits by affiliates in their nations of domicile can be treated either as a tax credit or a tax deduction by the parent organization in the calculation of its U.S. taxes. To the degree that a tax paid on profits to a foreign government is treated as a tax credit, the net effect of a company paying taxes on its profits in a foreign country is that these taxes are essentially paid for by the U.S. government foregoing an equivalent amount of U.S. source based tax revenue.

Obviously, taxes paid to foreign governments must pass certain criteria set forth by the Internal Revenue Service to be considered for a tax credit. Foreign tax credits apply to taxes paid on foreign source profits calculated in a conventional way as U.S. source profits. Tax credits are also available for foreign government withholding taxes on dividends, interest payments, and royalties paid by a foreign-based affiliate to a U.S. parent company.

There is a maximum permissible limit on tax credits linked to the ratio of foreign source income to total worldwide income multiplied by the tax liability of U.S. operations. This effectively limits the foreign tax credit to the U.S., not the foreign, tax rate. A company doing business in a nation with a higher tax rate on profits than in the United States does not receive a tax credit equal to the taxes paid to the foreign government.

The tax credit is based on the U.S. tax rate. With U.S. tax rates being lower than in most other industrialized nations, U.S. based global companies are not being fully compensated by tax credits on foreign income taxes. This may provide an incentive to shift taxable income back to the United States through changes in transfer prices. The U.S. tax authorities permit a credit for taxes paid on profits to other nations under the notion of tax equity and tax neutrality.

The principle of tax equity implies that a U.S. taxpaying entity with an operation in another nation should not pay more in taxes than having the operation domiciled in the United States. Were the equity principle absolutely true, a U.S. taxpaying entity would be indifferent, or neutral, to whether the operation was located in another nation or in the United States. Some maintain that the U.S. tax code does not adhere to the tax neutrality principle because a company doing business in New York City does not obtain a tax credit on its federal taxes for taxes paid to the state and city of New York on profits made in their jurisdiction.

A company with an affiliate in another nation not only receives a tax credit, which neutralizes its foreign and U.S. income taxes, but does not have to pay U.S. taxes on its foreign source earnings until those earnings are remitted to the parent in the form of a dividend, a royalty payment, or an equivalent thereof. As long as foreign source profits remain in the coffers of the affiliate, no taxes are due to the U.S. government, even though, under special circumstances, the affiliate may lend these funds to the parent company.

Deferral of dividend payments is essentially an interest-free loan made by the U.S. government to the foreign affiliate of a U.S. parent company on the amount of U.S. taxes due if, and when, these funds are repatriated to the U.S. parent. The principles of equity and neutrality built into the U.S. tax code were designed to provide an incentive for U.S. firms to invest overseas as part of the national policy of rebuilding war-torn nations. U.S. companies would be better off confining their activities within the United States, and would not invest in foreign affiliates, if the profits of these foreign affiliates were exposed to double taxation.

Qualified foreign taxes, which cannot be utilized as tax credits, may be used as a tax deduction. A tax deduction is not as valuable as a tax credit. Tax deductions apply when there are not sufficient U.S. taxes to be shielded by tax credits, or where the overall limitation on tax credits has been exceeded. Tax deductions can be carried back or carried forward, whichever is more useful.

REIN VOICING CENTERS

Some companies have set up rein voicing centers to manage all intra company trading of products. A rein voicing centre is at a single location, buying the output of the manufacturing affiliates and selling it to the marketing affiliates. Each affiliate receives or pays in its own currency, thus concentrating all intra company transaction currency exposure at the rein voicing centre.

The centre possesses the necessary data to assess the net currency exposure of intra company transactions and can enter into appropriate currency hedges. The centre may also receive better quotes from currency exchange dealers because all intra company currency exchange transactions are done at one location. The rein voicing centre can mark up the price of all products flowing through the centre to cover its administrative expenses. If there is little or no profitability associated with the operations of a rein voicing centre, it does not matter where the rein voicing centre is located from a tax viewpoint. However, it is possible to increase the markup to the point where corporate profit can be diverted from the nations where the goods are manufactured and marketed to the nation where the rein voicing centre is located. Now the location of the rein voicing centre is critical from a tax viewpoint.

In the 1960s, the U.S. government became concerned with the accumulation of profits in rein voicing centers located in tax havens. Tax havens were characterized as nations imposing no, or a very low, tax on profits, having a high degree of bank secrecy, and little or no currency controls. These nations consider financial activities of importance to their economy, provide modern communication facilities, and promote themselves as offshore financial centers.

Bahamas, Bermuda, Cayman Islands, Liberia, Panama, and Vanuatu have been identified as tax havens. It is possible to "run" a rein voicing centre through these nations without a physical presence of personnel or products. Profits can be easily diverted to tax havens by increasing the markup on selling prices, thus reducing tax liabilities to the nations where the products are manufactured and marketed.

If the criterion for determining a tax haven is satisfied, then the income earned by a rein voicing centre, or any corporate entity in the declared tax haven, is deemed Subpart F income. This income flows directly to the U.S. parent corporation and is taxed as though the income was earned in the United States.

TAXATION IMPACT ON TRANSFER PRICING

Companies operating in the United States are guided by Section 482 of the Internal Revenue Code when setting transfer prices. Specifically, the IRS, through the Secretary of the Treasury, has the right to "distribute, apportion, or allocate gross income, deductions, credits, or allowances... between or among... businesses, if he determines that such distribution, apportionment, or allocation is necessary in order to prevent evasion of taxes. The IRS has been granted wide latitude to do whatever it wants if the IRS deems that dealings between a U.S. parent and its affiliates do not meet its standards. For instance, the IRS can reallocate income and deductions if loans have been made between a parent corporation and an affiliate at an unrealistic interest rate. Unrealistic interest rates are those that would not occur for similar transactions between unrelated third parties.

This also applies to charging for services and use of property, and transfers of tangible and intangible property including lease payments and royalties. A reference to IRS guidelines has already been made in discussing R&D and intangible costs in setting transfer prices by the production cost approach. Basing transfer pricing on published data rather than corporate derived prices is another example of the close working relationship, voluntary or not, between tax authorities and managers responsible for transfer prices.

In general, the IRS standard for determining transfer pricing, and other dealings between a parent and its affiliates, is whether it is an "arm's-length" transaction—one that would occur between a company and a third party having no affiliation other than the commercial transaction under consideration. This is independent of whether the transfer price is based on the cost of production or on market prices.

If the transfer price between affiliates is seemingly out of line with a price that would have been charged to an unrelated party, then the IRS has the right to reallocate income or deductions according to what it feels to be the appropriate transfer price.

The IRS specifies various methods for establishing an appropriate transfer price. The preferred one is the comparable uncontrolled price method where prices are the same for goods sold to affiliate and to nonaffiliated companies. The price for goods sold to an unrelated third party establishes the transfer price for goods transferred to an affiliate.

This method does not work when goods are not sold to third parties, but are totally transferred between affiliates. Under these circumstances, the second method for setting the transfer price is the resale price method. This is the price for which the company would sell the item to an unspecified third party. The third party would add the same comparable value as the affiliate and sell the completed product with an appropriate markup.

By netting the market price of the appropriate markup and the value added to the product by an affiliate, one can "back into" an appropriate transfer price from the point of view of the tax authority. The third method is the "cost plus" method, where the IRS permits three different ways of allocating costs (full absorption, direct cost, and incremental cost).

All these methods leave some margin of discretion as to what is the appropriate transfer price. If all these fail, as they frequently do for high-technology products, customised components, or subassemblies, then so-called fourth methods are permitted, such as determining transfer pricing on the basis of a predetermined profit for the foreign firm's operations and, through a netting process of accounting for applicable costs, establishing an appropriate transfer price.

Regardless of the methodology, the burden of proof in supporting a transfer price is with the taxpayer, not the IRS.

To confuse matters more, there have been occasions when the tax courts have rejected the notion of arm's-length transfer pricing in settling tax disputes between corporations and the IRS.

OTHER NATIONS' POLICIES CONCERNING TRANSFER PRICING

The tax authority in Canada views transfer pricing of goods similar to the way the United States does. Transfer pricing for services differs in that it is based on a pro rata sharing of actual incurred costs between the parent corporation and its affiliate, and not necessarily at an arm's-length price. Tax authorities in Japan follow a system comparable to that of the United States.

German tax code provisions permit the reallocation of domestic source income if revenue or income has been shifted to another nation through a transaction that is different from those that would have been entered into by unrelated parties. In other words, transfer pricing should be arm's-length, although the code is not specific in defining arm's-length pricing.

The United Kingdom is similar to Germany in not specifically defining arm's-length pricing. The Inland Revenue may adjust taxable income based on fairness and arm's-length criteria. Disputes between corporations and Inland Revenue agents are frequently settled by negotiation, resulting in some sort of compromise between the two parties. This is unlike in Germany, where the adjustments made by the tax authorities are considered final, and unlike in the United States, where adjustments are litigated in tax courts.

Tax authorities in many nations are currently taking a much closer look at transfer pricing practices. Recently, the U.K. Inland Revenue recast the accounts of one non-British company operating in the United Kingdom and assessed back taxes of nearly 2 billion pounds. In the United States, there is growing political pressure for the IRS to take more vigorous action against foreign-owned companies operating through U.S. based affiliates.

This pressure stems from the realization that the aggregate expenses for foreign-owned businesses operating in the United States exceed aggregate revenues. This means that, in the aggregate, foreign-owned subsidiaries are claiming to operate at a loss, although individual foreign-owned subsidiaries may be paying taxes on profits.

Some foreign-owned affiliates operating in the United States have a twenty-year string of consecutive losses. This is not considered a realistic appraisal of performance because there are few profit-motivated foreign-based parent companies that would support twenty years of successive losses were they real. Poor or nonexistent profits for foreign-based affiliates operating in the United States are blamed on transfer pricing.

Transfer price manipulation is felt to have resulted in tax underpayments of between $12 and $50 billion. Legislation was passed in 1989 to require foreign-owned businesses in the United States to keep records, in English, of transactions with foreign related parties. Much of this legislation has to do with substantiating transfer pricing on either a cost or arm's length transaction with an unrelated third party.

A growing risk associated with manipulating transfer prices for the purpose of tax minimization. The risk is that the tax authorities will recast the company's statements with their own version of the proper transfer price, thus exposing a company to the risk of double taxation. Most nations have entered into tax treaties with various other nations with regard to taxing of affiliates of parent organizations domiciled in the treaty nations.

These treaties determine withholding taxes on dividends, interest, and royalties; relief from double taxation; and the types of taxes and organizations covered by the treaty. Overall exposure to taxation can be reduced by judicious structuring of the legal corporate entities of a parent company and its affiliates in accordance with the provisions of these treaties.

Some of these treaties contain formal agreements for the mutual examination of the tax returns of affiliates of a parent company. The tax returns of affiliates and parent organizations are exchanged and examined by the tax authorities to determine correct tax liabilities, detect tax avoidance maneuvers, scrutinize transfer pricing practices, and exchange information useful to the tax authorities.

These treaties also provide a forum for one tax authority to complain about the actions taken by another, when these actions are deemed detrimental to its interests. Recent developments in international cooperation of tax authorities include the establishment of a formal agreement on transfer prices.

The mutual agreement of various nations to reference a published source for tanker rates in determining oil company tax liabilities is an example of this. Australia and the United States are attempting to grant "advance determinations" of the proper transfer price for Australian companies' dealings with their U.S. affiliates.

A recent survey has shown that about half of IRS tax examinations of multinational companies involve transfer prices. If a mutually agreeable methodology could be arranged between a company and the IRS, many of these tax examinations could be eliminated. The IRS is attempting to develop a procedure whereby a company and the IRS would mutually agree to a transfer-pricing agreement covering the distribution of finished goods, sales of raw materials and components, general and administrative expenses, and managerial and technical services.

If the taxpayer develops an acceptable transfer-pricing methodology, then the taxpayer and the IRS would enter into an advance-pricing agreement.

The IRS would limit its examinations to an audit to ensure that the taxpayer has complied with the agreement. However, the taxpayer is obliged to submit pricing data of independent transactions, or an adequate substitute, to show that the transfer price possesses the necessary attributes of an arm's-length transaction.

The taxpayer is also responsible to show that the agreed transfer-pricing methodology is generating acceptable transfer prices from an arm's-length perspective. The preference of tax authorities in many nations for arm's-length transfer pricing may act as an inducement to switch from the cost-of-production to the market price approach in setting transfer prices because, presumably, they are one and the same.

The financial and taxation departments of multinational, or global, companies must deal daily with what are considered to be the most pressing issues in international accounting today. Those involved with transfer pricing must measure the consequences of their transfer-pricing decisions both on corporate profits and on current and potential tax liabilities.

Potential tax liabilities, stemming from tax authorities rejecting management's transfer price decisions, and substituting their own, are enormous. This must weigh heavily on the shoulders of those responsible for setting transfer prices.

10

Regulating International Banking

RATIONALE, HISTORY AND FUTURE PROSPECTS

International agreement on the regulation of global financial institutions is a relatively recent phenomenon. The collapse of the Bretton Woods international monetary system, beginning in 1971, and the increase in cross-border investments by multinationals, as well as the problem of recycling petrodollars, have caused bank supervision agencies in various countries to recognize the need for greater cooperation to reduce the risks to the global financial system. The Basle Accord of July 1988 was a major step in moving toward a convergence of supervisory regulations governing the capital adequacy of international banks. Since that time, the United States has legislated major reform of deposit insurance with the passage of the FDIC (Federal Deposit Insurance Corporation) Improvement Act of 1991, and U. S. banks have experienced an unparalleled period of profitability. The creation of the European Monetary Union, which promises to bring about changes in the structure and organization of banking in Europe, will undoubtedly impact the global environment for cooperation among bank supervisory agencies.

The final decade of the twentieth century offered a window of opportunity for global cooperation in the regulation of international banking. The rationale underlying interna-tional banking regulation, review the history of such regulation, and provide observations on the future prospects for global bank supervisory agreements.

REGULATING MULTINATIONAL BANKS

To understand the rationale for regulating multinational banks, it is first important to review the history of the regulation of domestic banks. Though the detailed history varies widely from country to country, the earliest banks were not the same kind of institutions that we have today. Currently, banks serve both deposit and lending functions; that is, they issue liabilities that are a convenient medium of exchange, and are intermediaries between borrowers and lenders. The great early banking houses loaned out their own capital, not other people's money. There existed other specialized institutions that accepted deposits for safekeeping. It is only later that the two functions, lending and deposit taking, were fused into banking institutions--usually connected to the needs of the sovereign for financing expenditures. The intertwining of these two functions necessarily implies that banks are subject to the problem of banks runs, since the funding source for assets is mostly depositors' funds and, to a much lesser extent, the bank's capital. In the early nineteenth century, banks operated with capital ratios in the 40 percent range in Europe and 70 percent in North America. In the United States, as the state or federal government began to play a greater role in the prudential regulation of banks, the capital ratios declined dramatically. Because banks also lacked transparency, they were prone to runs.

In the United States, the involvement of the federal government in banking regulation began during the Civil War. The purpose of the National Banking Act was to create a safe and uniform currency but, and just as important, provide a source of demand for government debt. During the Great Depression, the U. S. financial system was compartmentalized into commercial banks, investment banks, savings and loans, and so on, and deposit insurance was implemented. Though a few U. S. banks had an international presence, it was not until after World War II that international banking began to expand. The Marshall Plan, which encouraged U. S. foreign direct investment, provided the impetus for the expansion of global banking. However, bank regulation changed slowly--understandable perhaps in a world with a system of fixed exchange rates and dominated economically by the United States.

Domestic events and concerns dominated banking supervision and regulation. As it developed over 150 years in the United States, the rationale for the prudential regulation of domestic financial institutions can be summarized as

- The protection of (unsophisticated) depositors, monetary stability,
- The promotion of an efficient, competitive financial system, and
- Consumer protection. It is not the purpose of domestic banking regulation to prevent all bank failures, to substitute government decision making for private bank decisions, or to favour certain groups over others.

In the United States, federal deposit insurance and a strengthened Federal Reserve System provided the protection and the stability. Promoting an efficient and competitive system was much more difficult to achieve because it implied that, since market forces could not be fully relied upon, regulatory policy would have to be implemented that replicated a "market" solution. Geographical and product restrictions, as well as enforced compartmentalization, conflicted with the goal of efficiency in the provision of financial services. At the same time, the prudential regulation of banks provided an opportunity to expand regulation to include questions of disclosure and consumer protection. The result in recent years has been an increase in complaints from banks about the regulatory burden. It would appear that the rationale for international banking regulation would follow a similar development. Actually, however, the demand for international banking regulation originated from the bankers who believed that there was an absence of a level playing field, which could be rectified by the passage of laws. Thus, in the United States, we have the International Banking Act of 1978, which placed foreign and domestic banks on an equal footing in the United States with respect to branching, reserve requirements, and other regulations. The problem, as the history of federal government versus state government banking regulation aptly demonstrates, is that competition in regulation does not necessarily promote safety, stability, or efficiency in the financial system. The experience of the "free banking" period in the United States, between 1836 and 1863, provides a lesson on what happens in the absence of uniform bank regulation and supervision.

Thus" since World War II, and especially in the past quarter century with the move to floating exchange rates, the world has been in a period with similarities to the free banking era in the United States. However, it is not currently possible to employ the national banking solution to the present-day global environment because there is no global government and no single global regulatory agency for international banking. Hence, the only alternative is the requirement that the national bank supervisory agencies cooperate to achieve the goals of regulation.

Another important difference is that the protection of the unsophisticated depositor and consumer protection are not presumably goals of global regulation. In principle, unsophisticated depositors should not be involved in international banking, and there is no need for consumer protection legislation (e. g. , truth in lending). This leaves two principal rationale for global banking regulation: monetary stability and the promotion of efficiency and competition. In practice, these two goals are intertwined into the fundamental problem of systemic risk. Systemic risk has been defined "the likelihood of a sudden, usually unexpected, collapse of confidence in a significant portion of the banking or financial system with potentially large real economic effects". Three important components of prudential regulation are regular bank examinations for safety and soundness, lending and investment restrictions, and maintenance of adequate capital. In practice, the problems of international banking have been dealt with through agreements among bank supervisors on the fundamentals of bank regulation and supervision and the mandating of minimum capital adequacy standards.

Countries vary widely in the range of activities that are permitted for banks (investment banking, insurance, and so on), and therefore there has been to date no consensus on whether to impose a specific model, such as universal banking, as part of an international agreement. Edward Kane and others have pointed out the principal-agent problems involved in domestic banking regulation. The regulators are presumed to be acting in the interest of the public (or taxpayers), but it is difficult to implement an incentive scheme that would produce regulation at a minimum cost to the public. The problem, in essence, is that regulators cannot typically be held personally liable for losses in the banking system during their watch. Incentives be built into regulators' contracts as a way to minimize bad behaviour for which the regulators could escape the consequences. The problem is that regulators really have a mix of public and private motivations for being regulators. In the case of global regulation, the regulators are presumably acting in the interest of global depositors.

This raises a dilemma if regulators bail out large financial institutions where presumably the creditors of the institution are not unsophisticated investors. This requires that the regulators rely upon systemic risk or bank contagion--the fear that the collapse of one financial institution may lead to the collapse of otherwise solvent institutions--as the rationale for bailing out large institutions. In bailing out large institutions, the regulators must provide reasoning why the private institutions did not adequately prepare for the default of an institution of which they are a creditor. This creates a problem of moral hazard since the institution's behaviour may mean that it takes on more risk under such circumstances. Alan Greenspan stated that optimal bank regulation is "regulation designed to assure a minimum level of prudential soundness". This view is based on the assumption that banks manage risks and, at the same time, play an important role in the payment system. Given this view of banks, the regulators must supervise banks to control risk to prevent a systemic crisis. According to George Benston and George Kaufman, banking regulation should seek to mimic the operation of free markets. Optimal regulation would involve a policy whereby regulators would invoke prompt corrective action when capital-asset ratios reach specified levels. Model of optimal regulatory behaviour based on a double moral hazard dilemma. Optimal regulation involves an incentive structure which leads regulators to intervene only when bad management results in underperformance by a bank manager.

Our view, although not inconsistent with the above ideas, differs somewhat from each. In its strictest sense, banking regulation refers to the framework of laws and rules under which banks operate--these are the rules of the game. Supervision in its strictest sense refers to the banking agencies' monitoring of financial conditions at banks under their jurisdiction and to the ongoing enforcement of banking regulation and policies.

Optimal supervision would promote allocative efficiency in the carrying out of the regulations, assuming, if we wish, self-interest-motivated behaviour of the regulatory agencies. In the regulation of international banking (as also in domestic banking), regulators must balance the problems of prudential regulation, market discipline, and moral hazard. In practice, this implies regular examinations, greater transparency, and capital adequacy standards.

HISTORY OF SUPERVISORY COOPERATION

The Bretton Woods international monetary agreement, which established the post-World War II system of fixed exchange rates among the major Western economies, collapsed in March 1973 when the United States unilaterally floated the dollar. Although President Richard Nixon did not begin to engineer the official demise of the system in August 1971, it was clear by the late 1960s that the end was near for the fixed exchange quasi-gold standard that had operated for a quarter of a century. The demise of fixed exchange rates, and the floating of the major currencies, set the stage for difficulties in the international payments system. In 1972 an informal group of banking supervisors in the European Economic Community (EEC) established an informal and autonomous group within the EEC with responsibilities for operational banking supervision. The principal aim of this group, known as the Group de Contact, was to achieve greater understanding and cooperation among the bank supervisory agencies in the EEC.

Table: A Chronological History of the Regulation of International Banking, 1972-1999

Date	Group/Event	Rationale/Accomplishment
972	Groupe de Contract	To achieve closer understanding and practical cooperation between the supervisory authorities of the EEC
September 1974	Basle Committtee of Sipervisors created	Established in the aftermath of serious disturbance in international currency and banking markets (notably the failure of Bankhaus Herstatt in West Germany).
February 1975	Basle Committee first meeting	The first task was to consider methods of improving "early-warning" systems.
December 1975	Basle Concordat	Five key principles established for international supervisory cooperation
July 1979	International Conference of Banking Supervisors	Bank of England-host
May 1983	Basle Committee:	"Principles for the Supervision of Bank's Foreign Establishments" Set down the principles for sharing supervisory responsibility for bank's foreign branches, subsidiaries and joint ventures between hoast and parent (or home) supervisory authorities.

June 1983	EEC Advisory Banking Committee	Directive on consolidated supervision
July 1988	Basle Accords	Capital measurement system was approved by the G-10 central bank Governors and released to the banks.
April 1990	Supplement to the 1983 Concordat was issued	Intended to improve the flow of prudential information between banking supervisors in different countries.
November 1991	The 1998 capital framework was ammended	To give greater precision to the definition of those general provisions or general loan-loss reserves which could be included in capital. (BCCI failure)
September 1993	Basle Committee	A statement was issued confirming that all the banks in the G-10 countries with material international banking business were meeting the minimum requirements laid down in the Accord.

The rules of the game had changed for global banking and weaknesses in the international payments system were exposed with the collapse of Bankhaus Herstatt in 1974. Henceforth, greater coordination of banking regulation and supervision would be necessary in the post-Bretton Woods era. The failure of Bankhaus Herstatt occurred after the irrevocable settlement of the Deutsche Mark leg of foreign exchange transactions, but before the settlement in dollars had occurred. "This left Herstatt counterparties expecting the dollars facing non-payment and caused major disruption to the operations of the Clearinghouse Interbank Payments System (CHIPS)". Confidence in the counterparty system was badly shaken, and the risk resulting from the nonsimultaneous settlement of the two legs of a cross-currency settlement became known as a "Herstatt risk". As a result of the failure, CHIPS adopted new risk control measures.

Along with the Herstatt bank failure, there was the failure of the Franklin National Bank of New York and the British-Israel Bank of London in 1974. According to Ethan Kapstein, it was these three failures that led to the formation of a G-10 committee on banking regulations and supervision that eventually became known as the Basle Committee. The governors of the world's central banks issued a statement in September 1974: "[W]hile it was not practical to lay down in advance detailed rules and procedures for the provision of temporary support to banks experiencing liquidity difficulties, the means were available for that purpose and would be used if and when necessary". The governors also created a new standing committee--the Committee on Banking Regulations and Supervisory Practices. The first meeting of this committee, which became known as the Basle Committee, took place in February 1975.

January 1996	a formal Amendments to the Capital Accord,	Designed to incorporate within the Accord the market risks arising from banks' open positions in foreign exchange, traded debt securities, equities, commodities and options.
May 1996	Basle Committee and IOSCO released a Joint Statement	Responded to a number of concerns expressed by 6-7 Ministers of Finance at the 1995 Halifax Summit and described the steps banking and securities regulators were taking together to preserve the stability of the financial system.
June 1996	International Conference Of Banking Supervisors (ICBS)	supervisors from one hundred and forty counties attended
October 1996	Basle Committee	Released a report drawn up by a joint working group also containing supervisors from offshore centers, which presented proposals for overcoming the impediments experienced by banking supervisors in conducting effective consolidated supervision of the cross-border operations of international banks.
September 1997	Core Principles	Core Principles for Effective Banking Supervision issued by the Basle Committee
July 1999	Basle Committee release on credit risk	Capital adequacy standards revised.

The low inflation, rapid growth, and exchange rate stability of the postwar period was replaced in the 1970s by inflation and volatile interest and exchange rates. At the same time, in the United States and other G-10 countries, a process of deregulation of industry began that included the financial services industry. In the United States, the International

Banking Act of 1978 was passed, which sought to put domestic and foreign banks on an equal footing, and the Depository Institutions Deregulation and Monetary Control Act of 1980 was enacted, which placed various financial institutions on a more equal and efficient footing. American money-centre and superregional banks had increased their overseas branches from 100 in the 1950s to over 800 by the early 1980s.

THE BANK FOR INTERNATIONAL SETTLEMENTS AND THE BASLE COMMITTEE

The Basle Committee was formed under the auspices of the Bank for International Settlements (BIS), which was established in 1930 by a de cision of the Hague Conference, which dealt with the German reparations payments after World War I. The central banks of the world were the members of the BIS, although it was not until September 1994, when Federal Reserve Chairman Alan Greenspan assumed the seat reserved for the United States, that the United States formally acknowledged the role of the BIS in maintaining the stability of the international financial system. The BIS is a public limited company whose thirty-three shareholders comprise almost all European central banks, plus the central banks of Australia, Canada, Japan, and South Africa. The bank is managed by a seventeen-member board of directors that, since 1994, has included the chairman of the board of governors of the Federal Reserve System and the president of the Federal Reserve Bank of New York. The present (1999) general manager is Andrew Crockett of the Bank of England. One of the most important functions of the BIS is to promote voluntary cooperation between central banks.

The Basle Committee on Banking Supervision, as noted above, was established to compare and, if possible, harmonize national rules on supervision in order to bolster confidence in the banking system. The two major tasks confronting the committee were

- To adapt the national supervisory system within each country in order to cope with the wider dimensions of their major banks' businesses and
- To promote close cooperation between national authorities in monitoring the activities of the overseas branches, subsidiaries, and affiliates of their own banks, as well as the offshoots of foreign banks in their own territories. The fundamental problem with international cooperation and coordination is that each country has grown up with its own particular, perhaps unique, banking supervisory structure. In some countries banking supervision is separated from the monetary authority, and in others it is not. Some countries have detailed statutory frameworks; others rely more on informal and flexible arrangements.

The former general manager of the BIS, Alexandre Lamfalussy, explained the importance of cooperation in bank supervision: The essential point is that, nowadays, the central banks cannot ensure proper supervision of banking without an international association of supervisory authorities, because the major banks are active all over the world; certainly where it is a question of providing appropriate assistance for wealthy customers and international business. And the working day never ends any more. During a twenty-four hour period, the banks just move along their positions on the stock markets to the next time zones. . . . [this] justifies the existence of the BIS: an impartial party is the best intermediary for everyone. That is how the G10 arrives at agreements of such quality that almost all central banks in the world automatically impose them on their own banking systems.

The Basle Committee comprises representatives from Belgium, Canada, France, Germany, Italy, Japan, Luxem-bourg, the Netherlands, Sweden, Switzerland, the United Kingdom, and the United States. In the concordat on international supervisory cooperation adopted in 1975, the committee established two principles for its work on international banking supervision:

- That no foreign banking establishment could escape supervision" and

That the supervision should be adequate". It is important to note that the concordat does not address, and was never intended to address, the issue of lender of last-resort facilities to the international banking system. Indeed, there is no necessary and automatic link between banking supervision and the lender of last-resort provision. The recommendations of the concordat, as summarized by Cooke, include the following:

- The supervision of foreign banking establishments should be the joint responsibility of host and parent authorities.
- No foreign banking establishment should escape supervision, each country should ensure that foreign banking establishments are supervised, and supervision should be adequate as judged by both host and parent authorities.
- The supervision of liquidity should be the primary responsibility of host authorities since foreign establishments generally have to conform to local practices for their liquidity management and must comply with local regulations.
- The supervision of solvency of foreign branches should be essentially a matter for the parent authority. In the case of subsidiaries, while primary responsibility lies with the host authority, parent authorities should take account of the exposure of their domestic banks' foreign subsidiaries and joint ventures because of the parent banks' moral commitment in this regard.
- Practical cooperation would be facilitated by transfers of information between host and parent authorities on the territory of the host

authority. Every effort should be made to remove any legal restraints (particularly in the field of professional secrecy or national sovereignty) which might hinder these forms of cooperation.

Though the concordat was an important first step, according to Richard Dale, placing the primary responsibility for supervision with the host country conflicts with the committee's recommendation that the supervision of international financial institutions should occur on a consolidated basis. The problem was that host countries might expect parent authorities to supervise local subsidiaries, while home countries might expect those subsidiaries to be supervised by the host country. Another apparent weakness in the agreement was the failure to address the differing supervisory standards among countries. These and other confusions delayed the final release of the concordat to the public, even though it had been adopted five years earlier by the central bank governors.

In July 1979, an International Conference of Banking Supervisors was held at the Bank of England. It was attended by bank supervisors from about eighty countries. The topics discussed included supervisory cooperation, division of supervisory responsibility, capital and liquidity adequacy, foreign exchange controls, monitoring on a consolidated basis, and the role of offshore banking centers. This first worldwide meeting of bank supervision personnel was followed by various regional and more specialized meetings including a meeting of G-10 supervisors in Basle in October 1980 on the issue of offshore banking centre supervision.

Beginning in 1981, the committee began issuing an annual Report on International Developments in Banking Supervision. To remedy the problems with secrecy laws in a number of countries, such as Germany and Switzerland, the committee developed the concept of "consolidated supervision as a means of giving practical effect to the principle of parental responsibility". The failure of Banco Ambrosiano in Italy pointed to the deficiency in the concordat mentioned above; namely, who has responsibility for a subsidiary? The Italian authorities argued that they had no responsibility for the liabilities of the Banco Ambrosiano subsidiary in Luxembourg because it was not a bank. The Italian authorities, however, provided full backing for the Banco Ambrosiano liabilities in Italy.

At the time of the Banco Ambrosiano failure, there was also the announcement in August that Mexico would be unable to make the interest payments coming due to foreign banks. The fear was that international trade would be disrupted and that capital inadequacy would lead to the collapse of a number of large banks. Since 1984 there has been an annual examination of the provision made by the commercial banks of the G-10 in regard to sovereign credit risk of loans to debtor countries.

In May 1984 Continental Illinois required a $6 billion infusion of Federal Reserve funds to meet its financial obligations, but it failed nevertheless. The subsequent guarantee of all deposits led many to fear that a policy of "too big to fail" had been firmly established in the United States. This failure also exposed the inadequacies of the U. S. capitaladequacy standards, which were simplistic when compared with those in other G-10 countries such as Belgium, France, and Great Britain. These countries had already established "risk-weighted" capital standards requiring banks to hold more capital with riskier portfolios. At first the United States resisted the idea of risk-weighted capital standards partly because of the large number of American banks--over 10,000 at the time. The European system of determining capital adequacy on a case-by-case basis could not be applied in the United States. In January 1986 the United States released for public comment its proposal for a "supplementary" risk-weighted capitaladequacy standard for commercial banks. At the same time, the European Community had been discussing the harmonization of capital standards. In July 1986 the United States and the United Kingdom began to discuss an agreement on the evaluation of capital adequacy and announced, in January 1987, that they had reached common standards. This accord provided a common definition of capital, the adoption of a riskweighted system for evaluating capital adequacy, and the inclusion of all off-balance-sheet commitments in capital-adequacy determinations. These standards were released in September 1997.

This agreement set the stage for the Basle Accord, and on December 10, 1987, the committee announced that it had reached agreement on a proposal for "international convergence of capital measurements and capital standards". The committee members met again to discuss revisions of the preliminary agreement, and the final version was released on July 15, 1988. The accord received high praise.

The Basle Capital Accord of 1988 helped to reverse a prolonged downward tendency in international banks' capital adequacy into an upward trend in this decade. . . [and] effectively contributed to enhanced market transparency, to international harmonization of capital standards, and thus, importantly, to a level laying field within the Group of Ten (G-10) countries and elsewhere. Has this accord made a difference? A recent study conducted by John Wagster examined the causes of the international credit crunch of 19891992. Wagster examined four hypotheses that could explain the reduction in loans experienced over that period. Included in the hypotheses was the impact of the Basle Accord capital standards. Since larger amounts of capital are required for loans when compared to marketable securities, implementation of the standards may have been a major factor. The study also examined the hypothesis that additional regulatory scrutiny may have been a major factor in explaining the reduced availability of lending services. The study indicates that implementation of the international capital standards may have contributed to the credit crunch, although the strongest support was presented for increased regulatory scrutiny. Examination of the movements in capital following the implementation of the Basle Accord standards led Wagster to question the effectiveness of the capital standards.

Wagster's results indicated that banks increased their systemic risk following the implementation of the standards and led him to question the effectiveness of the standards.

CORE PRINCIPLES FOR EFFECTIVE BANKING SUPERVISION: BASLE COMMITTEE ON BANKING SUPERVISION,

PRECONDITIONS FOR EFFECTIVE BANKING SUPERVISION

- Clear responsibilities and objectives for each agency involved.

LICENSING AND STRUCTURE

- The permissible activities must be clearly defined.
- The licensing authority must have the right to set criteria.
- Review and reject any proposals to transfer significant ownership
- Corporate affiliations or structures do not expose the bank to undue risks.

PRUDENTIAL REGULATIONS AND REQUIREMENTS

- Banking supervisors must set prudent and appropriate minimum. capital adequacy requirements for all banks. For internationally active banks, these requirements must not be less than those established in the Basle Capital Accord and its amendments.
- Evaluation related to the granting of loans and investments
- Evaluating the quality of assets and the adequacy of loan loss provisions and loan loss reserves.
- Banking supervisors must be satisfied that banks have management information systems that enable management to identify concentrations within the portolio and supervisors must set prudential limits to restrict bank exposures to single borrowers or groups of related borrowers.
- Banks to lend to related companies and individuals on an arm's-length basis.
- Procedures for identifying, monitoring and controlling country risk and transfer risk reserves against such risks.
- Accurately measure, monitor and adequately control market risks.
- Comprehensive risk management process where appropriate, to hold capital against these risks.
- In place internal controls that are adequate.
- Strict "know-your-customer" rules, that promote high ethical

and professional standards Methods of Ongoing Banking Supervision

- On-site and off-site supervision.
- Regular contact with bank management.
- Prudential reports and statistical returns.
- Validation of supervisory information.
- Supervise the banking group on a consolidated basis.

INFORMATION REQUIREMENTS

- Each bank maintains adequate records drawn up in accordance with consistent accounting policies and practices. Formal Powers of Supervisors
- Banking supervisors must have at their disposal adequate supervisory measures to bring about timely corrective action when banks fail to meet prudential requirements. Cross-border Banking
- Global consolidated supervision over their interna-tionally active banking organizations.
- Information exchange with the various other supervisors involved.
- Local operations of foreign banks to be conducted to the same high standards as are required of domestic institution.

Wagster found that Canadian, U. K. , and German banks lowered capital and may have achieved a competitive advantage over U. S. and Japanese banks. These, and other concerns about the original accord, have led to a revised proposal that has been distributed for discussion and debate.

THE 1999 BASLE PROPOSAL

The Asian crisis of 1998 underlined that weak supervision can have severe repercussions on financial stability. In this environment, the Basle Committee has submitted for comment a proposal to address the limitations of the current regulations. Since the accord proposal was put into place, securitization has become more significant in the financial landscape. Banks have been able to limit their capital requirements through increased use of securitization. The current standards do not appear to be effective in classifying risks in loans. Regardless of market rating, all corporate loans carry the same risk weighting. The proposal calls for changing the risk-weighting structure based on external credit ratings provided by agencies such as Moody's and Standard & Poor's. The highest rated loans would have a weighting of 20 percent; the lowest rated claims, a weighting of 150 percent. Loans that are not rated would have a 100 percent weighting.

The proposal includes some discussion of substitution of a bank's credit evaluation system if it can be demonstrated to be effective. The proposal calls for greater supervisory review of a bank's risk management and capital allocation procedures, suggesting that, in some instances, greater amounts of capital than called for by the committee could be required. Finally, the proposal calls for greater disclosure of risks by commercial banks. This view is consistent with the call for extended use of market discipline and increased transparency.

OTHER INTERNATIONAL AGREEMENTS

The difficulties of integrating international banking supervision can be illustrated by the problems found in the European Community (EC), which currently comprises fifteen European nations covering most of Western Europe. The EC created the framework for a single European market for retail banking services on January 1, 1993. The purpose of the integrated market is to increase competition in banking services and improve the efficiency of financial institutions. The European Commission issues regulations and directives, both of which are binding on member countries. The first directive, issued in 1977,

sought to establish the rules for banks to establish branches in member countries. The host-country rule that was adopted requires the bank to gain permission from the supervisory authorities in the host country before they are allowed to operate in the host country. The Second Banking Directive, adopted in 1989, mandated the harmonization of standards for prudential supervision, mutual recognition by member states in the way in which they apply those standards, and home country control and supervision. The mutual recognition of a single banking license eliminates the need for EC banks to obtain banking charters from the host country. Home-country rule requires that host regulators give up primary regulatory responsibility for foreign institutions to the home country.

The motivation for changes in EC banking is to remove barriers to cross-border banking services and to increase competition in retail banking. The system that was in place prior to the initiatives was highly nationalized with a focus on collusion and regulatory capture rather than competition. Large price differentials were prevalent for retail banking services among the EC members. Implementation is predicted to lower costs for retail services in the countries with the most significant barriers. Increased competition is expected to reduce profitability for banks in member states. Increased competition is also expected to result in some concentration since smaller, less efficient banks will not be able to compete.

Implementation of the directives for a single market in banking has been quite successful. Based on a study of twelve member states on ten key banking directives, 82 percent of the states had properly transposed the directives into national statutes by the end of 1983. In many states in which statutes had not yet been enacted, actions were in process.

THE FUTURE OF INTERNATIONAL BANKING REGULATION

There are three basic approaches to international banking regulation in the future: the first would be a move toward greater reliance on the discipline of the market system, the second would be the establishment of a supranational regulatory agency, and the third would be a continuation of what we have--a combination of reliance on market discipline, an expandable role for banks' internal controls, and international supervisory cooperation. The third appears to be the preferred approach for the foreseeable future.

Alan Greenspan sketched this framework for bank regulation and supervision in the future in a speech to the American Bankers Association on October 11, 1999. The key components are disclosure and market discipline, internal risk assessment, and capital adequacy. Chairman

Greenspan made the following points regarding the future of banking regulation:

- The scope and complexity of prudential policies should conform to the scope and complexity of the bank entities to which they are applied.
- Policymakers must be sensitive to the tradeoffs between more detailed supervision and regulation, on the one hand, and moral hazard and the smothering of innovation and competitive response, on the other.
- Supervisors have little choice but to try to rely more--not less--on market discipline--augmented by more effective public disclosures--to carry an increasing share of the oversight load.
- The most cost-effective approach to prudential oversight would have supervisors tap into that bank's internal risk assessments and other management information.
- New examination guidance encouraging the largest and most complex banks to carry out self-assessments of their capital adequacy in relation to objective and quantifiable measures of risk.
- The need to make regulatory capital requirements more risk-focused as well.

Greenspan thus argues that the increased difficulties of banking regulation and supervision will require that regulators ensure that banks have their own internal control mechanisms in place. The logic of this strategy is that, today, international markets are so instantaneously interconnected that intervention by regulators when a crisis erupts is always a second-best solution. The way to minimize problems in the future is to make banks take all precautions to protect themselves in a competitive environment.

This view is consistent with those who believe that there should be a greater reliance on market forces in disciplining banks. In a speech given in 1996, Thomas Hoenig, president of the Federal Reserve Bank of Kansas City, suggested limiting the safety net to banks that are not involved in the more exotic nontraditional activities such as derivatives. He also suggested a second element to improve regulation by reducing systemic risk through limiting large interbank exposure in the payment system and interbank deposit markets. The advantages limiting the safety net to banks that are involved only in traditional activities would include reduced regulatory and compliance costs and improved efficiency.

For example, consider the Basle Committee's recent revision to the capital adequacy standards to incorporate market risk. The Committee's capital standards allow banks to use their own value-at-risk models to determine the amount of capital necessary to protect them from market risk. Clearly, banks need to use their own models to effectively manage risk. To effectively supervise banks that use their own models, however, examiners need to have the expertise to judge the adequacy of the models and the risk management practices. At a minimum, this requires understanding the quantitative aspects of the model, such as its statistical structure, its accuracy in valuing assets, and the adequacy of the stress tests used to determine the financial consequences of large movements in interest rates and asset prices. In addition, examiners must understand the qualitative aspects of a risk management strategy, such as how management uses the model's information and ensures compliance with its risk management strategy.

Undoubtedly, bank examiners must be well trained. Recent changes in examination procedures at the U. S. bank regulatory agencies have placed Ph. D. economists on the examination teams. This, together with greater reliance on competition, may promote more effective supervision that also minimizes the problems of systemic risk. At a recent conference held at the Federal Reserve Bank of Chicago, numerous central banking officials concurred in the need for a larger role for market discipline for large financial institutions. Federal Reserve Board Governor Laurence Meyer spoke of the need for greater disclosure, as did Thomas Hoenig. The Basle Committee, in its latest proposal on the overall state of global bank capital standards, also echoes this view.

Will there indeed be a greater reliance on market discipline? The lesson from history is that we will continue to need a lender of last resort, and the nonbank institutions that compete with banks in the payment system will eventually be regulated as banks. Though Gilbert recognizes that market discipline is important for enhancing the effectiveness of supervision, it is not sufficient to prevent recurring panics and crises. History has also shown that the move toward greater regulation and supervision has often occurred during periods of financial distress.

What does this imply for international banking regulation--which, as we have seen, has also been driven by financial crises? In the first place, it implies that the domestic bank regulatory agencies will expand their turf to include financial institutions that today are not considered banks. Hence, in the United States, the result of legislation to expand the scope of the operations of banks will lead to the regulation of the nonbank competitors. This will also require some restructuring of the activities and responsibilities of the various financial institution regulatory agencies--including the Securities and Exchange Commission, the Commodities Future Trading Corporation, and so on, in addition to the Federal Reserve, the Comptroller of the Currency, the FDIC, and Office of Thrift Supervision.

Could international banking crises lead to the expansion of the role of the BIS or the International Monetary Fund (IMF) or the World Bank?

In recent years, the IMF and the World Bank have placed increasing emphasis on the importance of financial systems as crucial infrastructure. Both agencies have enormously expanded staff in the area of banking regulation and supervision. At the same time, both agencies have come under criticism for continuing to exist when the reason for their existence is questionable. The BIS has seized the initiative in global arrangements on banking regulation and supervision. Though there is unlikely to be a global chartering agency, the IMF could conceivably provide expertise to examine global banks. It could do this under the authority granted by nation-states, or as part of the revised IMF Articles of Agreement. The IMF, even more than the World Bank, has searched for a new mission in the post-Bretton Woods era.

As technological change and economic growth generate the potential for systemic crises, assuming domestic bank examiners are not up to the task, the IMF could find its new mission to include the examination of global banks. The probability of a rationale of parceling out global financial regulatory and supervisory responsibilities among the various nation-state agencies and the global agencies is low. Such an outcome would require a breakdown in national governments and an international agency up to the task of assuming new responsibilities. What is more likely is a gradual progress based on a cooperative effort for international banking regulation that periodically will be accelerated by shocks to the financial system--payments crises, for example--and the resultant collapse of one, or several, large financial institutions.

SEBI GUIDELINES RELATING TO CAPITAL ISSUES

In the case of new companies with foreign equity participation, the public offer should not be less than 20% of the issued capital, and the Indian promoter's share should not be more than 40% of the issued capital. For new companies without any foreign equity participation, the public offer is required to be at least 60% of the issued capital. Finance companies would be eligible to make an issue only if they have a minimum track record of 2 years operations or they have been granted registration as a non-banking financial company by RBI or as an intermediary by SEBI.

Stock exchanges are required to ensure that the companies concerned, have a valid acknowledgment card issued by SEBI. SEBI vets the offer document, to ensure that all disclosures have been made by the company, in the offer document, at the time the company applies for listing of its securities to the stock exchange.

Following the abolition of the office of Controller of Capital Issues and the consequent removal of administrative control over the pricing of new issues, the capital markets now enjoy a considerable degree of freedom. New companies, being set up by existing companies; with a five year track record of profitability, are free to price issues, provided the participation of the promoters is not less than 25% of the equity of the new company and the pricing is made applicable to all new investors symmetrically. Where a new company is set up by existing private sector companies along with a state level agency, or a government company, or a foreign collaborator, it will be sufficient if the private sector companies alone satisfy the requirements of five year track record of profitability. Existing profitable companies issuing capital for augmenting their own capital base are free to price their issue. At the same time, the practice of making preferential allotment of shares, unrelated to the prevailing market prices was stopped by SEBI.

In any capital issue to the public, there is a specified minimum capital contribution to be made by the promoters. To reduce the cost of the issue, underwriting by issues has been made optional, subject to the condition that if an issue is not underwritten, and is not able to collect 90% of the amount offered to the public, the entire amount collected would be refunded to the investors.

Where fully convertible debentures (FCDs) are to be issued, the interest rate can be freely determined by the issuer. Companies are required to create a Debenture Redemption Reserve (DRR) equivalent to 50% of the amount of debenture issue before debenture redemption commences. The cost of issuing capital, as of December 1992, was estimated at approximately 9-19% of the issue. This included fees for issue management, underwriting fees, stationary costs, advertisement and publicity costs, mailing costs, brokerage, etc. Companies have a variety of options which entail lower issue costs, such as GDR issues, private placement, and bought-out deals.

SEBI's intention of passing on some part of its responsibility to the lead managers is reflected in the new guidelines announced in May 1995.

The major decisions were:

- SEBI has decided to stop vetting of rights issues all together. The onus of this responsibility will now rest with Th. lead managers. The procedure for clearance would be that the merchant banker would have to file the offer document with SEBI six weeks prior to the proposed date of offer of rights issue. If SEBI does not ask for clarifications within 21 days from the date of filing, the company and the lead manager can proceed with the issue.
- SEBI revised the guidelines for reservation in public issues. As per the new guidelines which took effect from 1 June 1995, half of the

net public offer should be reserved for small applicants, i.e. those applying for less than 1,000 shares/securities. The other half would be reserved for the corporate applicants.

- A committee comprising chiefs of senior executive directors of the five divisions of SEBI has been formed which will clear all public issues which are more than Rs. 1 billion. Formerly, all the issues were cleared by the primary markets division. Issues less than Rs. 200 million would be cleared by the division chiefs, those between Rs. 200 million and Rs. 500 million by the executive directors and those between Rs. 500 million and Rs. 1 billion by the senior executive director.

Index

L

M

N

O

P

Q

R

S

U

V

W